Hiding
from
Humanity

Hiding from Humanity

Disgust,

Shame,

and the Law

MARTHA C. NUSSBAUM

**Princeton
University
Press**
Princeton and Oxford

Second printing, and first paperback printing, 2006
Paperback ISBN-13: 978-0-691-12625-8
Paperback ISBN-10: 0-691-12625-9

The Library of Congress has cataloged the cloth edition of this book as follows

Nussbaum, Martha Craven, 1947–
Hiding from humanity : disgust, shame,
and the law / Martha C. Nussbaum.
p. cm.
Includes bibliographical references and index.
ISBN 0-691-09526-4 (alk. paper)
1. Law—Psychological aspects. I. Title.

K346.N87   2004
340'.1'9—dc22   2003061013

British Library Cataloging-in-Publication Data
is available

This book has been composed in New Baskerville

Printed on acid-free paper. ∞

pup.princeton.edu

Printed in the United States of America

3 5 7 9 10 8 6 4

For David Halperin

O my body! I dare not desert the likes of you in other men and
women, nor the likes of the parts of you,
I believe the likes of you are to stand or fall with the likes of the
soul, (and that they are the soul,)
I believe the likes of you shall stand or fall with my poems,
and that they are my poems.
—Walt Whitman, "I Sing the Body Electric," 9.129–131

Human beings are not by nature kings, or lords, or courtiers, or
rich. All are born naked and poor; all are subject to the
miseries of life, to sorrows, ills, needs, and pains of every kind.
Finally, all are condemned to death. . . . It is the weakness of the
human being that makes us sociable; it is our common miseries
that turn our hearts to humanity; we would owe humanity
nothing if we were not human. Every attachment is a sign of
insufficiency. If each of us had no need of others, he would
hardly think of uniting himself with them. Thus from our weakness our fragile happiness is born. . . . I do not conceive how
someone who needs nothing can love anything. I do not
conceive how someone who loves nothing can be happy.
—Jean-Jacques Rousseau, *Emile*, Book IV

"The alarming thing about equality is that we are then both
children, and the question is, where is father? We know
where we are if one of us is the father."
—B, patient of Donald Winnicott, analysis published as
Holding and Interpretation

Contents

Chapter 2. **Disgust and Our Animal Bodies** 71

Chapter 3. **Disgust and the Law** 124

Chapter 4. **Inscribing the Face: Shame and Stigma** 172

Chapter 5. **Shaming Citizens?** 222

Acknowledgments

This book began as the Remarque Lectures, delivered at the Remarque Institute at New York University in March 2000. I owe thanks to Tony Judt, the institute's director, for the invitation and the occasion to present material to a very stimulating audience. Jair Kessler was an invaluable support in the practical arrangements surrounding the visit.

The general chapter on emotions and law draws on an article, "Two Concepts of Emotion in Criminal Law," that Dan M. Kahan and I published in the *Columbia Law Review* (96 [1996], 269–374). I am most grateful to Kahan for getting me started on this track years ago, and for the unfailing helpfulness and intelligence of his contributions on the topic. The present book is in large part a record of disagreements that increasingly emerged as we pursued our common interest, and therefore may seem to contain a rather large measure of criticism of Kahan. I should make clear, however, the large amount it owes, as well, to his insight and energy.

The material on disgust began as a review of William Miller's *The Anatomy of Disgust*, in the *New Republic*. I am very grateful to Miller for provoking my reactions by his insightful work, and for generous comments on the work in progress. The work then took shape as an article in a volume on emotions in the law edited by Susan Bandes ("'Secret Sewers of Vice': Disgust, Bodies, and the Law," in *The Passions of Law* [New York: New York University Press, 1999], 19–62). I am most grateful to Bandes for encouraging me to begin this project. The paper has been presented as a Katz Lecture at the University of Chicago Law School, and at quite a few other universities. The material on shame has also been presented at a number of occasions, including the American Society for Political and Legal Philosophy at the Eastern Division of the American Philosophical Association, and as the Kadish Lecture at Boalt Hall, University of California. For formal comments on the former occasion, I am grateful to Dan Kahan and Sandy Levinson; for comments at the latter, I am grateful to Seana Shiffrin and Chris Kutz. The manuscript in progress was also presented as a series of lectures at Syracuse University and as the Hourani Lectures at SUNY-Buffalo.

For very helpful comments on these and other occasions, or in response to reading a draft, I am most grateful to Kate Abramson, Louise Antony, Marcia Baron, Michael Blake, John Brademas, John Braithwaite, Talbot Brewer, Susan Brison, Alisa Carse, Peter Cicchino, Ruth Colker, Richard Craswell, John Deigh, Joshua Dressler, Barbara Fried, Robert Goodin, Virginia Held, Dan M. Kahan, Mark Kelman, Benjamin Kilborne, Carolyn Korsmeyer, Maggie Little, Tracey Meares, Winfried Menninghaus, Jeffrie Murphy, Charles Nussbaum, Rachel Nussbaum, Eric Posner, Richard Posner, Bernard Reginster, Deborah Rhode, Sibyl Schwarzenbach, Nancy Sherman, Jerry Siegel, Laura Slatkin, Marc Spindelman, Gopal Sreenivasan, Michael Stocker, Cass Sunstein, David Velleman, and James Whitman.

Three readers of the manuscript for the Princeton University Press supplied invaluable written comments: Seana Shiffrin, Robin West, and an anonymous reviewer. I thank them warmly, and I also thank Mitchell Berman, Dan Markel, Cass Sunstein, and Stephen Schulhofer, who did the same at a later stage.

Finally, I was lucky enough to have wonderful research assistance at various stages in the genesis of the project. I am exceedingly grateful to Sonya Katyal, Felise Nguyen, and Mark Johnson for their energy and creativity.

This book is dedicated to my long-time friend, David Halperin, scholar and activist, one of the founders of the rigorous academic study of sexual orientation. Although I know that he disagrees with a lot that is in it, both methodologically and substantively (as I disagree with some of what he writes), our disagreements over the years, and our agreements, have been undergirded both by my deep gratitude for the experience of being understood and seen, which is very rare in friendship, and which I hope is in some sense reciprocal, and by a passionate shared commitment to equal human dignity.

Hiding
from
Humanity

**I. Shame and Disgust:
Confusion in Practice
and Theory**

A California judge orders a man convicted of larceny to wear a shirt stating, "I am on felony probation for theft." In Florida, convicted drunk drivers are required to display bumper stickers reading "Convicted D.U.I." Similar stickers have been authorized in other states, including Texas and Iowa.[1] Penalties like these, involving public shaming of the offender, are becoming increasingly common as alternatives to fines and imprisonment.

Jamie Bérubé was born with Down syndrome. As a result of changes enacted under the Individuals with Disabilities Education Act, he has an Individualized Education Plan that provides for him to be "mainstreamed" in a regular public school classroom, albeit with a monitor. The teacher and monitor work to ensure that Jamie need not live as a shamed and stigmatized person, and his condition need no longer be the object of humiliation.[2] Stephen Carr, a drifter lurking in the woods near the Appalachian Trail, saw two lesbian women making love in their campsite. He shot them, killing one and seriously wounding the other. At trial, charged with first-degree murder, he argued for mitigation to manslaughter on the grounds that his disgust at their lesbian lovemaking had produced a reaction of overwhelming disgust and revulsion that led to the crime.[3]

In a 1973 opinion that still defines the law of obscenity, Chief Justice Warren Burger wrote that the obscene must be defined in a manner that includes reference to the disgust and revulsion that the works in question would inspire in "the average person, applying contemporary community standards." To make the connection to disgust even clearer, Justice Burger added a learned footnote about the etymology of the term from Latin *caenum*, "filth," and cited dictionary definitions defining obscenity in terms of disgust (as will be discussed in chapter 3).[4]

Shame and disgust are prominent in the law, as they are in our daily lives. How do, and how should, they figure in law's formulation and administration? Even in this small sampling of cases, the role of the two emotions seems complicated and hard to pin down. Shaming penalties encourage the stigmatization of offenders, asking us to view them as shameful. At the same time, current trends in our treatment of the disabled, typified by the case of Jamie Bérubé, discourage persistent habits of stigmatization and shaming, in the name of human dignity and individuality. Other previously excluded groups, such as gays and lesbians, have also fought against social stigmatization with some success.

Of course there is no obvious contradiction between these two trends, because it is consistent to hold that the disabled are blameless, and therefore should not be shamed, while criminals should be. It is also consistent to hold that those who commit consensual sexual acts, however controversial, should not be stigmatized, while those who harm others should be. But there may yet be a deeper tension between support for punishments that humiliate and the general concern for human dignity that lies behind the extension of stigma-free status to formerly marginalized groups—and, in general, between the view that law should shame malefactors and the view that law should protect citizens from insults to their dignity.

Disgust, too, functions in complicated ways. It serves, sometimes, as the primary or even sole reason for making some acts illegal. Thus, the disgust of the reader or viewer is one primary aspect of the definition of obscene materials under current obscenity laws. Similar arguments have been used to support the illegality of homosexual relations between consenting adults: they should be illegal, it is alleged, because the "average man" feels disgust when he thinks about them. It is used to justify the criminalization of necrophilia; it has been proposed as a reason for banning human cloning. And disgust has also been taken to be an aggravating factor in acts already illegal on other grounds: the disgust of judge or jury at a murder may put the defendant into a class of especially heinous offenders. On the other hand, disgust also plays a role in mitigating culpability. Although Stephen Carr did not succeed in his attempt to win a reduction on the ground of his disgust, and was convicted of first-degree murder, other offenders have succeeded in winning mitigation with a similar defense.[5]

Again, there appears to be no real inconsistency here, since the disgust of an observer is obviously distinct from the disgust of a perpetrator. It seems consistent to hold that citizens should be shielded by law from what disgusts them, and yet that overwhelming disgust might serve as a mitigating factor in the case of a violent act. Nonetheless, the cases still leave us in some confusion about what the role of disgust really is, and why it should play the role that it does.

If we turn to the theoretical literature, our sense of perplexity only grows, because there is considerable debate about whether shame and disgust ought to play the roles they currently play. Furthermore, both supporters and opponents of these roles use a variety of distinct arguments that are not always mutually consistent. Thus, shaming penalties are frequently defended as valuable expressions of social norms by political theorists whose general position might be described as communitarian, in the sense that it favors a robust role for strong and relatively homogeneous social norms in public policy. Both Dan M. Kahan, the leading advocate of such penalties, and general social critics such as Christopher Lasch and Amitai Etzioni have defended the revival of shaming on the grounds that society has lost its communitarian moorings by losing a shared sense of shame at bad practices. Shame penalties, they argue, would promote a revival of our community's common moral sense. Etzioni memorably suggests that society would improve if young drug dealers, caught in a first offense, were "sent home with their heads shaved and without their pants."[6] In a similar vein, though without even requiring an offense, William F. Buckley, Jr., suggested in 1986 that gay men with AIDS should be tattooed as such on their buttocks.[7] On the other hand, another influential defender of public shaming, John Braithwaite, insists that the goal of such punishments ought to be not stigmatization or humiliation, but the reintegration of offenders into the community. Is Braithwaite taking a different view about the same thing, or is he talking about a very different set of legal practices?

Nor do opponents of shaming penalties agree about what the best rationale for opposition is. Some hold that the penalties are inappropriate because of their assault on human dignity.[8] Others hold instead that the problem with such penalties is that they constitute a form of mob justice, and are for that reason inherently unreliable and uncontrollable.[9]

The theoretical debate about shaming penalties becomes all the more difficult to figure out when we consider the theoretical basis for a wide range of legal practices that currently protect citizens from shame: laws protecting personal privacy, for example, and the new laws promoting a dignified education for disabled children. Typically, these practices are defended on liberal grounds, with appeal to the idea, typical of classical liberalism, that each individual citizen deserves a life with as much dignity and self-respect as can be provided, taking into account the fair claims of others.[10] Are these ideas inconsistent with the use of shame in punishment, as some theorists believe? Or is the tension between shaming and classical-liberal norms merely apparent?[11]

Disgust is equally perplexing in theory. The appeal to disgust in law has its most famous defense in Lord Devlin's *The Enforcement of Morals,* an influential work of conservative political thought. Lord Devlin argues that the disgust of average members of society (the "man on the Clapham omnibus") gives us a strong reason to make an act illegal, even if it causes no harm to others. This is so, he claims, because society cannot protect itself without making law in response to its members' responses of disgust, and every society has the right so to preserve itself. (I shall analyze his views in detail in chapter 2.) More recently, legal theorist William Miller, while apparently disagreeing with Devlin about some concrete policy matters, supports his general line, arguing that a society's hatred of vice and impropriety necessarily involves disgust, and cannot be sustained without it.[12] But a significant role for disgust has also been supported from a viewpoint that is, while communitarian, nonetheless self-described as "progressive." In his article "The Progressive Appropriation of Disgust," Dan M. Kahan argues that a liberal society, concerned with the eradication of cruelty, needs to build law on the basis of disgust. Kahan's aim, he announces, is "to redeem disgust in the eyes of those who value equality, solidarity, and other progressive values."[13] We should not cede the "powerful rhetorical capital of that sentiment to political reactionaries" just because prominent defenders of disgust have often used it to defend conclusions that appear reactionary from a liberal perspective.

II. Law without the Emotions?

One possible reaction to this confused situation is to say that emotions are irrational anyway, and it is always a mistake to take much account of them in constructing legal rules. There is a popular commonplace to the effect that the law is based on reason and not passion—a view recently imputed to Aristotle in the fictional Harvard Law School classroom in the movie *Legally Blond*. This commonplace, or something like it, has been endorsed by some liberal legal thinkers, responding to the appeals to emotion that I have just been discussing.[14] Let us call it the "No-Emotion" proposal. If we take such a general line, we seem to cut through the theoretical and practical debates—although it is not terribly clear what the result of so doing will be for many well-entrenched practices.

This shortcut is a mistake, however. First of all, law without appeals to emotion is virtually unthinkable. As chapter 1 will argue, the law ubiquitously takes account of people's emotional states. The state of mind of a criminal is a very important factor in most parts of criminal law. The state of mind of a victim (of rape, blackmail, et cetera) is also often relevant in determining whether an offense occurred, and, if so, of what magnitude. More deeply, it is hard to understand the rationale for many of our legal practices unless we do take emotions into account. Without appeal to a roughly shared conception of what violations are outrageous, what losses give rise to a profound grief, what vulnerable human beings have reason to fear—it is very hard to understand why we devote the attention we do, in law, to certain types of harm and damage. Aristotle once said that if we imagine the Greek gods as depicted in legend—all-powerful, all-seeing creatures who need no food and whose bodies never suffer damage—we will see that law would have no point in their lives. What need would they have, he said, for making contracts, paying back deposits, and so on? We might add, what need would they have for laws against murder, assault, and rape? We humans need law precisely because we are vulnerable to harm and damage in many ways.

But the idea of vulnerability is closely connected to the idea of emotion.[15] Emotions are responses to these areas of vulnerability, responses in which we register the damages we have suffered, might suffer, or luckily have failed to suffer. To see this, let us imagine beings who are really invulnerable to suffering, totally self-sufficient. (The Olympian gods aren't quite like this, insofar as they love their mortal children and have quarrels and jealousies among themselves that give rise to many types of mental and physical suffering.) Such beings would have no reason to fear, because nothing that could happen to them would be really bad. They would have no reasons for anger, because none of the damages other people could do to them would be a truly significant damage, touching on matters of profound importance. They would have no reasons for grief, because, being self-sufficient, they would not love anything outside themselves, at least not with the needy human type of love that gives rise to profound loss and depression. Envy and jealousy would similarly be absent from their lives.

The Greek and Roman Stoic philosophers draw on this idea when they ask us all to become such self-sufficient people, insofar as we can, extirpating the emotions from our lives. They argue plausibly that human beings can achieve something like the imagined invulnerable condition if they simply refuse to value anything outside of that which they control—their own will, their capacity for moral choice.[16] By shifting our attachments and what we consider valuable, we also shift the emotions we are liable to experience. Although few of us would fully share the Stoic project of withdrawing our attachments from the world, considering that project is a good way of measuring the large role that attachments to insecure aspects of our world—other people, the material goods we need, social and political conditions—play in our emotional life. It also helps us, correspondingly, to measure the large role that emotions such as fear, grief, and anger play in mapping the trajectory of human lives, the lives of vulnerable animals in a world of significant events that we do not fully control. If we leave out all the emotional responses that connect us to this world of what the Stoics called "external goods," we leave out a great part of our humanity, and a part that lies at the heart of explaining why we have civil and criminal laws, and what shape they take. (In other words, we can see why and how our vulnerability entails emotion by seeing how the denial of emotion entails a denial of that vulnerability.)

As Rousseau argues in the passage from *Emile* that I have quoted as an epigraph to this book, our insecurity is inseparable from our sociability, and both from our propensity to emotional attachment; if we think of ourselves as like the self-sufficient gods, we fail to understand the ties that join us to our fellow humans. Nor is that lack of understanding innocent. It engenders a harmful perversion of the social, as people who believe themselves above the vicissitudes of life treat other people in ways that inflict, through hierarchy, miseries that they culpably fail to comprehend. Rousseau asks, "Why are kings without pity for their subjects? It is because they count on never being human beings." Emotions of compassion, grief, fear, and anger are in that sense essential and valuable reminders of our common humanity.

Such emotions typically play two distinct but related roles in the law. On the one hand, these emotions, imagined as those of the public, may figure in the justification for making certain sorts of acts illegal. Thus, any good account of why offenses against person and property are universally subject to legal regulation is likely to invoke the reasonable fear that citizens have of these offenses, the anger with which a reasonable person views them, and/or the sympathy with which they view such violations when they happen to others. (Typical is Mill's account of the foundations of legal constraint, in chapter 5 of *Utilitarianism,* which traces the "sentiment of justice" to "the impulse of self-defence, and the feeling of sympathy.")

On the other hand, such emotions figure, as well, in the account of what is legally relevant about a criminal's state of mind, which, of course, has many other nonemotional elements (such as negligence, premeditation, intention). A prominent way in which emotions figure in assessing an offender's mental state, and the one that will concern me, both in discussing anger and fear in chapter 1 and in the later discussion of disgust, is as a mitigating factor: a putatively criminal offense may be judged less heinous, or not even a crime at all, if it is committed under certain "emotional circumstances." If, for example, a killer's anger is deemed to be that of a "reasonable man" encountering a serious provocation, the level of his culpability may be judged lower. It is easy to see that this role for emotions in the law is closely related to the more general role in justifying legal norms that I have just described. It is precisely because anger at certain violations is understood to be reasonable that we both have laws against these violations and mitigate the culpability of those who lash out when provoked by one of them. It is precisely because one of the main points of law is to protect us against death and bodily injury (because the fear of these is reasonable) that killing in self-defense, in circumstances of reasonable fear, is not a crime, and that committing a crime under duress may mitigate fault. Disgust has similarly been invoked in a two-sided way: as the emotion of a public, justifying the illegality of certain acts, and as the emotion of a putative offender, allegedly mitigating fault. Here, too, the two roles are closely linked: it is precisely because a certain type of disgust is judged so reasonable that it can be the basis for criminalizing certain sorts of acts and that its presence in the mind of an alleged criminal might be thought to mitigate fault.

A valiant attempt to defend an antiemotion program in law has been made by some scholars in the Utilitarian tradition. These scholars have indeed tried to imagine a pure emotion-free system of law, by substituting considerations of deterrence for consideration of the offender's state of mind. In penalizing a given case of homicide, for example, we are to think only of how our penalties will affect the likely future behavior of this offender and other possible offenders.[17] We do not consider the offender's state of mind (including his emotions), or whether that state mitigates culpability. Such a view (which, note, does away with much more than appeals to emotion, since it also removes appeals to intention and other mental states) seems problematic in many ways, not least on grounds of fairness. A person who lashes out because her child has just been murdered seems importantly unlike a person who commits premeditated murder; the intrinsic quality of her act seems very different. The pure deterrence view—whether or not it leads to the same conclusion about this person's punishment (as it might, by saying that such impulsive killings cannot be deterred by heavy punishments)—does not seem to capture this intrinsic difference. Similarly, the idea that only deterrence is relevant to distinguishing between inadvertent and deliberate acts, or between negligent and fully premeditated acts, seems problematic on grounds of fairness even if the proposed results might end up looking relatively similar.

A larger problem with such views, however, is that they really do not fulfill their promise. They dispense with emotion in one place, in judging the state of mind of the offender; but they leave it in another and more fundamental place, in explaining why criminal sanctions exist at all. (Thus Mill, Utilitarian though he is, still feels the need to explain the foundations of the law in terms of emotion.) The deterrent role for punishment cannot be explained without some account of why certain acts are bad. Such an explanation is bound to refer to human vulnerability and our interest in flourishing. But then we are already dealing with and evaluating emotions. If a certain offense is a serious assault on human life or flourishing, that very judgment entails that it is to be feared, and that it is an appropriate target of anger. As I shall argue at greater length in chapter 1, the very content of such emotions includes such evaluative judgments, and it would seem, as well, that one cannot consistently have such evaluative judgments without having the corresponding emotions. (Can one judge that death is importantly bad for one, and yet not fear death? I believe not, however much one may think one is above mere fear.) Thus, the Utilitarian-deterrence version of the antiemotion view does not really take us away from appealing to emotions; it just denies the appeal to emotion in one area, that of the criminal's state of mind. And this denial then appears peculiar and unfair: for if we judge that it is reasonable to fear death, so much so that we use that as a reason in justifying laws against homicide, then why shouldn't the reasonableness of a person's fear be relevant in assessing the putatively criminal act that he or she performs?

Such considerations suggest that a system of law that did not include a substantial normative role for certain sorts of emotions, and for norms of reasonableness in emotion, would be difficult to conceive; at the very least it would be utterly unlike current known systems of law. That, then, is a first problem with the antiemotion proposal. Moreover, the proposal, which brands all emotions as "irrational," is both unclear and unconvincing. "Irrational" is a slippery word. It may mean "devoid of thought," as when we say (perhaps wrongly) that a fish, or a human infant, is "irrational." In that sense, as chapter 1 will argue, it is quite unconvincing to suggest that all emotions are "irrational." Indeed, they are very much bound up with thought, including thoughts about what matters most to us in the world. If we imagine a living creature that is truly without thought, let us say a shellfish, we cannot plausibly ascribe to that creature grief, and fear, and anger. Our own emotions incorporate thoughts, sometimes very complicated, about people and things we care about.[18] Grief, for example, is hardly just a tug in the gut—its wrenching character cannot be explained without bringing in the thoughts we have about the person who has been lost, and who has been, let us say, a vital daily presence in our life. Similarly, the emotions that are most frequently invoked in the law, for example anger and fear, are obviously thought-laden. If I yield to a blackmailer out of fear, that fear is not just an electric impulse jolting through me: its painful character comes from the thoughts it contains about the damage I may sustain. If I attack a person who has just raped my child, my anger, again, is not just a mindless impulse. It involves a thought about the terrible damage my child has just suffered, and the wrongfulness of the offender's act. So if Dworkin's proposal is to neglect emotions because they are impulses without thought, that proposal is quite implausible.

"Irrational," however, can also be defined in terms of thought that is *bad thought* in some normative sense. Thus, the person who says that two plus two is five, even after repeated teaching, is irrational, because he thinks badly. So, too, in a different way, we typically hold that racism is irrational, based on beliefs that are false and ungrounded. Perhaps, then, we can reformulate Dworkin's proposal as the proposal that emotions are always irrational in the sense that they embody defective thought, thought that should never guide us in important matters.

The Greek Stoics had such a view. Because they held that all emotions involve high evaluation of aspects of the world that we do not fully control, and because they thought that such evaluations are always mistaken, they did hold that emotions were normatively irrational as a class. A person who thinks well will have none of them. But, as I have already said, that is a view that few people have ever found plausible. More important for our purposes, it is not a view on which a system of law could plausibly be based. Law has the function of protecting us in areas of significant vulnerability. It makes no sense to have criminal laws if rape, murder, kidnapping, and property crime are not really damages, as a strict Stoic would require us to believe. So the Stoic reason for holding that all emotions are irrational is not available to any thinker who wants to defend a legal system that is at all like the systems we know. What law might be for godlike Stoics is a question of some theoretical interest; it is irrelevant, however, to thought about the criminal and civil law of a real contemporary nation.

We can bring this out by thinking, once again, about some cases of emotion that our legal system has typically found reasonable. Anger at an assault—either on oneself or on a family member—is often treated as paradigmatic of what a "reasonable man" would feel. So, too, is fear for one's life or reputation or well-being. These doctrines internal to criminal law will be further investigated in chapter 1. More globally, the whole structure of criminal law might be said to imply a picture of what we have reason to be angry at, what we have reason to fear. The law of homicide itself might be said to express reasonable citizens' outrage at homicide, just as the law of rape responds to the reasonable fear of rape and expresses outrage at rapes that take place. The very fact of the law is a statement that these attitudes are indeed reasonable.

Of course many particular instances of anger or fear may indeed be irrational in the normative sense. They may be based on false information, as when someone gets angry at X in the belief that X has assaulted her child, but no such crime has occurred (or someone else did it). They may also be irrational because they are based upon false values, as would be the case if someone reacted with overwhelming anger to a minor insult. (Aristotle's example of this is anger at people who forget one's name.) The law needs to take a stand on what really is a significant damage, what a reasonable person would and would not find a ground for anger. As we shall see, the law does so in many ways. But such judgments are typically particularistic. They do not say, "All anger and fear are irrational." They say, "This instance of anger is not the anger of a reasonable person," "This instance of fear is ill-grounded." So they take place against the background of a shared judgment that emotions are sometimes reasonable, in the normative sense. In other words, these emotions are justified by what has happened, against the background of reasonable views about what matters. As I shall argue, judgments of reasonableness in the law are normative judgments, using a hypothetical image of the "reasonable man." Not surprisingly, these images are responsive to existing social norms. And yet they may also play a more dynamic role, by either shoring up faltering norms or calling them into question. Law, then, does not just describe existing emotional norms; it is itself normative, playing a dynamic and educational role.

If, however, we cannot imagine a system of law that does not frequently advert to the emotions, and that does not, furthermore, treat at least some of them as reasonable, then we seem to be back where we started. We cannot cut our way through the confusion surrounding shame and disgust by simply discarding all legal analysis framed in terms of emotion, and we thus seem to have no way, as yet, of sorting through the theoretical and practical debate.

III. Two Problematic Emotions

A much more promising way of proceeding—the way I shall be following in this book—is that of looking much more closely at the type of emotion in question, asking about its structure, its thought-content, and its likely role in the economy of human life. This is what judges and juries implicitly do all the time with anger and fear. They have an implicit picture of anger as a response to a damage, and of fear as a response to imagined bad possibilities. They then use this picture in evaluating the specific cases of anger and fear put before them. There is reason to think that making these pictures more explicit, raising public awareness about what is actually in question, can help sort through at least some difficulties. For example, the traditional law of self-defense has been effectively challenged by battered women, who use an explicit account of fear in order to illustrate their claim that one may act out of self-defense even when not lethally menaced at that very moment (say, when the woman's batterer is asleep).

Similarly, looking closer at disgust and shame, and offering a more explicit analysis of their thought-content, their genesis, and the variety of roles they play in our social life will, I believe, help us greatly in deciding what we want to say about the controversies concerning the roles they play in law. That is the project that I shall undertake in this book. During the past fifty years there has been a great deal of good work on these two emotions, not only in philosophy, but also, empirically, both in cognitive psychology and in the clinical treatment of patients by empirically minded psychoanalysts. (I shall in general bring experimental psychology and clinical psychoanalytical accounts together, and shall rely on psychoanalytic accounts where they are consistent with other empirical data and offer valuable insights.) My analyses will draw on this recent scientific and humanistic work, though ultimately I shall be proposing a philosophical analysis of my own, with strong links to the empirical literature.

My general thesis will be that shame and disgust are different from anger and fear, in the sense that they are especially likely to be normatively distorted, and thus unreliable as guides to public practice, because of features of their specific internal structure. Anger is a reasonable *type* of emotion to have, in a world where it is reasonable to care deeply about things that can be damaged by others. The question about any given instance of anger must then be, are the facts correct and are the values balanced? On the other hand, one could argue that jealousy is always suspect, always normatively problematic as a basis for public policy (however inevitable or even at times appropriate in life) because it is likely to be based on the idea that one is entitled to control the acts of another person, an idea reinforced by centuries of thought that have represented women as men's property. Both its general cognitive content and its specific history in Western societies make it a dubious emotion to invoke, either in justifying criminal regulation of conduct (adultery, for example) or in mitigating blame for a criminal act (the murder of a spouse's lover, for example). This is the sort of case I shall be making about disgust, and, with much qualification, about shame.

Disgust, I shall argue, is very different from anger, in that its thought-content is typically unreasonable, embodying magical ideas of contamination, and impossible aspirations to purity, immortality, and nonanimality, that are just not in line with human life as we know it. That does not mean that disgust did not play a valuable role in our evolution; very likely it did. Nor does it mean that it does not play a useful function in our current daily lives; very likely it does. Perhaps even the function of hiding from us problematic aspects of our humanity is useful; perhaps we cannot easily live with too much vivid awareness of the fact that we are made of sticky and oozy substances that will all too soon decay. I shall argue, however, that a clear understanding of disgust's thought-content should make us skeptical about relying on it as a basis for law. That skepticism should grow greatly as we see how disgust has been used throughout history to exclude and marginalize groups or people who come to embody the dominant group's fear and loathing of its own animality and mortality.

I shall ultimately take a very strong line against disgust, arguing that it should never be the primary basis for rendering an act criminal, and should not play either an aggravating or a mitigating role in the criminal law where it currently does so. The valuable role for disgust in the law, it seems to me, is confined to areas such as nuisance law and zoning where it seems legitimate to allow offense, not just harm, to play a guiding role.

Shame is much more complicated, in two ways. First, it arrives on the scene earlier in human life. It is relatively easy to do experimental research on disgust because children acquire it after they acquire at least some linguistic capacity. Shame probably arrives earlier, so in order to study it, and to describe its relation to guilt and other relatives, we must construct hypotheses about the mental lives of preverbal infants. Fortunately, we need not do so in a vacuum. There is by now a rich experimental literature on infancy that has formed a valuable partnership with clinical psychoanalysis of both children and adults, and this literature helps us to construct a convincing, if complicated, story of the development of shame out of the infantile demand for control over all the important aspects of its world.

Shame is more complicated than disgust in another way as well: there is much more to be said about its positive role in development and social life, in connection with valuable ideals and aspirations. Thus my story about shame will ultimately be quite complex, and will involve distinguishing different varieties of shame, some more and some less reliable. I shall argue that what I shall call "primitive shame"—a shame closely connected to an infantile demand for omnipotence and the unwillingness to accept neediness—is, like disgust, a way of hiding from our humanity that is both irrational in the normative sense, embodying a wish to be a type of creature one is not, and unreliable in the practical sense, frequently bound up with narcissism and an unwillingness to recognize the rights and needs of others. Even though this sort of shame can be in many ways transcended, such favorable outcomes do not always take place. Moreover, all human beings very likely carry a good deal of primitive shame around with them, even after they in some ways transcend it. For this reason, and other reasons I shall offer, shame is likely to be normatively unreliable in public life, despite its potential for good. I shall then argue that a liberal society has particular reasons to inhibit shame and to protect its citizens from shaming.

Thus, although this book concerns two emotions and their place in law, especially criminal law, it is ultimately far broader in its concerns and aims. The positions that it criticizes are widespread social attitudes, influential in many times and places. They are currently enjoying renewed attention in contemporary American culture. It will be my contention that these attitudes are profound threats to the existence and stability of a liberal political culture. Through criticizing them I hope to offer, as well, a partial account of attitudes that do sustain liberalism.

Thus the book is intended, ultimately, as an essay about the psychological foundations of liberalism, about the institutional and developmental conditions for the sustenance of a liberal respect for human equality. It is inspired by Rousseau's profound contention that political equality must be sustained by an emotional development that understands humanity as a condition of shared incompleteness. But its liberalism is ultimately more Millian than Rousseauian, valuing liberty as well as equality, space for human creativity as well as decent material conditions of life for all.

Rousseau and Mill both understood that just institutions, if they are to be stable, require support from the psychology of citizens. Both therefore emphasized the role of education in producing a society decently attentive to human equality. I am concerned with that educational project, and the analyses in the present book contain many suggestions for how public education in a liberal society might grapple with the problems I diagnose.[19] But individuals and institutions are mutually supporting. Institutions must be sustained by the good will of citizens, but they also embody and teach norms of what a good and reasonable citizen is. They are sustained by the psychology of real people, but they also embody, teach, and express a political psychology, through norms of the reasonable citizen and the proper role for law. My argument in this book, though full of implications for the educational side of the issue of equal respect, is primarily concerned with its legal and institutional aspect: what sort of public and legal culture will embody the "political psychology" appropriate to a liberal regime? What norms of reasonableness in emotion are the right ones to build into the law, both expressing and nourishing appropriate emotions in citizens?

Mill had answers to these questions, but, as chapter 7 will argue, they were not quite the right answers for a pluralistic society; they placed too much emphasis on the creative contributions of out-standing individuals, too little on the importance of removing stigma and hierarchy wherever they occur. Thus his account of the moral foundations of the criminal law, though in my view basically correct in substance, is defective in rationale. I hope to provide at least one part of a better rationale for something like Mill's "harm principle," while at the same time offering a psychological and philo-sophical diagnosis of some underlying dangers endemic to any lib-eral society. It will emerge, I hope, that this same analysis offers us a convincing rationale for public policy in general toward traditionally stigmatized and marginalized groups. Thus its treatment of issues of sexual orientation and disability will range well beyond the criminal law to include broader questions of nondiscrimination and educa-tion law.

What I am calling for, in effect, is something that I do not expect we shall ever fully achieve: a society that acknowledges its own hu-manity, and neither hides us from it nor it from us; a society of citi-zens who admit that they are needy and vulnerable, and who discard the grandiose demands for omnipotence and completeness that have been at the heart of so much human misery, both public and private. To that extent, its spirit is less Millian than Whitmanesque: it constructs a public myth of equal humanity, to substitute for other pernicious myths that have long guided us. Such a society remains elusive because incompleteness is frightening and grandiose fictions are comforting. As a patient of Donald Winnicott's said to him (in an analysis that I shall analyze in detail in chapter 4), "The alarming thing about equality is that we are then both children, and the ques-tion is, where is father? We know where we are if one of us is the fa-ther."[20] It may even be that such a society is unachievable, because human beings cannot bear to live with the constant awareness of mortality and of their frail animal bodies. Some self-deception may be essential in getting us through a life in which we are soon bound for death, and in which the most essential matters are in fact beyond our control. What I am calling for is a society where such self-deceptive fictions do not rule in law and in which—at least in crafting the in-stitutions that shape our common life together—we admit that we are all children and that in many ways we don't control the world.

This, it seems to me, is a good way to proceed in a liberal society, by which I mean one based on a recognition of the equal dignity of each individual, and the vulnerabilities inherent in a common humanity. If we cannot fully achieve such a society, we can at least look to it as a paradigm, and make sure that our laws are the laws of that society and no other.[21]

Chapter 1
Emotions and Law

[N]o defendant may set up his own standard of conduct and justify or excuse himself because in fact his passions were aroused, unless further the jury believe that the facts and circumstances were sufficient to arouse the passions of the ordinarily reasonable man.

—*People v. Logan,* 164 P. 1121, 1122 (Cal. 1917)

Nor, on the other hand, must the provocation, in every case, be held sufficient or reasonable, because such a state of excitement has followed from it; for then, by habitual and long continued indulgence of evil passions, a bad man might acquire a claim to mitigation which would not be available to better men, and on account of that very wickedness of heart which, in itself, constitutes an aggravation both in morals and in law.

—*Maher v. People,* 10 Mich. 212, 81 Am. Dec. 781 (1862)

I. Appeals to Emotion

Frank Small had a quarrel with C. R. Jacoby in Keyser's Saloon. Jacoby walked out of the saloon and down the street with his wife. As he was walking away, Small came up to him, put a pistol to his head, and shot him. Jacoby died two days later. In an attempt to mitigate the grade of the homicide from murder to manslaughter, Small argued that he had been impelled to kill by an intense surge of anger that persisted from the time of the quarrel until the fatal attack. On appeal from his conviction for first-degree murder, he argued that the trial court had erred in failing to instruct the jury that some people calm down more rapidly than others after a quarrel. The Pennsylvania Supreme Court rejected the argument: "Suppose then we admit testimony that the defendant is quick-tempered, violent and revengeful; what then? Are these an excuse for, or do they even mitigate crime? Certainly not, for they result from a want of self-discipline; a neglect of self-culture that is inexcusable."[1]

Judy Norman had been physically and mentally abused by her husband for years. He forced her to engage in prostitution and he frequently threatened to kill her. One evening her husband beat her with unusual severity, called her a "dog," and made her lie on the floor while he lay on the bed. Norman took the baby to her mother's house and came back with a pistol. She shot her husband, fatally, while he slept. At trial, a defense expert testified that Norman killed because she feared that if she did not she would "be doomed . . . to a life of the worst kind of torture and abuse" and that "escape was totally impossible." The North Carolina Supreme Court affirmed the trial court's refusal to instruct the jury on self-defense. The majority opinion held that the evidence "would not support a finding that the defendant killed her husband due to a reasonable fear of imminent death or great bodily harm"; the dissent maintained that the husband's "barbaric conduct reduced the quality of the defendant's life to such an abysmal state that . . . the jury might well have found that she was justified in acting . . . for the preservation of her tragic life."[2]

In 1976, the U.S. Supreme Court declared the North Carolina death penalty statute unconstitutional because it did not allow defendants an opportunity to present their life history at the penalty phase and thus to appeal to the compassion of the jury. The possibility of compassion, the Court wrote, is an essential part of the process of appropriate criminal sentencing:

> A process that accords no significance to relevant facets of the character and record of the individual offender or the circumstances of the particular offense excludes from consideration in fixing the ultimate punishment of death the possibility of compassionate or mitigating factors stemming from the diverse frailties of humankind. It treats all persons convicted of a designated offense not as uniquely individual human beings, but as members of a faceless, undifferentiated mass to be subjected to the blind infliction of the penalty of death.[3]

In a 1986 California case, citing this precedent, the Court discussed a California jury instruction that cautions jurors that they "must not be swayed by mere sentiment, conjecture, sympathy, passion, prejudice, public opinion or public feeling."[4] They agree that the instruction is constitutional only if it is interpreted to ask jurors to disregard "untethered" sympathy; that is, "the sort of sympathy that was not rooted in the aggravating and mitigating evidence introduced during the penalty phase."[5] It would clearly be unconstitutional were it interpreted so as to ask jurors to disregard *all* compassionate emotion.[6]

Appeals to emotion are prominent in the law. Moreover, there is general agreement that emotions can be evaluated not just as stronger or weaker, but also as more and less reasonable, more and less in accordance with the hypothetical legal norm of the "reasonable man." As my examples make clear, this norm is contested. Frank Small tried to win for his own unusually irascible and violent character the recognition that courts have traditionally accorded only to the "ordinarily reasonable" citizen. Judy Norman's fear for her life is depicted as perfectly reasonable by her attorneys and the dissenting judge, but attacked as unreasonable by the prosecution and the majority. The Supreme Court grants that a certain sort of compassion is reasonable, but the opinions present evidence that prosecutors frequently mislead juries on this point, suggesting that the only reasonable stance is one utterly without emotion.

Interestingly enough, all parties appear to be agreed that emotions can be evaluated for reasonableness and appropriateness, and that, to that extent, they are parts of a character that one might deliberately cultivate. The judge hearing Small's appeal writes that his conduct shows "a want of self-culture that is inexcusable." The Norman defense lays heavy emphasis on the features of her life that made it utterly reasonable for her to fear both inescapable degradation and an early death; the other side argues that these factors do not show that she acted on the basis of "reasonable fear of imminent death or great bodily harm." Operating in a tradition in which self-defense is defined with reference to the notion of reasonable fear, the parties have no interest in even exploring the possibility that fear is nothing but an impulse that cannot plausibly be assessed as reasonable or unreasonable. The Supreme Court seems to assume that compassion has a close relation to thought: it is based on evidence, and it can be "tethered" to limit its purview to the evidence presented at the penalty phase of a criminal trial.

Because my overall project in this book is to conduct a detailed and highly critical evaluation of two specific types of emotion, it is important, first, to gain an understanding of the prevailing attitude to emotions in general in the Anglo-American legal tradition, and of the conception of emotions on which this attitude is implicitly based. This tradition, as we shall see, connects emotions closely with thought about important benefits and harms, and thus, as well, with prevailing social norms concerning what benefits and harms are rightly thought important. Because I believe that this conception of emotion is basically correct, I shall offer some arguments in its favor, and show the advantages it offers for a picture of social emotion and moral education.

After providing an account of the merits of the traditional conception, I shall look more closely at three areas of law in which the conception has played an interesting role: the law of "reasonable provocation," the law of self-defense, and the role of appeals to compassion in criminal sentencing. These are intended as examples, only, to show how the appraisal of emotion typically functions. There are many other areas of both criminal and civil law that could have been chosen for a similar analysis.[7]

Because emotions as I shall characterize them make reference to social norms, a question naturally arises at this point: to what extent should a society committed to a liberal respect for pluralism be in the business of evaluating emotions, and therefore the norms they embody? I shall conclude the chapter by briefly sketching the conceptions of political liberalism and the justification of law that I favor, and shall then argue that the evaluation of emotion plays a limited but still significant role inside a political liberalism so understood.

What are we talking about when we talk about emotions? Although there are many differences of opinion about how to analyze emotions, it is significant that there is a large measure of agreement about what the category includes. A long Western tradition, both philosophical and popular, has agreed that certain human experiences that people commonly call "emotions" or (especially earlier) "passions" can usefully be classified together, since they share many common features.[8] The major emotions, both in this philosophical tradition and in related popular and literary thought, typically include joy, grief, fear, anger, hatred, pity or compassion, envy, jealousy, hope, guilt, gratitude, shame, disgust, and love.[9] Non-Western traditions appear to classify experience in a roughly similar way.[10] More recently, research on emotion in evolutionary biology and in cognitive psychology has come up with a very similar list.

The point of this grouping is to distinguish this group of experiences from bodily appetites such as hunger and thirst, and also from objectless moods, such as irritation and certain types of depression. The emotions on the standard lists seem to have a lot in common with one another, and to be distinct in structure, in ways that I will shortly describe, from appetites and moods. Of course there are also many distinctions among members of the category of emotions; the classification of certain cases remains a matter of dispute. The consensus about central members of the family across differences of time and culture is, however, striking.[11]

I have said that emotions are "human experiences," and of course they are that; but most contemporary researchers, and many in the ancient world, also hold that some nonhuman animals have emotions, at least of some types.[12] Obviously the differences in cognitive ability among species create corresponding differences in their emotional lives, and some emotion-types prove easier to ascribe to nonhuman animals than do others. Many animals probably have fear; a smaller number probably have anger and grief; a still smaller number

appear to have compassion, since that emotion usually requires perspectival thinking, that is, the ability to assume, mentally, the position
of another person or creature.[13] These questions should not be neglected in any theoretical account of emotions, difficult though it is
to decide how to ascribe emotions to creatures who do not use language. There is compelling evidence that the ascription of a wide
range of emotions is essential to explaining animal behavior. I shall
leave that issue to one side for now, however, focusing on the human
emotions that are the standard material of law.

II. Emotion and Belief,
Emotion and Value

When we think about our emotions, they frequently seem to us like
forces that take over, so to speak, from outside. Frequently they seem
to have little connection with our thoughts, evaluations, and plans.
If, then, we are going to defend the traditional picture of emotions,
which has its roots in ancient Greek conceptions of emotion and of
their contribution to a good character, we need to understand why
the idea of emotions as unthinking forces is ultimately inadequate,
despite its first-blush intuitive plausibility.

Let us, then, think about Judy Norman's fear. Very likely it was accompanied by at least some powerful feelings and bodily changes.
What, nonetheless, would make us think that this is not all her emotion
contained?

First of all, her fear has an *object*. It is focused on something:
namely, the prospect of being killed by her husband (and beaten
and degraded, even if she is not killed). It is a fear *of* those terrible
possibilities. If we remove from her feelings that character of being
focused on bad events in the future, they become something else—
not fear, but a mere pain or shaking. Indeed, it is interesting that we
do not really know, or perhaps greatly care, exactly what Judy Norman's bodily feelings were. (Did she tremble? Did she have a pain in
her stomach? Was her heart racing? Perhaps all of these, at different
times?) What we care about, what makes us convinced that she felt
fear, is the way we imagine her focusing on those future possibilities.

Furthermore, the object of her emotion is what philosophers generally call an *intentional object*: that is, its role in the emotion depends on the way in which it is seen and interpreted by the person whose emotion it is. Let us explore this point using a less contested case, and then return to Judy Norman. A mother is told that her only child, whom she loves very much, has just died. She reacts with intense grief. The point is that her grief is based on the way *she sees* her situation, namely, as that of a woman who has just lost her beloved child. Her view of the situation might be factually correct or it might be incorrect: for example, perhaps the child is alive and well, and the person who told her the news is mistaken or lying. In that case, her grief is based on a false belief, but it is still grief, because that is how she sees her situation.

A separate issue is the issue of reasonableness. Suppose she believes that her child is dead because the news is brought to her by a person whom she trusts and whom she believes to be in a very good position to know how things are with her child. In that case, her belief that the child is dead might still be false, but it seems to be reasonable. If, on the other hand, she believes the news because she hears a casual rumor from a very untrustworthy person, her belief is unreasonable, whether it happens to be true or not. In that way, the issue of reasonableness is independent from the issue of truth: reasonableness concerns issues of evidence and reliability, in a way that truth does not.

Now let us return to Judy Norman. Her fear was based on the way she saw her situation—as one in which her life and safety were threatened by her husband. The two sides in the case disagreed about whether her belief that her husband was likely to cause her serious bodily harm was reasonable. They did not raise the issue of truth, presumably because her belief was about the future, and to that extent its truth could not be ascertained. What they were asking was whether it was reasonable of her, based on her past experience and the evidence available to her, to believe her life or bodily safety threatened.

This discussion already brings out a third feature of emotions that makes them unlike the unintelligent feelings and bodily forces with which we began. That is, they involve beliefs, and sometimes very complex beliefs, about their object. Aristotle insists on this point in the *Rhetoric*, where he gives advice to young public speakers about how to create emotions in their audience.[14] They create emotions, or take them away, he argues, by making the audience believe certain things about their situation. Suppose I want to make my audience feel fear.[15] Then, he says, I must convince them that serious bad things are in the offing, threatening them or their loved ones, and that it is not entirely clear that they will be able to ward these bad things off. If I am to make them angry with someone—let's say, with the Persians—I must convince them that the Persians have damaged some aspect of their well-being (or that of their loved ones or allies) in a serious way, and that the damage was not simply inadvertent, but willingly and wrongfully inflicted.[16]

Changing any element in these complex families of beliefs can bring about a change in the audience's emotions. For example, suppose the orator now wants to remove fear. He can try to convince his audience that, after all, the damage they fear is not really serious. (We do not fear the loss of trivial items, such as paper clips and toothbrushes.) Or he can convince them that it is not really likely to occur. (We typically don't fear an invasion from Mars.) Or he can convince them that, if the bad thing does occur, they can surely ward it off and prevent any serious damage. (In this way, we don't fear dying of a tooth abscess, even though we know that, left untreated, cavities can lead to an abscess that can go straight to the brain, because we are sure that we can take effective action long before the really bad thing happens.) Similarly, he can remove their anger against the Persians by altering any member of the relevant family of beliefs: he can convince them that the damage was done by the Scythians, not the Persians; or he can convince them that it was trivial, not serious; or he can convince them that it didn't happen at all; or he can convince them that the Persians did the bad thing by accident, not in a culpable way.

Aristotle's account is convincing: beliefs are essential bases for emotion. Each type of emotion is associated with a specific family of beliefs such that, if a person doesn't have, or ceases to have, the beliefs in the relevant family, she will not have, or will cease to have, the emotion. That is why political rhetoric is emotionally powerful. Obviously enough, politicians have no way of directly influencing the bodily states and the feelings of their audience. What they can influence is the beliefs people have about a situation. But those beliefs appear to be necessary for emotions such as fear and anger. In many cases, they appear to be sufficient as well: that is, just getting someone to believe that she faces threatening prospects will be enough to make her have fear; the beliefs themselves will probably trigger whatever further bodily changes and feelings occur. (Ultimately, in order to give an adequate account of emotions of human children and nonhuman animals, we probably should understand the notion of "belief" extremely broadly and elastically, as any cognitive state that involves seeing X as Y.)

Another important point, much stressed by Aristotle and other philosophers who write on this topic, is that the beliefs are connected to the emotions in a very intimate way: they appear to be part of what the emotion itself is. That is to say, if we try to give a definition of an emotion such as anger, in which we mention everything that is absolutely essential to anger and what differentiates anger from other painful emotions, we will find, he suggests, that we cannot succeed in this task if we mention only the way anger *feels*. Many negative emotions involve rather similar feelings of pain: fear, pity, envy, jealousy, anger—can we really differentiate these in a reliable way by associating each with a characteristic type of feeling? In order to differentiate them, we seem to need to bring in, as well, the beliefs that are characteristic of each. Fear involves a belief about bad possibilities imminent in the future. Anger involves a belief about damage wrongfully inflicted. Pity requires a belief about someone else's significant suffering. And so forth. The same is true of the so-called positive emotions: they may all be associated with some pleasing feeling, but it would be difficult indeed, probably impossible, to distinguish love, joy, gratitude, and hope with references to these nice feelings alone without mentioning the family of beliefs characteristic of each.

Indeed, we might go one step further than Aristotle and point out that the feelings don't actually help us very much in defining emotions because the feelings associated with a given type of emotion vary greatly, both between people and in the same person over time.[17] Think of Judy Norman's fear. She probably had a kaleidoscopic series of feelings while she was fearing for her life. It is hard even to imagine them. Sometimes she probably did tremble and her heart was racing. At other times she may have felt numb, or exhausted. And if this is so with fear, one of the simpler emotions, it is all the more clearly true of people who are experiencing grief or anger. People also differ from one another: one person may experience anger in connection with a boiling feeling; another may experience a dull ache. And love? The experience of loving someone, whether a friend or a child or a partner, is surely rich in feeling, but it would be too limiting to say what specific feeling it must always contain.

Sometimes, indeed, an emotion may be present without the presence of any specific feeling associated with it. We do not need complex accounts of emotional repression in order to acknowledge that many of our beliefs are operative, motivating our behavior, without our being conscious of them all the time. The belief that things dropped fall to the ground; the belief that my lectern is a solid object through which my hand will not pass; the belief that if I want to move the lectern I will have to lift it or push it—all these beliefs and countless others are affecting my actions while I give a lecture, even though I am not conscious of them. The same thing is true of emotions. My grief for a lost parent, my fear of my own death, my love for my child—each persists in the fabric of my life, explaining actions of many different kinds, even though I am not aware of them at all times, and therefore not aware of any particular feeling-state associated with them.

We cannot, then, regard the thoughts involved in emotion as simply concomitants or causal prerequisites. If they are needed to identify or define an emotion, and to distinguish one emotion from another, this means that they are part of what the emotion itself *is,* constitutive of its very identity. They are, moreover, parts that appear to be more stable and susceptible of analysis than the fluctuating and variable feeling-components. We should conclude, then, that Aristotle and the legal tradition are on the right track when they focus on the thoughts involved in emotion, and when they ask the questions they do about the reasonableness or the unreasonableness of those thoughts.

If a view of the object, and thoughts about that object, are integral to the experience of emotion, what sort of thoughts must those be? I have suggested that most emotions involve a complex family of thoughts. But if we look back at our examples, we find that there is an interesting overlap among them. All the emotions involve appraisals or evaluations of the object, and all appraise the object as significant rather than trivial. We do not fear trivial losses. We do not get angry over trivial slights (or, when we do, it is because we think them more important than they are). We do not grieve for the loss of something that seems to us utterly unimportant. Sometimes, indeed, the experience of emotion reveals patterns of evaluation of which we had previously been unaware. A reaction to the death of a friend might inform a person about the real importance that friend had in her life. Anger at an insult to a person's appearance might reveal to her that she ascribes more importance to her looks than she might have admitted to herself.

The value seen in the object is of a particular sort: it seems to make reference to the person's own well-being, or to that of some group to which the person feels attached. People do not go around fearing any and every catastrophe in the world: they fear those that affect them in significant ways. They do not grieve for any and every death, but only those that play a central role in their own lives. This does not mean that emotions are always selfish: for people can and do attach great importance to things and people outside themselves, and to that extent they will feel fear, and anger, and grief about what befalls those things and people. The point is, though, that we have emotions only about what we have already managed to invest with a certain importance in our own scheme of goals and ends.

Now we can see why it seems important to distinguish emotions, as a class, from both appetites and objectless moods. Emotions are distinct from appetites, such as hunger and thirst, because belief plays a far more important role in them: they involve far more thought about their object. Hunger and thirst are based on an antecedent bodily condition, and they go on desiring their object, typically, until gratification ensues. Argument and change of belief influence them hardly at all. As Sextus Empiricus said, "One cannot produce by argument in the hungry man the conviction that he is not hungry." And Adam Smith pointed out that, for this reason, we do not become hungry just because we imagine the hunger of another person, the way we often become sad, or angry, by putting ourselves in someone else's shoes. Taking on the other person's belief is insufficient, because hunger requires a bodily condition that we are simply not in.[18] Smith's view entails what Aristotle would readily grant: that there can be no political oratory designed to whip up hunger, the way there is political oratory designed to whip up anger and fear.

We should not deny that beliefs and norms can influence appetite in some ways: thus it is plausible that hungers for certain specific foods are the product of social teaching. The sexual appetite is even more deeply affected by social learning than hunger and thirst. Moreover, when there is some degree of physical hunger, or sexual lack, rhetoric that draws attention to it can greatly augment it. To the extent that sexual desire is more emotion-like, more ideational, than food-desire, there will be a correspondingly large space for sexual pornography, and a relatively small space for food-pornography. Pornography operates on the borderline between appetite and emotion, exploiting the ideational or emotion-like aspects of an appetite. (It also offers, through masturbation, a gratification of the appetite, another reason why food-pornography does not play a large role in most lives.) So the distinction between emotion and appetite should not be drawn crudely, in a way that negates these possibilities. Nonetheless, the distinction itself remains illuminating.

With moods such as sadness, irritation, and endogenous depression, the issue is more subtle. The distinction we want to get at is that between states that are focused on an intentional object and states that are not, but it is difficult to draw this distinction correctly in any particular case. Some genuine emotions may have an extremely vague object: thus one may have a generalized fear about one's future, or a generalized depression about one's prospects in life. These are emotions and not mere moods, because they have an object, and to that extent we can imagine what it would be to change the state by changing the beliefs involved in it. But we may not be able to tell readily in a particular case whether there is no object, or a vague and highly general object. The problem becomes still deeper once we recognize that people frequently cannot identify the object of their emotion. I may think I am angry at the person who treated me rudely just now, but the intensity of my anger may betray to me, if I study my reactions more systematically, that I am really experiencing a pervasive anger about my job, or my marriage, or bad treatment in the distant past.[19] I may also feel a love, or a jealousy, toward a person in the present that is crucially conditioned by, and in many ways about, a person in the past. These phenomena can lead to many confusions between emotions and moods. If I am feeling depressed, it may be very difficult to know whether my depression is simply endogenous, and perhaps primarily chemical in origin, or whether it has an object in my past or present that I can't readily grasp. Depression occasioned by belief will of course have chemical effects, thus compounding the difficulty. Often the only way to tell will be to see what forms of treatment prove effective—and yet even this does not settle the matter, because treatment that relieves symptoms may do a lot of good without addressing underlying causes.[20] At any rate, however, the conceptual distinction we are after is clear: emotions involve a focus on an intentional object and evaluative beliefs about that object.

III. Emotions, Appraisal, and Moral Education

We have said that emotions involve appraisal or evaluation. We can now see that this is so in two distinct ways. First, as I argued, emotions contain within themselves an appraisal or evaluation of their object. Judy Norman's fear appraises her own death as a serious bad thing that may befall her. A bereaved person's grief appraises the death of a loved one as a terrible loss. The Athenians' anger at the Persians appraises the damage the Persians did to them as an important and terrible damage.

But this means, as I have already suggested, that emotions can themselves be appraised. We can point out that someone's emotion rests on beliefs that are true or false, and (a separate point) reasonable or unreasonable. Furthermore, what we can now see is that such judgments can be made not only about the factual component of the emotion-beliefs, but about their evaluative or appraisal component as well. Take the bereaved person's grief. In appraising it I will of course ask whether it is *true* that the person's loved one has really died, and (a separate point) whether her belief that the death has occurred is *reasonable;* that is, whether she believes this on the basis of good evidence or authority. But I will also ask a further question: Is the death of a loved one the sort of thing about which it is reasonable to be upset? Is her view that this loss is a terrible and significant loss a reasonable view to have? Most of us will unhesitatingly answer, "Yes, of course." The ancient Greek Stoics would have answered, "No, it is not right to be upset at anything that lies outside of our control." In short, our appraisal of her grief must depend on what we think in general about the norms and values that it seems right to hold. Most of us think that it is right to attach great importance to loved ones, and to think such a death terrible. The Stoics differed because they had a different set of norms, according to which any attachment to people and events outside our control is a weakness and a defect.

Or take the Athenians' anger at the Persians. One thing we will ask is: What did the Persians really do, and are the Athenians right about the facts? The emotion of the Athenians might be criticized by saying that they got the facts wrong, or that they formed their view much too hastily, without waiting to sift the evidence. Here again, though, we will also ask a different kind of question: Is what the Persians allegedly did a really bad thing, something that it's right to get really upset about? Maybe what they did was to damage crops in one of the Athenians' colonies. Well, we now have to ask, how bad, really, was that? How upset should they be about it? Is it the sort of thing that is really worth making a big deal about? Again, maybe one of their leaders said something that sounded a little insulting: well, we have to ask ourselves how big a deal that is, whether it's the sort of thing that reasonable people will take to heart, get very angry about, maybe even go to war about.

People care about all kinds of things, and we constantly make appraisals of what they care about. We think, for example, that people are behaving unreasonably if they get very, very upset about being cut off in traffic. "Calm down, it's not such a big deal," we might say to such a person. In his work *On Anger*, Seneca reports that he himself gets very angry when a host seats him at a place at a dinner table that he considers not the most honorable place.[21] He says that he knows he was unreasonable to react this way: this is just not something about which a reasonable person should get angry. Similar judgments are made about fear. Aristotle said that it would be pretty unreasonable to be afraid of a mouse making a noise; but, then and now, many of us are quite afraid of mice.[22] We probably won't spend much time criticizing our friends for their fear of mice, but often a misplaced fear is socially significant. Suppose a colleague of mine crosses the street in fear every time he sees an African-American male walking toward him in Hyde Park, and I want to convince him that it is unreasonable to fear every person of a given race. First, I will point out that such fears probably reflect confused factual beliefs—perhaps he's confusing the fact that a large proportion of crime in Hyde Park is committed by African-American males with the false view that a large proportion of the African-Americans in Hyde Park commit crimes. Next, I will suggest that his emotion probably reflects, as well, some deeper beliefs about race that are equally irrational (in the normative sense I identified in the Introduction): that black men are all a menace to the community, perhaps even that criminality has a hereditary connection to race. By calling these evaluative beliefs "irrational" or "unreasonable," we mean to say that they are groundless, based on mistaken thinking that a closer and more rigorous scrutiny would show to be bad thinking.

So far I have made things too simple. In appraising the evaluative component of a person's emotion, we need, ultimately, to distinguish truth from reasonableness, as we did with the factual beliefs.[23] A person, for example, might hold an evaluative view that is true but unreasonable ("irrational" in the normative sense), if she came by the true view about what is important hastily or carelessly, through a defective process of reasoning. She might also hold a view that is false but reasonable, if she formed the false view on the basis of evidence or teaching that she had good reason to trust. This latter category is important in thinking about change of norms over time. For we typically think that people are reasonable if they accept the standard norms of their society. At any rate, as we shall see, the law typically thinks this, routinely equating the "reasonable man" with the "average" or "ordinary" man. And yet, we all know that such norms may be mistaken. In another era, they would have endorsed judgments that women and members of other races are not equally human. Today we probably hold some views that are just as mistaken as these, but it is difficult to know which views these are, and if we are somewhat merciful with ourselves we might say that if we have made a good-faith effort to be reasonably independent critical thinkers, we are not unreasonable for holding such mistaken normative beliefs as we hold. Thus, if a man in ancient Athens believed that women are inferior, we may judge his view to be mistaken but reasonable, or at least not unreasonable, while such a belief in today's America would be both mistaken and unreasonable.

These appraisals of evaluative beliefs are central to the roles played by emotion in law. We can understand how they work still better if we observe that they are deeply entrenched in our practices of moral education of children. If emotions were not connected to beliefs, if they were just mindless surges, like electric currents, then a parent or teacher could influence a child's emotions only by a process of behavioral conditioning, the way we might teach a rat to run through a maze. We could hope that by attaching rewards and punishments to the behavior associated with the emotion in question we could encourage appropriate emotions and discourage those that are inappropriate.

But of course this is not how real parents behave, at least once their children reach a certain age. Like Aristotle's public speaker, but with much more intimate knowledge of the children who are their audience, they influence emotions by influencing beliefs. If a child gets very angry when another child snatches away his toy, we encourage that anger, up to a point. We tell the child that this is the sort of thing that is unfair, and it's right to be angry at that—not *too* angry, perhaps, but somewhat angry. If, on the other hand, he gets angry because another child wants to take turns using a toy that belongs to the school, we tell him it's not right to get angry at this. That child deserves her turn, it isn't your toy anyway, it is there for all the children to share.

As children get older, we teach them ever more sophisticated appraisals of emotion-related situations. We teach children that it is right to fear certain situations that might not seem to them dangerous at all, as when a smiling stranger offers them a ride in a car. We also teach them that things that seem to them dangerous are not really dangerous: thus it is silly, beyond a certain age, to be afraid of the dark, there isn't anything really bad about the dark. Children don't have a natural fear of people whose skin color is different from their own. Indeed, they hardly notice it as a salient fact about people, unless that fact is made salient to them by adults.[24] But suppose they have acquired somehow the view that people with black skin are to be feared: a parent or teacher will talk to them and try to show them that there is no foundation for such beliefs.

Indeed, thinking about how we grapple with racism and sexism in society helps us understand further the reasons we have for thinking of the emotions in the Aristotelian way I have outlined. For we really don't think that racial fear and hatred are just unreasoning urges that can be dealt with only by suppression. We think that they can be reasoned with: we think that people will change emotionally once they get rid of—or, far better, never acquire—the mistaken beliefs about matters of both fact and value that form the basis for these hatreds.

We need not think that such change is easy. Beliefs taught early in life become deeply habitual, and unlearning them requires a patient effort of attention and self-transformation. Every time we find ourselves seeing the object in the old, defective way, we have to work to shift our perception and substitute a different way of seeing.[25] There is no guarantee that this process will be successful, especially since most people do not have the patience and determination to focus on it consistently over time. There may also be deeper roots to some types of unreasonable emotion. Stephen Carr (the murderer, described in the Introduction, who shot two lesbian women) maintained that his hatred of lesbians derived from his early childhood, when his mother became a lesbian and then abandoned him. Whether this story is true or not, it is the type of story that sometimes happens, and that guarantees a rocky road for even the most determined practitioner of moral self-improvement, which Stephen Carr most certainly was not.[26] Thus holding the view that emotions change in response to changes in belief does not commit us to the absurd view that such change is easy or quick.[27]

Moreover, we may come to think that the very structure that is typical of human life gives rise to some tendencies to unreasonable emotion. In other words, we may believe that there are certain structural obstacles to reasonableness that make the struggle to achieve appropriate emotions something of an uphill battle in all human beings. That is what I shall be arguing in my chapters on disgust and shame. The history of a human being is an odd one. We spend our infancy in a state of physical powerlessness that is virtually unparalleled in animal species, and we remain comparatively powerless throughout our lives, in terms of the ability to meet our own physical needs without assistance. Throughout infancy and childhood, our maturing ability to grasp our world through mind and sense is not matched by physical ability to get what we want for ourselves; we remain for a long time in a state of extreme dependency on others. Moreover, we are also aware of our limits to a much greater extent than are the other animals. After a certain age, we are aware of the fact of death. We fear death and brood about it, and hope that we really will not die. In all these ways, our life story has conflict and ambivalence written into it. It is not surprising that we conceive of ways to deny our mortality and human animality, nor is it surprising that our emotions reflect these struggles.

Thus, though the law tends to operate with the fiction that the "reasonable man" is more or less the same as the "average man," I shall be arguing that it is important for thinkers about law to go behind this assumption and to question it. The average man, being also a human being, exhibits a lot of tension, ambivalence, and, in normative terms, unreasonableness. If we can show that certain emotions are especially likely to be repositories of that unreasonableness, we will have some special reasons to scrutinize their legal role with a particular skepticism.

In short, the Aristotelian view of emotions that I have been defending, the view that is central to the common law tradition, need not be combined with Aristotle's sanguine assumption that most people become fully virtuous and reasonable if they are given a basically good education. It can be combined with a much richer and more accurate view of infancy and childhood, one that does justice to the complex ambivalences and tensions that arise in a typical human process of development. Aristotle, like most men in Greece in his day, did not have much interest in children, and probably never looked closely at them.[28] When we do, we learn some things about the genesis of our own emotions that may lead us to criticize legal practices that are, in at least some areas, too deferential to prevailing norms in emotion.

IV. Emotion and the "Reasonable Man": Manslaughter, Self-Defense

I have argued that our legal tradition works, for the most part, with a view of emotions that has great plausibility and intuitive power.[29] According to this picture, emotions are not mindless surges of affect, but, instead, intelligent responses that are attuned both to events in the world and to the person's important values and goals.[30] They both contain appraisals of items in the world and invite the appraisal of others. It is now time to illustrate the way in which these ideas inform areas of legal doctrine.

In this section I shall focus on the emotions of the alleged malefactor, but we should not forget that the emotions of a "reasonable man" typically play a related role in justifying the underlying contours of the criminal law. On the picture of emotions that I have presented, there will be a close logical relation between the belief that murder, rape, and the like are important damages to human beings and the idea that it is reasonable to fear them when they are impending, to be angry about them when they occur, and to feel compassion when they happen to another. It would be difficult, then, to have any account of why these offenses should be legally regulated that did not at least entail a role for these reasonable emotions, whether that role is emphasized or not.

The standard legal doctrine of voluntary manslaughter holds that a defendant charged with murder may win a reduction of the offense to manslaughter if he can show that: the homicide was committed in response to a provocation by the victim of the crime; that the provocation was "adequate"; that the defendant's anger was that of a "reasonable man"; and that the homicide was committed "in the heat of passion" without sufficient "cooling time." The doctrine mitigates rather than offering a complete exculpation. The most plausible reason for this difference between voluntary manslaughter and self-defense is that, in the manslaughter case, the person's own life is not being threatened and he could and should therefore have summoned the law to his aid. Nonetheless, the doctrine holds that something about his situation and his emotions makes this crime less bad than a murder would be. What makes the difference?

The defendant, we said, must show that he committed the violent act as the result of a provocation, and that the provocation meets a test of legal adequacy. Moreover, he has to have been provoked by the victim of the crime. If A is provoked by B and then kills C, he gets no mitigation under this doctrine.[31] The typical situation is one in which B commits a serious harmful act against A and A retaliates with violence. The early common law authorities defined "adequate" provocations as a matter of law. The distinctions between provocations that were adequate and those that were not were often quite fine. For example, a blow to the face was adequate, a boxing of the ears not.[32] Adultery with a man's wife was adequate, while adultery with a man's girlfriend was not.[33]

Contemporary authorities have tended to abandon such fixed definitions of adequate provocation, leaving these determinations to the judge or jury. The reason for this, according to one influential case, is that the analysis of adequate provocation "must vary with, and depend upon the almost infinite variety of facts presented by the various cases as they arise. The law cannot with justice assume, by the light of past decisions, to catalogue all the various facts and combinations of facts which shall be held to constitute reasonable or adequate provocation."[34] Insofar as this approach is still contested, with many jurisdictions preferring rigid categories, the reason for the controversy is concern to avoid inflammatory prejudicial effect. Although it seems eminently reasonable to permit judges and juries to evaluate matters for themselves, this interest must be balanced against the worry that when they do so they will do so in a way that is unfair and unbalanced.

Even when the doctrine of a jurisdiction does leave a lot of room for judges and juries to insert their own analyses of provocations that are and are not adequate, therefore, some provocations have been ruled inadequate as a matter of law. That is how the Pennsylvania judge ruled when Stephen Carr sought to admit evidence of his overwhelming disgust at witnessing lesbian lovemaking: "[the law] does not recognize homosexual activity between two persons as legal provocation sufficient to reduce an unlawful killing . . . from murder to voluntary manslaughter." "A reasonable person," the court concluded, "would simply have discontinued his observation and left the scene; he would not kill the lovers."[35] Implicit in the judge's remarks is the fact that the women had done nothing at all to provoke Carr except to exist and be lesbians in his presence. They had not harmed him or committed any aggressive act against him. And such an aggressive act is a necessary condition for the application of the doctrine of reasonable provocation.

Thus, although the law does not require defendants to show that their emotions were *actually* the emotions of the reasonable person (an inquiry that would be hopelessly subjective and indeterminate), they do require them to show that their situation was such that it would have provoked extremely strong anger or a related emotion in a reasonable person. (Moreover, it does require a showing that the defendant was under *some* strong emotion.) The showing of reasonable provocation always requires the showing of some aggressive or harmful act by the victim against the defendant, and an act that reaches a certain level of seriousness. What is going on is presumably this: we do not want to hold up social norms that encourage wanton killing. And in general we do not condone any homicide not committed in self-defense. We hold that the reasonable person would never actually take the law into his own hands in a situation of provocation. But we do want to give public and legal recognition to the fact that reasonable people become enraged at certain types of damages to themselves or their loved ones, and we therefore build into the legal doctrine a reduction for those who commit a violent act under such circumstances. The homicidal act is not justified, but it is partially excused, in the sense that a lesser punishment is given for it. The reason is not simply that the person's emotion is comprehensible. It is that the emotion itself, though not the act chosen under its influence, is appropriate.[36]

Notice that the judge in Carr's case does not say that Carr was not disgusted, that his disgust was not extremely strong, or that it did not prompt his homicide. He says, rather, that these are not the reactions of a reasonable person. A reasonable person, whether disgusted or not, would not have been so overwhelmed by emotion that he would be inclined to violence. The law in this way contains a model of what provokes a reasonable person to extreme emotion and what does not. As the case that provides the epigraph to this chapter, *People v. Logan,* puts the point: "[N]o defendant may set up his own standard of conduct and justify or excuse himself because in fact his passions were aroused, unless further the jury believe that the facts and circumstances were sufficient to arouse the passions of the ordinarily reasonable man."

Similar is the case of Frank Small, described at the opening of this chapter. Small insisted that his anger was very strong because he was just a more angry fellow than most people. The judge did not dispute this claim, but said that the law does not reward people for permitting themselves to get into this condition. Small's extreme emotions, the court noted, "result from a want of self-discipline; a neglect of self-culture that is inexcusable."[37] We do not reward people for allowing themselves to be provoked by trivial slights.[38]

What about the doctrinal requirement that the killing must be done "in the heat of passion" and without sufficient "cooling time"? These doctrines might be taken to show that legal authorities think of the emotions as impulses that have to run their course and that disable reason only briefly. This, however, cannot be the right understanding of the doctrine. Carr's and Small's emotions may have been very strong, but they did not get a reduction. Nor does a defendant even need to show that extreme emotion was actually present in order to win a reduction. What seems important is that the situation is such that the reasonable man would have extreme emotion in it. But then, if the defendant has been adequately provoked by a wrongful act committed by the victim, and his anger is thus that of the hypothetical reasonable man, why shouldn't he get the reduction to manslaughter if he kills the victim after a long time has passed? Surely his anger at the wrong done to him does not become inappropriate after a passage of time. Let us suppose that someone has just murdered G's child. G comes upon the murderer right after learning of the crime; she shoots and kills him. G will be very likely to get mitigation under the doctrine. If, however, she waits three weeks and then, having tracked down the murderer, shoots him, she will not. Why not? Surely a reasonable person will remain extremely angry at the murderer, perhaps for the rest of her life.

To solve this puzzle, we have to think not only of the emotion but of its relationship to other concerns. I have already said that the doctrine mitigates, and does not fully exonerate, because it is never right to take the law into one's own hands. In this sense, G's *anger* is that of a reasonable person, but she is not in every respect a reasonable person. A reasonable person would also have other thoughts and emotions: a respect for the law, a sense of anticipatory guilt about homicide, a fear of punishment. In many circumstances, these other thoughts and emotions would step in, preventing G from killing the murderer. She would call the police instead. In the bewildering and jarring moments immediately following her discovery of the murder, we forgive her for not getting her priorities straight, and for not noticing the reasons she has to restrain herself. We do, however, expect people to think about the big picture after a while, and not to be so wrapped up in a single emotion that they forget what they owe to society. So, I think, the doctrine is most plausibly understood.[39]

Self-defense is different. Here we feel that people do not act wrongly when they kill, because a threat to life (or a threat of serious bodily injury) gives people a right to kill. Thus self-defense provides complete exculpation. But the doctrine, once again, defines carefully the limits of the circumstances in which a reasonable person will fear for his life or safety. As Blackstone put it, "[t]he law of self-defense is a law of necessity." The right begins only when the necessity is present, and extends only as far as the necessity. To quote a modern summary of the doctrine:

> There must have been a threat, actual or apparent, of the use of deadly force against the defender. The threat must have been unlawful and immediate. The defender must have believed that he was in imminent peril of death or serious bodily harm, and that his response was necessary to save himself therefrom. These beliefs must not only have been honestly entertained, but also objectively reasonable in light of the surrounding circumstances. It is clear that no less than a concurrence of these elements will suffice.[40]

From the earliest stages of the doctrine the importance of these limits is emphasized:

This right of natural defence does not imply a right of attacking: for, instead of attacking one another for injuries past or impending, men need only have recourse to the proper tribunals of justice. They cannot therefore legally exercise this right of preventive defence, but in sudden and violent cases; when certain and immmediate suffering would be the consequence of waiting for the assistance of the law. Wherefore, to excuse homicide by the pleas of self-defence, it must appear that the slayer had no other possible means of escaping from his assailant.[41]

Some such discussions (the Judy Norman case, for example) refer to the defendant's reasonable *fear* of death or harm, some simply to a reasonable *belief* that he or she might face death or serious bodily harm.[42] Our analysis suggests that it is not surprising that there is this easy substitution, since the belief is one element in the fear, and the most pertinent one for legal purposes. (Another belief that plays a role in fear in such cases, the belief that one's own life is extremely important, is taken for granted throughout, and its reasonableness is the basis of the entire doctrine.)

The general sense of the doctrine is that intense fear for one's life or bodily safety is, all by itself, not sufficient to justify the use of deadly force. We require in addition that the fear be reasonable; that is, based on reasonable beliefs about the situation. We can easily see here that reasonableness, and not truth, is the relevant category. If an intruder threatens me with a gun, it is usually reasonable for me to believe that the gun is a real gun and loaded with real ammunition, even though it might turn out that it was a toy gun, or loaded with blanks. I will be able to plead self-defense even though my belief turns out to have been false.

There are many questions about how the reasonableness standard should be further defined. For example, should the belief be one that it would be reasonable for any person to hold, or should it be reasonable in the light of the person's particular history and experience? This issue was debated in the case of Bernard Goetz, who was tried for attempted murder after having shot and wounded four young men in the New York subway after one or two of them approached him and asked for $5.[43] Goetz maintained that his belief that his life was in danger was reasonable in the light of his own particular history of assault. This contention was essentially repudiated by the New York Court of Appeals, which maintained that the standard of reasonableness was an objective and not a subjective standard, and that an honest belief, based on prior history, was not necessarily enough to meet the reasonableness standard.[44] Questions are also prompted by different formulations of the standard in different legal sources. The Model Penal Code, for example, omits the crucial word "reasonable," and reformulates the doctrine so that a defendant whose belief was negligently formed, for example, could be convicted only of the lesser charge of negligent homicide. New York is an example of a state which, though following the general approach of the Model Penal Code, has reinserted the word "reasonable" into the relevant statute. In one way or another, the tradition remains one that invites assessment of the reasonableness of a defendant's fear, and the beliefs grounding that fear.

I have said that the doctrine assumes the significance of one's own life, and the legitimacy of caring greatly about protecting it. But the appraisals it involves are actually much more complex. For it is not only a threat to life that may give rise to a successful claim of self-defense. As we have seen, serious bodily injury is also typically included. But there are still other important items that a defendant is allowed to use violence in order to protect. In some jurisdictions, one may plead self-defense if one uses deadly force to avoid rape or even robbery.[45] Such statutes implicitly appraise bodily integrity and property as significant goods for which it is reasonable to fight. Again, although some jurisdictions impose a duty to flee or retreat before turning and fighting, others do not. The refusal to impose this requirement clearly has its roots in a nineteenth-century conception of honor: it would be demeaning to require "'a true man . . . to fly from an assailant, who by violence or surprise maliciously seeks to take his life or do him enormous bodily harm.'"[46] Such a high valuation of honor has been criticized, but many jurisdictions still allow a fear of disgrace to be favorably appraised in this sort of situation.[47] Similar thoughts about honor and identity inform the prevailing notion that one need not flee an assault within one's own home: it would be an indignity for a man to be made "a fugitive from his own home."[48]

Finally, I am allowed to plead self-defense if I intervene in order to prevent death or injury to another—but states are divided about what, exactly, the person has to believe in order to get this excuse. Some hold that the defendant will be exculpated if he reasonably believed he had to attack in order to save the person he reasonably took to be the victim. Others impose the stronger requirement that the person on whose behalf he intervenes must in fact have had the right to use deadly force.[49] Such doctrines also involve social norms about the relationship in which we stand to one another, and the type of caution that a potential rescuer needs to exercise.

Let us now turn to Judy Norman's case. Battered women have for some time attempted to portray homicide of the battering spouse as an act of self-defense. The difficulty is that the act is at least sometimes committed at a time when the victim is temporarily not posing any direct threat to the woman's life. It is important to point out that this is not the typical case; the idea that it is is a media construction. In the best recent survey of such cases, 80 percent of the battered women who killed their spouse killed him during a direct confrontation.[50] Thus traditional self-defense doctrine proves adequate to account for the majority of such cases. Nonetheless, the remainder constitute an important minority, and recent legal thought has been grappling with the doctrine in order to deal adequately with these cases. It is evident that women who live in fear of their batterers, and are usually much weaker physically, often believe that they can successfully defend themselves only if the battering spouse is sleeping or otherwise inattentive at the time. Such beliefs seem very reasonable. And yet the idea that it is self-defense to kill a man in his sleep fits badly with the narrow boundaries of the tradition. Another issue is that of escape: it seems to legal authorities very odd to say that the battered woman cannot escape, if, in fact, the battering spouse is sleeping and she can just walk out the door. Judy Norman did walk out the door, dropping her child off somewhere else before returning to kill her husband.

For such reasons, courts have been reluctant to allow battered women to plead self-defense. In a case shortly before Judy Norman's, the Kansas Supreme Court held that it was error to give the jury a self-defense instruction in a case similar to Norman's, where the defendant had shot her spouse while he was sleeping:

In order to instruct a jury on self-defense, there must be some showing of an imminent threat or confrontational circumstance involving
an overt act by an aggressor. There is no exception to this requirement where the defendant has suffered long-term domestic abuse
and the victim is the abuser. In such cases, the issue is not whether the
defendant believes homicide is the solution to past or future problems with the batterer, but rather whether circumstances surrounding the killing were sufficient to create a reasonable belief in the
defendant that the use of deadly force was necessary. . . . Under such
circumstances, a battered woman cannot reasonably fear imminent
life-threatening danger from her sleeping spouse.[51]

Similarly, Judy Norman's actions seemed to the judge to show that
she did not have a reasonable belief that her life was in imminent
danger: she was able to, and did, leave the house; when she attacked,
her husband was sleeping.

Such cases suggest that the doctrine, crafted to deal above all with
the situation of men confronted with a threat of violence from other
men, is not very well designed to confront the situation and circumstances of the battered woman. She may in fact have no reasonable
hope of a life apart from her spouse. If she leaves, he is very likely to
pursue her, and in any case she usually has no livelihood apart from
him. She may also fear for the safety of children if she leaves. Experts
on battered women have added psychological analyses of the emotional condition of battered women, who become emotionally de-
pleted and helpless in a relationship in which they are constantly
subjected to abuse.[52] In one 1980 case, in which the State had successfully excluded expert psychological testimony on battered women,
the New Jersey Supreme Court reversed the defendant's conviction
for murder, holding that this testimony was pertinent to establishing
the objective reasonableness of her belief that her life was endan-
gered.[53] This area of law remains debated, however. The divided opinions in Judy Norman's case show the depth of controversy about how
the reasonableness standard should be understood in these circumstances. Meanwhile, it has become increasingly common for juries to
acquit defendants in such cases, even where the formal requirements
of the doctrine are not met.[54]

V. Emotions and Changing
Social Norms

Keith Peacock returned home unexpectedly one evening and discovered his wife making love with another man. He shot her dead several hours later. Upon Peacock's plea of guilty to voluntary manslaughter, Judge Robert Cahill sentenced Peacock to eighteen months' imprisonment in a work release program. The judge expressed sympathy for Peacock, stating that he could imagine nothing that would provoke "an uncontrollable rage greater than this: for someone who is happily married to be betrayed in your personal life, when you're out working to support the spouse."[55] "I seriously wonder how many men married five, four years," Cahill continued, "would have the strength to walk away without inflicting some corporal punishment."[56]

The only remarkable thing about this story is that anyone viewed it as remarkable. For centuries, adultery has been regarded as a provocation adequate to mitigate the killing of either the paramour or the unfaithful spouse to voluntary manslaughter; for centuries, men convicted of this offense have been sentenced leniently. Yet Judge Cahill's sentence and remarks set off a storm of controversy. Newspapers ran critical editorials. Protesters picketed the courthouse, calling for Cahill's removal. Formal disciplinary proceedings were initiated.[57]

What was once settled in the law—that marital infidelity can provoke a reasonable man to homicidal rage—is now contested. Until 1973, the Texan who killed his wife's paramour had a complete statutory defense to homicide.[58] By the time of its repeal, the statute was viewed as "an anachronism—a frontier idea whose time had gone" and which rendered "the state a legal laughing stock."[59] Other states, which expressed leniency through mitigation rather than complete exculpation, have undergone a similar shift, as the public criticism of Judge Cahill indicates.

Presumably the public does not doubt the genuineness or the intensity of the rage of the betrayed husband. People object, rather, to the judgment that this emotion is reasonable, the sort of emotion a reasonable man would have. Because emotions involve appraisal, the appraisal of those emotions will reflect a society's norms. When a society asks what cases of fear and anger it should deem reasonable, the emotions that the hypothetical reasonable man would have in such a situation, it implicitly asks what it is reasonable to value deeply, and the answer to that question is typically given in terms of prevailing normative standards. Such normative appraisals are, then, likely to shift as society's norms undergo change. Even if marital infidelity continues to be viewed as a serious moral wrong, something it is right to get angry about, few today would assert what was typically asserted in defense of the traditional doctrine, namely, that adultery is "the highest invasion of a man's property."[60] (Notice that this shift may be closely connected to a shift in view about whether adultery is properly judged a criminal offense.)[61] Presumably the current view is that it is reasonable to care about one's spouse and her fidelity, but not *in the way* that the homicidal husband does. Anger is reasonable, but not the sort of anger that leads to homicide. He is treating his wife as a piece of property that is his to control, rather than a person who has made a free choice, however unfortunate from his point of view.

In the case of the jealous husband, a new understanding of marriage has altered norms of male authority and control that underlay the old application of the reasonableness standard. A similar shift is at work in the area of domestic violence. As we have seen, the self-defense doctrine was crafted to deal with a common situation confronting males: their life is imminently threatened by an adversary or an intruder. (Sometimes, of course, females faced similar dangers, but references to the "true man" and to the idea of the man as homeowner show that the threatened male was taken to be the standard case.) In this paradigm scenario, there is good reason to insist that the threat to life be imminent. Legal authorities did not want to encourage people to track down an adversary hours later and kill him in the belief that they would be completely exonerated. Such a killer might possibly get a reduction to voluntary manslaughter, but he would never be able to plead self-defense. This seems perfectly logical.

Now, however, we have a better understanding of domestic violence than previous generations had, and we have decided to focus on it as a social problem of great importance. Study of the problem suggests that a woman may reasonably believe her situation inescapable and

that she has no alternative but to use deadly force, even if her husband is asleep or otherwise not threatening her with a weapon at
that particular moment. (The reasonableness of such beliefs is supported by the evidence that batterers often track and violently attack
their partners, even after the partner has left.) Such issues remain
deeply controversial. One might plausibly hold, for example, that a
woman in the position of Judy Norman deserves a reduction to voluntary manslaughter, on the grounds that the abuse was adequate
provocation, but does not deserve complete exculpation on the basis
of self-defense. Such difficult issues should be worked out over time.
But it is clear that the threat to life, bodily integrity, and dignity that
is posed by domestic violence has greatly risen in visibility, and that,
as a society, we now accord these issues much more importance than
we previously did. We have a better understanding of the harm domestic abuse does, and we are no longer inclined to think of a woman
as in any sense her husband's subordinate. Such shifts in norms alter
the valuation of the anger and fear of the battered woman.

VI. Reasonable Sympathy:
Compassion in Criminal Sentencing

So far we have focused on the emotions of the criminal defendant. I
have argued that anger and fear play a significant role in the process
of evaluating putatively criminal acts. While such emotions are not in
any way error-proof, and while the doctrine itself insists that they
may be inappropriate in a variety of ways, the doctrine also holds
that at times these emotions can be "reasonable," based on a correct
appraisal of facts and a reasonable account of important values. When
this is so, they may either mitigate or, in the case of self-defense, provide a complete exculpation for violent behavior. The reason these
emotions play the role that they do inside the process of criminal ad-
judication is that they respond to significant harms or damages, and
there is general agreement that harms and damages are appropriate
areas for legal regulation. As I have mentioned, these judgments are
closely linked to a set of judgments about the emotions of the public
at large: namely, that it is in general reasonable for a citizen to have

fear of and anger at certain sorts of damages. Such ideas are deeply embedded in the justification of the criminal law.

Now, however, we turn directly to spectatorial emotions, as we consider the role played by compassion in the process of criminal sentencing. It is obvious that compassion *can* play a role in criminal sentencing. It is natural to consider the defendant's life at this time, and to adjust the penalty if we think that a specific history—for example, a history of childhood sexual abuse—might have destabilized the personality, making criminal conduct more understandable and to that extent less heinous, even if it does not give rise to a successful plea of diminished capacity under today's very restrictive insanity criteria. Such judgments are routinely made, both in informal public assessment of highly publicized cases and in actual deliberations by judges and juries. For example, Susan Smith, a mother who killed her children after a long history of child sexual abuse, was convicted of first-degree murder but given a life sentence rather than the death penalty. That judgment mirrored widespread public sentiment in favor of some degree of leniency in sentencing on account of this history.[62]

The question we need to press, however, is whether this role for compassion is regarded by the legal tradition as reasonable and good. One can easily imagine arguments against allowing it to play this role: people's sympathies are unpredictable and inconstant; they may have antecedent biases against certain types of defendants and in favor of others that will influence the way in which they hear the defendant's story. Despite these perils, however, a long Anglo-American tradition in the criminal law has insisted on a place for compassion in sentencing, constructing a notion of "tethered" or reasonable compassion that is analogous to the law's conceptions of reasonable anger and reasonable fear.

Before we can examine this tradition, however, we need to say more about the emotion itself.[63] Compassion, like the other emotions we have discussed, contains thoughts. Standard analyses of the emotion, from Aristotle on, emphasize that compassion requires the thought that another person is undergoing something seriously bad. In the emotion itself, then, we evaluate the other person's predicament as serious, as having "size," as Aristotle put it. The estimate of

"size" may echo the suffering person's own estimate, but that need
not always be so. We have great compassion for people whose very
predicament is that they are rendered unconscious or mentally damaged, and who thus may be unable to comprehend the seriousness of
their loss. We also withhold compassion from people if we think that
they are just "spoiled," moaning and groaning over something that is
not really so bad. In according compassion to another, we already,
then, begin to assume the posture of a "judicious spectator," forming
an estimate of the person's misfortune as best we can. Of course we
may do this hastily or wrongly, and thus may fail to be the fully "judicious spectator" that Adam Smith envisaged when he coined the
term, but compassion's spectatorial nature already contains at least
an invitation to reflective evaluation.

The second thought that compassion generally contains is one
that Aristotle emphasized in connecting compassion to tragic drama:
that the person is not fully to blame for his or her plight.[64] There may
be some blame, but, insofar as we feel compassion, we are judging that
the predicament is out of proportion to the blame.

The tradition further emphasizes that compassion typically involves the thought that we ourselves are vulnerable in similar ways. It
thus connects the suffering person to the sympathizer's own possibilities and vulnerabilities. This creation of a community of vulnerability is among the great strengths of compassion, as a motive for
helping; but it also explains why people who think that their possibilities are utterly above those of others may fail to have compassion for the plight of those others. Rousseau said that the kings and
nobles of France lack compassion for the lower classes because they
"count on never being human beings," subject to all the vicissitudes
of life. Typically this thought of similarity is reinforced by acts of empathetic imagining, where we put ourselves in the other person's
own shoes.

I would argue that neither the judgment of similar possibilities
nor empathetic imagining are strictly necessary for compassion. We
may have compassion for the sufferings of animals without thinking
that their possibilities are similar to our own and without imagining
that we are them—although we surely need to make sense of their
predicament somehow. We can also imagine an omnipotent God

feeling compassion for human suffering despite God's utter difference in possibility. Many religious traditions have held that imagining requires a body, thus limiting the ways in which God can imagine human suffering. (According to Aquinas, for example, God [the Father] could form the concepts involved, but without imagining the particulars.) We should surely grant, however, that both the acknowledgment of similarity and empathetic imagining are very strong psychological aids in getting flawed human beings to feel compassion for others. Experimental work on the emotion by C. Daniel Batson has shown clearly the power of a vivid narrative presentation of the suffering person's predicament in the generation of compassionate emotion and helping behavior.[65]

One further thought must, I believe, be added if we are to have compassionate emotion: it is what I call the *eudaimonistic judgment*, that is, the thought that the person in question is important to the person who has the emotion. Our emotions take their stand where we are, from within the perspective of our most significant concerns. We grieve for those for whom we care, not for those for whom we don't care. We fear for calamities that may befall ourselves or those for whom we care, not for distant calamities—unless we have managed to make them part of our circle of care and concern. Even though compassion has the potential to connect us to a larger group of humans, it will not do so without a moral achievement that is at least coeval with it, in which we focus on the suffering person or people as among our significant goals and ends, as part of our circle of concern. That focusing may happen contemporaneously: thus, Batson has shown that a vivid story of a stranger's predicament may generate a lively concern for that person, leading to both emotion and helping behavior. Such focusing may prove unstable, however: Adam Smith wryly comments that people who feel compassion for the victims of an earthquake in China will lose that emotion completely if they are distracted by a pain in their little finger. The uneven and perspectival character of compassion poses problems for moral education and for ethics.[66]

Now that we have laid out these four judgments, we can see how and why compassion is likely to go wrong. It may go wrong by getting the seriousness of the predicament wrong—either because of misinformation as to what has actually happened, or because of confusion about how serious the bad event is. (Sociologist Candace Clark finds that many Americans list being stuck in traffic as a major occasion for compassion, along with illness and impending death.)[67] It may go wrong because of errors about fault, blaming people for things that they did not bring on themselves, or failing to hold them responsible for things that they did. (Clark shows that Americans are strongly inclined to blame the poor for their poverty, despite the fact that it would be difficult to support this judgment with convincing reasons.) It may go wrong, finally, by including too few human beings (and, indeed, other creatures) in the circle of concern.

Most societies will contain serious disagreements about what instances of compassion are reasonable and appropriate. Are the poor to blame for their poverty? How serious a hardship is unemployment? How far should one be concerned with the well-being of people outside one's own nation? We can expect controversy to continue over these and many other cases, and it would probably be unwise to build legal norms on any definite answer to such highly controversial propositions. On the other hand, it is also clear that some central instances of compassion can be agreed to be reasonable, and that at least some of these have a role in criminal sentencing. Certain sorts of abuse in childhood, for example, are understood to be serious wrongs that a child suffers through no fault of its own. If the legal process directs the judge or juror to focus on the fortunes of such a person, we may expect compassion to be the result, and this sort of compassion would be generally agreed to be reasonable.

Let us now consider criminal sentencing, and let us focus on one case that has already been introduced, *California v. Brown*. At issue was a state jury instruction that asked jurors not to be swayed by "mere sentiment, conjecture, sympathy, passion, prejudice, public opinion or public feeling." The issue was whether this instruction was unconstitutional on grounds that it asked jurors to disregard "'its constitutional duty to consider "any [sympathetic] aspect of the defendant's character or record," whether or not related to the offense for which he is on trial, in deciding the appropriate penalty.'"[68] Notice that from the beginning there is a general agreement that defendants have a constitutional right to present such compassion-eliciting evidence at the penalty phase, and that to be deprived of this right is a constitutional violation (of the Eighth Amendment's guarantee against cruel and unusual punishment). Thus nobody questions the fact that a certain sort of compassion, based upon the evidence presented during the penalty phase, must be available as a part of the process of capital sentencing if such sentencing is to be constitutional.

Albert Brown had been found guilty of forcible rape and first-degree murder in the death of a fifteen-year-old girl. At the penalty phase, the prosecution presented evidence of a prior crime. The defense presented the testimony of family members, who attested to his usually peaceful nature, and also the testimony of a psychiatrist, who stated that Brown "killed his victim because of his shame and fear over sexual dysfunction." Brown himself testified, saying that he was ashamed of his conduct, and asking for mercy from the jury.[69] The case did not concern the adequacy of this testimony to mitigate punishment from death to life imprisonment; again, all sides admitted that this *sort* of testimony was pertinent, and that the jury should be allowed to consider it and decide for itself.

What was at issue was whether the jury instruction would mislead jurors and dissuade them from duly considering this pertinent evidence, thus fulfilling their constitutional mandate. The majority held that the word "mere" in the instruction modified all the words after it, not just "sentiment," and that jurors were thus asked to disregard only "mere sympathy," by which was meant "untethered sympathy," that is, sympathy not based upon the testimony actually presented at the penalty phase. The majority argues, further, that an average juror would understand that this was the intent of the instruction, and would not be misled. "[W]e hold that a reasonable juror would not interpret the challenged instruction in manner that would render it unconstitutional."[70] The dissenters argue (plausibly, in my view) that the instruction is confusing on its face: a juror could easily conclude that "mere" modified only "sentiment" and that they were thus being asked to disregard all sympathy. (This confusion would be fostered by the fact that there is no good form of prejudice to be contrasted with "mere prejudice.") Moreover, the textual confusion is made greater by the characteristic behavior of prosecutors, who browbeat jurors into disregarding sympathy-eliciting testimony by offering a confusing reading of the instruction. Thus, in a typical example, a prosecutor said, "'As the Judge will instruct you, you must not be swayed by sympathy.'"[71] Another said, "'[S]ympathy is an interesting thing, because even though you try not to consider it, this decision you are going to make has emotional overtones to it. It would be very hard to completely filter out all our emotions, make the decision on a rational basis. Although the instruction says you are to try to do that.'"[72] Agreeing with the majority that the defendant has a constitutional right to present sympathy-inducing evidence and to have the jury duly consider it, with the possibility that it will elicit a compassion leading to mercy, the dissenters conclude that Brown's constitutional rights are violated by the instruction, which can easily confuse the jurors into disregarding their constitutional duty.

"Tethered" or "reasonable" compassion is, then, a part of the sentencing process about which all agree. Such compassion is based on testimony presented at the penalty phase, rather than any extraneous feature, and it is based on a reasonable juror's evaluation of that evidence. In Brown's case, for example, a reasonable juror might hear all the evidence and not react with compassion, since it would be perfectly reasonable to think that sexual dysfunction is not a predicament sufficiently grave to explain, in any mitigating way, an upsurge of homicidal anger. Had Brown's childhood included serious sexual abuse, there would be a greater likelihood that compassion would be elicited. In any case, to have the chance to present evidence that *might* possibly elicit compassion is every defendant's right, as *Woodson* asserted in 1976, holding that this process is part of what it is to treat defendants as "uniquely individual human beings."

There remain some serious unresolved issues about this role for "tethered compassion." For example, if it is constitutionally required, and if, at the same time, there is other evidence showing that any discretionary death penalty process is likely to be biased on grounds of race, doesn't this entail that there is no constitutional way to administer the death penalty? (I believe that the answer to this question is "yes," and that, among the several reasons for thinking the death penalty unconstitutional, this is one argument that may possibly persuade adherents who are not persuaded by more direct moral arguments.)

Another question that we must face is the proper role of compassion for victims in the sentencing process. There has been a strong trend toward the introduction of "victim-impact statements" at the penalty phase, and it has been argued by some legal defenders of compassion that anyone who supports the *Woodson* argument must, in all consistency, support victim-impact statements.[73] In other words, if the defendant has a chance to appeal to the jury for sympathy, the victim's survivors should have this opportunity too. On the other hand, one can argue, plausibly in my view, that the penalty phase is about the defendant (who has already been convicted), and about whether that individual should live or die. Any evidence about the level of crime the defendant has committed has already been introduced in the main part of the trial. Extra evidence of impact on relatives is of unclear relevance, whereas evidence of serious developmental damage to the defendant is of admitted and obvious relevance. Moreover, victim-impact statements may exacerbate the problems of forming a correct "eudaimonistic judgment"; that is, focusing with due concern on the defendant. For victims are very often more like jurors than defendants are, and they may have an easier time feeling compassion for them, but this alliance drives a wedge between the jury and the defendant.[74] Finally, the use of victim-impact statements treats victims unequally, since people who have surviving relatives are represented in a way that isolated people are not. For all these reasons it seems perfectly consistent to support the *Woodson* tradition of a "tethered compassion" for defendants while remaining skeptical about victim-impact statements.

Once again, however, this is a debate about *what* a reasonable compassion is, and precisely what role it should play, not about *whether* there is a reasonable compassion, or whether elicitors of such emotions are important parts of the process of sentencing.

Compassion has many potential roles in public life. It can provide crucial underpinnings for social welfare programs, for foreign aid and other efforts toward global justice, and for many forms of social change that address the oppression and inequality of vulnerable groups. I have focused here on just one small part of its function important in the criminal law. It has been my aim to show that even the most cautious jurists agree that compassion is built into the sentencing process, and that any attempt to eliminate it violates fundamental rights. (So much, I shall argue, is not true of disgust and shame.)

VII. Emotions and Political Liberalism

When we evaluate people's emotions and judge that some are based on a more reasonable appraisal of important goods than others, a worry naturally arises. This worry is that the resulting conception of law will be illiberal, imposing on some people the view of the good that others hold. This worry grows particularly strong when we recognize that in the typical case the view respected by the law is the view of the majority. Are we not simply inviting the majority to tyrannize over the minority, saying that minority values are less legitimate or less important than majority values?

This worry will not trouble political thinkers who are basically communitarian in their orientation. The communitarian position (as typified, for example, in the "communitarian manifesto" of Amitai Etzioni, and in his other work) typically prizes homogeneity of values as a very important social good.[75] Communitarians are often willing to sacrifice both diversity and, to a certain extent, liberty in order to pursue that good. With respect to the law, Etzioni clearly regards it as an advantage in a view of law that it does curtail diversity and even inhibit some people's freedom, while at the same time promoting homogeneity in values. That is what a "monochrome society" (the title of his most recent book) is supposed to be: a society in which we identify ourselves with what we have in common, rather than with what divides us. Such thinkers will still have questions to face about how far liberty may be curtailed in the name of shared values, but the general enterprise of imposing shared norms through law will not seem troubling at all.

The liberal is in a very different position. Typically, liberals follow John Stuart Mill in thinking that the liberty of individuals to choose, proclaim, and live by norms of their own choosing is an extremely important social good. Some liberals emphasize, along with Mill, that respect for individual liberty produces yet other goods. Mill argued, for example, that we are likely to get more truth by protecting the expression of unpopular opinions, because it is only in the climate of free debate that the merits of each position are likely to be clearly seen. (I shall discuss this position in chapter 7.) Other liber-. als focus, instead, on the intrinsic importance of a person's choices as a part of what a person is, and thus connect respect for liberty to a more general norm of respect for persons. A society that tells people what they should think and say in important matters is lacking in respect for what may be at the heart of each person's search for the meaning of life.[76] Both sorts of liberals, however, will be made very nervous by the idea that law should take sides with some norms against others, saying that these are good norms to hold (and on which to base one's emotions) and that those are not.

This book does not defend one of these political approaches above the other, at least not directly or systematically, but the perspective from which it is written is that of a liberal who believes that respect for persons requires considerable respect for and deference to their conceptions of what is valuable in life. Following both Mill and John Rawls, I argue elsewhere that the tyranny of majority over minority opinion is a major danger in political life, and that one of the great strengths of the classical liberal tradition is its respect for spheres of freedom within which individuals choose the goals that they think most important.[77] I therefore need to confront the imagined liberal objection to my view of the role of emotions in law.

To reply to the objection, we could simply say that it is inevitable that the law will take cognizance of the valuations inherent in the emotions of both perpetrators and victims, and judge some as more pertinent than others. It would appear that this imagined opponent cannot stop short at removing appeals to emotion only; he or she will have to object to evaluative judgments passed on all mental states, especially those that have, internally, an intentional and value-laden character. Thus not only anger and fear, but also intention, motive, and other nonemotional mental states will have to be rejected. The alternative (to focus for now on the criminal law) would thus be to have a strict-liability standard for all criminal conduct, which would mean a radical and more or less unimaginable change in current practices. In other words, we would have to say that homicide is homicide, whatever states of mind accompany the bodily movement of killing. We would have to treat a killing in self-defense as no different, under the law, from a malicious premeditated killing. Such an approach would mean a complete transformation in the criminal law. When we think about crimes such as murder and rape, as well as fraud, larceny, and blackmail, we are making value judgments all the time, classifying different levels of offense by their gravity, and recommending different levels of sentence for different offenders within a given offense. Often, these evaluations involve evaluation of emotion and state of mind. In fact, without evaluation it would be difficult to know how we would even describe offenses: the terms "murder," "rape," and "blackmail" already involve evaluation of states of mind, and if we would assiduously avoid such judgments we would have to find a new language for the description of these acts. So we could reply that it looks as if liberals are already living with a legal regime in which value judgments are made about emotions, and have no realistic prospect of doing otherwise.[78] Moreover, this legal regime has been understood, where compassion is concerned, to be constitutionally required.

Could we imagine an objector who was content to allow the law to allude to, and to evaluate, mental states such as intentions, motive, negligence, and premeditation, objecting only to the evaluation of emotions, and the valuations they contain? Certainly the criminal law proceeds in this way in many areas; the question is, however, whether we could defend an approach that did so in all, including the areas we have just been discussing. Well, anything is possible, but it would be somewhat difficult to understand what the rationale for this distinction would be. (Nor would it remove troublesome issues of evaluation, nor even evaluation directed at states that have, internally, an intentional and value-laden character.) As I have mentioned in the Introduction, the most common form of the antiemotion position today is a Utilitarian position that denies all appeal to mental states. Nonetheless, if we did encounter such a position, we would still be able to say that this position would transform many doctrines in the criminal law: not only the doctrines of premeditation and self-defense, and the appeal to compassion in the context of sentencing, but also others that I have not discussed here, for example the doctrine of duress. So the onus would be on the objector to give a coherent account of the criminal law without such doctrines in their current form.

Moreover, as I have already stressed in the Introduction, such objections to evaluating the emotional states of alleged malefactors typically leave in place a substantial role for emotions, and the valuations they contain, in the underlying justification of the criminal law. Thus, even if we do away with a role for fear and anger inside the evaluation of a criminal defendant, we are left with a large role for notions of reasonable fear and reasonable anger in describing the contours of legal regulation and justifying the very existence of laws against theft, assault, murder, and so forth. If those appeals themselves should be sidelined by the objector, he would have to take on the much larger task of saying why these crimes are bad without alluding to the attitudes people have to the damage they do. Again, this would be a large task, involving considerable revision of traditional understandings. I myself believe that any coherent account of why murder, assault, and the like are bad will at least *entail* that citizens reasonably fear such crimes and are reasonably angry when they occur, whether these entailments are emphasized or not. Would it then not seem a little peculiar, however, to avoid mentioning these facts about the "reasonable man" when evaluating malefactors' states of mind?

Such an answer, resting as it does on traditional understandings, would not be fully satisfactory in the context of the present project, since I shall be proposing some significant alterations in settled legal practice. It would be inconsistent to recommend these changes and then to fall back, when it suits my purposes, on current ways of doing things, though it must be noted that the changes I shall propose are small and subtle by comparison to the radical change that would be required if we were to remove the evaluations of emotions altogether from the criminal law and its justification. Fortunately, however, we can make a much stronger response to the objection from a liberal perspective.

Liberalism, in valuing freedom of choice as a very great good, is not committed to complete neutrality or agnosticism about matters of value. Indeed, the very fact that it is committed to freedom of choice as a great good shows that it is not neutral about value. And in general, the political culture of a liberal society is not free of value judgments. It is best conceived of as a partial moral conception, not a conception in which the moral has no place.

To make this idea more precise, let us consider one of the strongest recent forms of liberalism, the "political liberalism" of Charles Larmore[79] and John Rawls.[80] Political liberalism is based on a norm of respect for persons, which is understood to require respecting their diverse conceptions of what is good and valuable in life. Seeing that there are many religions and many secular views of how to live in any modern society, and seeing that the disagreements among these views do not appear to be going away, political liberals hold that there is a measure of "reasonable disagreement" among people on matters of ultimate value (matters, for example, such as the immortality of the soul, and the particular content of a list of personal virtues). Political liberals are not skeptics: they do not hold that no position is better than any other. They simply hold that many disagreements are reasonable disagreements among reasonable people. This being the case, it is right for political society to respect those differences, as a part of what respect for persons requires. This respect for difference, however, does not lead the political liberal to believe that political life should be value-free. On the contrary, respect for persons is a very basic *value* about which the political liberal is not in the least neutral. And it has implications for many other aspects of political society.

For example, if we respect persons, and respect them as equal in worth—the version of mutual respect that political liberals typically defend—we will naturally be led to endorse a form of political society that gives all persons certain basic religious, political, and civil liberties. We will want those liberties to be both extensive and in some sense equal: Rawls captures this by saying that we will choose the most extensive liberty that is compatible with a like liberty for all. We will also, Rawls argues, want all citizens to be supplied with other "primary goods" that are prerequisites for getting on with any plan of life whatever. Thus, we will want a distribution of income, wealth, and opportunity that permits all citizens to pursue their plans of life. The details of Rawls's particular proposal are controversial, and need not concern us here. What should concern us is the idea that all citizens will be asked to endorse society's arrangements, both with regard to liberty and with regard to other basic goods, and to endorse them *as good,* not just as a mere modus vivendi, something that they have to put up with in order to have peaceful coexistence. Thus citizens are asked to share a partial conception of what is good and valuable.

How can this be compatible with liberalism, one might ask? The answer is that liberalism has always stood for something, and has always asked people to endorse something: the equal worth of persons, and their liberty. Rawls argues that the different views that currently exist in a complex modern society such as that of the United States are not so different that the holders of those views cannot concur on a core set of norms in these areas. He suggests that the different religions and other views of how to live life can still endorse the political values of liberty and opportunity *as one part* of what their overall view of life includes. He uses a striking image: the values of the political culture are a "module" that can be attached onto the rest of what Catholics, Protestants, Jews, Buddhists, atheists, and others believe. It can be so attached because it does not take stands on controversial religious matters (such as the nature of the soul). Further, the holders of the different views will want to attach it to their views in this way because they will see that it is a view that respects them and answers well to their desire to live with others on a basis of both freedom and mutual respect. In this way, Rawls envisages the coming into being of an "overlapping consensus" that will include all the major conceptions of value prevalent in a pluralistic society.

There may be views that refuse to join the consensus: religions, for example, that preach intolerance, or conceptions holding that blacks, or women, should not have equal political and civil rights. The holders of such views will not be persecuted, because strong norms of free speech apply to all citizens, but they will rightly be regarded as "unreasonable," in conflict with the basic social consensus. Their proposals, insofar as they do conflict with that consensus, will not be able to come up for straightforward majority vote: constitutional principles entrenching the basic freedoms and rights of the consensus will prevent (as they now do) the U.S. Congress from debating a motion to restore slavery, or to remove women's right to vote.

I have presented the idea of political liberalism in some detail because, now that we have it before us, we can easily see that the type of appraisal of emotion and value discussed here need not be in any tension with it. Political liberalism asks us to value certain basic rights and liberties for all citizens. It also asks us to value certain "primary goods" that are prerequisites for leading a flourishing life.[81] So it is easy to see that such a liberalism will have a strong interest in laws that protect those rights and liberties for all citizens, and also in laws that protect other primary goods, such as property.[82] Laws against homicide, rape, and theft are natural expressions of the overlapping consensus, as are judgments that distinguish deliberate from inadvertent or merely negligent offenses. Indeed, respect for persons seems to require that we protect them from violations of their rights. Whether we think of the criminal law in retributive, deterrent, or expressive terms, it seems eminently reasonable to make the standard distinctions of level of offense.

Our three areas of criminal law fit very nicely into such a liberal approach. The person who receives mitigation under the "reasonable provocation" doctrine values goods such as life, bodily integrity, and the life and bodily integrity of her loved ones, that were threatened by the wrongful act of the victim. Valuing these goods is part of the political conception. It is because the victim in this way violated her rights, rights that we all agree belong to all citizens, that she deserves mitigation for her violent act. The person who kills in self-defense kills in defense of a central good—life or bodily safety—that is similarly central to the political conception. In other words, the goods at stake in these two cases are common ground between the liberal and the communitarian, and up to that point there should be no difference between them that will affect the endorsement of the traditional legal doctrine. As for compassion, I have argued in *Upheavals of Thought* that a liberal society may construct a variety of roles for compassion in connection with support for a set of basic entitlements.[83] With regard to our present concern, the possibility of compassion in the criminal sentencing process is understood as required by the Eighth Amendment's guarantee against cruel and unusual punishment.

Liberalism may, however, make a difference to our thinking about some aspects of these doctrines. We can easily see that a version of the voluntary manslaughter doctrine based on the idea that wives are property would be rejected by the political liberal, for whom the equality of all citizens is a key part of the political conception. The plea of the battered woman for either mitigation or exculpation may get a more favorable hearing from the liberal than from at least some types of communitarians if it can be argued that such changes in law are important to securing women's full equality as citizens. The traditional norms of manly honor that inform other aspects of self-defense doctrine are likely to be regarded by the political liberal with at least some skepticism. Do we really want to make such views of honor, which license violent acts against another human being, part of the core set of values that we endorse for political purposes? Many conceptions of value that citizens actually hold endorse such ideas of manly honor. What we will need to ask is whether those ideas fit well with the egalitarian ideas of political community we share and, even if they do, whether they are sufficiently central that they ought to be attached to the restricted "module" of the political conception, rather than being optional matters about which citizens may simply disagree. Since the history of the doctrine shows, indeed, that reasonable citizens *do* strongly disagree about the worth of such honor-norms, the liberal might be inclined to detach them from the core of the doctrine.

In general, liberalism invites us to ask whether the evaluations in question lie in the core of the political conception, which we ask all citizens to share, or outside it, in areas of reasonable disagreement. For the liberal, unlike the communitarian, this is a fundamental distinction. The liberal thinks it illegitimate to promote or enforce homogeneity of values outside of the core, whereas the communitarian typically thinks that homogeneity across the board is a good thing. Many evaluations concerning honor and status, for example, do not appear to lie in the core of the political conception of either the United States or other political cultures, and yet they may be very influential, as the history of the self-defense doctrine shows they have been. The liberal and the communitarian will be likely to differ about the role of law vis-à-vis such valuations.

In another, more general way, endorsement of a liberal conception of politics influences the judgments one will be inclined to make about the role of emotions in law. Liberals, while not straightforwardly committed to John Stuart Mill's "harm principle," are likely to view it with considerable sympathy. Mill held that a necessary condition of the legal restriction of conduct is that it be harmful to nonconsenting others.[84] Conduct that is potentially harmful only to the self, or to others who freely agree to join in, cannot rightly be restricted. Mill, while defending the freedom of the gambler and the sex worker, was ambivalent about certain cases in which the actor could be said to do indirect harm. He considered expanding his principle to permit legal penalties against the pimp and the person who keeps a gambling house on the grounds that these people typically exploit the weaknesses of others and ultimately cause harm. (The gambler may harm his family by squandering money that is rightly theirs; the pimp harms the women he recruits and then exploits.) Thus the scope of this principle remains controversial, and contemporary political liberals continue to debate such cases. They also debate cases in which the freedom at issue seems trivial: thus, many political liberals would not mind laws requiring seat belt use or motorcycle helmets, on the grounds that such intrusions on freedom of choice do not touch on an important area of liberty, and may save society a lot of money in medical costs.[85]

In general, however, political liberals are likely to be sympathetic to Mill's idea, because they typically hold that freedom is a very great good, and they believe that people are entitled to the greatest freedom that is compatible with a like freedom for others. The freedom to harm others obviously limits the freedom of those who are harmed. It also renders that freedom unequal, in that physical force and the ability to defraud are unequal. So allowing rape and theft would not just limit freedom, it would limit freedom in unequal ways. Certain basic rights and liberties, moreover, are prerequisites for getting on with any meaningful life, and harmful acts violate these rights. Even if rape limited the freedom of all citizens equally, it would still be injurious to the ability of all to get on with their lives.

So the liberal can easily justify the restriction of conduct that harms others. Restriction of conduct that does no harm to others is much more difficult to justify along liberal lines.

There are many difficulties in the way of understanding Mill's principle precisely. How imminent and how likely must the harm be? What counts as a harm? Is there a salient distinction to be drawn between harm and offense? Mill believed that the harm, to fall under his principle, had to be both imminent and very likely, and that it had to be harm with regard to certain antecedently demarcated areas of fundamental "constituted rights."[86] So, for Mill, harm was a notion clearly distinct from mere offense, and harm was a very narrow category, defined in terms of a menu of basic rights that were fundamental to his political conception.[87] Fundamental to his entire project in *On Liberty* was the protection of people such as atheists, gamblers, and prostitutes, whose conduct was clearly very offensive to the majority, but who did no harm in the limited sense Mill gave that term; that is, did not commit theft, larceny, assault, rape, and so forth.

The liberal who wants to grapple with the role of emotions in the law will have to take some stand on Mill's principle. Does she endorse the principle itself in general terms? And, if so, does she interpret it in more or less the way Mill did, or does she recognize a broader category of harms, and, if so, how does she define this broader class? What, in her view, are the most important types of freedom protected by the principle? Might there be others sorts of freedom that are not so fundamental, concerning which we are less reluctant to regulate self-regarding conduct?

I shall be arguing from a fundamentally Millian starting point, and I shall interpret Mill's principle more or less the way he does, defining the relevant harms in terms of a limited menu of rights that are central to the political conception, although in chapter 3 I shall argue that a limited class of direct bodily offenses are sufficiently harm-like to be relevant to legal regulation. I shall not offer a full defense of Mill's view, and in chapter 7 I shall criticize a major line of argument Mill offers for his principle, though I shall try to show at various points why it is an attractive starting point for people attached to liberty as a good.

Mill's conception of the foundations of criminal law is controversial. The U.S. legal tradition has never fully endorsed it.[88] Restriction of conduct that does no harm to nonconsenting third parties has never been repudiated at the highest level in our legal system. Although both state and appellate courts have delivered Millian judgments, using a Millian rationale, in areas such as homosexual activity and nude dancing, the U.S. Supreme Court continues to uphold the constitutionality of restrictive laws in these areas. In an opinion overruling the Seventh Circuit Court of Appeals, which had found an Indiana ordinance against nude dancing unconstitutional, Chief Justice Rehnquist insists that the bare idea of "moral disapproval" is a perfectly appropriate basis for law.[89] And in a concurring opinion of typical pungency, Justice Scalia states—correctly, so far as historical description is concerned—that the Millian principle (which he imputes to Thoreau, not Mill) has never been regarded by our nation as an appropriate basis for thinking about the limits of the law:

The dissent confidently asserts that the purpose of restricting nudity in public places in general is to protect nonconsenting parties from offense; and argues that since only consenting, admission-paying patrons see respondents dance, that purpose cannot apply, and the only remaining purpose must relate to the communicative elements of the performance. Perhaps the dissenters believe that "offense to others" ought to be the only reason for restricting nudity in public places generally, but there is no basis for thinkng that our society has ever shared that Thoreauvian "you-may-do-what-you-like-so-long-as-it-does-not-injure-someone-else" beau ideal—much less for thinking that it was written into the Constitution. The purpose of Indiana's nudity law would be violated, I think, if 60,000 fully consenting adults crowded into the Hoosierdome to display their genitals to one another, even if there were not an offended innocent in the crowd. Our society prohibits, and all human societies have prohibited, certain activities not because they harm others but because they are considered in the traditional phrase "contra bonos mores," i.e., immoral. [The] purpose of the Indiana statute [is] to enforce the traditional moral belief that people should not expose their private parts indiscriminately, regardless of whether those who see them are disedified. Since that is so, the dissent has no basis for positing that, where only thoroughly edified adults are present, the purpose must be repression of communication.

Some of what I shall say about disgust and shame will presuppose a general Millian outlook on the limits of the law. On the other hand, I cannot, and shall not, assume that this perspective is shared by my reader. I shall therefore be as explicit as I can be about which of my arguments rest on Mill's idea and which do not. But I shall also hope to show readers who are skeptical about Mill's idea some further reasons they might have for supporting it. When we understand more fully some of the reasons why people are as eager as they are to seek the criminalization of harmless acts, when we see some of the more general social attitudes that are inextricably woven into such laws, we will have some reasons for being skeptical about at least some non-Millian laws even when we do not antecedently accept Mill's principle. Thus I shall argue that even someone who is initially sympathetic with Lord Devlin's views about the role of disgust in the law (mentioned in the Introduction and to be discussed in detail in the next chapter) may rethink that allegiance once she reflects more fully about the cognitive content of disgust and its typical role in social life.

VIII. How to Appraise Emotions

According to the picture I have been presenting, appraisal of the norms that play a role in emotions must take place on a number of distinct levels. To see this, let us consider a specific case of anger: a parent who kills (immediately, or without long delay) the person who has just killed her child. Our question is whether her anger is the sort of emotion that a "reasonable man" would have, and whether, accordingly, we should give her a reduction in level of homicide from murder to manslaughter.

First, we have to ask about the particulars of the act and its circumstances. Did the parent get the facts about the murder of the child right? If not, was her belief that the victim was the murderer sincere, and not just sincere and honest, but also reasonable? Was she reasonable, furthermore, in thinking the murder of her child adequate provocation for some sort of retaliation? Is the murder of a child the sort of thing that has serious importance? Is that sort of case typically recognized in the traditional doctrine, and, if it is not, is this a case where we believe that social norms have evolved in such a way that it ought to be? All these questions must be answered before we can say whether the anger was the sort of anger that should be regarded as reasonable under the doctrine of reasonable provocation.

This is all we are likely to ask, if we are on a jury in such a case, because the doctrine exists, and our job is to apply it. We do have a constructive role, because the provocations that are deemed "adequate" are not fixed as a matter of law; one of our jobs will be to determine whether the case before us meets that general test. In the process, we are likely to be sensitive to changes in social norms, insofar as they seem to affect an objective judgment of reasonableness and adequate provocation. But this will be the limit of our questioning.

If, however, we are assessing the case from a more detached point of view, we must ask further questions. First, we will ask about the whole idea that an emotion that prompts a homicide is "reasonable." Will a "reasonable man" ever kill? We all know that it is possible to restrain the impulse to retaliate with homicidal violence. Isn't this what the reasonable man should really do? Isn't the entire doctrine an archaic survival of a frontier mentality? In other words, we will assess the *type of anger* that is involved in such cases, and the *role* of that anger in giving defendants mitigation.

Moving one further step up in level of generality, we will ask about the idea that anger can often be a reasonable emotion. Here we will have to try to get a general account of anger, and we will probably come up with something like Aristotle's account, in which anger involves the belief that one has been harmed or damaged, in some serious way, by another person or persons' wrongful act, and that the act was committed not inadvertently but willingly. Let us say that this is the account we favor. Looking at this account, we will ask whether this is the sort of emotion that might well be reasonable if the facts about the harm and its seriousness are all correct. Some people who agree with the ancient Greek Stoics may at this point say that anger is never reasonable, because anything that can be damaged by another is not really of serious importance in human life. Only one's own virtue is really important, and that can never be damaged by another. Most of us, however, will judge that anger can often be reasonable, because there are many important things in any human life that can be damaged by another.

Finally, we must ask whether anger is the sort of emotion that can frequently be reasonable, not in terms of any conception of life we happen to have, but in terms of the core conception that informs our political and legal doctrine. If we are asking the question from the point of view of the type of Rawlsian political liberalism I described in section VI, we will answer that very frequently anger can be reasonable, because political liberalism recognizes certain rights, liberties, opportunities, and other primary goods as very important, and obviously these can be damaged by another person's wrongful act. Whether or not we agree with Mill that harm in such areas of "constituted right" is a necessary condition of legal regulation, we probably do think that it is usually a sufficient condition for such regulation. That is, whatever else we think the state ought to do, we do think that it ought to protect people's rights in certain core areas.

Often in legal matters our questions will remain relatively concrete, because it is obvious that the emotion is of a sort that is legally relevant if the facts are all correct. Anger and fear, for example, seem to be in this category: the question is not *whether* a "reasonable man" would be motivated by them in areas of legal salience, but rather *what sort* of anger and fear we want to recognize as reasonable in various specific areas of law.

Sometimes, however, we may have questions about the whole emotion category. Rightly or wrongly, jealousy has sometimes been held to be an emotion based on an inappropriately possessive relation to another person. The jealous person is not simply fearful about a possible loss of love. In addition, he has the thought that it is good to control the actions of the beloved by removing the threat posed by a rival. One may think that a person with a balanced view of love would not have those possessive thoughts: thus, jealousy is not the emotion of a "reasonable person." We might also add that these possessive thoughts have been especially pernicious aspects of the relation of men to women, and part of a picture of women as men's property. None of this means, of course, that jealousy is not ubiquitous in human life, but if one holds that it does betray an inappropriate set of attitudes toward another person, one will have reason to question its role in the formation of law and public policy. Thus one would very likely oppose, for example, granting mitigation on grounds of "reasonable provocation" to a person who kills a rival or an adulterous spouse.

The sort of argument I shall be making about disgust and, to a limited extent, shame is similar to this hypothetical argument about jealousy. I shall argue that the cognitive content of disgust is deeply problematic, and that the same is true of at least one basic type of shame, which I shall call "primitive shame." I shall not argue that disgust and shame can, or even should, be eliminated from human life. Like jealousy, disgust and primitive shame are deeply rooted in the structure of human life, and are probably impossible to eradicate. This is so, I shall suggest, because both of these emotions are ways in which we negotiate deep tensions involved in the very fact of being human, with the high aspirations and harsh limits that such a life involves. But their cognitive content is problematic, and their social operations pose dangers to a just society.

Chapter 2
Disgust and Our Animal Bodies

The Professor of Gynaecology: He began his course of lectures as follows: Gentlemen, woman is an animal that micturates once a day, defecates once a week, menstruates once a month, parturates once a year and copulates whenever she has the opportunity.

I thought it a prettily-balanced sentence.

—W. Somerset Maugham, *A Writer's Notebook*

Was there any form of filth or profligacy, particularly in cultural life, without at least one Jew involved in it?

If you cut even cautiously into such an abscess, you found, like a maggot in a rotting body, often dazzled by the sudden light—a kike!

—Adolf Hitler, *Mein Kampf*[1]

If a man had been able to say to you when you were young and in love: "An' if tha shits an' if tha pisses, I'm glad, I shouldna want a woman who couldna shit nor piss . . ." surely it would have helped to keep your heart warm.

—D. H. Lawrence to Ottoline Morrell,
quoting from *Lady Chatterley's Lover*

I. Disgust and Law

Disgust is a powerful emotion in the lives of most human beings.[2] It
shapes our intimacies and provides much of the structure of our
daily routine, as we wash our bodies, seek privacy for urination and
defecation, cleanse ourselves of offending odors with toothbrush
and mouthwash, sniff our armpits when nobody is looking, check in
the mirror to make sure that no conspicuous snot is caught in our
nose-hairs. In many ways our social relations, too, are structured by
the disgusting and our multifarious attempts to ward it off. Ways of
dealing with repulsive animal substances such as feces, corpses, and
rotten meat are pervasive sources of social custom. And most societies teach the avoidance of certain groups of people as physically
disgusting, bearers of a contamination that the healthy element of
society must keep at bay.

Disgust also plays a powerful role in the law. It figures, first, as the
primary or even the sole justification for making some acts illegal.
Thus, sodomy laws have frequently been defended by a simple appeal to the disgust that right-thinking people allegedly feel at the
thought of such acts. The judge at Oscar Wilde's second criminal
trial said that he would prefer not to describe "the sentiments which
must rise to the breast of every man of honour who has heard the details of these two terrible trials," but his virulent condemnation of
the defendants made his disgust amply evident.[3] Lord Devlin famously argued that such social disgust was a strong reason to favor
the prohibition of an act, even if it caused no harm to nonconsenting others; he applied his conclusion explicitly to the prohibition of
consenting homosexual acts.[4] In his recent work on disgust, legal
theorist William Miller, while not supporting Devlin's concrete policy recommendations, gives support to his general line by arguing
that the degree of civilization in a society may properly be measured
by the barriers it has managed to place between itself and the disgusting.[5] Legal barriers, in such a view, could easily be seen as agents
of the civilizing process. Most recently, conservative bioethicist Leon
Kass, who now heads a commission charged by President Bush with
examining moral issues relating to stem-cell research, has argued

that in general society will do well to trust to "the wisdom of repugnance" when pondering new medical possibilities. In an essay supporting bans on human cloning, he suggests that disgust "may be the only voice left that speaks up to defend the central core of our humanity."[6]

One area of the law in which judgments of the disgusting are unequivocally central is the current law of obscenity: the disgust of an average member of society, applying contemporary community standards, has typically been taken to be a crucial element in the definition of the obscene. The Supreme Court has noted that the etymology of the word "obscene" contains the Latin word for filth, *caenum,* and that two prominent dictionaries include the term "disgusting" in their definition of the term.[7]

The disgust of society also figures in legal arguments about categories of acts that are already considered illegal on other grounds. The disgust of a criminal for a homosexual victim may be seen as a mitigating factor in homicide.[8] The disgust of judge or jury has frequently been regarded as relevant to the assessment of a homicide where potentially aggravating factors are under consideration.

On one view of these matters, the emotion of disgust is highly relevant to law and a valuable part of the legal process. For Devlin, society cannot defend itself without making law in response to its members' responses of disgust, and every society has the right to preserve itself.[9] Every society, therefore, is entitled to translate the disgust-reactions of its members into law. For Kass, disgust embodies a deep wisdom that "warn[s] us not to transgress what is unspeakably profound."[10] If we do not heed that wisdom, we are in danger of losing our humanity. For Miller, a society's hatred of vice and impropriety necessarily involves disgust, and cannot be sustained without disgust. Disgust "marks out moral matters for which we can have no compromise."[11] It should follow that for Miller disgust plays a legitimate role in the criminal law, and perhaps in other areas of law as well, although Miller does not discuss these further implications.

All of these arguments favoring disgust are conservative. But Dan M. Kahan has recently argued that disgust is of importance to progressive legal thought, as well, and ought to be permitted to play a larger role in the criminal law than most legal theorists currently want it to play. Disgust is "brazenly and uncompromisingly judgmental,"[12] indeed "essential to perceiving and condemning cruelty."[13]

These are plausible theses, which should not be easily dismissed. Nor, as I have argued in chapter 1, should they be dismissed by a blanket condemnation of all appeals to emotion in law, or by the strong and misleading contrast between emotion and reason that we all too frequently hear when legal theorists discuss appeals to sympathy, or indignation, or overwhelming fear. If, as seems plausible, all these emotions involve complex evaluative cognitions, then they cannot be called "irrational" as a class. Instead, we must evaluate the cognitions they embody, as we would any class of beliefs, asking how reliable they are likely to be given their specific subject matter and their typical process of formation. There seem to be no reasons to think that the cognitions involved in emotion are generally and ubiquitously unreliable.

Usually, I have argued, the appraisal of emotion must focus on concrete cases, asking questions about the person's assessment of the situation and the values contained in it. Anger as a whole is neither reliable nor unreliable, reasonable or unreasonable; it is only the specific anger of a specific person at a specific object that can coherently be deemed unreasonable. I have also argued, however, that we may sometimes judge that a particular emotion-type is always suspect or problematic, in need of special scrutiny, given its likely aetiology, its specific cognitive content, and its general role in the economy of human life. In chapter 1 I suggested that we might raise such questions about jealousy. This is the type of argument I shall be making about disgust in this chapter. I shall argue that the specific cognitive content of disgust makes it of dubious reliability in social life, but especially in the life of the law. Because disgust embodies a shrinking from contamination that is associated with the human desire to be nonanimal, it is frequently hooked up with various forms of shady social practice, in which the discomfort people feel over the fact of having an animal body is projected outwards onto vulnerable people and groups. These reactions are irrational, in the normative sense, both because they embody an aspiration to be a kind of being that one is not, and because, in the process of pursuing that aspiration, they target others for gross harms.

Where law is concerned, it is especially important that a pluralistic democratic society protect itself against such projection-reactions, which have been at the root of gross evils throughout history, prominently including misogyny, anti-Semitism, and loathing of homosexuals. Thus while the law may rightly admit the relevance of indignation, as a moral response appropriate to good citizens and based upon reasons that can be publicly shared, it will do well to cast disgust onto the garbage heap where it would like to cast so many of us.

Specifically, I shall argue (in chapter 3) that the disgust of a defendant for his alleged victim is never relevant evidence in a criminal trial; that disgust is an utter red herring in the law of pornography, occluding the salient issues of harm and even colluding in the perpetuation of harms; that disgust is never a good reason to make a practice (for example sodomy) illegal; that even where one homicide seems worse than another because it is unusually disgusting, this disgust-reaction should itself be distrusted, as a device we employ to deny our own capacities for evil.

II. Pro-Disgust Arguments: Devlin, Kass, Miller, Kahan

We must begin by understanding the pro-disgust position in greater detail. Since in actuality it is not a single position, but a family of positions, we need to scrutinize one by one the main arguments that have been advanced in favor of allowing disgust an ample legal role.

The most influential pro-disgust argument has been Lord Devlin's, in his famous lecture "The Enforcement of Morals" (1959). Devlin, a judge, took as his occasion the Wolfenden Report released in 1957, which had recommended the decriminalization of homosexual relations between consenting adults and had opposed the criminalization of prostitution, which was not then illegal. In support of its recommendations, the commission made a more general case against the legal regulation of "private immorality." Basically, they took Mill's line:

society has no right to use the law to regulate personal conduct that does no harm to others. Devlin's counterargument is complex. He agrees with the commission that in general personal liberty should be extensive: "There must be toleration of the maximum individual freedom that is consistent with the integrity of society."[14] He then goes on to argue, however, that societies cannot last if they cease to have an "established morality" that is broadly shared. Although Devlin does not hold that this morality can never change,[15] he does hold that "[t]here is disintegration when no common morality is observed and history shows that the loosening of moral bonds is often the first stage of disintegration, so that society is justified in taking the same steps to preserve its moral code as it does to preserve its government and other essential institutions."[16]

Now at this point it would obviously be open to the supporter of Mill's principle (and the authors of the Wolfenden Report) to reply that of course society needs a shared morality, but this shared morality may be found in the core set of political values that define citizens' basic constitutional rights and entitlements, and in whatever other principles are required to protect citizens from harm in respect of those "constituted rights," to use Mill's term.[17] Thus liberals need not and should not hold that society can do without a shared morality; they need only say that the shared morality should be a political-liberal morality, one that makes a distinction between shared political and constitutional values and other aspects of people's comprehensive conception of the good life. These other aspects would include matters of religion and, harm to the nonconsenting aside, matters of sexual conduct and desire. Liberals may add that the protection of liberty in areas of deep personal significance is itself a moral norm and a shared value, one of the most cherished values in many societies. Thus Devlin sets things up in a misleading way at the start, suggesting that we have only two alternatives: either use law to enforce personal sexual morality and other areas of personal moral conduct, or forgo the whole project of using law to enforce moral norms. We obviously have a further alternative: we may use law to enforce all and only the core values of a liberal society, which prominently include the protection of areas of personal liberty.

Devlin thus needs to show the liberal that the core liberal values are insufficient to hold society together, that society will fall apart unless it protects values going beyond—and in some ways directly against—these core liberal values. And indeed Devlin does use a very specific picture of social disintegration to support his case. Throughout this essay and related essays, Devlin focuses on specific types of private immorality: nonstandard sexual conduct, drunkenness, and the use of drugs. Using these examples, he paints a very particular picture of the danger that might be caused to society by the spread of "vice": namely, one in which important activities cannot be carried out because people are too distracted by their "vices" to perform them. Nonstandard sexual conduct figures in his argument as a type of addiction (homosexuals, he writes, are in fact "addicts"), which makes the personality incapable of carrying out its ordinary business. Thus he writes that "men who are constantly drunk, drugged or debauched are not likely to be useful members of the community."[18] Even more vividly, he argues that "[a] nation of debauchees would not in 1940 have responded satisfactorily to Winston Churchill's call to blood and toil and sweat and tears."[19] Thus he attempts to convince the Millian that immorality does grave social harm, eroding the type of self-control and purposiveness that we need to expect from the average citizen if major activities of the society are to be carried out.

There is at least a case to be argued on this basis, if we think about alcohol abuse and drug abuse, though whether the legality of these substances is a social danger of the sort Devlin contemplates (causing widespread social decay through the "contagion" of their abuse) is most unclear. Where homosexuality is concerned, however, his argument seems to partake of a type of "moral panic" that we shall have occasion to investigate in chapter 5.[20] The idea that public toleration of homosexuality will in some vague and unspecified way erode the social fabric is hardly new. Nor is it old. Shortly after September 11, 2001, the Reverend Jerry Falwell issued a national statement ascribing responsibility for the bombing of the World Trade Center to "gays and lesbians"—presumably thinking in Devlin's way that their presence somehow weakens America.[21] Such claims, though we still hear them, are both outrageous and completely implausible. We should bear this feature of Devlin's argument in mind, for much that he says appears to rest on false factual premises concerning same-sex conduct and its effect on the personality. He certainly does not portray heterosexuals as "addicts," or depict their sexual preference as an addiction that saps society's vital force.[22]

Not all threats to a society's moral code are sufficiently serious to warrant legal intervention, according to Devlin, given the importance of personal liberty. Devlin therefore proposes a test to determine when the point is reached beyond which society should not be asked to tolerate immoral conduct. To find an appropriate standard, Devlin turns to the well-known legal fiction of the "reasonable man," whom he also describes as "the man on the Clapham omnibus."[23] When this person reacts to the self-regarding conduct of others with a very intense form of disapproval, the conduct in question may be prohibited by law. Devlin terms the intense emotion "intolerance, indignation, and disgust." These, he says, "are the forces behind the moral law"; without them society has no right to deprive individuals of freedom of choice.[24] Although Devlin thus lists three very different sentiments, the content of his argument would appear to focus on disgust, as I shall define it. Indignation, as I shall argue, is typically understood to be a response to a harm or a damage that has been wrongfully inflicted; but Devlin does not insist that any such harm be present, and indeed his entire argument is directed against Mill's contention that only such a harm justifies legal regulation. Later in his argument he alludes only to disgust, saying that the question to be asked about homosexuality is "whether, looking at it calmly and dispassionately, we regard it as a vice so abominable that its mere presence is an offence."[25] He thus suggests, albeit unclearly, a two-stage inquiry: first, the "reasonable man" feels disgust at homosexual conduct; next, he steps back and asks himself calmly whether he is really right to feel that way.

Why does Devlin think disgust a reliable basis for lawmaking? Even if we grant him that there are some vices that, sufficiently disseminated, would erode society's capacity to function, why should we suppose that disgust is a reliable index of which activities have that property? Miscegenation has been the object of widespread disgust—and yet even Devlin, who seems happy with any form of heterosexual marriage, would not presume to argue that this disgust tracks social danger in a reliable way. The very presence of the mentally handicapped and the physically disabled in our communities, functioning in the public eye, has often occasioned disgust; and yet it would be difficult to maintain that they pose a danger to the social fabric. On the other side, there are forms of conduct that are clearly dangerous to the social fabric, but that do not tend to elicit disgust, because they are widespread and even popular. Racism and sexism have had that role in many societies; greed and sharp business practices can even elicit admiration. So at a crucial point in the argument we are left adrift; nor does Devlin offer us any further analysis of either the emotion's content or its likely objects that would assist us in assessing his position further. We must therefore leave Devlin at this point, turning to other authors who may have answers to some of these questions.

Leon Kass has a position very close to Devlin's, but one that offers a little more in the way of reflection about the emotion of disgust and its social role. Kass does not advance a general theory of legal regulation, but it is safe to say that he is no Millian. Society clearly may prohibit conduct without ascertaining that it is "other-regarding" in Mill's sense, affecting adversely the "constituted rights" of nonconsenting others. But Kass's view of the danger to society is different from Devlin's, as is his argument about why disgust is important. The danger that worries Kass is not the disintegration of society's capacity to act and plan that might be caused by widespread "debauchery." Instead, he worries that in a more subtle way core human values may be eroded by the increasing acceptance of practices that treat human beings as means to the ends of others. The world he fears is a world "in which everything is held to be permissible so long as it is freely done, in which our given human nature no longer commands respect."[26] So far, Kass seems to argue squarely within the liberal tradition: for surely a respect for human dignity must be among the core political values of any viable form of political liberalism. (The words "given human nature," however, go beyond the political idea of human dignity in suggesting a specific metaphysical or religious view of humanity.) And surely a liberal can easily grant that one of the main dangers a liberal society must guard against is the danger that humanity will be used only as a means, and not as an end. If we could be convinced that disgust is reliably correlated with violations of human dignity, we would at least be on the way to viewing it as relevant to legal regulation.[27]

According to Kass, there is a "wisdom" in our sentiment of "repugnance," a wisdom that lies beneath all rational argument. When we contemplate certain prospects, we are disgusted "because we intuit and feel, immediately and without argument, the violation of things that we rightfully hold dear." Repugnance "revolts against the excesses of human willfulness, warning us not to transgress what is unspeakably profound."[28] Kass admits that "[r]evulsion is not argument," but he thinks that it gives us access to a level of the personality that is in some ways deeper and more reliable than argument. "In crucial cases . . . repugnance is the emotional expression of deep wisdom."[29]

Kass now lists six acts that we allegedly find revolting, arguing that any attempt to give an argument for our revulsion would itself be suspect, a superficial attempt to "rationalize away our horror."[30] His examples: father-daughter incest (even with consent), having sex with animals, mutilating a corpse, eating human flesh, rape, and murder. We are immediately in difficulty, for most of these acts are squarely within the purview of Mill's principle, causing harm to nonconsenting others. Rape and murder, obviously; father-daughter incest, because a minor child is rightly regarded as incapable of giving consent, especially when the seducer is her own father; sex with animals because it usually inflicts tremendous pain and indignity on animals, using them as instruments of human whim. (Mill, a great defender of the legal rights of animals, who left much of his fortune to the SPCA, would surely agree.) Eating human flesh doesn't take place unless the human being has been killed first. If we really do imagine a situation in which the person has died from natural causes, with no form of coercion involved, it becomes simply a gruesome variant of the corpse-mutilation case. Mutilating a corpse does indeed raise real moral questions, as to whether and on what grounds it ought to be prohibited. I shall return to those questions in chapter 3. But it is a complicated issue once we state clearly that the corpse is an inert heap of stuff and not the living person. Kass offers no arguments on this issue—and yet this case is the only one in which he has even putatively gone beyond the bounds of Mill's principle. It seems to me that what we want to do with this case is to reflect and argue about it, not to assume that our repugnance contains a subrational wisdom.

Moreover, Kass's example of argument that is nothing more than superficial rationalization is a most unfair one: it is the claim that incest is wrong only because of the "genetic risks of inbreeding." This argument might conceivably be advanced by someone concerned with the legal status of first-cousin incest, or even adult brother-sister incest; it is hardly the natural first argument to make about fathers and daughters, where the harm to the daughter is usually considered central. Moreover, adult incest between first cousins or even brother and sister typically does not inspire disgust. Indeed, some of our most cherished cultural paradigms of romantic love, such as Siegmund's love for Sieglinde in Wagner's *Die Walküre*, rest on the profound seductiveness of the brother-sister relation. The lovers are drawn to one another not in spite of the tie, but precisely because of it: they seem to see their own faces in one another, and to hear their own voices. So if we want to find reasons to make that sort of adult consensual incest illegal, disgust will not help us, and arguments about health issues are perhaps exactly what we need.

So far, then, Kass has not convinced us that disgust is reliably correlated with serious violations of human rights or human dignity. Nor does Kass at all consider cases where our sentiments of repugnance appear to give very poor guidance. He speaks of the way in which "some of yesterday's repugnances are today calmly accepted—though, one must add, not always for the better."[31] It seems safe to conjecture that he is thinking of homosexual relations, a topic on which he holds strong negative views. So, in his view, the sentiments about homosexuality to which Devlin also refers *were* good guides when we had them, and it is too bad that we have lost the guidance they proffer. Many readers will strongly disagree. But what about other former targets of widespread repugnance, such as Jews, or mixed-race couples, or the novels of James Joyce and D. H. Lawrence? Will Kass say that these earlier instances of disgust contained wisdom? What about the disgust many people feel even now when they see the mentally handicapped in public settings, or when they see people who are physically deformed or obese? Kass now faces a dilemma. Either he will say that in all these cases disgust gave and gives good guidance, in which case he will strike most readers as making a preposterous and morally heinous assertion; or he will say that in some of them disgust actually gave bad guidance, in which case he will have acknowledged that he needs a criterion to distinguish good from bad cases of disgust. Kass never faces up to this dilemma: thus he gives us no information as to how we tell when and how far disgust is reliable. But his argument requires a strong claim that it is highly reliable: for its whole point is to persuade us to take our current alleged repugnance at the prospect of human cloning as good reason to ban the practice, without engaging in further reflection or argument.

What, in any case, does someone need to believe in order to believe that disgust gives good guidance in the realm of law, a guidance that is deeper and more reliable than that of rational argument? One way of defending such a claim would be Devlin's, namely that disgust is a cultural product and thus a good index of what we have come to care about socially. That cannot be Kass's view, however, for in Kass's view the culture itself is corrupt, and we turn to disgust precisely because we cannot trust the culture. His position credits disgust with an extracultural authority. But on what grounds? If the view is that disgust is a part of our evolutionary heritage, then it seems implausible to credit it with *moral* authority on those grounds. Nor is Kass likely to make this move, given his deeply religious orientation. It seems that Kass must think that disgust has a divine origin, or is in some way fortunately implanted by a wise teleology of nature, in order to curb the "willfulness" that the Judaeo-Christian tradition equates with original sin. If this is his view, it is a startling and novel theological position. But in a political-liberal state such a position can carry no weight, unless it can be translated into terms that would persuade someone who does not accept that particular religious teleology. We find no such translation in Kass's argument.

Miller's position on disgust is somewhat more complicated than those of Devlin and Kass. Unlike these two writers, Miller conducts an extensive analysis of disgust, to which I shall refer frequently in my own subsequent analysis. He believes that disgust has a definite cognitive content, and that it gives guidance through that content, not by being a subterranean force beneath or apart from argument. Although he holds that disgust toward certain "primary objects"—bodily wastes, spoiled food, corpses—has an evolutionary origin and is very widespread, he also holds that societies have considerable latitude in shaping the extension of disgust from primary objects to other objects. The core idea involved in disgust, according to Miller (and I shall support this), is the idea of contamination: when one advances disgust as a reason for prohibiting a practice, one is trying to prevent oneself, or one's society, from being contaminated by the presence of that practice. This analysis is probably compatible with the positions of Devlin and Kass, but it is considerably more specific. Finally, Miller argues at some length that disgust is closely connected with traditions of social hierarchy: most if not all societies construct strata of human beings, deeming some to be tainted and disgusting. Often the ones at the bottom are Jews or women. Miller is inclined to hold that the establishment of hierarchies is intrinsic to disgust: disgust deems its object base and low, thus constructing levels of persons and object.[32]

Even this sketchy overview of Miller's argument shows that he is well aware that disgust can give problematic guidance. (For Miller is critical of the hierarchies that disgust constructs.) Why, nonetheless, does he give it qualified endorsement? The normative aspect of Miller's book is brief and thin, and there is almost nothing in the book about legal regulation, so any answer to this question must be rather speculative, but it would seem that he makes two key claims. First, he makes a general claim that disgust may be used as an index of progress as civilization advances: the more things a society finds disgusting, the more advanced it is. I shall examine this claim in detail later in this chapter. But it is not clear how it relates to legal regulation, so I now turn to the second thesis. This is what Kahan has appropriately called Miller's "moral indispensability thesis."[33] This is the claim that disgust is essential to motivating and reinforcing opposition to cruelty. We cannot "put cruelty first among vices" without attending to our reactions of disgust and allowing them to influence us in lawmaking.[34]

Now it would seem that this claim does little to support legal regulation of the sort that interests Devlin and Kass; that is, regulation of self-regarding conduct that lies outside of Mill's principle. Not even Devlin and Kass believe that homosexuality is a form of cruelty—if they did, surely they would not spend so much time finding non-Millian ways to justify making homosexual acts illegal. Nor does Miller make such a claim; it is evident that he does not think that disgust always signals the presence of cruelty, and so should be trusted on that account. By his own account, disgust typically signals the presence of something deemed a contaminant, but there are many harmless and noncruel contaminants, as he himself insists. (He cites male semen and female bodily fluids as two major objects of disgust, and he stresses the historical evidence that disgust has been used to target vulnerable and innocent people and groups.) Nor does he offer any argument that cruelty always disgusts. Such argument would be difficult to produce in the light of the evidence he himself cites concerning the pleasure societies take in inflicting cruel forms of subordination on powerless people and groups. So his thesis cannot be that disgust reliably signals the presence of cruelty. It must be a more indirect thesis: for example, that disgust is a part of our moral equipment without which we could not respond well to cruelty. But that thesis, whether plausible or not, gives no support to the use of disgust as a basis for legal regulation. For we could always retain disgust in our personalities but base the case for legal regulation on other factors.

Miller's case for disgust is thus incomplete, and he seems to have little interest in the issues of legal regulation that concern us.[35] Dan M. Kahan, however, discussing Miller's book, has extended his argument to address legal questions.[36] Kahan begins by granting that the appeal to disgust is usually made by conservative legal theorists defending traditional values. But he points out, plausibly enough, that there is no necessity that this be so. Given Miller's thesis that the objects of disgust change over time, it is also possible that proponents of new social orderings might use the appeal to disgust to downgrade those that they think low or base, and to build up nontraditional people and values. So Kahan concludes that progressive legal thinkers have prematurely dismissed disgust: it is a pervasive moral sentiment, and progressives might as well use its power in their own cause.

But why the appeal to disgust in the first place, one might ask? Since by Kahan's own account (following Miller) disgust is connected with hierarchy and the unequal ranking of persons as to their worth or value, why should we listen to it at all when we make law, rather than basing law on other or different sentiments? At this point Kahan's argument becomes somewhat unclear. For, unlike Devlin and Kass, he does not defend the use of disgust to render "self-regarding" acts illegal. He does not oppose such "morals laws" either, and for all we know he might support the use of disgust as a criterion supporting the regulation of some forms of "self-regarding" action, such as drug use, solicitation, and gambling. To judge from his examples, however, his focus is entirely on crimes that meet Mill's test easily. Throughout the article, indeed, he focuses on murder, and accepts Miller's view that cruelty is the worst form of evil. We do not need to appeal to disgust to tell us that murder and cruelty are bad.

Kahan's position seems to be, however, that certain murders are worse than others, and that trusting our sentiments of disgust is a good way to rank murders and, especially, murderers. We can rely on disgust to identify legally significant aggravating features, or to judge that certain murderers are especially base or vile. Disgust, then, plays a role in sentencing; in that way it reinforces our condemnation of and opposition to cruelty. (I shall examine this claim in detail in chapter 3.) Although I shall not accept it, it has a kind of limited plausibility, because Kahan has allowed disgust to operate, in this case, only within the context of acts that are defined as illegal on other, more Millian grounds.

Let us pull all this together. We now see that the pro-disgust position is actually many positions. For all these writers, however, disgust is at least sometimes a useful legal criterion, giving us information that is relevant to the legal regulation of certain types of acts. We may now insist on one important distinction. None of these four writers is thinking of disgust as simply a limited type of harm to persons, of the sort typically addressed by nuisance laws. Nuisance laws penalize those who inflict upon others a particularly painful sort of intrusion that often takes the form of disgust: for example, a disgusting smell that affects the neighbors of the person who creates it. That is one way in which disgust figures in the law (and I will discuss it in chapter 3). For all four of our authors, however, disgust has a much broader and more foundational significance. Disgust, for each, is not itself a harm to be regulated: it is, rather, a criterion we use to identify the bad, indeed the very bad, and hence (they argue) the regulable. We use the idea of the disgust of the "reasonable man" to identify acts that may be (or should be) legally regulated, whether or not they actually occasion disgust as a painful nuisance in any person who is really present when the act itself is committed. Indeed, notice that most of the cases contemplated by Devlin and Kass will not occasion disgust of the sort covered by nuisance law, since they are performed in private. Those who don't like them are not around to be offended. Disgust, instead, is a moral thread or criterion we follow when we ask how immoral the act is; that judgment of immorality (also, for all four thinkers, a judgment of social danger) is itself what is relevant to the legal regulation of conduct.

Beyond this point, the four authors differ as to what the most pressing social dangers are, and as to how disgust helps us to cope with them. Since Miller has no clear normative position, I shall focus on the other three from now on. Kahan's view—at least for the purposes of these writings on disgust—appears to be a recognizable liberal view of the sort favored by Mill, in which legal regulation is based in the first instance upon harm to others. He uses the appeal to disgust only in connection with acts that are very harmful. Within that context, however, disgust is used to measure not the level of an act's harmfulness, but something different: how base and vile the criminal is. Kahan here departs from Mill, though far less so than do Devlin and Kass.

For Devlin and Kass, disgust sweeps much more broadly. Although most of Kass's examples of the disgusting do in fact involve harm to others, it is plain that he does not accept Mill's limiting principle, and that he is prepared, with Devlin, to regulate harmless conduct. The argument he uses to defend regulation is, however, a very different argument from Devlin's, using a very different picture of why disgust should be thought to be reliable. For Devlin, disgust is socially engendered, and is valuable because it informs us about deeply held social norms. For Kass, disgust is presocial or extrasocial, and is valuable because it warns us about dangers to our humanity that a corrupt society may have obscured from view. Both, however, conclude that disgust gives us information we would not have without it.

They also agree that it is pertinent to legal regulation whether or not its deliverances stand the scrutiny of rational argument.

As I have already shown, these positions have internal problems. They all contain gaps, and they do far too little to confront possible counterexamples. But they have been influential and persistent enough that the issue they raise seems worthy of further investigation. It seems obvious that such an investigation should begin with as good an account of disgust and its operations as we can produce, since only such an account can answer some of the questions we have raised about disgust's reliability and its social role.

III. The Cognitive Content of Disgust

Disgust appears to be an especially visceral emotion. It involves strong bodily reactions to stimuli that often have marked bodily characteristics. Its classic expression is vomiting; its classic stimulants are vile odors and other objects whose very appearance seems loathsome.[37] Nonetheless, important research by psychologist Paul Rozin has made it evident that disgust has a complex cognitive content, which focuses on the idea of incorporation of a contaminant.[38] His core definition of disgust is "[r]evulsion at the prospect of (oral) incorporation of an offensive object. The offensive objects are contaminants; that is, if they even briefly contact an acceptable food, they tend to render that food unacceptable." Similarly, Winfried Menninghaus speaks of disgust as a "crisis of self-assertion against unassimilable otherness," a repudiation of a "closeness that is not wanted," in which an object is "assessed as contamination and violently distanced from the self."[39] The objects of disgust must be seen as contaminants, not merely as inappropriate to ingest. Thus paper, marigolds, and sand are found inappropriate, but not disgusting.[40]

Rozin does not dispute that disgust may well have an underlying evolutionary basis; in fact he accepts Darwin's argument that disgust was originally a type of rejection, primarily of unwanted foods, closely connected to strong negative sensory experiences.[41] He shows, however, that it is distinct from both *distaste,* a negative reaction motivated by sensory factors, and (a sense of) *danger,* a rejection motivated by anticipated harmful consequences. Disgust is not simple distaste, because the very same smell elicits different disgust-reactions depending on the subject's conception of the object.[42] His subjects sniff decay odor from two different vials, both of which in reality contain the same substance; they are told that one vial contains feces and the other contains cheese. (The real smells are confusable.) Those who think that they are sniffing cheese usually like the smell; those who think they are sniffing feces find it repellant and unpleasant. "It is the subject's conception of the object, rather than the sensory properties of the object, that primarily determines the hedonic value."[43] In general, disgust is motivated primarily by ideational factors: the nature or origin of the item and its social history (e.g., who touched it). Even if subjects are convinced that ground dried cockroach tastes like sugar, they still refuse to eat it, or say it tastes revolting if they do.

Nor is disgust the same as (perceived) danger. Dangerous items (e.g., poisonous mushrooms) are tolerated in the environment, so long as they will not be ingested; disgusting items are not so tolerated. When danger is removed, the dangerous item will be ingested: detoxified poisonous mushrooms are acceptable. Disgusting items remain disgusting, however, even when all danger is removed. People refuse to eat sterilized cockroaches; many object even to swallowing a cockroach inside an indigestible plastic capsule that would emerge undigested in the subjects' feces.

Disgust concerns the borders of the body: it focuses on the prospect that a problematic substance may be incorporated into the self. For many items and many people, the mouth is an especially charged border.[44] The disgusting has to be seen as alien: one's own bodily products are not viewed as disgusting so long as they are inside one's own body, although they become disgusting after they leave it. Most people are disgusted by drinking from a glass into which they themselves have spat, although they are not sensitive to saliva in their own mouths. The ideational content of disgust is that the self will become base or contaminated by ingestion of the substance that is viewed as offensive. Several experiments done by Rozin and colleagues indicate that the idea involved is that "you are what you eat": if you ingest what is base, this debases you.[45]

The objects of disgust range widely, but the focus is on animals and animal products. Angyal argued more specifically that the center of disgust is animal (including human) waste products, which we see as debasing.[46] Rozin has confirmed experimentally our preoccupation with animal matter, but he adds that disgust may be transferred to objects that have had contact with animals or animal products—a major source being contact with "people who are disliked or viewed as unsavory." We shall discuss these extensions shortly. Rozin also insists, along with Miller, that disgust focuses on decay as well as waste: thus corpses are as much at the core of the disgusting as feces.[47] It is difficult to explain why plant products (apart from decayed and moldy specimens) are typically not found disgusting, but Angyal, Rozin, and Miller all conclude that the motivating idea has to do with our interest in policing the boundary between ourselves and nonhuman animals, or our own animality.[48] Hence tears are the one human bodily secretion that is not found disgusting, presumably because they are thought to be uniquely human, and hence do not remind us of what we have in common with animals.[49] Feces, snot, semen, and other animal bodily secretions, by contrast, are found contaminating: we do not want to ingest them, and we view as contaminated those who have regular contact with them. (Thus those formerly called "untouchables," in the Indian caste system, were those whose daily function was to clean latrines; oral or anal reception of semen, in many cultures, is held to be a contamination and a mark of low or base status.) Insofar as we eat meat without finding it disgusting, we disguise its animal origin, cutting off skin and head, cutting the meat into small pieces.[50]

Angyal, Rozin, and Miller all conclude that disgust pertains to our problematic relationship with our own animality. Its core idea is the belief that if we take in the animalness of animal secretions we will ourselves be reduced to the status of animals. Similarly, if we absorb or are mingled with the decaying, we will ourselves be mortal and decaying. Disgust thus wards off both animality in general and the mortality that is so prominent in our loathing of our animality. Indeed, we need to add this restriction in order to explain why some aspects of our animality—for example, strength, agility—are not found disgusting. The products that are disgusting are those that we connect with our vulnerability to decay and to becoming waste products ourselves. As Miller puts it: "[U]ltimately the basis for all disgust is *us*—that we live and die and that the process is a messy one emitting substances and odors that make us doubt ourselves and fear our neighbors."[51]

In light of this analysis, it should not surprise us that in all known cultures an essential mark of human dignity is the ability to wash and to dispose of wastes. Rozin points to analyses of conditions in prisons and concentration camps that show that people who are forbidden to clean themselves or use the toilet are soon perceived as subhuman by others, thus as easier to torture or kill.[52] They have become animals. And this same recognition led a Massachusetts District Court, in 1995, to find that conditions in the Bridgewater State Prison violated the prisoners' Eighth Amendment right to be free from "cruel and unusual" punishments. The primary condition complained of by the prisoners was the disgusting condition of the chemical toilets, which regularly overflowed and generated disgusting sights and smells that they could not escape.[53]

This analysis of disgust is the result of contemporary psychological research, but it coheres well with earlier reflections, prominently including Freud's classic analyses in *Civilization and Its Discontents,* and a variety of other passages and letters.[54] For Freud, the history of disgust must be understood together with the history of upright walking. Whereas for many animals smell is an especially keen sense, and one closely connected to sexual interaction with other animals, the human being has broken away from this animalistic world of excretion, smell, and sexuality, and has raised its nose on high. From this point on, the human animal has a problematic relationship to the smells of the genital area: it retains attraction to them, but must repress them for the sake of civilization. Thus, children must learn disgust toward them. I shall later return to this developmental history. It is enough here to show that there is a substantial measure of convergence between Freud's psychoanalytic account and more recent accounts developed in cognitive psychology.

Freud's account of disgust focuses less on mortality and decay than on our bodily commonality with the "lower" animals. Psychoanalyst Ernest Becker, however, argues convincingly that, at least after a certain age, human disgust reactions are typically mediated very powerfully by the awareness of death and decay. In developing a disgust toward bodily wastes, a young human is reacting against "the fate as well of all that is physical: decay and death."[55] In a revealing discussion of Jonathan Swift's poetry of disgust, Becker concludes that "[e]xcreting is the curse that threatens madness because it shows man his abject finitude, his physicalness, the likely unreality of his hopes and dreams."[56] Thus, here again, psychoanalytic accounts of disgust converge with the more recent findings of experimental psychology.[57]

Rozin's research, then, has broad support both from other experimental research and from other experientially attuned theories. His theory of disgust seems clearly preferable to its most famous theoretical alternative, Mary Douglas's theory of purity and danger.[58] For Douglas, disgust and impurity are socially contextual notions, and the guiding idea is that of an anomaly. An object may be pure in one context, impure in another: what makes it impure-disgusting is its violation of socially imposed boundaries. Douglas's theory does important work in making us aware of social factors surrounding disgust, on which we shall shortly comment further. And no doubt surprise is one factor that governs our sense of the disgusting. Nonetheless, the theory has a number of defects that make it problematic as an account of *disgust,* however insightful it may be about the operation of taboos and prohibitions.[59] First of all, it runs together the idea of purity and the idea of disgust, two very different concepts. It is obvious that an item may be impure without being disgusting. Second, Douglas tends to assimilate disgust and danger: thus sorcery, along with disgusting foods and fluids, is classified as a violation of social boundaries. Third, the account is *too* contextual: wastes, corpses, and most bodily fluids are ubiquitously objects of disgust. Societies have great latitude to determine how ideas of contamination extend to other objects, but they seem not to have latitude to make these primary objects nondisgusting. Fourth, the idea of anomaly is too weak to explain why we find some things disgusting. Feces and corpses are disgusting but in no way anomalous. On the other hand, a creature like a dolphin is an anomaly in nature, being a sea-dwelling mammal, but nobody finds dolphins disgusting. There seems to be more going on in disgust than merely the idea of surprise or departure from social norms. That something is plausibly captured in Rozin's idea of anxiety about animality.

Rozin's theory, however, has its own problems, which must now be examined. I believe that they can be remedied in a way that is fully consistent with the general spirit of his account. First of all, his focus on the mouth as boundary seems much too narrow: disgust-relevant contamination may occur through the nose, the skin, the genitals. That is why I have downplayed from the beginning that part of Rozin's theory. Much more plausible, and consistent with the general spirit of Rozin's account, is David Kim's suggestion, in his important and very well-argued study, that the key idea is that of crossing a boundary from the world into the self; disgust would thus be closely connected to all three of the senses that the philosophical tradition regards as "tactile" senses rather than mediated or distance senses: i.e., touch, smell, and taste, rather than sight or hearing. As Kim says, all three of the contact senses are touch-like, in the sense that smells become disgusting through the idea that the disgusting stench has made its way into the nose, is sitting there in contact with it.

The "animal-reminder" idea also needs work. We are not repulsed by all animals, or all reminders of our own animality. As I have said, strength, speed, and animals who exemplify those traits are far from disgusting. So we need to add what Rozin at times, but not consistently, does add: that what we are anxious about is a type of vulnerability that we share with other animals, the propensity to decay and to become waste products ourselves. As we see, Becker was already on to that point, and his insights need to be brought in to give shape to Rozin's vaguer account of the basis for disgust. Once we hold firmly to this point, we may also answer two other questions that David Kim poses to Rozin's theory. Kim asks why insects are so frequently disgusting, and feels that the "animal-reminder" theory does not fully account for that focus. Insects are, however, especially likely to be linked with the disgust-properties that signal decay—stickiness, sliminess and other signs of our animal mortality and vulnerability.

A second, and more difficult question is why people often feel disgust or aversion toward people with disabilities. To a great extent, this disgust is socially constructed, and thus our discussion of it belongs in our subsequent treatment of the social extension of disgust. But it may be (though we really do not know) that there is some primary disgust attaching to the sight of a person with a stump instead of a limb, or a person whose face and bearing show signs of developmental delay. These disabilities are, of course, reminders of our own vulnerability. Rather than having a rational soul that is invulnerable, we have mental faculties that can encounter arrest; even before we die, we can lose bodily parts.[60] I conclude that the spirit of Rozin's theory survives, although more work was needed to give it good answers to some plausible questions.

Disgust, then, begins with a group of core objects, which are seen as contaminants because they are seen as reminders of our mortality and animal vulnerability. Disgust at these objects is mediated by concepts and to that extent it is learned, but it appears to be ubiquitous in all human societies. Disgust, however, soon gets extended to other objects, through a complicated set of connections. A prominent feature of these extensions, as studied by Rozin, is the notion of "psychological contamination." The basic idea is that past contact between an innocuous substance and a disgust substance causes rejection of the acceptable substance. This contamination is mediated by what Rozin, plausibly enough, calls laws of "sympathetic magic." One such law is that of *contagion:* things that have been in contact continue ever afterwards to act on one another.[61] Thus, after a dead cockroach is dropped into a glass of juice, people refuse to drink that type of juice afterwards. Well-washed clothing that has been worn by someone with an infectious disease is rejected, and many people shrink from all secondhand clothing.[62] As Rozin and his coauthors remark, "The law of contagion as applied to disgust is potentially crippling; everything we might eat or touch is potentially contaminated." We deal with this problem, they conclude, by adopting complex sets of ritual prohibitions defining the relevant zones within which contamination will be recognized.[63]

In this way it is possible to connect to Rozin's core analysis the more helpful aspects of Douglas's social analysis. Douglas, we recall, argues that our idea of the contaminating typically involves the idea of a boundary violation, violation of accepted categories, or "matter out of place." Her theory proves inadequate as an account of the core notions involved in disgust.[64] The core or primary objects of disgust are reminders of animal vulnerability and mortality. But through the law of contagion all kinds of other objects become potential contaminants. The extension of contamination is mediated by social boundary-drawing, with the result that the disgusting is only what transgresses these boundaries.[65]

A second law by which disgust is extended is the law of "similarity": if two things are alike, action taken on one (e.g., contaminating it) is taken to have affected the other. Thus, a piece of chocolate fudge made into a dog-feces shape is rejected, even though subjects know its real origin; subjects also refuse to eat soup served in a (sterile) bedpan, to eat soup stirred with a (sterile) flyswatter, to drink a favorite beverage stirred by a brand-new comb.[66] Because similarity is a very elastic notion, this law is also highly mediated by social rules and boundaries.

Disgust appears not to be present in infants during the first three years of life. Infants reject bitter tastes from birth, making the gaping facial expression that is later characteristic of disgust. But at this point disgust has not broken off from mere distaste; nor has danger even appeared on the scene. The danger category seems to emerge in the first few years of life, and full-blown disgust is present only from around four years of age onward. Children do not show rejection of feces or vomit in early life; if anything, children are fascinated and attracted by their feces, and disgust, learned later, is a powerful social force that turns attraction to aversion.[67] Nor before the age of three or four is there any evidence for the rejection of smells, other than those that are actually irritants. Disgust, then, is taught by parents and society. This does not show that it does not have an evolutionary origin; many traits based on innate equipment take time to mature. Yet it does show that with disgust, as with language, social teaching plays a large role in shaping the form that the innate equipment takes.

Usually this teaching begins during toilet training; and despite all the interest psychoanalysts have taken in this process, we still need more close empirical studies of its workings.[68] Cross-cultural studies would be of particular interest. It is obvious that parents in most if not all societies communicate to children powerful messages of both distaste and disgust in regard to their feces, and that these messages convert attraction into aversion, or at least cause the very strong repression, behind aversion, of whatever attraction persists. There is, however, a lack of clarity about the stages through which children typically pass on their way to full adult disgust. Rozin holds, tentatively, that children do not immediately develop full-blown disgust toward their feces; instead, reacting to parental cues, they first develop distaste only. After repeated displays of disgust by parents and others, however, they eventually come to share that full-blown disgust.[69] The disgust levels of children correlate strongly with those of their parents, and, as Rozin's empirical surveys show, there is considerable individual variation in levels of disgust toward primary objects.[70]

Would it be possible to raise children who did not have disgust toward their bodily wastes? Clearly there are evolutionary tendencies at work that might make this a difficult task. Nor would it necessarily be wise to attempt it. Disgust provides an additional emphasis to the sense of danger, motivating the avoidance of many items that are really dangerous. Even though the disgusting does not map precisely onto the dangerous, the mapping is a good enough heuristic for many daily purposes, and even today we do not have the option of testing our environment in each case for germs and bacteria. Beyond these evolutionary links, disgust toward primary objects embodies, and does so more and more as a person's understanding of death and decay matures, an avoidance of issues that really are difficult to live with. It seems unlikely that we could ever be at ease with our own death and the decay that surrounds it; insofar as disgust grows out of our uneasy relationship with decay and mortality, it seems likely to surface sooner or later, and it may be necessary in order to live.

One question that remains unanswered is to what extent disgust toward primary objects is accompanied by attraction to the same objects. Freud plausibly argues that a child is attached to its feces, and retains this attraction behind the disgust that represses it. The strength of this retained attachment, however, may well differ greatly across individuals and, indeed, societies. It is likely to be influenced by toilet training, during which parents often praise a child for producing a bowel movement, and the child comes to view the product as a gift that he has given his parent. We still need to know much more about these phenomena. Where disgust toward other primary objects is concerned, it is less clear whether we should posit any initial attraction. Vomit, snot, slimy animals, decaying substances, corpses: do these allure us, or do they simply disgust us? And, insofar as they are objects of allure or fascination, is this simply because they are forbidden, or is the attraction prior to the prohibition?

These questions probably have no simple or single answer. Children certainly enjoy slimy things even while finding them disgusting. But sometimes, too, they enjoy them precisely to the extent that parents indicate that they are disgusting. And although most of us feel no attraction to corpses, they have sometimes been objects of attraction. Thus, Plato expects his readers to recognize as a central example of appetitive attraction that of Leontius, who desires to stare at the exposed corpses of dead soldiers, although he knows that he should not do it.[71] Most modern American readers find the passage puzzling: why didn't Plato choose an appetite with which we're all familiar if he wanted to illustrate the conflict between appetite and moral indignation? Yet Plato must have been able to rely on an audience for whom the desire to look at the decaying corpse was keen— perhaps because Greek traditions held that an exposed corpse was so profoundly disgraceful. Thus, in this case and in others, it seems likely that there is considerable individual and societal variation in the degree to which the disgusting exercises allure, and especially in the degree to which this allure is itself a construct of social prohibitions.

Whatever the full story is about the development of disgust toward primary objects, it is clear that the ideas of indirect and psychological contamination that are so prominent in the adult's experience of disgust develop much later, when children become capable of the more complicated types of causal thinking involved: thought, for example, about contagion and similarity. Both parental and social teaching are involved in these developments. Disgust, as Rozin says, is therefore an especially powerful vehicle of social teaching. Through teaching regarding disgust and its objects, societies potently convey attitudes toward animality, mortality, and related aspects of gender and sexuality. Although the cognitive content and aetiology of disgust suggest that in all societies the primary objects—feces, other bodily fluids, and corpses—are likely to be relatively constant, societies have considerable latitude in how they extend disgust-reactions to other objects, which they deem to be relevantly similar to the primary objects. Thus, although it seems right in a sense to say that there are some "natural" objects of disgust, in the sense that some broadly shared and deeply rooted forms of human thinking are involved in the experience of disgust toward primary objects, many objects become objects of disgust as a result of highly variable forms of social teaching and tradition. In all societies, however, disgust expresses a refusal to ingest and thus be contaminated by a potent reminder of one's own mortality and decay-prone animality.

This refusal, as we shall see in section V, has about it an urgency that leads to the anxious extension of disgust to other objects in an effort to insulate the self yet further from contamination by the primary objects. From the time (perhaps around age seven or eight) when children somehow learn to play with those ubiquitous paper devices known as "cootie-catchers," pretending to catch foul bugs from the skin of children who are disliked or viewed as an out-group, children practice a form of disgust-based social subordination known to all societies, creating groups of humans who allegedly bear the disgust-properties of foulness, smelliness, contamination. These subordinate humans create, so to speak, a "buffer zone" between the dominant humans and the aspects of their animality that trouble them.

Before we can say more about the social extension of disgust, however, we must confront the relationship between disgust and anger or indignation: only then will we be in a position to ponder the use of disgust in apparently moralizing contexts, and to dissect the relationship between this moralism and the creation of human buffer zones.

So far I have treated disgust as a cultural universal—and psychological research indicates that there are robust commonalities in disgust across cultural boundaries—but the general account of emotions I have developed in *Upheavals of Thought* indicates that societies vary not only in what objects they deem appropriate for a given emotion, but also, to some extent, in their more precise understanding of the emotion itself and its relation to other emotions. Since disgust has a cognitive content, it is no exception to this rule. One example must suffice to show the degree to which disgust is not a single thing, but an overlapping family. In an important study of the emotion of *fastidium* in ancient Rome, Robert Kaster argues that it overlaps considerably with English "disgust," and fits closely, up to a point, the Rozin analysis.[72] Thus people express *fastidium* toward a similar range of "primary objects," and then extend this emotion to people who are viewed as relevantly similar to the primary objects. There is a significant difference, however: for the same term, *fastidium*, also denotes an experience that is recognized (by Romans themselves) as somewhat different from the disgust-like *fastidium*; it involves looking down on a person with a kind of delicate hauteur, maintaining one's distance above something perceived as low. This sort of *fastidium* has close links to contempt, and also to an aristocratic sense of proper rank and hierarchy.

Kaster now shows in convincing detail that the fact that a single term names two admittedly different experiences is not irrelevant to the history of each: the two categories of experience begin to overlap and crisscross, so that people perceived as low in the hierarchical sense of *fastidium* can then easily have disgust-properties imputed to them; and people who are associated with a disgust-property will be ranked low and looked down on. All of this is not exactly strange to the English-language term, since disgust pervasively constructs social hierarchies, but the peculiar blend of aristocratic disdain with disgust, and the movement back and forth between the two, seems to be a distinctively Roman construct, giving rise to some experiences and judgments that are subtly different from those in other societies.

Good work of this sort, precise in its cultural analysis, shows us that with disgust as with other emotions, analysis and criticism ought to begin with the specifics of the culture in question, delving deeply into its specific understandings of what is human and what foul. Nonetheless, disgust appears to be an emotion with great transcultural overlap; it also has had an influential Western cultural formation that has itself ensured considerable similarity across both time and place. Therefore, with awareness that all such generalizations are incomplete, we may continue to treat it as a single phenomenon.

IV. Disgust and Indignation

Disgust, as we can see by now, is distinct not only from fear of danger, but also from anger and indignation. The core idea of disgust is that of contamination to the self; the emotion expresses a rejection of a possible contaminant. The core objects of disgust are reminders of mortality and animality, seen as pollutants to the human. Indignation, by contrast, centrally involves the idea of a wrong or a harm. Philosophical definitions of anger standardly involve the idea of a wrong done, whether to the person angered or to someone or something to whom that person ascribes importance. Thus, the standard ancient Greek definitions reported and discussed in Seneca's *On Anger* are "desire to avenge a wrong," "desire to punish one by whom one believes oneself to have been wronged," and "desire for retaliation against someone by whom one believes oneself to have been wronged beyond what is appropriate."[73] (Aristotle's earlier account is very similar.)[74] Notice that the idea of a (believed) wrong is so important that the last Stoic definition includes it twice-over, by adding "beyond what is appropriate" to the word "wronged." Most subsequent definitions of anger and indignation in the Western philosophical tradition follow these leads,[75] and psychology has taken a similar line.[76]

Because the notion of harm or damage lies at the core of anger's cognitive content, it is clear that it rests on reasoning that can be publicly articulated and publicly shaped. Damages and harms are a central part of what any public culture, and any system of law, must deal with; they are therefore a staple of public persuasion and public argument. This has been frequently observed in the history of philosophy. Thus, as I mentioned in chapter 1, Aristotle's *Rhetoric* gives the aspiring orator elaborate recipes for provoking indignation in an audience through the presentation of reasons they can share with regard to a putative wrong. He also gives the orator recipes for taking indignation away that involve convincing the audience that they had not in fact been wronged in the way they thought.[77]

As chapter 1 has argued, the reasons underlying a person's anger (or nonanger) can be false or groundless, and this in several distinct ways. Perhaps the damage did not occur at all. Perhaps it did occur, but it was done by someone other than the current target of the person's indignation. Perhaps it did occur, and that person did it, but it was not the wrongful act the person believes it to be. (It might, for example, have been an act of self-defense.) More subtly, perhaps the item damaged or slighted was not as important as the person believes it to be. Thus, Aristotle notes that many people get upset if someone forgets their name, though this is not as important as they think it is. As we saw, Seneca notes that he himself gets angry if a host has given him a place at a dinner table that he considers insufficiently honorable; again, he criticizes himself for overvaluing these superficial signs of honor. More deeply, most of the Greek and Roman philosophers think that people standardly overvalue certain types of "external goods," such as honor and money. Many of their angry reactions are based upon these overvaluations, and to that extent their anger will be unreliable as a source of public reasons. They might also undervalue something that is important: Aristotle mentions people who do not get angry when their relatives are subjected to indignity, although they ought to get angry. We might add that we often fail to get angry at wrongs done to people who live at a distance, or who are different from ourselves. Sometimes we don't even see a wrong as a wrong. Thus slavery didn't seem wrong to most of the people who practiced it; the rape of women within marriage was for many centuries considered just a man's exercise of his property rights.

In all of these ways, then, anger (and nonanger) may be misguided, but if all the relevant thoughts stand up to scrutiny, we can expect our friends and fellow citizens to share them and to share our anger. In that way, as Adam Smith remarked, indignation is very different from romantic love: "If our friend has been injured, we readily sympathize with his resentment, and grow angry with the very person with whom he is angry. . . . But if he is in love, though we may think his passion just as reasonable as any of the kind, yet we never think ourselves bound to conceive a passion of the same kind, and for the same person for whom he has conceived it."[78] Because love is based upon idiosyncratic reactions that usually cannot be put into words at all, much less shared by another, we cannot expect our friends to share our love—though, as Smith goes on to note, they may of course share lovers' anxieties and hopes about the future.[79] By arguing that the judicious spectator will experience anger on another's behalf, but not love, Smith suggests that anger, unlike erotic love, is well suited to ground public action in a society that aims to base its judgments on the public exchange of reasons.

Disgust is very different from anger, and in crucial ways more like erotic love. Although some disgust reactions may have an evolutionary basis and thus may be broadly shared across societies, and although the more mediated types of disgust may be broadly shared within a society, that does not mean that disgust provides the disgusted person with a set of reasons that can be used for purposes of public persuasion. You can teach a young child to feel disgust at a substance—by strong parental reactions and by other forms of psychological influence. Imagine, however, trying to convince someone who is not disgusted by a bat that bats are in fact disgusting. There are no publicly articulable reasons to be given that would make the dialogue a real piece of persuasion. All you could do would be to depict at some length the alleged properties of bats, trying to bring out some connection, some echo with what the interlocutor already finds disgusting: the wet greedy mouth, the rodentlike body. But if the person didn't find those things disgusting, that's that.[80]

Again, imagine trying to convince someone who didn't find gay men disgusting that they are in fact disgusting. What do you do? As the campaign in favor of Amendment 2 in Colorado showed, you can do two things.[81] On the one hand, you can try shifting from the ground of disgust to the ground of more reason-based sentiments such as fear (they will take your children away from you) or indignation (they are being given "special rights"). On the other hand, if you remain on the ground of disgust, you will have to focus on alleged properties of gay men that inspire disgust. And, in fact, the proponents of the referendum circulated pamphlets in which it was stated that gay men eat feces and drink human blood.[82] But such appeals to revulsion are not public reasons on which differential treatment under law can reasonably be based. The proponents of Amendment 2 seemed well aware of this, and thus were reluctant to admit to the tactics they had used. Their direct testimony focused on "special rights" and dangers to society; it was the plaintiffs, on cross-examination, who introduced evidence of the campaign's appeal to disgust.

Disgust is problematic in a way that indignation is not, and for more than one reason. First of all, indignation concerns harm or damage, a basis for legal regulation that is generally accepted by all. Disgust concerns contamination, which is far more controversial as a source of law. Indignation, again, is typically based on ordinary causal thinking about who caused the harm that occurred, and ordinary evaluation, about how serious a harm this is. Disgust, by contrast, is usually based on magical thinking rather than on real danger. As Rozin has shown, it is insensitive to information about risk, and not well correlated with real sources of harm. Finally, indignation, in its general nature, responds to the fact that we are vulnerable to damage, and that even things we care about most can be harmed by another's wrongful act. This is a salient fact about human life, and few would deny that it is true.[83] Disgust, by contrast, revolves around a wish to be a type of being that one is not, namely nonanimal and immortal. Its thoughts about contamination serve the ambition of making ourselves nonhuman, and this ambition, however ubiquitous, is problematic and irrational, involving self-deception and vain aspiration.

It may well be that all known societies police the borders of human animality with this strong emotion; it may even be that in our evolutionary history such policing proved valuable insofar as it succeeded in bounding off a group against its neighbors and promoting clannish solidarity. Perhaps even today societies need this policing in order to flourish, because people cannot endure the daily confrontation with their own decaying bodies. But it cannot be denied that the policing itself, in its social extension, works in ways that cannot stand the scrutiny of public reason. There is something wrong with disgust as a basis for law in principle, not just in practice.

At this point, it is important to remember the distinction between disgust as criterion and disgust as a putative harm. Sometimes being forced to be in the presence of a deeply offensive substance may inflict something that looks very much like a harm or a damage: offensive odors and substances are typically regarded as creating a "public nuisance," and, as I have mentioned, prisoners have argued, successfully, that being forced to live with overflowing chemical toilets was "cruel and unusual punishment."[84] These cases of disgust are important, and in chapter 3 I shall support some legal regulation in this area.

What we are dealing with for the most part in this argument, however, is another type of appeal to disgust: a use of disgust as a criterion for behavior that might be legally regulated, whether or not it inflicts anything at all on nonconsenting parties, and whether or not they are even aware of its presence. It is what Mill called a "merely constructive" injury: the injury a person imagines he would feel if he were present at such acts.[85] This is the type of appeal to disgust we have found in the arguments of Devlin and Kass. Of course the very imagining of such acts may indeed cause genuine distress, but this case must be carefully distinguished from the case in which a person is unwillingly subjected to the presence of an object he or she finds disgusting. Not all such cases give good grounds for legal regulation, as I shall argue. But the "merely constructive" type of case is problematic across the board and probably should never provide the basis for legal regulation.

The boundary between disgust and indignation is sometimes obscured by the fact that disgust can come packaged in a moralized form. As we shall see later, the judge at Oscar Wilde's trial represents himself as expressing a moral sentiment about the badness of sodomy; to that extent he took himself to be offering a type of public reason. Rozin and other psychologists have found that the term "disgusting" is very often applied to moral phenomena in a way that seems interchangeable with words indicative of damage, such as "horrible" and "outrageous." At first, writes Rozin, his tendency was to think this an accident of English usage, simply careless locution of some type.[86] Further study revealed, however, that speakers of other languages, too, made the same sort of extension. How, then, to understand the phenomenon? Is there still a distinction to be drawn between indignation and disgust in these moralized cases?

Here we should say, I think, that several different things are going on. Some cases are probably best explained as loose or careless usage, explained, to at least some extent, by the fact that English has no affectively strong adjective with which to express anger. ("That's outrageous!" seems pretty prissy and bland, so "that's *disgusting*!" sometimes substitutes.) In other cases, such as the Wilde case, the moralism seems to be a cloak for a quite familiar type of disgust, expressing contamination from the presence of an allegedly vile creature, an inhabitant of the human buffer zones that we shall discuss in section V. In other cases, a genuine moral judgment is linked to a disgust-judgment: thus a grisly murder will be found both very bad in the damage sense, and disgusting because of the gore and blood. (I shall discuss this sort of case in chapter 3.) In still other cases, there probably is a genuine extension, but the idea of distancing oneself from a contaminant is still central. Thus, people who say that crooked politicians are "disgusting" are saying something different from what they say when they express anger or outrage against these same people.[87] They are saying not that the politicians have done harm, but that they are contaminants to the community, rather like slimy slugs whom we would like simply to banish. Similar sentiments might be expressed about racists, sexists, and the like.

This last type of disgust raises some interesting questions, which we need to investigate sympathetically. Because I am so critical of disgust in this chapter, for the sake of fairness let me illustrate this point with an example of disgust that deeply moves me, and with which I identify, namely the famous "cry of disgust" in the third movement of Mahler's Second Symphony. Words cannot fully capture this musical experience, but, to cite Mahler's own program, the idea is that of looking at "the bustle of existence," the shallowness and herdlike selfishness of society, until it "becomes horrible to you, like the swaying of dancing figures in a brightly-lit ballroom, into which you look from the dark night outside. . . . Life strikes you as meaningless, a frightful ghost, from which you perhaps start away with a cry of disgust."[88] This disgust, we might think, is a valuable moral response to the deadness of social interactions, very close to an emotion of indignation at the wrongs done to people by hypocrisy, stifling ossified customs, and the absence of genuine compassion. Mahler's response to it, in the next movement, is to focus on pure compassion for human suffering, embodied in a text from folk poetry and music that alludes centrally to Bach.[89] Doesn't this mean that there is a type of disgust that offers some very good public reasons to criticize some social forms and institutions?

I believe not. However close the "cry of disgust" lies to indignation, its content is antisocial. Its content is, "I repudiate this ugly world as not a part of me. I vomit at those stultifying institutions, and I refuse to let them become a part of my (pure) being." Indignation has a constructive function: it says, "these people have been wronged, and they should not have been wronged." In itself, it provides incentives to right the wrong; indeed it is typically defined as involving a desire to right the wrong. By contrast, the artist who runs away from the world in disgust is at that moment not a political being at all, but a romantic antisocial being.

Thus Mahler's turning to compassion in the ensuing movement of the symphony does not grow directly out of his disgust; in fact, it requires him to overcome disgust, as he dramatizes by depicting the compassionate sentiments as embodied in the mind of a young child, who simply lacks that emotion. "O small red rose, humanity lies in the greatest need," begins the lyric: and the figure of the delicate flower is its own antidote to the disgust that has preceded. We are now viewing humanity as delicate, vulnerable, flowerlike: we have overcome the momentary temptation to vomit at its imperfections. Thus I would argue, with Mahler, that even the moralized form of disgust is an emotion that is highly problematic. It must be contained and perhaps even surmounted, on the way to a genuine and constructive social sympathy.

My own experience of moralized disgust takes the following form. When politics proves too gross and vile, I imagine, and sometimes seriously entertain, the thought of moving to Finland, a nation in which I have spent eight summers working at a United Nations institute— a nation, therefore, that I know pretty well, but not too well. I imagine it, not altogether falsely, as a land of clear, pale blue lakes and unsullied forests, and, at the same time, as a land of social democratic virtue, unsullied by greed, aggression, and corruption. In short, my fantasy is an escape fantasy, having more to do with back-formation from current discontents than with constructive engagement with

Finnish society. Anger at U.S. politicians tends in the direction of protest and constructive engagement. Disgust at U.S. politicians leads to escape and disengagement.

Might there be a type of disgust, directed at oneself and one's current society, that is productively connected with moral improvement?[90] Prophetic rhetoric does sometimes evoke disgust with current bad ways, as well as anger at them. And it is at least possible that using disgust-imagery about one's current self might be connected with a helpful move away from that defiled self. But I am skeptical: for if the imagery is that of disgust, then the statement that is made is that the self is filthy. Is that ever a helpful attitude to have toward oneself? Doesn't it suggest that the self just has to be discarded as hopeless, rather than the constructive idea that it should atone for its bad deeds and develop its potentiality for good? I suspect that all too many religious and political uses of such ideas are too much connected to ideas of self-loathing and self-abasement, rather than to the constructive amelioration of the self. Moreover, the fantasy of self-transcendence that may accompany such thoughts is all too likely to be a fantasy of impossible strength or purity, in which crucial elements of the human are lacking.[91]

But, Dan M. Kahan will now argue, why not use disgust's undeniable power for good?[92] If all societies contain disgust, and in all societies it is a potent moral sentiment, then why not harness it, teaching people to feel disgust at racism, sexism, and other genuinely bad things? One initial problem with this proposal is that disgust does not remain focused on an act. Anger at a bad act is compatible with the desire to rehabilitate the offender and with respect for the offender's human dignity. Disgust, because of its core idea of contamination, basically wants to get the person out of sight. And it seems to me that we should not have that attitude toward racists and sexists. We should distinguish carefully between persons and their acts, blame people for any bad or harmful acts they commit, but retain a respect for them as persons, capable of growth and change. So I think that the response that says, "Let's get those disgusting rats out of here" is not a helpful one for a liberal society, even when directed at people who may have bad motives and intentions.

Nor, as my Finland story illustrates, is there anything constructive about this fantasy of purity. What we should ask of racists and corrupt politicians is good behavior, and, even better, reform. When they do something bad they should be punished. What helpful course is even suggested, however, by the idea that they are like vomit or feces? Obviously we aren't going to send them into exile, and should not even if we could. So disgust both hooks us on an unrealizable romantic fantasy of social purity and turns our thoughts away from the real measures we can take to improve race relations and the conduct of politicians. Nothing is gained by treating any group of citizens like dirt, even if they are immoral. And of course, as the ensuing section argues, such treatment can also all too easily lead to the victimization of groups and harmless persons, through the magical thoughts of contagion and similarity. Is it good that Americans should feel disgust against terrorists? No, I would argue, not least because it can so easily spread outward, making us think that we must toss all Muslims and Arab-Americans into internment camps, or banish them from our borders. Anger and determination to rectify the situation—these are appropriate sentiments. Disgust is more problematic. Next door to the fantasy of a pure state is a highly dangerous and aggressive xenophobia.

V. Projective Disgust and Group Subordination

If disgust is problematic in principle, we have all the more reason to regard it with suspicion when we observe that it has throughout history been used as a powerful weapon in social efforts to exclude certain groups and persons. So powerful is the desire to cordon ourselves off from our animality that we often don't stop at feces, cockroaches, and slimy animals. We need a group of humans to bound ourselves against, who will come to exemplify the boundary line between the truly human and the basely animal. If those quasi-animals stand between us and our own animality, then we are one step further away from being animal and mortal ourselves. Thus throughout history, certain disgust properties—sliminess, bad smell, stickiness, decay, foulness—have repeatedly and monotonously been associated with, indeed projected onto, groups by reference to whom privileged groups seek to define their superior human status. Jews, women, homosexuals, untouchables, lower-class people—all these are imagined as tainted by the dirt of the body.

Let us look at some of these remarkable constructions more closely. The stock image of the Jew, in anti-Semitic propaganda from the Middle Ages on, was that of a being disgustingly soft and porous, receptive of fluid and sticky, womanlike in its oozy sliminess. In the nineteenth and twentieth centuries, such images were widespread and were further elaborated, as the Jew came to be seen as a foul parasite inside the clean body of the German male self. Particularly influential was the book *Sex and Character* by Otto Weininger, a self-hating homosexual and Jew, who died by suicide in 1903. Weininger argues that the Jew is in essence a woman: "[S]ome reflection will lead to the surprising result that Judaism is saturated with femininity, with precisely those qualities the essence of which I have shown to be in the strongest opposition to the male nature." Among the Jewish-feminine traits he explores is the failure to understand the national state as the aim of manly endeavor: thus Jews and women, he argues, have an affinity for the ideas of Marxism. They also fail to comprehend class distinctions: they are "at the opposite pole from aristocrats, with whom the preservation of the limits between individuals is the leading idea."[93]

Such ideas, already influential in the late nineteenth century, became extremely influential in the wake of the devastation of World War I. No doubt propelled by a fear of death and disintegration that could not help making itself powerfully felt at that time, many Germans projected onto Jews, as well as women, misogynistic disgust-properties that they both feared and loathed. The clean safe hardness of the true German man (often praised in images of metal and machinery) was standardly contrasted with female-Jewish-communistic fluid, stench, and muck.[94] As Klaus Theweleit argues in his impressive study of the letters and memoirs of a group of the Freikorps, a group of elite German officers of this period, "The most urgent task of the man of steel is to pursue, to dam in, and to subdue any force that threatens to transform him back into the horribly disorganized jumble of flesh, hair, skin, bones, intestines, and feelings that calls itself human—the human being of old." The aspiration to get away from messy, sticky humanity is well described in a novel of Ernst Jünger, *Kampf als inneres Erlebnis* (Battle as Inner Experience):

> These are the figures of steel whose eagle eyes dart between whirling propellers to pierce the cloud; who dare the hellish crossing through fields of roaring craters, gripped in the chaos of tank engines . . . men relentlessly saturated with the spirit of battle, men whose urgent wanting discharges itself in a single concentrated and determined release of energy.
>
> As I watch them noiselessly slicing alleyways into barbed wire, digging steps to storm outward, synchronizing luminous watches, finding the North by the stars, the recognition flashes: this is the new man. The pioneers of storm, the elect of central Europe. A whole new race, intelligent, strong men of will . . . supple predators straining with energy. They will be architects building on the ruined foundations of the world.[95]

In this fascinating passage, Jünger combines images of machinery with images of animal life to express the thought that the new man must be in some sense both powerful beast and god, both predatory and invulnerable. The one thing he must never be is human. His masculinity is characterized not by need and receptivity, but by a "concentrated and determined release of energy." He knows no fear, no sadness. Why must the new man have these properties? Because the world's foundations have been ruined. Jünger suggests that the only choices, for males living amid death and destruction, are either to yield to an immense and ineluctable sadness or to throw off the humanity that inconveniently inflicts pain. Disgust for both Jews and women became for such men a way of asserting their own difference from mere mortal beings.

As we can see, disgust is thus closely linked to experiences of vulnerability and shame. Underlying this obsessive focus on images of steel and metal is the sense that our mere mortality is something shameful, something we need to hide or, better yet, to transcend altogether. It is no surprise that such complex emotions were unleashed by the devastation of World War I—but of course they might arise in many different circumstances, given that human beings so often aspire to an invulnerability that they cannot achieve. Disgust therefore points backwards, in the human life cycle, to earlier experiences of helplessness, and of shame concerning helplessness. As I shall argue in chapter 4, both primitive shame and aggressive responses to it are deep and archaic features of most human histories, although some cultural and familial histories cause them to take a milder and more harmonious form than do others. Theweleit's and other related work establishes that the social and familial construction of the German male self at this time was closely linked to a type of pathological and narcissistic shame that bodes ill, as I shall argue, for relations with others.[96]

It is in this antithesis between the disgusting fluid and sticky, feminized Jew and the clean healthy German male body that we find the origins of Hitler's claim, in the epigraph to this chapter, that the Jew is a maggot in a festering abscess, hidden away inside the apparently clean and healthy body of the nation. Related images of Jews as slimy and disgusting are ubiquitous in the period, and even make their way into fairy tales for children, where Jews are standardly represented as disgusting animals who have the stock disgust-properties.[97] In a related development, medical discourse of the time standardly dehumanized Jews (and communists) by depicting them as cancer cells, tumors, bacilli, "fungoid growths." And in a remarkable inversion, cancer itself was described as a socially subversive group within the healthy body—even, more precisely, as "Bolshevists" and "spongers" (a stock description for Jews).[98]

The case of the Jews shows us that disgust toward groups frequently relies on elaborate social engineering. This engineering need not even rely on broadly shared human responses. Although disgust toward Jews seems to have had deep roots in experiences of shame, fear, and devastation, the fact that it was directed toward Jews in particular is an artifact of the social success of Jews, combined with elaborate ideological campaigning aimed at putting them down. One sure way of putting a group down is to cause it to occupy a status between the fully human and the merely animal. It is not because in some intrinsic way Jews were actually or "originally" or "primarily" found disgusting that they came to be associated with stereotypes of the disgusting. The causality is more the other way round: it was because there was a need to associate Jews (or at any rate *some* group, and for various reasons Jews came readily to mind) with stereotypes of the animal, thus distancing them from the dominant group, that they were represented and talked about in such a way that they came to be found disgusting.

However these causal chains worked, it came to be widely believed that Jews' bodies were actually different, in crucial ways, from the bodies of "normal people."[99] From the nineteenth century onward, a corpus of pseudoscientific literature described the allegedly unique properties of the Jewish foot, the Jewish nose, allegedly diseased Jewish skin, and allegedly Jewish diseases (such as hereditary syphilis).[100] The Jewish nose was widely linked to animality (the sense of smell being allegedly the most animal of the senses), to female odors and sexuality, even to menstruation; and Jews were widely believed to give off a distinctive and repulsive odor, often compared to the alleged smell of a woman during her menstrual period.[101]

And, indeed, the locus classicus of group-directed projective disgust is the female body. Misogynistic disgust has some empirical starting points that help to explain why this form of projection turns up with such monotonous regularity in more or less all societies. Women give birth, and are thus closely linked to the continuity of animal life and the mortality of the body. Women also receive semen: thus, if (as research suggests) semen disgusts males only after it leaves the male body, males will very likely come to view women as contaminated by this (to them) disgusting substance, while the male will view himself as uncontaminated, except insofar as he is in contact with her. In connection with these facts, women have often been imagined as soft, sticky, fluid, smelly, their bodies as filthy zones of pollution. Miller argues that misogyny lies very close to the ideational core of disgust. While it might have been some minority other than the Jews who could have been viewed as slimy and smelly, it is no accident that women are so viewed more or less ubiquitously, because males are disturbed by birth and especially by their own sexuality and bodily fluids. Miller argues that men find semen both distressing and deeply disgusting: thus, any being who receives it is contaminated. Following Freud, he then argues that men will always have great difficulty seeing their sex object as anything but debased, and will tend to seek already-debased objects, so that they can indulge their desires—understood as entailing the debasement of the object who receives those fluids—without guilt at inflicting debasement on one not debased. Miller does hold that love causes the relaxation of disgust, but only briefly, and to a limited extent.[102] In general, because the woman receives the man's semen, she "is what she eats" (whether in the sense of oral or vaginal incorporation); she becomes the sticky mortal part of him from which he needs to distance himself.[103]

One may wonder whether Miller has uncovered a universal phenomenon; and certainly the idea that semen is paradigmatic of the disgusting is one that does not find universal assent. But in its general outlines, his account of male disgust tracks a long-lasting and widespread type of misogyny. In very many cultures and times, women have been portrayed as dirt and pollution, as sources of a contamination that allures and must somehow, therefore, be both kept at bay and punished.[104] In Tolstoy's *Kreutzer Sonata,* closely linked to Tolstoy's own struggles with sexuality, the killer-husband describes sex as inevitably linked to revulsion with the woman who has inspired desire, and thence with rage and hatred for the subjection to desire that is intrinsic to any sexual relationship. He represents his murder of his wife as the natural consequence of the sex act, renunciation of sex as the only hope for relations between men and women not marred by hatred and disgust. For Schopenhauer, whose views are very similar, woman embodies the force of animal nature, striving to preserve itself; her allure is a primary obstacle to male projects of contemplation and detachment, and revulsion at her animality is thus closely linked to rage and hatred. Weininger developed such ideas in elaborate detail, arguing that woman, unlike man, is entirely sex and sexual, and that she is in effect the man's animality, from which he unevenly tries to distance himself, with reactions of both disgust and guilt: "Woman alone, then, is guilt; and is so through man's fault. . . . She is only a part of man, his other, ineradicable, his lower part."[105] Because the Jew is a woman, and disgusting in the way that women are disgusting, Jewish women, according to Weininger, are doubly disgusting, hyperanimal beings who exercise a fascinating allure but who must be warded off.[106]

One may find variants on these themes in more or less all societies, as women become vehicles for the expression of male loathing of the physical and the potentially decaying. Taboos surrounding sex, birth, menstruation—all these express the desire to ward off something that is too physical, that partakes too much of the secretions of the body. Consider the professor of gynecology, quoted by Maugham in my epigraph: for him woman is emblematic of all the bodily functions; she is, in effect, the male's body, and her receptive sexual eagerness is the culmination of her many disgusting traits. Anne Hollander's witty account of the history of the tailored suit gives a trenchant narrative of the way in which women's skirts were widely thought to hide a disgusting zone of filth and pollution, from which it was good to be safely distanced by wide voluminous skirts made of yards of fabric. Only recently have women been permitted to show their legs, revealing that they have human anatomy similar to that of males, not a foul cesspit of fluids.[107]

Consider, finally, the central locus of disgust in today's United States: male loathing of the male homosexual. Female homosexuals may be objects of fear, or moral indignation, or generalized anxiety, but they are less often objects of disgust. Similarly, heterosexual females may feel negative emotions toward the male homosexual—fear, moral indignation, anxiety—but again, they rarely feel emotions of disgust. What inspires disgust is typically the male thought of the male homosexual, imagined as anally penetrable. The idea of semen and feces mixing together inside the body of a male is one of the most disgusting ideas imaginable—to males, for whom the idea of nonpenetrability is a sacred boundary against stickiness, ooze, and death. The presence of a homosexual male in the neighborhood inspires the thought that one might oneself lose one's clean safeness, become the receptacle for those animal products. Thus disgust is ultimately disgust at one's own imagined penetrability and ooziness, and this is why the male homosexual is both regarded with disgust and viewed with fear as a predator who might make everyone else disgusting. The very look of such a male is itself contaminating—as we see in the extraordinary debates about showers in the military. The gaze of a homosexual male is seen as contaminating because it says, "You can be penetrated." And this means that you can be made of feces and semen and blood, not clean plastic flesh.[108] (And this means: you will soon be dead.)

Both misogynistic and homophobic disgust have deep roots in (especially male) ambivalence about bodily products and their connection with vulnerability and death. These reactions certainly involve learning and social formation, but they are likely to be broadly shared across cultures in a way that disgust at Jews is not. We do not have the sense in these cases, as we do in the case of anti-Semitic disgust, that the actual physical properties of the group were more or less totally irrelevant to their choice as disgust object: a broadly shared anxiety about bodily fluids finds expression in the targeting of those who receive those fluids. On the other hand, disgust in these cases is surely compounded by the element of deliberate construction that characterizes anti-Semitic disgust. The interest in having a subordinate group whose quasi-animal status distances the dominant group further from its own animality leads, here too, to a constructing of the woman, or the gay man, as disgusting by the imputation of further properties found disgusting. Bad smell, sliminess, eating feces—these are projected onto the group in ways that serve a political goal.

One recent example of the political role of disgust, which brings together all these areas, combining them with an anxious image of national purity, is the use of disgust to motivate violence by Hindus against Muslims in Gujarat, India, in March 2002.[109] Hindu nationalist rhetoric typically uses ideas of purity and contamination, with Muslims often portrayed as outsiders who sully the body of the nation. This general idea of purity takes an insistently bodily form, as Muslim men and women are portrayed as hypersexual animal beings, whose bodily fertility threatens the control of the pure Hindu male.[110] Pamphlets circulated during the rioting obsessively develop this sexual imagery, and imagine retaliation against the bodies of Muslim men and women in terms of a violation of their sexual parts (anus and vagina) by fire and metal objects. These tortures were enacted on the bodies of women, who were gang-raped, tortured with large metal objects inserted into their vaginas, and then burned alive.[111] This example, like so many others, clearly shows the connection between disgust and a type of aggression whose animating fantasy is that of ridding the nation of a contaminant.

VI. Disgust, Exclusion, Civilization

William Miller, following sociologist Norbert Elias, argues that the more things a society recognizes as disgusting, the more advanced it is in civilization.[112] He holds this thesis even though he grants Rozin his distinction between disgust and genuine danger, and even though he grants everything I have just said about the connection between disgust and the hatred of Jews, women, homosexuals, and other groups who become emblematic of the animal. Nor does he confine his claim to cases of moralized disgust like my Mahler example; it is at least arguable that we might measure social progress by the degree to which people learn to be disgusted by racism and other forms of social injustice. Miller's focus, however, is simply on the bodily. His claim is that the more we focus on cleanliness and the more intolerant we become of slime, filth, and our own bodily products, the more civilized we are.

This claim is utterly unconvincing, both descriptively and historically. The claim is descriptively unconvincing because it posits a unilinear progress in the area of disgust, ignoring the great vicissitudes of societies across the ages in the toleration they exhibit for bodily wastes and other disgust-substances. Focusing on a narrow period in European history, Elias and Miller fail to note that ancient Roman sanitary practices were in many respects well in advance of those that obtained in Great Britain until very close to the present day, if not now as well. The common Roman soldier stationed in Northumberland, in the north of England, among the most remote outposts of the empire, had a toilet seat to sit on below which flowed running water in which he might immerse his wiping sponge. Romans in major cities all had copious running water carried by aquifers whose engineering was remarkable, and the system separated water used for cooking and drinking from water used for toilet-flushing.[113] Both at home and abroad, baths of many kinds were widely available, and the average level of bodily cleanliness, to judge from documentary and archaeological evidence, was very likely high. By contrast, courtiers in Elizabethan England urinated and defecated in corners of palaces, until the stench made it necessary to change residences for a time. And the weekly bath was the most English people of all classes typically knew until extremely recent times.

In general, customs of cleanliness vary greatly in today's world. Americans are shocked by the English custom of rinsing dishes in the same soapy dirty water the dishes have been washed in, and also by English contentment with rinsing the body in the same tub water in which one has washed oneself. Indians of all classes wash with soap and water after defecating and find the institution of toilet paper in America and Europe substandard. (Similarly, the average toilet stall in Finland has a sink with a spray nozzle inside the stall, to promote such washing.) So we don't seem to find a uniform advance in the direction of greater sensitivity to the bodily fluids.

Normatively, it seems difficult to connect the kind of disgust-sensitivity on which Miller focuses with any kind of genuine social advance. It seems plausible enough that as society advances it will identify more things as physically dangerous, and so protect itself better against germs and bacteria, although one should note that such a policy is not always wise, excessive disinfecting being tentatively associated with a rise in asthma and other diseases with an immune-deficiency component. (Thus a child's resistance to finding dirty things disgusting might confer a health advantage.) Miller's normative claim is not a claim about danger, however. His claim is that the magical thinking characteristic of disgust is itself a sign of social progress.

If any such sweeping thesis can be entertained, surely the more plausible thesis is that the moral progress of society can be measured by the degree to which it *separates* disgust from danger and indignation, basing laws and social rules on substantive risk and harm, rather than on the symbolic relationship an object bears to anxieties about animality and mortality. Thus the Indian caste system was less civilized than the behavior of Mahatma Gandhi, who cleaned latrines in order to indicate that we share a human dignity that is not polluted by these menial functions.[114] Similarly, the behavior of D. H.

Lawrence's character Mellors to Lady Chatterley is much more civilized than the behavior of all the upper-class men around her. They
evince disgust at her body and its secretions; Mellors tells her that he
would never like a woman who did not shit and piss. Lawrence remarks to Ottoline Morrell that such attitudes help to "keep [the]
heart warm": they help constitute the relationship between male and
female as deeply reciprocal and civilized, rather than based on self-
loathing and consequent denigration of the female.

We might, with Walt Whitman, go still farther: the really civilized
nation must make a strenuous effort to counter the power of disgust,
as a barrier to the full equality and mutual respect of all citizens.[115]
This will require a re-creation of our entire relationship to the bodily. Disgust at the body and its products has collaborated with the
maintenance of injurious social hierarchies. The health of democracy therefore depends on criticizing and undoing that social formation. The job of the poet of democracy therefore becomes that of
singing "the body electric," establishing that the locus of common
human need and aspiration is fundamentally acceptable and pleasing—still more, that it is the soul, the locus of personal uniqueness
and personal dignity. Slave's body, woman's body, man's body, all are
equal in dignity and beauty:

> The male is not less the soul nor more, he too is in his place,
> ·
> The man's body is sacred and the woman's body is sacred.
>
> No matter who it is, it is sacred—is it the meanest one in the
>   laborer's gang?
> ·
> Each belongs here or anywhere just as much as the well-off, just as
>   much as you,
>
> Each has his or her place in the procession.
>   ("I Sing the Body Electric," 6.75, 83–84, 87–88)

Whitman sees that the realization of this idea requires an elaborate
undoing of disgust at the parts of bodies that we typically find problematic: hence the remarkable long conclusion of the poem, in which
he enumerates the parts of the body from top to bottom, outside to
in, depicting them all as parts of the soul, as clean and beautiful, to

be encountered with "the curious sympathy one feels when feeling with the hand the naked meat of the body." Curious sympathy takes the place of disgust, and the traversal of the body triumphantly ends:

> O I say these are not the parts and poems of the body only, but of
>   the soul,
> O I say now these are the soul!
>
> ("I Sing the Body Electric," 9. 164–65)

Whitman makes it clear that this recuperation of the body is closely linked to women's political equality. Because misogyny has typically seen the female as the site of the disgusting, a decontamination of the body, especially in its sexual aspects, is an essential part of undoing sex-based inequality (and the closely related inequality of the homosexual male). Responses to Whitman's poetry on its publication show us the depth of the problem. In a fashion typical of the American puritanism of the time, reviewers could not describe the poetry's focus on the sexual without describing it as disgusting. Thus the defenders against the charge of filth proceeded by denying the poems' sexual content: "I extract no poison from these leaves," wrote one Fanny Fern, contrasting Whitman's poems with popular romances in which "the asp of sensuality lies coiled amid rhetorical flowers." Edward Everett Hale, praising the book's "freshness and simplicity," insisted that "there is not a word in it meant to attract readers by its grossness."[116] What is striking about these reviews is their total lack of any way to talk about sexual longing other than in the language of disgust.

Whitman's response, throughout his career, was to represent the receptive and "female" aspects of sexuality as joyful and beautiful, indicating at the same time that in present-day America this joy can be realized only in fantasy. Thus in section 11 of *Song of Myself* he offers what he calls a "parable." By placing it immediately after an account of a slave's body, he invites us to ponder its connection to the theme of political equality:

> Twenty-eight young men bathe by the shore,
> Twenty-eight young men and all so friendly;
> Twenty-eight years of womanly life and all so lonesome.

She owns the fine house by the rise of the bank,
She hides handsome and richly drest aft the blinds of the window.

Which of the young men does she like the best?
Ah the homeliest of them is beautiful to her.

Where are you off to, lady? for I see you,
You splash in the water there, yet stay stock still in your room.

Dancing and laughing along the beach came the twenty-ninth
    bather,
The rest did not see her, but she saw them and loved them.

The beards of the young men glisten'd with wet, it ran from their
    long hair,
Little streams pass'd all over their bodies.

An unseen hand also pass'd over their bodies,
It descended tremblingly from their temples and ribs.

The young men float on their backs, their white bellies bulge to
    the sun, they do not ask who seizes fast to them,
They do not know who puffs and declines with pendant and bending
    arch,
They do not think whom they souse with spray.

                                    (*Song of Myself,* 11. 199–216)

These lines depict female sexual longing, and the exclusion of the
female, by morality and custom, from full sexual fulfillment, and
from public recognition as a sexual being. Their placement invite us
to see the woman as a figure for the excluded black man, who must
also hide his desire from the white world and who also runs the risk
of being seen as a metaphor for the feared intrusion of the sexual.
But there is another excluded party who also hides behind the cur-
tains. In the depiction of the woman's imagined sexual act, linked, as
it is, to other oral-receptive imagery in other poems about the allure
of the male body, Whitman also refers to the exclusion of the male
homosexual, whose desire for the bodies of young men must be concealed even more than must female desire. The easy joy of these
young men depends on their not knowing who is watching them

with sexual longing; and this is true of the situation of the homosexual male in society, at least as much as it is of the black man gazing
erotically at the white woman, or the female gazing erotically at the
male. As he says in "Here the Frailest Leaves of Me," from *Calamus:*
"Here I shade and hide my thoughts, I myself do not expose them, /
And yet they expose me . . ." (2–3). The woman, then, is also the
poet, caressing in fancy bodies that in real life shun his gaze.

The woman's gaze, like the gaze of the poet's imagination in the
earlier section, is tenderly erotic, caressing the bodies in ways that
expose their naked vulnerability, their soft bellies turned upward to
the sun. And she caresses something more at the same time. The
number twenty-eight signifies the days of the lunar month and also
of the female menstrual cycle. The female body, in whose rhythms
Whitman sees the rhythms of nature itself, is immersed in finitude
and temporality in a manner from which the male body and mind at
times recoils. (Havelock Ellis, writing eloquently about this passage,
cites the elder Pliny's remark that "nothing in nature is more mon-
strous and disgusting than a woman's menstrual fluid.")[117] In caressing the twenty-eight men, the woman caresses her own temporality
and mortality, and at the same time sees it in them, approaches and
makes love to it in them, rather than turning from it and them in
disgust.

Whitman suggests that the willingness to be seen by desire entails
a willingness to agree to one's own mortality and temporality, to be
part of the self-renewing and onward-flowing currents of nature. It is
because it touches us in our mortality that sex is deep and a source
of great beauty. In the final poem of *Leaves of Grass,* he imagines em-
bracing a male comrade, and says, "Decease called me forth." The
deep flaw in Whitman's America, then, the flaw that for him lies at
the head of hatreds and exclusions, is disgust at one's own softness
and mortality, of the belly exposed to the sun; the gaze of desire
touches that softness, and must for that reason be repudiated as a
source of contamination. Over against this flawed America Whitman
sets the America of the poet's imagination, healed of disgust's self-
avoidance and therefore truly able to pursue liberty and equality.

Whitman's America is a fiction. No real society has triumphed
over disgust in the way depicted here. Nor should we hastily con-

clude that such a society is even an ideal norm we should endorse. Should human beings really try to rid themselves of disgust insofar as they possibly can, in every aspect of the fabric of our lives? Several considerations suggest that this may not be such a good idea.

First of all, as we have mentioned, disgust very likely played a valuable role in our evolutionary heritage, steering us away from real danger. Even if it does not track real danger perfectly, it does give an added emphasis to the sense of danger, and thus we might well want to rely on it in parts of our lives where ascertaining danger is likely to be difficult and uncertain. Thus it would very likely be a mistake to try to eat all foods, even those that initially disgust us. Disgust toward feces and corpses is probably a good thing to teach children, as a device to steer them away from genuine danger at an age when they cannot be expected to calculate the dangers. Nor are adults always very good at washing their hands, for instance, because it is the prudent thing to do, so doing it because feces are disgusting may be a good backup motive on which to rely.

Second, we have reason to believe that in at least many cultures at many times, or at least for many people within cultures, the disgusting and the attractive are interwoven in a complex manner. Would a sexuality free of all sense of the disgusting be feasible and imaginable? And even if it is so for many people, it might not be for all. Whitman's hygienic picture of the body does not seem very sexy: so we need to ask whether the disgust-free attitude does not remove too much.

This brings us to the third and most significant point. What Whitman asks of us is, in the end, a simple relationship to our own mortality and its bodily realization. We are to embrace with neither fear nor loathing the decay and brevity of our lives. But to ask of humans that they not have any shrinking from decay or any loathing of death is to ask them to be other than, possibly even less than, human. Human life is a strange mystery, a combination of aspiration with limitation, of strength with terrible frailty. To become a being who didn't find that mysterious or weird or terrifying would be to become some kind of subhuman or inhuman being, and it would also be to forfeit, very likely, some of the value and beauty of human life. At least we don't see clearly that it would not have this effect. If, however, the complex struggle we currently wage with mortality has disgust as its corollary, we should not expect to dismiss disgust utterly from our lives.

For all these reasons, it seems that we should think hard before endorsing Whitman's comprehensive program of disgust-extirpation. Nonetheless, to say that a certain motive should probably remain embedded in the fabric of human life is not to say that this motive gives good guidance for political and legal purposes. I have argued that disgust gives bad guidance for several reasons: because it does not well track genuine danger; because it is bound up with irrational forms of magical thinking; and, above all, because it is highly malleable socially, and has very often been used to target vulnerable people and groups.

Notice that these arguments do not give us strong reasons not to base laws on disgust where there is an actual bodily offense to a nonconsenting party that we can examine, asking how it was produced and how bad it is. In other words, the use of disgust in the area of nuisance law may still withstand the type of critique I have advanced, and in chapter 3 we shall see to what extent this is so. What the critique does call into question is the more nebulous and global argument made by Devlin and Kass—that disgust is an emotional criterion rooted in our personalities (or, in the case of Devlin, in our social order) that gives us reliable guidance by identifying types of acts that are beyond the pale and that should be prohibited, despite the fact that they cause no harm to nonconsenting parties. Disgust looks not at all reliable because of the way that it constructs groups of surrogate animals who represent to the dominant members of the community things about themselves that they do not wish to confront.

Now of course, as I argued in chapter 1, no emotion is reliable per se as a basis for law. Anger embodies judgments about harm that may well be misguided: for example, it once informed the cuckolded husband that infidelity is a harm justifying homicide. But at least anger makes a claim that is a pertinent one: this is a very serious harm, wrongfully inflicted. This is obviously a pertinent sort of claim to make in a context where we are contemplating legal regulation of conduct. If it stands up to scrutiny, we can expect the law to take it very seriously.

What claim is made by disgust? In the case we are envisaging, where disgust is used as a criterion to support the prohibition of harmless acts, the claim appears to be: "This act (or, more often and usually inseparably, this person) is a contaminant; it (he or she) pollutes our community. We would be better off if this contamination were kept far away from us." But that, as we have seen, is a very vague claim. If it is meant literally—for example, if the claim is that someone has actually polluted a neighbor's water supply with harmful material—then we have moved onto the terrain of harm, as I shall argue in the following chapter. If, however, we just say, "These men having sex in their bedrooms are a pollution in our community, even though I don't see them or encounter their act," or, "These Jews going around our city streets are a verminous pollution, even though they don't take harmful action against us," in such cases the idea of contamination and pollution is extremely vague and nebulous—what Mill called "merely constructive."

What exactly are we saying? That the presence of such people and their acts in our community will cause its downfall? Why should we think this? Because we don't like them? That is hardly a sufficient reason for legal regulation. And if we were to uncover and state what really seems to be in the background, namely, "We have chosen these people as surrogate animals in order to distance ourselves from aspects of animality and mortality that appall us," then that reason, once brought out into the light, would provide absolutely no ground for legal regulation. Instead, it would prompt the further question, "Why don't we criticize ourselves for treating a group of people in such a blatantly discriminatory manner?" The real content, in short, would prompt criticism of the disgusted rather than of the constructed cause of their disgust.

Let us now turn to specific legal issues to see whether we can uncover there the signs of the problems we have found, and to see whether our critical attitude will offer useful legal guidance.

Chapter 3
Disgust and the Law

[The law] does not recognize homosexual activity between two persons as legal provocation sufficient to reduce an unlawful killing . . . from murder to voluntary manslaughter. . . . A reasonable person would simply have discontinued his observation and left the scene; he would not kill the lovers.

—*Commonwealth v. Carr,* Pennsylvania 1990

There is no doubt of the general proposition that a man may do what he will with his own, but this right is subordinate to another, which finds expression in the familiar maxim, "Sic utere tuo ut alienum non laedas." . . . Ever since Aldred's Case . . . it has been the settled law, both of this country and of England, that a man has no right to maintain a structure upon his own land, which, by reason of disgusting smells, loud or unusual noises, thick smoke, noxious vapors, the jarring of machinery, or the unwarrantable collection of flies, renders the occupancy of adjoining property dangerous, intolerable, or even uncomfortable to its tenants. No person maintaining such a nuisance can shelter himself behind the sanctity of private property.

—*Camfield v. U.S.,* 1897

"A mass of stupid filth . . ."

—Early review of Walt Whitman's *Leaves of Grass*

I. Disgust as Offense,
Disgust as Criterion

We have seen some reasons to be particularly mistrustful of disgust as a guide to the legal regulation of conduct. Even though it is evidently a very strong emotion, Leon Kass's contention that it contains a wisdom that steers us reliably in moral matters is not supported by our analysis of its cognitive content and its social history. Indeed, its propensity for magical thinking and its connection to group-based prejudice and exclusion make it look particularly unreliable. Devlin's position is, so far, less damaged by our analysis, because he grants that disgust is based on social norms. He does not maintain that it contains a moral wisdom that goes beneath or beyond the current deliverances of society. But surely even his position has been called into question by the evidence of the sheer irrationality of social disgust and the gratuitous harms it inflicts upon others. As for the position of Miller and Kahan, that disgust helps motivate opposition to cruelty, we have seen that even the moralized form of disgust partakes in the demand for purity and freedom from contamination, a demand that is all too easily connected to the denigration of persons and groups who are unpopular, and too little tethered to any concrete issue of wrongdoing, for which evidence might be offered and examined.

When we turn to specific areas of law with these concerns in mind, we should bear in mind the distinction drawn in chapter 2, between the use of disgust as an actual offense, a type of damage or harm, and the use of disgust as criterion to identify types of acts that might be regulated, whether or not they cause any harm to nonconsenting parties. It is not always easy to make this distinction. Sometimes people feel damaged because they have a certain view about a type of conduct: thus a person may feel damaged by an attempted homosexual seduction because of beliefs of the sort that underlie the legal prohibition of sodomy. Similarly, the reading of offensive material often causes actual offense, even though obscenity law uses the hypothetical standard of an average or reasonable man to calibrate the offensiveness of the questionable material. Public nudity is a particularly difficult case: it seems possible to maintain that it causes harm, at least to children, but it is also possible to maintain that the person feels harmed only because of what they imagine. (Because this case seems more in the ballpark of shame than in that of disgust, I will discuss it in a later chapter.)

There are clear cases of both types, however. The nuisance cases itemized in my second epigraph fall clearly into the disgust-as-harm category. In section V, I shall discuss the relationship between disgust and harm in these cases, and the related link between disgust and danger. On the other end of the spectrum, the use of disgust to support laws against consensual homosexual acts that take place in private is clearly one of the "purely constructive" or hypothetical type. If there is actual offense, and there often is, it is offense occasioned by *imagining* what is going on, or thinking about the fact that the law permits this sort of thing to go on, not by any direct infliction of offense on a nonconsenting person. I shall argue that the use of disgust as criterion has no legal value; the appeal to disgust would be better replaced by other notions, especially notions of damage or harm, and by a search for evidence of such harm. My position on disgust-as-harm will be more complex. I shall argue that many such cases are indeed rightly regulated by law, and that Anglo-American nuisance law, in its general outlines, is a reliable repository of criteria for legal regulation. Sometimes, however, the claim that a certain sort of person, or a person's act, is a nuisance to the community, or a provocation to an individual, is itself based upon the type of irrational group prejudice I have dissected in chapter 2. We should therefore confine even the appeal to direct disgust to cases where disgust lies very near to strong distaste and/or danger.

II. Disgust and the Offender: The "Homosexual-Provocation" Defense

Should a criminal's reaction of disgust ever help his cause, when he has committed a violent crime? As we saw in chapter 1, the defense of "reasonable provocation" appeals to the emotion of the offender in order to argue for a reduction in level of homicide from murder to voluntary manslaughter.[1] Usually, however, the emotional state invoked is anger, and the anger involved has to be of a very specific sort, pertaining to a serious wrong or aggression committed by the victim against the defendant. To win a reduction, the defendant must show that he acted "in the heat of passion" after a provocation by the victim of the crime, that the provocation was "adequate," and that the emotion he exhibited was that of a "reasonable man." The sheer intensity of the defendant's emotional excitation will not suffice to mitigate crime; such a policy would reward people for "evil passions."[2] A person of "a cruel, vindictive, and aggressive disposition will seize upon the slightest provocation to satisfy his uncontrolled passions by forming a design to kill."[3]

For this reason, as we saw, evidence of the defendant's emotional state is standardly not admitted into evidence unless the provocation meets a standard legal definition of reasonableness. The account of what would provoke a "reasonable man" to violence has shifted over time, as we saw, but it always involves some serious aggression and harm done to the defendant by the victim: bodily assault, adultery with the person's wife, and domestic abuse are three salient examples. Although a reasonable belief that such a harm has occurred might fulfill the general legal standard, mitigation typically requires establishing that the harm in question actually occurred. The idea behind the defense is that if the reasons for being angry are good enough and such as to command broad public agreement, then a reduction in level of crime is warranted.

Earlier, as we saw, what counted as an adequate provocation was defined as a matter of law. Offenses of certain specific types were defined as legally adequate or inadequate. More recently, jurors have been given some latitude to judge the offense for themselves. But courts still sometimes define certain types of provocation as insufficient as a matter of law, refusing to let the jury hear this emotional evidence.[4] The question before us must now be whether the defendant's strong disgust for the victim may ever fulfill the legal requirements for a provocation defense.

There would appear to be argument on both sides of this question. On the one hand, disgust is a very strong response, and being disgusted can in some cases be a kind of harm, analogous to an assault or aggression. One's body feels invaded or contaminated by the disgusting object. Thus in nuisance law, as we shall later see in more detail, putting disgusting smells in another person's way can be an actionable offense on the grounds that it spoils their enjoyment of their property, which is a kind of harm. As previously noted, prisoners who were kept in the presence of stinking and overflowing chemical toilets were held to be so severely harmed by that disgusting circumstance that the punishment was held to violate the Eighth Amendment's guarantee against cruel and unusual punishment. A cruel and unusual punishment is surely a kind of harm or aggression against a person.

On the other hand, disgust looks different from anger, in the sense that it is a generalized response to the presence or characteristics of the person, not to the person's aggressive or wrongful act. While we can see good reason for mitigation in the case where the victim provoked the defendant first by a serious harm or aggression against either the defendant or the defendant's loved ones, we do not see why the mere presence of a person in the vicinity, not doing anything wrong or aggressive to the defendant, should be reason to mitigate the defendant's harmful act against that person, disgusting though that person may have been. Being disgusting to look at is not an invitation to violence. Chapter 2, furthermore, has shown that disgust is frequently the result of socially learned prejudice, so by offering mitigation on the grounds of disgust we would be reducing the disincentive to the commission of hate crimes.

An adequate response to this dilemma requires making several distinctions. The first distinction that seems important is that between sensory disgust at "primary objects," a disgust lying close to distaste and danger, and the socially mediated disgust that people so often feel toward members of unpopular groups, such as Jews, women, racial minorities, and homosexuals. We can imagine that no education in the world, and no socialization in the world, would make the presence of an overflowing stinking toilet nondisgusting. Even if disgust at feces does have to be learned, it is a universal property in all known societies, and it is a reasonable response to unpleasant sensory properties and/or dangers posed by feces. Disgust at unpopular groups, by contrast, is mediated by magical thinking about contamination and purity, and, as we have seen, usually involves the projection onto the group in question of characteristics that do not belong to those human beings any more than to other human beings. The unpopular become the vehicles for a contamination we all actually share. Moreover, such projections are not only irrational, they are also objectionable because they are part of the systematic subordination of those people and groups. We might think, then, that the law ought to be more sympathetic to disgust at primary objects than to the projective form of disgust.

The second distinction that seems pertinent is that between aggression and just being there. Insofar as the provocation defense makes sense at all, it makes sense because we think that the victim did something violent—usually something criminal—to the defendant, something that, in the heat of the moment (before thoughts of calling in the law intervene) seemed to justify a similarly violent response. But the bare fact that a person is in the area is not an act of aggression. Thus the idea that in the heat of passion the defendant could consider no other option but that of violence against the source seems prima facie less plausible. The defendant is the first aggressor, and in general that is a weak position. (Compare the theory of just war, in which justification must derive from a prior act of aggression against the nation in question.)

If the first of our distinctions leads us to think that the law should look more kindly on those who claim that they are injured by a disgust directed at "primary objects," the second distinction leads us to think that even such a primary disgust is unlikely to support a provocation defense in the absence of an aggressive act by the victim.

Finally, a third distinction seems pertinent: between cases where one may avoid the unpleasantness by going away from it and those where it is inflicted upon one in a way that seems difficult to avoid. The standard provocation defense involves a hostile or aggressive act that has been inflicted upon the defendant; it seems that he cannot avoid being the target of this act, either because it has simply happened to him, as when someone in a bar hauls off and hits someone else, or because the nature of the relationship in question makes the aggressive act unquestionably and irrevocably a part of the person's life, as when someone has raped the defendant's child. (Compare the role of inevitability in self-defense, where there is frequently a duty to retreat if retreat is possible, the salient exception, as we saw in chapter 1, being one's own home.) Thus, even if a person has actual distaste-properties—for example, the person is smeared in urine and filth—it is usually possible to get out of the person's way.

With these three distinctions in mind, let us begin with an area in which a disgust-based provocation defense has actually been considered in recent cases, and then try to arrive at a more general formulation. Does a person's disgust at the mere presence of a homosexual fulfill the legal criteria for a provocation defense? One would think not, if my reasoning above is correct. Just by being in the world as a homosexual, the homosexual has not committed an aggressive or harmful act against the offended person. If a person's psychology is such that the mere physical proximity of such a homosexual person feels like an assault, the solution of a "reasonable" such person (if such there can be!) would be to get out of the area, not to kill the homosexual person. Violence is no more excusable than it would be if someone shot someone because they didn't like the person's face, or ethnicity, or skin color, or physical defect, all properties that may occasion actual disgust in some people. A homosexual does not have actual physical properties that constitute a nuisance in the narrow sense intended in nuisance law, nor is his or her presence an aggressive act.

As the reader will recall, Stephen Carr, a drifter, was lurking in the woods near the Appalachian Trail when he saw two lesbian women making love in their campsite. He shot them, killing one of them. At trial he argued for mitigation to manslaughter on grounds of reasonable provocation, arguing that his disgust at the sight of their lesbian lovemaking provoked his response. He sought to introduce psychiatric evidence to explain, on the basis of his childhood history, this unusually strong disgust-reaction. The judge rightly refused to admit such evidence: "[the law] does not recognize homosexual activity between two persons as legal provocation sufficient to reduce an unlawful killing . . . from murder to voluntary manslaughter. . . . A reasonable person would simply have discontinued his observation and left the scene; he would not kill the lovers."[5] Carr's disgust was inadmissible as a matter of law because it did not fulfill the legal requirement of harmful and aggressive action.

Returning to our three distinctions, we notice that Carr's disgust was of the purely constructive kind: no distaste-properties belonging to primary objects of disgust were salient in the case. With regard to the aggression–just-being-there distinction, the women, who were not even aware of Carr's presence, clearly committed no act of aggression against him. And the third distinction also goes against Carr's contention: as the judge said, he could have walked away any time.

Carr's case is unusually clear, because the women did nothing at all in relation to him, and did not know he was there.[6] More legally problematic has been a group of cases in which defendants seek mitigation on grounds of a homosexual advance allegedly committed by the victim, which allegedly occasioned a disgust that led to the ensuing violence. Although judges have sometimes refused to admit evidence of such alleged provocation, quite a few such defendants have been able to present this defense, and have gotten a reduction to voluntary manslaughter or a very light sentence for murder.[7] Does such an advance ever justify mitigation? Should the law accept the idea that a "reasonable person" would react to such an advance with violence?

An initial problem with such defenses is that the facts are usually very difficult to establish. There may be many witnesses to a physical assault or to a history of domestic battery. The homosexual advances that such defendants allege typically occur without witnesses, and there may be more than a shadow of a suspicion that the defendant has used the victim's sexual orientation as a convenient occasion to allege an advance in order to seek mitigation. Let us stipulate, however, that the facts are all true as the defendants narrate them, considering only noncoercive and nonthreatening forms of sexual approach. Does disgust at an attempted homosexual seduction provide a legally adequate basis for mitigation?

Jerry Volk and his friend John Hamilton arrived in Minneapolis broke and with no place to stay.[8] They planned to pose as gay prostitutes, pick up a homosexual man, and rob him. They picked up a Mr. Traetow. Some hours later Traetow was found shot dead in his own apartment; his hands and legs had been taped. Volk's thumbprint was on a broken vodka bottle on the floor. Volk admitted being present at the scene, and at least being an accomplice in the homicide (although there remained a disagreement between Volk and Hamilton as to which of them actually shot Traetow). His story was that when Traetow made a homosexual advance, he was "revolted" and provoked to homicide. Hamilton also described Volk as "pretty disgusted." On appeal, Volk claimed that the trial court improperly refused to instruct the jury on a heat-of-passion manslaughter defense.

The court disagreed. "Assuming for argument the truth of these circumstances, there was no provocation sufficient to elicit a heat of passion response. A person of ordinary self-control under like circumstances would simply have left the scene." In other words, seduction is not assault or gross harm, so long as there is neither intimidation nor duress. If a sexual advance is found disgusting, just leave, don't kill the seducer.

Thinking again of our three distinctions, we notice that, once again, the disgust is constructive: that is, it is disgust at the mere thought of a homosexual act, not at anything that was actually taking place or inflicted upon the defendants. (And the defendants' claim of disgust is a little hard to square with the fact that they had actively solicited the advance by posing as gay prostitutes.) The aggression–being-there distinction is a little more difficult to apply than in Carr's case, because Traetow did do something to Volk, namely ask him for sex. But it was not a coercive or violent or harassing approach. It was, by all accounts, just a seduction or proposition—and one of a kind that they had solicited by posing as gay prostitutes. So in the relevant sense it is more like being there than like aggression.[9] And the unpleasant situation was hardly unavoidable; as the judge said, they could simply have left.

In this case the judge ruled disgust irrelevant as a matter of law, but other cases have gone the other way. Consider, for example, *Schick v. State*.[10] A young man, out drinking with his friends, hitched a ride home with another man, the victim. Together they drove around looking for women for sex. After a while the young man asked, "Where can I get a blow job?" The victim replied, "I can handle that." They drove around some more, then went to a baseball field at a local school. The victim pulled down his pants, but the young man kicked him and stomped on him, took his money, and left him to die on the baseball field.[11] Before leaving he carefully wiped the victim's car clean of his fingerprints. At trial the defense argued that the homosexual advance was sufficient provocation to explain the killing; the prosecutor did not object, and the judge permitted the defense. (The theft and the wiping of fingerprints were described as afterthoughts.) The jury convicted the young man of voluntary manslaughter.[12]

In this case, as in *State v. Volk,* the homosexual advance had been actively encouraged by the defendant and was neither coercive nor harassing. All the victim did was to pull down his pants and wait for the other man to pull his down. Insofar as the "advance" was disgusting, the defendant's disgust was a purely constructive disgust, not one connected to sensory properties of primary disgust objects. And, finally, the defendant might have left at any time. We may add that he was so far from showing revulsion in the first instance that he apparently agreed to a sex act; and he was so far from being out of control with passion that he acted, after the crime, with cool deliberation. The success of a provocation defense in these circumstances shows the level of irrational disgust many people in American society currently feel at the very thought of same-sex acts.

The traditional doctrine of voluntary manslaughter is basically rational and consistent, although some of its recent applications are not. The doctrine offers perfectly clear reasons why some emotional reactions are relevant to mitigation while others are not. When the emotion is that of the "reasonable man," the defense provides not a justification, but a partial excuse.[13] Indignation is relevant to mitigation under certain circumstances, where it is a reasonable response to an adequate provocation.[14] Disgust is totally irrelevant, because feeling contaminated or "grossed out" by someone is never a "reasonable man's" emotion of the sort that excuses violent conduct against that person. (If it's a reason to do anything, it's a reason to move away.) On my account of the two emotions, this is as it should be: society has wisely recognized, for the most part, that people's disgust is totally irrelevant to the justification of violence. As Robert Mison concludes, "[a] murderous personal reacton toward gay men should be considered an irrational and idiosyncratic characteristic of the defendant and should not be allowed to bolster the alleged reasonableness of the defendant's act."[15] Because the "reasonable man" is not simply the average man, but a normative social ideal, we should not admit that gay-bashing disgust is ever the emotion of that hypothetical person.

We see the wisdom of this judgment when we think of disgust directed against Jews, women, blacks, or people with disabilities. In none of these cases would we—in America today—even briefly entertain the thought of a heat-of-passion defense for someone who happens to find members of that group and their romantic advances disgusting. In other times and places, this would not have been so. Indeed, we can all too easily imagine the loathesomeness of a Jew's advances being used in exactly the way Volk used the alleged advance by Traetow.[16] The fact that, as a society, we are conflicted about the disgust issue as applied to homosexuals shows us that this group is currently a focus of our desire to cordon ourselves off from the viscous, the all-too-animal. That, I would argue, is an even stronger reason for us to be skeptical of those emotional responses, and to refuse as a matter of law to admit them into evidence.

III. Disgust and the
"Average Man": Obscenity

Should disgust ever be a central factor in rendering a practice illegal? Here we are squarely in Devlin-Kass territory. Disgust is not being seen as the actual offense for which law might offer a remedy. (Obscenity law does not give a cause of action for damages to readers who have been personally disgusted by a book.) Disgust is instead a criterion: asking whether a "reasonable" or "average" man would find the item in question disgusting is a way of asking about how bad it is, and therefore how important it is to keep it away from those who might actually like it. Usually the exercise is purely hypothetical: the "man on the Clapham omnibus" is imagined as not at all the sort of man who goes looking for pornographic films, or acts of sodomy and necrophilia. But his respectable reaction, rather than the reactions of those who actually do seek out such materials or acts, is thought a reliable index of what should be legally permitted.

We can begin our consideration with the law of obscenity, which makes some of the salient issues especially clear. Legal accounts of the obscene typically refer to the disgusting properties of the work in question as they relate to the sensibilities of a hypothetical "average man." The legal standard set by *Miller v. California* in 1973 holds that a work may be subject to state regulation "where that work, taken as a whole, appeals to the prurient interest in sex; portrays, in a patently offensive way, sexual conduct specifically defined by the applicable state law; and, taken as a whole, does not have serious literary, artistic, political or scientific value."[17] This determination is to be made from the point of view of "the average person, applying contemporary community standards." Disgust enters the picture in two ways: as a way of articulating the notion of the "patently offensive," and also as a way of thinking about what "prurient interest" is: it is to be understood as a "shameful or morbid interest in nudity, sex, or excretion."[18]

In order to make these connections clearer, the Court analyzes the concept of obscenity in a fascinating and significant footnote. Criticizing an earlier decision for not offering a precise definition of the obscene, the Court discusses the etymology of "obscene" from Latin *caenum*, "filth."[19] Next, Justice Burger cites the *Webster's Third New International Dictionary* definition of "obscene" as "disgusting to the senses . . . grossly repugnant to the generally accepted notions of what is appropriate . . . offensive or revolting" and the *Oxford English Dictionary* definition of "obscene" as "[o]ffensive to the senses, or to taste or refinement, disgusting, repulsive, filthy, foul, abominable, loathsome."[20]

This, however, is not the end of the matter. The note now adds that the materials being discussed in this case are "more accurately defined" as "pornography" and "pornographic materials." In other words, the concept of the "obscene" now undergoes further refinement and analysis via the concept of the "pornographic."[21] The etymology of "pornography" from the Greek term for "harlot," or female "whore," is now discussed, and pornography is defined (via

Webster's dictionary) as "a depiction of licentiousness or lewdness: a portrayal of erotic behavior designed to cause sexual excitement."

The mingling of ideas in this account is truly fascinating. In order to offer a "precise" account of the *Roth* notion of "prurient interest," the Court brings in the concept of the disgusting, as it is used in dictionary definitions of obscenity. This concept, in turn, is rendered "more accurately" by reference to the concept of the female whore and the related idea of a "portrayal of erotic behavior designed to cause sexual excitement." In other words, that which appeals to prurient interest is that which disgusts, and that which disgusts (at least in the area of sex) is that which (by displaying female sexuality) causes sexual excitement. The pornographic is a subclass of the disgusting, the subclass that deals with female sexuality in an exciting way. But why this linkage? Aren't disgust and sexual arousal very different things?

The nexus has in fact caused some legal conundrums. In a 1987 case in the Fourth Circuit concerning films depicting intercourse with animals, the defense argued that the materials in question were not obscene because they were surely not sexually arousing to the "average man"; indeed, the "average man" would find films like *Snake Fuckers, Horsepower,* and *Horny Boar* pretty revolting.[22] Undaunted by this difficulty, the unanimous three-judge panel responded that the obscene *is* the disgusting, and it surely would be inconsistent with the spirit of the law to find milder materials obscene because they arouse average people, and to let more deeply revolting materials off because they disgust average people:

> [T]he offensiveness requirement in the Miller test is more than minimally met, however, the greater the number of people who would react to the material with revulsion and disgust. Surely Guglielmi is right that the reaction of most people to these films would be one of rejection and disgust, not one of sexual arousal, but that cannot lead to the conclusion that the most offensive material has constitutional protection while less offensive material does not.[23]

In other words, when the averagely arousing and the averagely disgusting point in different directions, the disgusting takes precedence for purposes of interpreting the *Miller* standard: for surely the worse cannot get more protection than the less bad, and the disgusting is surely worse than the merely arousing.

The two standards suggested in *Miller* do not always point in the same direction, clearly, and they leave many problems of interpretation for courts to sort out. But why, we might ask, should one ever have supposed that these ideas would go together? What is sexy about the disgusting, and what is disgusting about the activities of a female whore? The answer should by now be all too evident. In this confused nexus of concepts we discern the time-honored view that sex itself has something disgusting about it, something furtive and self-contaminating, particularly if it is the body of a female whore (receptacle of countless men's semen) that inspires desire. Justice Burger records and endorses a conceptual linkage crafted by the long tradition of misogyny and misanthropy that I discussed in chapter 2, a tradition brilliantly described by such disparate writers as William Miller and Andrea Dworkin.[24] The female body is seen as a filthy zone of stickiness, sliminess, and pollution—disgusting to males because it is the evidence of the male's own embodiment, animality, and mortality. Disgust for oneself as animal is projected onto the "female whore" whose activities typify, for Justice Burger, the sexually arousing and hence the disgusting. In Adam Smith's words, "When we have dined, we order the covers to be removed." The presence of that reminder of "our" (meaning male) sexuality is disgusting if it remains around in the community to haunt us.

This conceptual nexus is ubiquitous in the post-Victorian period in attacks on sexually explicit artworks. Typical is an early review of Joyce's *Ulysses:*

> I have read it, and I say that it is the most infamously obscene book in ancient or modern literature. The obscenity of Rabelais is innocent compared with its leprous and scabrous horrors. All the secret sewers of vice are canalized in its flow of unimaginable thoughts, images and pornographic words. And its unclean lunacies are larded with appalling and revolting blasphemies directed against the Christian religion and against the holy name of Christ—blasphemies hitherto associated with the most degraded orgies of Satanism and the Black Mass.[25]

The attack on the novel focused on Molly Bloom's monologue, whose frank depiction of a woman's nonmarital sexual desires—combined, as they are, with ruminations about her menstrual period, deflationary thoughts about the penis, and memories of love—are indeed shocking to those in the grip of the disgust-misogyny I have outlined.[26] Indeed, we can see the operations of disgust-misogyny in the very strange response of this reader (hardly unusual) to the work he purports to have read.

Joyce believed that our disgust with our own bodily functions lay at the root of many social evils, including nationalism, fanaticism, and misogyny. Like Lawrence he held that a healthy society would be one that comes to grips with its own mortal bodily nature and does not shrink from it in disgust. Joyce's novel, of course, is the opposite of disgusting to one who reads it as it asks to be read. Like Lawrence's *Lady Chatterley's Lover,* it presents the body as an object of many emotions—desire, humor, tender love, calm acceptance. But one emotion that is conspicuously absent from both writers (and the invitation they give to their readers) is that of disgust. The novels of Joyce and Lawrence were found disgusting precisely because the society that read them was so deeply in the grip of a kind of loathing of its own animality that it could not actually read the works. Writers who wish to present the body without disgustingness have usually encountered such reactions.[27] They are found threatening precisely because they ask their readers to look at the body. The reader's antecedent disgust with the body (especially the female body) gets projected back onto the work, as a way of warding off the challenge it poses.

We have good reason, then, to doubt whether the disgust of the "average man" would ever be a very reliable test for what might be legally regulable in the realm of art. If indeed disgust is frequently a defensive projection stemming from a fear of confronting the naked body, especially when the body is presented in a nondisgusting way, then we have reason to fear that loathing of sexuality and animality may render unreliable many judgments that are made about works of art. Any society that pursues sex equality should be deeply skeptical of this conceptual nexus, and protective of works that seek to separate the arousing from the disgusting. (It should also be protective of works, like those of contemporary performance artist Karen Finley, that explore critically the conceptual nexus between the arousing and the disgusting.) Were it true that the "average man" feels disgust at such works, a society committed to equality should worry about the "average man" and his education, rather than about the works to which he reacts.

In short: the legal definition of obscenity actively colludes with misogyny, has the root concepts of misogyny embedded in it.

It seems to me that Catharine MacKinnon and Andrea Dworkin are entirely right in their argument that the serious moral issue posed by pornographic materials is not the issue of sexual explicitness and its alleged disgusting excitingness.[28] Even if some citizens in a liberal society continue to believe that sex is disgusting, the presence of sexually explicit materials in society is no more harmful to them than the presence of texts defending a religion different from their own. They can simply avoid those materials, and, at most, demand that they not be easily available to children, or displayed in public in a way that accosts unwilling viewers. (Similarly, parents can reasonably request that children not be required to attend teachings of a proselytizing sort in a religion not their own, and that public education not accost them with sectarian devotional materials.)

The issue that a society committed to the equality of its female citizens should take seriously is the issue of subordination, humiliation, and associated harms. These aspects of pornography threaten core elements of a liberal society, elements on which citizens who otherwise differ in religion or comprehensive vision of life can agree. Much pornography, it is no news to say, depicts sexuality in a way designed to reinforce misogynistic stereotypes, portraying women as base and deserving of abuse, as wanting and asking for abuse, and as outlets for the male's desire to humiliate and abuse. It is this that we should take seriously, as a moral statement that conflicts pretty directly with the equality of women. Pornography is in this sense similar to anti-Semitic literature or racist literature: it makes a statement that directly conflicts with ideas of equal worth and equal protection that are basic to a liberal social order. But of course this feminist concept of the pornographic as the subordinating is profoundly at odds with the legal concept of the obscene. It doesn't just reorient "our" thought, it implicitly shows up the misogyny inherent in "our" previous thought.

Exactly what the consequences of this reorientation should be for the law is a question that may be disputed. By thinking of the analogous case of anti-Semitic literature, we can see that liberal societies have taken a range of differing positions on the protection to be extended to speech and expression of this kind. Germany has seen fit to ban such items, and to sequester items published in earlier eras in special archives, from which photocopies may not be taken. The United States has protected such speech and expression, except where there is an imminent danger of public disorder. John Rawls suggests extending this protection yet further: the speech of the "unreasonable" (those who endorse a view of life at odds with the liberal society's constitution) will be protected except in a grave constitutional crisis where the stability of the constitutional order itself is in jeopardy.[29] On the other hand, the U.S. tradition has sometimes been read as supplying stronger protection for political speech than for other forms of expression.[30] If we take such a tack, we will then have to ask whether violent subordinating pornography counts as political speech and, if it does not, what level of protection it ought to enjoy. It seems initially plausible to think that we should categorize it the same way we categorize anti-Semitic and racist speech, given the MacKinnon-Dworkin analysis, although we would need to consider duly arguments that reach a different conclusion. Then we will have to ask, in each case, whether the subordinating speech counts as political speech; if it does not, we will have to ask what level of protection it ought to have.

For reasons that should be clear from the foregoing analysis, few U.S. feminists support outright censorship of subordinating pornography, and it must be stressed again and again (because this fact has been much misunderstood) that MacKinnon and Dworkin do not support censorship. What they do support is an ordinance that gives individual women a civil cause of action for damages if they can show that they have been harmed by men in a way that crucially involves pornography.[31] They envisage two classes of plaintiffs: actresses and models who have suffered abuse in the making of pornography, and women abused by men who were turned on by, or who were copying the scenarios depicted in, pornography. Such women can of course already bring criminal charges against their abusers, but the MacKinnon-Dworkin ordinance allows them to sue for damages the makers and distributors of the pornographic materials, and also to get an injunction against them. The injunction would result in suppression of some pornographic materials: that is where something like censorship comes into the picture. The analysis, however, is that pornography is a dangerous harm-causing product, and an individual plaintiff must always make a showing of harm. Modeled on laws passed prior to Prohibition that allowed women to bring damage suits against the makers and distributors of alcohol if they could show that they had been abused by men in a way that involved alcohol as a crucial agent, these laws also bear a strong resemblance to more recent dangerous-product damage suits against the tobacco and firearms industries. MacKinnon and Dworkin have amply demonstrated that there are many cases where the relevant harms can be plausibly attributed to pornography.[32] Nor should the critic demand an unreasonable level of proof for the causal connections in question: we typically do not require a showing of either necessity or sufficiency when we hold other dangerous items responsible for a damage.[33]

We may still argue about whether the ordinance would be either effective or wise. Will courts interpret it well, or will they use it to go after unpopular materials, such as lesbian and gay materials? Is its account of the pornographic so broad that it will end up targeting the wrong materials?[34] If makers and distributors of a work are held responsible for copycat enactments of its content, won't this suggest that authors who depict murders and suicides are legally responsible for copycat murders and suicides (which certainly have existed for writers as eminent as Goethe and Dostoyevsky)? MacKinnon and Dworkin are aware of these questions, and have made plausible replies to them, which it is not my concern to assess here. My point is simply that one may disagree about the specifics of the ordinance, and even about its general wisdom, while granting that they have reoriented the moral and political debate in an extremely salutary way, from the alleged inherent disgustingness of sex (and of women) to issues of equality, subordination, and associated harms and damages.

The progressive pro-disgust position must now be heard, however. Dan M. Kahan's position would surely be that disgust has a valuable role to play even in this revised feminist program of scrutiny. Let us consider a case in which the pornographic materials in question are patently offensive to feminists and an assault on women's equality. We might call them "disgusting," using the term in the richer moral sense we recognized in chapter 2. Kahan would hold that this richer moral disgust is progressive and productive, but even in such cases, I would argue, the emotion of disgust is typically a confusion and a distraction from the serious moral issues that ought to be considered. In 1984, a suit was brought against *Hustler* magazine for publishing features depicting Andrea Dworkin in a derogatory manner:

> The February Feature is a cartoon, which, as described in the plaintiffs' complaint, "depicts two women engaged in a lesbian act of oral sex with the caption, "You remind me so much of Andrea Dworkin, Edna. It's a dog-eat-dog world." The March Feature is a ten page pictorial consisting of photographs of women engaged in, among other things, acts of lesbianism or masturbation. Some of the photographs depict obviously staged scenes that include posed violence and phony blood. One photograph, supposedly of a Jewish male, has a caption stating: "While I'm teaching this little shiksa the joys of Yiddish, the Andrea Dworkin Fan Club begins some really serious suck'n'squat. Ready to give up the holy wafers for Matzoh, yet, guys?" The December Feature was included in the "Porn from the Past" section of the magazine. It shows a man performing oral sex on an obese woman while he masturbates. A portion of the caption states: "We don't believe it for a minute, but one of our editors swears that this woman in the throes of ecstacy [*sic*] is the mother of radical feminist Andrea Dworkin."[35]

I shall not comment here on the central legal issues in the case, which were the definition of the concept of a public figure for the purposes of the law of libel and slander, and the distinction between statements of fact and privileged statements of opinion. What interests me is a side-argument in which the court considers the issue of obscenity. The court's conclusion is that the materials in question involve political speech and thus cannot be obscene under the *Miller* test: "Because the Features expressed opinions about matters of public concern, they did not lack 'serious literary, artistic, political, or scientific value.' It follows that they are not obscene." Again, I shall leave to one side, for purposes of my argument here, the question of whether this claim of political value is plausible.

What interests me is that on the way to her conclusion, and immediately prior to her description of the Features attacking Dworkin, Judge Hall feels it important to express her disgust with the materials in the case and the periodical in general. "Hustler Magazine is a pornographic periodical. Much of its content consists of what we have recently described as 'disgusting and distasteful abuse.'" So the Features attacking Dworkin are "disgusting," and thus might have been candidates for obscenity had the political-speech issue not intervened. The question is, what is this disgust about, and is it relevant to the serious issues in this case?

On one reading—we may call it the Kahan reading—the disgust felt by the judge at *Hustler* and the Dworkin Features is a tough, uncompromising moral sentiment that should be honored as highly relevant to the legal regulation of expression, even if, in the present case, other arguments prevented this reaction from determining the outcome. I believe that this is the position that Kahan should logically take, given his overall view. But I am dubious. The morally salient issue in the case, it seems to me, is one of harm, humiliation, and subordination. Dworkin is being treated as a plaything of male fantasies of humiliation and domination; in retaliation for her feminist criticism of men, *Hustler* is taking pleasure in portraying her as both disgusting and contemptible. What Dworkin is claiming is that she has been harmed by this representation. The appropriate reaction to such a harm is outrage and indignation, not disgust. We don't vomit at subordination and inequality, we get mad. Here as elsewhere, disgust expresses the thought that the object is contaminating and must be kept at a distance. It does not adequately register the thought that a harm has occurred. In short, disgust seems not quite the relevant emotion. It does not respond to harms that are alleged and well supported by the evidence.

In addition to the sheer irrelevance of the issue of contamination, there is another issue: what is the disgust really about, and what sentiments, more precisely, does it express? What is found disgusting by Judge Hall, it would seem, is the physical grossness of what is depicted—both the grossness of the men's depicted behavior and, I cannot help thinking, the grossness of the image of Andrea Dworkin's mother so displayed. *Hustler* is disgusting, in short, because it shows obese people copulating, inviting our disgust at their obesity. The response of disgust, far from being a repudiation of *Hustler,* is exactly what the periodical solicits and reinforces: male disgust at the body of Andrea Dworkin's mother represented as obese. The whole idea of the Features is to humiliate feminists and feminism by implying that Andrea Dworkin's mother's body (and no doubt, by extension, Dworkin's own body) is disgusting, in a very traditional misogynistic sense. When the judge says "disgusting," then, she is at least in part colluding in the magazine's project. It is difficult to believe that she would use the same words about a slender model of the *Playboy* type. Insofar as she does distance herself from the magazine, she does so in a way that expresses class-based disdain for the lower-class males depicted in *Hustler:* she finds their appearance and behavior disgusting. And this, too, colludes in the magazine's enterprise: for it standardly portrays itself, with pride, as the sex-magazine for "regular guys" who would be scorned and found disgusting by the readers of upmarket porn like *Playboy.* In neither case does her disgust record an emotion that is morally relevant to what is really going on in the case. At worst, she joins in the humiliation of Dworkin. At best, she makes some disdainful comments about lower-class men that are altogether irrelevant to the legal issues before her.

In short, even when disgust appears to support values that we prize, we should scrutinize it very closely. Its focus on contamination and pollution appears inadequate and irrelevant to the salient issues of harm that typically confront us in cases involving sexist obscenity; and its strong link to traditional misogyny makes it a slippery and double-edged way of (apparently) expressing feminist sentiments.

Although disgust remains central to the Anglo-American analysis of pornography, it is extremely interesting that Germany has recently adopted an approach much more like the one that I favor, focused on issues of dignity, subordination, and objectification. To begin with, the relevant section of the criminal code, which used to be called "Offenses against Morality" (*Straftaten wider die Sittlichkeit*), is now called "Offenses against Sexual Autonomy." And the analytical focus has correspondingly shifted, from concern with community

morality to a concern with offense against the dignity of individuals.[36] There are many interesting consequences of this redirection of
emphasis, especially in areas such as rape, prostitution, and child
abuse. But to focus on the immediate topic, the 1973 reform legalized the distribution of pornography among adults, focusing on restricting its distribution to children and the use of children in it.
(Germany has tough laws, for example, on the distribution of child
porn over the Internet.)

This, however, is not the end of the issue. For German law remains
concerned with the objectification of adult women in pornographic
materials. Although for the reason given this issue does not come
under the criminal law, an extremely interesting 1981 decision of the
German Federal Administrative Court upheld an agency denial of a
trading license to a club for operation of a peep show in which a
woman would perform nude for the pleasure of patrons.[37] The
Court focused on the issue of human dignity, as guaranteed by Article 1 Section 1 of the German Constitution, and held that the peep
show did inflict a dignitary offense on the actress appearing in it.[38]
What was particularly fascinating was that the Court drew a distinction between the traditional strip tease and the peep show. The
striptease, the Court argued, stands in a long tradition of erotic performance, and the fact that the woman performing it can move
around, look at the audience, relate to the whole group, and be seen
from many different perspectives makes her retain a kind of live humanity: her dignity is allowed "to pass untouched."[39] By contrast, in
the peep show she is turned into a thing, a mechanical object, a
mere commodity for the use of a single purchaser. Pointing to the
isolation both of the woman and of the viewer in his booth, they conclude that the woman has been converted from live performer to a
mere "object for the arousal and satisfaction of sexual desires" (*An-
regungsobjekt zur Befriedigung sexueller Interessen*); thus her dignity has
been injured. The Court rejects the argument that the woman con-
sented to appear in the show: for dignity, they argue, is an objective
and not a subjective matter, and cannot be alienated at will.[40]

I do not wish to defend everything in this judgment: in particular,
the distinction the Court draws between striptease and the peep
show is too quick, I believe, nor does the Court reflect convincingly

about the extent to which a liberal society should permit people to choose potentially degrading activities. I would be inclined to consider the model's decision protected from legal penalty, whether or not it was a choice to surrender human dignity (though I am not sure that Millian arguments have much weight when we are simply talking about licensing and not criminal penalties).[41] What I want to say, however, is that the German Court is in the right ballpark of analysis: it has found the morally significant issues, which are issues of human dignity, objectification, and subordination. Disgust has nothing to do with it.

Pornography raises issues that are salient for any liberal society attached to the equality of all citizens: issues of equality, subordination, and humiliation. It also raises issues of personal morality that may be salient for individual citizens or groups of citizens, depending on the content of their moral and religious views. But citizens who object to the moral content of a book or film, whether on grounds of sexual explicitness or on grounds of religious or political doctrine, may deal with this problem by avoiding the works in question and by trying to ensure that the works do not confront citizens in public space and that they are not paraded before the impressionable young. This seems to be the way that a pluralist democracy ought to deal with moral differences of the sort occasioned by the novels of Joyce and Lawrence. Issues of subordination are different, because they touch on values that lie at the core of a pluralist society, values that are part of the political consensus on which the society's basic principles are based. Some nations, for example Germany in the case of anti-Semitic speech, respond to this difference by an outright ban on the speech in question. The United States has followed a different course, one that protects politically heinous speech. The MacKinnon-Dworkin approach does not directly contest that doctrine, but rather attempts to find a remedy for individual plaintiffs who have been harmed by the speech in question. Whether we think this remedy adequate or wise, we should recognize that it is well within the group of remedies being discussed and implemented by advanced liberal democracies today.

Whatever legal response we prefer to the dilemmas posed by violent sexist pornography, we ought to recognize that the issue it raises is not that of sexual explicitness merely, and the alleged disgusting excitingness of that. Indeed, it would appear that disgust has nothing to do with the matter. To violations of the equality of a fellow citizen, the appropriate response is anger, not disgust. Kahan's progressive pro-disgust argument appears to hold that this anger is too fragile to survive without disgust.[42] I believe that people tempted to this position should think harder about the ambiguity of the disgust-response and its tendency to reinforce precisely those harms to which anger responds.

IV. Disgust as a Reason for Illegality: Sodomy, Necrophilia

But are Kass and Devlin ever right? Is the disgust of a "reasonable man" at a particular practice ever sufficient reason to make it illegal? Prima facie we might think that disgust, involving as it does ideas of contamination and pollution, would offer good reasons for the disgusted person to avoid the practice or people in question, just as disgust at a particular food or animal gives us good reasons to avoid that food or that animal. There seems to be no evident prima facie reason to take action against the practice or people, any more than people's disgust at specific foods or animals gives us reason to ban the food in question, or to kill or quarantine certain animals.

Devlin would respond at this point that it is not disgust of any and every sort that we are talking about here, but rather a strong disgust on the part of the "reasonable man," imagined as both average and, in some normative sense, normal, and going about his daily business as a productive member of society ("on the Clapham omnibus"). He argues that the strong disgust of this man does give us good reasons for legal regulation because such disgust indicates that a practice is destructive to the social fabric. It pollutes not just the life of an individual, but, through this individual's representativeness, the entire community. It shows us what we have to throw out if we want our community to survive.

As I have argued, it is not easy to tell exactly how the community is thought to be threatened by disgust-inspiring conduct. Devlin contends that there is a strong correlation between what the "reasonable man" finds disgusting and a type of "debauchery" so extreme that it marks incapacity to serve as a citizen. But this contention is not supported by argument, nor would it appear to square with the evidence. Jews, women, people in interracial marriages, homosexuals: all of these have been and are perfectly responsible citizens, and yet they have more frequently been the targets of disgust than people who are corrupt or greedy or egocentric. And yet the corrupt, greedy, and egocentric probably pose a significant threat to the social fabric of any democratic society.

Kass's argument is more difficult to criticize because he does not tell us whose disgust counts, or why. For Kass, disgust is a sign that a moral norm connected to "human nature" is being violated. But under what conditions? How widespread must the disgust be to play this evidentiary role? Disgust at miscegenation was surely very widespread, and there can be no doubt that it was widely taken as a sign that a moral norm inherent in nature was being violated. Indeed, the trial judge who heard the case of Richard and Mildred Loving, an interracial couple, defended Virginia's antimiscegenation law by appeal to just such an alleged precultural norm: "Almighty God created the races white, black, yellow, malay and red, and he placed them on separate continents. And but for the interference with his arrangement there would be no cause for such marriages. The fact that he separated the races shows that he did not intend for the races to mix."[43] It seems unlikely that this is the sort of moral norm Kass would endorse. And yet he offers us no way of distinguishing the disgust that lay behind antimiscegenation laws from the disgust that he endorses as a good legal criterion in the case of cloning, and, by suggestion, same-sex relations as well.

All we can do, then, is to study closely some cases where disgust continues to figure as the primary criterion for making some types of acts illegal, asking whether the reasoning underlying these prohibitions is sound or not, and how far the cases appear to support elements, at least, of a Devlin-Kass position.

Let us first consider sodomy laws. U.S. law retains a large number of laws against various types of consensual sexual relations, including adultery, fornication, and same-sex acts.[44] Sodomy is sometimes defined by reference to the same-sex nature of the act. Sometimes, instead, it is defined by reference to a type of sexual act, usually including all oral-genital and genital-anal conduct. This second type of sodomy law is neutral in appearance, applying to opposite-sex and same-sex acts alike. In *Bowers v. Hardwick*, however, the heterosexual couple who were originally joined in the suit were declared not to have standing to challenge the state's law on the grounds that they were in no danger of prosecution.[45] So on at least one plausible view of such laws, they are likely to be invoked today only against same-sex conduct, however they are worded. Until June 26, 2003, such laws remained on the books in quite a few states, and were the subject of at least some prosecutions.

The case against such laws is relatively easy to make. Even many people who strongly disapprove of homosexual relations oppose sodomy laws on the grounds that they are so rarely enforced that their enforcement, when it occurs, is arbitrary and capricious; they are just invitations to the police to engage in acts of harassment. Others hold a position closer to Mill's: moral disapproval is not a sufficient ground for the prohibition of an act that is carried out in seclusion, not inflicted on the unwilling, and not harmful to the nonconsenting. (Two other cases sometimes discussed in terms of Mill's principle, public nudity and public sex, will be discussed in chapter 5, since they raise issues of shame, rather than disgust.)

I have said that I will try to not presuppose Mill's principle in arguing against laws that flout it. So I cannot simply stop with the last type of reply. Nonetheless, it certainly seems fair to ask the defender of sodomy laws whether she would defend all the laws that have been democratically passed against unpopular sex acts of various types, including fornication and adultery, and, if not, on what grounds the continued illegality of homosexual sodomy can really be defended, especially in a pluralistic and religiously diverse society in which some groups and religions endorse such conduct and others do not. Most Americans are rightly wary of any simple appeal to majority sentiment in areas touching on personal conduct of a deeply meaningful kind, whether in sex or in religion. So the fact that we can muster some votes against it will seem insufficient. We need to have a stronger argument about what is really bad and damaging.

So: what have defenders of sodomy laws had to say about the badness of sodomy that would be persuasive? Devlin appeals to the need
to have a country that can fight a war. But by now we are well aware
that gays and lesbians have been excellent soldiers in many fine
armies around the world. Others have tried to find other harm-like
properties of same-sex conduct. It is fascinating to observe that
whenever restrictions on homosexual conduct are contemplated, a
parade of witnesses standardly comes forward to testify about alleged
harms of such conduct. In the trial of Amendment 2 in Colorado,[46]
the state introduced testimony on psychological self-harm, on child
abuse, on various types of alleged subversion of the civic fabric—all
in order to show what possible "compelling interest" the state might
possibly have in preventing homosexuals from enjoying the protection of nondiscrimination laws.[47] Similarly, in *Baehr v. Lewin* an unsuc-
cessful attempt was made to show that gay couples cause psychological
harm to children in order to support the claim of compelling state
interest in denying gays access to marriage.[48] In both cases, the prof-
fered testimony was convincingly refuted by other experts, whom the
judges in question found more reputable and credible. The claims
of danger were shown up as pathetically weak, and the issue came
down to disgust. Indeed, it became clear at trial that disgust lay behind the electoral success of Amendment 2. As we saw in chapter 2,
the proponents reluctantly admitted under oath that they had circulated materials that alleged that gays eat feces and drink human
blood—propaganda very similar to anti-Semitic propaganda from
the Middle Ages.[49]

When defenders of restrictions on homosexual activity introduce
testimony about actual harms, they are not conceding the value of
Mill's principle: for some of the harms they typically allege are harms
to self, and thus such debates do not beg the question in Mill's favor.
Paternalism (protecting people from harming their own interests) is
one thing, however, sheer disgust is another. The proponents of
Amendment 2 proved unable to offer convincing evidence even of the
sort of self-harm that Mill considered an inappropriately paternalistic basis for legal regulation. The psychiatric profession has long since
agreed that homosexuality is not a mental illness, and no evidence
produced convincingly showed any other sort of self-harm.[50] All that

the proponents of the amendment really seemed to offer was disgust, and their reluctance to argue on this basis suggests that they themselves recognized that disgust is a weak thread on which to hang legal restrictions. A showing of serious harm *of some type* is necessary; if the real motive has been disgust, one must put on a show to make people think it has been something else.

Let us now return to the third trial of Oscar Wilde; for it shows this point in an especially fascinating way. In his famous speech at sentencing, Mr. Justice Wills spoke as follows:

> Oscar Wilde and Alfred Taylor, the crime of which you have been convicted is so bad that one has to put stern restraint upon one's self to prevent one's self from describing, in language which I would rather not use, the sentiments which must rise to the breast of every man of honour who has heard the details of these two terrible trials. . . . I hope, at all events, that those who sometimes imagine that a judge is half-hearted in the cause of decency and morality because he takes care no prejudice shall enter into the case, may see that that is consistent at least with the utmost sense of indignation at the horrible charges brought home to both of you.
>
> It is no use for me to address you. People who can do these things must be dead to all sense of shame, and one cannot hope to produce any effect upon them. It is the worst case I have ever tried . . .
>
> I shall, under such circumstances, be expected to pass the severest sentence that the law allows. In my judgment it is totally inadequate for a case such as this. The sentence of the Court is that each of you be imprisoned and kept to hard labour for two years.[51]

Mr. Justice Wills maintains that decency prevents him from describing his real sentiments, which are also those of any "man of honour." A description would require "language which I would rather not use." He thus strongly hints that the emotion is a violent disgust that could only find appropriate expression in indecent language, like a kind of vomiting in speech.[52] He treats the prisoners as objects of disgust, vile contaminants who are not really people, and who therefore need not be addressed as if they were people. (At the conclusion of the speech, Wilde called out, "And I? May I say nothing, my lord?" His lordship made no reply, simply gesturing to the warders to remove the prisoners.) At the same time, however, Mr. Justice Wills appeals to public reason by claiming that he has combined judicial impartiality with "the utmost sense of indignation at the horrible charges brought home to both of you." The Justice tries to lay claim to the moral force of indignation; and yet his speech strongly suggests that indignation is but a public mask for disgust.

On what, we might now ask, could indignation be plausibly based? Wilde was convicted for "gross indecency."[53] He had had oral sex with a number of working-class men well above the legal age of consent (the youngest was eighteen and most were in their twenties). All sought out relationships with him, often in order to advance careers in literature and the theatre; he treated them with generosity, taking them on trips and buying them lavish presents.[54] Had the Justice attempted to show reasons for indignation that any person could share, it would have been very hard for him to point to wrongs done by this conduct, far less to show that it is "the worst case I have ever tried." Disgust hides behind the screen of indignation, but it is clearly disgust, not indignation at harm, that is driving the sentencing.

Moreover, the prosecution strongly linked disgust for same-sex conduct to disgust based on class: the lower-class origins of the younger men were often mentioned as evidence that the relationship in question was of an improper and disgusting sort. One exchange: "Did you know that one Parker was a gentleman's valet, and the other a groom?" "I did not know it, but if I had I should not have cared. I didn't care twopence what they were. I liked them. I have a passion to civilize the community." In this way disgust at same-sex conduct was linked to a kind of antimiscegenation disgust: sex should not join the upper classes with the lower.

In short, neither harm to others nor even any paternalist conception of self-harm is behind the sentiments expressed by the judge toward Wilde and Taylor. What is really being said is that "these are two slimy slugs whose type ought to be squashed before they insinuate themselves into our bodies."

Sodomy laws, the traditional focus of disgust-based lawmaking, thus do not stand up to serious scrutiny. Typically even their proponents have felt that disgust is too thin a basis for them to rest on, and have sought to introduce other more plausible, harm-based grounds.

When these collapse and the naked disgust is exposed, however, the sentiment seems extraordinarily capricious, linked to superstitions having to do with gender, class, and so on, rather than anything more publicly respectable. To appeal to disgust seems to be just to say "I don't like that," and to stamp one's foot vehemently. No reasons are advanced that would make debate about such laws a real piece of public persuasion.

The recent landmark Supreme Court decision in *Lawrence v. Texas* recognizes these points with an admirable clarity. Criticizing the historical and modern social analysis in *Bowers,* the Court argues that such an intimate adult consensual sexual relationship is "within the liberty of persons to choose without being punished as criminals." Therefore the state should not regulate it, "absent injury to a person or abuse of an institution the law protects." But this case involves neither minors nor coercion nor even the sort of relationship "where consent might not easily be refused." Citing a decision in the European Court of Human Rights and subsequent cases in a variety of European nations, the Court establishes that there is an emerging consensus that recognizes the right to engage in such consensual sexual relationships as an "integral part of human freedom." No reason has been given to support the idea that in the United States there is a particularly strong or urgent state interest in regulating such relationships.

Especially significant is the Court's recognition of a connection between liberty to engage in private sexual activities in one's own way and issues of dignity and respect. They understand that sodomy laws, whether or not enforced, have implications for employment, child custody, and a wide range of other social issues. To criminalize the form of sexual conduct people choose is to "demean" those persons. "The petitioners are entitled to respect for their private lives. The State cannot demean their existence or control their destiny by making their private sexual conduct a crime."

The Court understands the relationship between morality and law in a way that closely follows the political liberalism of John Rawls, which I have been defending throughout my argument. Recognizing that the religious condemnations of homosexuality are, for many citizens, "not trivial concerns but profound and deep convictions accepted as ethical and moral principles to which they aspire and which thus determine the course of their lives," the Court then distinguishes between these "comprehensive conceptions of the good" (to use Rawls's phrase) and the political principles that may be the permissible bases for law in a pluralistic society: "The issue is whether the majority may use the power of the State to enforce these views on the whole society through operation of the criminal law. 'Our obligation is to define the liberty of all, not to mandate our own moral code.'" Opposition to a Devlin-like view is thus based on the twin principles of respect for the dignity and liberty of persons and a recognition of social pluralism and the limits this pluralism suggests for the criminal law.

Sodomy laws are now a thing of the past, at least in the United States. There are, however, other acts that are still prohibited by way of an appeal to disgust. We need to look further, since it may be that not all cases are as weak as the one we have just considered. In particular, there is one sexual practice that apparently causes no harm—certainly not harm of Mill's sort—that seems so disgusting and awful that most people will immediately feel that it ought to be illegal, even if disgust is the only thing we have to say against it. This practice is necrophilia—in the words of one judge "the most loathsome, degrading and vile sexual activity imaginable."[55]

The first question that must be asked is whether necrophilia ought, in fact, to be illegal. The history of legislation regarding it is uneven. According to Richard Posner and Katharine Silbaugh's catalogue of sex laws as of 1996, thirty-six states have no law at all against it, and most such laws are of recent origin.[56] Most states have some laws against desecration of the corpse, but sexual desecration, though viewed as especially disgusting, is usually not singled out for especially harsh punishment. Indeed, some corpse-desecration statutes may not cover it at all: California's statute uses the words "willfully mutilates," and it is unclear whether this language applies to the damage done to the corpse during intercourse.[57] Rape statutes, meanwhile, have typically been interpreted to require a live victim, except in cases where the defendant mistakenly believes the person to be alive at the time of rape; even in alleged felony murders in which the murder is a prelude to a desired act of necrophilia, it has standardly been held that the defendant can be convicted only of attempted rape, not rape.[58] Necrophilia in which the perpetrator is not involved in the victim's death appears to be legally unprovided for in many jurisdictions; this state of affairs is sometimes defended on the grounds that necrophilia is a victimless crime.[59]

Here Kahan would be ready to step in. Surely my position against the legal relevance of disgust requires us to conclude that necrophilia should not be a crime, but just as surely our moral intuitions tell us otherwise. Here, then, may be a case in which our disgust is highly relevant to the determination that a practice should be illegal.

To answer this we must discuss the more general question of damage to corpses. We view these wrongs as grave wrongs primarily on account of the harm they cause to relatives and loved ones of the deceased. The corpse usually belongs to the survivors. It is an especially valuable and intimate type of property, like a precious sentimental or religious artifact. Any type of mutilation is heinous, but sexual mutilation is likely to be especially painful to the surviving family, because it gives the impression of treating the person who was with callous disregard, and even wanton cruelty. Where the dead person is without relatives and friends, we will still view necrophilia as an insult to the life of the person that was, and as an assault on religious or personal meanings that the state, by taking that person's corpse as its property, undertakes to protect from desecration.

In so judging we need not take any stand on the metaphysical issues connecting corpse and person; it is enough for us that people have religious beliefs and other deeply rooted ethical and emotional beliefs that are offended by the practice in question, and a right to complain in virtue of the fact that the corpse is their property.[60] In this sense, laws against corpse-mutilation are closely related to laws against the desecration of churches and religious artifacts: they are not just property crimes but an especially serious type of property crime, because they express a disregard for religious meanings that we have agreed, as a society, to protect. Even when they do not have such meanings, they may have emotional meanings that are especially central to the survivors. Necrophilia is especially horrible and outrageous to many people because we feel that use of these religiously charged objects for sexual purposes involves an especially deep profanation of their religious or emotional meaning (like the sexual profanation of a religious sanctuary).

A further relevant issue is that of consent. Whatever our metaphysical or religious beliefs, we typically understand a recent corpse to have an especially intimate connection with the person who was. Therefore, just as we abhor rape, including rape of a person who is asleep or in a coma, we also abhor sexual violation of the corpse. (This would include violations by relatives with whom the deceased did not have a sexual relationship, and would thus support prohibitions against necrophilia even by people who have lawful custody of the corpse.) Wisconsin straightforwardly takes this line. The relevant statute reads, "All sexual assault crimes apply whether a victim is dead or alive at the time of the sexual contact or sexual intercourse."[61]

Is this correct? It certainly seems that the person who has died is insulted by the postmortem rape, but this judgment raises difficult questions about when, if ever, an event that postdates the person's decease can be said to inflict a harm on that person.[62] If the distinction between being in a terminal coma and being dead is as important as it seems to be, it is unclear that the person who rapes a corpse has committed a criminal act. Such an act certainly says something very unpleasant about that person and his or her sexual fantasies. But it seems unclear to me whether this conduct should be criminal.

What about the special case where a person is both the lawful custodian of the corpse and a former sexual partner, such as a dead spouse? Here consent is not violated in precisely the same way, but, just as we feel that rape within marriage is still rape, so too we feel that this act with a nonresponsive object is a rape-like act. Whether or not such an act should be illegal, once again, it says something very unpleasant about the person in question. (Wisconsin's rape law is consistent with its antinecrophilia law, explicitly declaring that "a defendant shall not be presumed to be incapable of violating any sexual assault provisions because of marriage to the victim.")[63]

It seems to me that such considerations are the ones most relevant to the legal treatment of necrophilia. They are probably sufficient to justify some criminal penalties in the cases where property violations occur—including penalties that define necrophiliac violations as somewhat more severe than other forms of corpse desecration and vandalism of tombs. In other cases, the absence of consent is itself troubling, but it is unclear that it suffices to justify criminalization. In any case, necrophilia is altogether different from all the consensual sex acts that have been prohibited by appeal to disgust. Sodomy laws are wrong because they enact in law a disgust that neighbors feel toward the consensual practices of people whose lives are no business of theirs; necrophilia penalties are right, to the extent that they are, because the treatment of the corpse is the perfectly legitimate concern of whoever holds it as property, whether the state or private individuals. Where there is no individual holder, or where the holder is also the violator (the surviving spouse), we may have doubts about what to say legally, but we certainly can say that the act is morally peculiar, whether or not we ultimately decide to make it illegal.

Given this analysis, once again it would appear that disgust by itself is not the driving force behind whatever is legitimate about such laws. Four of the existing statutes do allude to it, using Devlinesque language such as "mistreats a corpse in a manner offensive to the sensibilities of an ordinary person."[64] This idea, however, seems to be both unnecessary to deliberation on the issue and a potential distraction from the serious questions that need to be considered. The issues we have discussed involve outrageous harms to the survivor and/or the deceased, property crimes and rape-like acts. What we feel when a religious sanctuary is violated is outrage: outrage because the protection of religion is a value to which we have deeply committed ourselves as a society. Similarly, what we feel when someone takes the corpse of our loved one and damages it is anger, because it is a particularly serious kind of harm, whether or not we also view it as similar to a rape. When the surviving spouse has sex with the corpse, we may feel pity, but we will also feel outrage that he was prepared to care so little about whether there was a living and consenting being there. In all of these cases, we may also feel disgust, but perfectly good reasons for whatever legal regulation we might wish to contemplate are contained in our response of outrage. It is the wrong done to people, not the sense we have that we are contaminated by vile sexual practices, that explains the legitimacy of some criminal penalties. Indeed, the immediate reaction of disgust at necrophilia tends to blur the issue, making us treat all cases as similar, when there seem to be crucial differences. Focusing on wrongs seems both more pertinent and more reliable than the focus on disgust, giving better guidance in this very difficult area.

V. Disgust and Nuisance Law

At this point we can turn to the area in which the appeal to disgust seems, and in a sense is, most straightforward: the law of nuisance. Here, as I have said, the law intervenes to protect people from an actual disgust-experience, which interferes with their use or enjoyment of their property. Disgust is treated as a type of harm: the maxim, as my epigraph from a typical case states, is *sic utere tuo ut alienum non laedas* (use your own in such a way that you do no harm to anyone else). Disgust, then, is the actual *harm* that occasions the legal prohibition, not a criterion allegedly showing how bad a certain type of act is. Because these cases appear to be straightforward, it might seem odd to treat them in the middle of my account of more complicated cases. But I think that the study of many varieties of disgust based on projection and group denigration helps us identify what, in the nuisance category, really is a straightforward case of disgust-as-harm, and what might be more problematic, both morally and legally.

The classic precedent, quoted in virtually all modern nuisance cases, is Aldred's Case (an English case from 1610) which holds that a man has "no right to maintain a structure upon his own land, which, by reason of disgusting smells, loud or unusual noises, thick smoke, noxious vapors, the jarring of machinery, or the unwarrantable collection of flies, renders the occupancy of adjoining property dangerous, intolerable, or even uncomfortable to its tenants." The enumerated instances all involve something from person A's property coming onto the property of person B: either a discernible substance (flies, smoke, vapors), or sound waves and smells that are not just imaginary or conceptual, but real physical presences. In other words, we are not on the terrain where B is upset and disgusted because he imagines A doing something on A's own property. Something real and definite has been inflicted upon B by A. Moreover, insofar as disgust is involved, the categories all involve disgust at "primary objects," frequently combined with real danger ("noxious vapors").

Cases in the modern tradition follow this lead. Many such cases involve water rights: neighbor A may not contaminate water that flows through B's land. The case law makes it clear that actual danger is sufficient but not necessary to constitute a nuisance: strong sensory disgustingness is enough.[65] Thus a swine farm located in a residential area created a nuisance even though it could not be shown to be injurious to health, and the odors were just the odors natural to pigs fed on good grains and vegetables.[66] A sewage lagoon for a hog confinement near a dairy farm was held to be a nuisance even though it could not be demonstrated that the cattle had actually contracted any disease from the effluences of the lagoon.[67]

Interestingly, lines are very carefully drawn: a factory that extracted fish oils and made fish pomace was held to constitute no nuisance, even though the process emitted "disagreeable smells," until the owners also started to manufacture phosphate manures from dried fish scrap, phosphate, sulphuric acid, and coal tar, a process that produced "nauseous and sickening stenches, which were diffused through the air, and large quantities of acrid tarry substances of filthy and disgusting smell were produced, . . . creating a nuisance to the then plaintiffs and a large part of the people of Milford."[68] Strong fishy odors, interestingly, were not enough, though the plaintiffs complained about them. The combination of noxious chemical odors was a different matter.

One further extension is traditionally allowed: if a disgusting substance has been placed in the water, and it is as yet imperceptible, but the knowledge of its presence nonetheless occasions disgust, then this too can be sufficient grounds for legal action. A common citation is a text on nuisances by Wood, which states:

> But in reference to [water rights], as with the air, it is not every interference with the water that imparts impurities thereto, that is actionable, but only such as impart to the water such impurities as substantially impair its value for the ordinary purposes of life, and render it measurably unfit for domestic purposes; or such as causes unwholesome or offensive vapors or odors to arise from the water, and

thus impairs the comfortable or beneficial enjoyment of property in
its vicinity, or such as, while producing no actual sensible effect upon
the water, are yet of a character calculated to disgust the senses, such
as the deposit of the carcasses of dead animals therein, or the erection
of privies over a stream, or any other use calculated to produce nau-
sea or disgust in those using the water for the ordinary purposes of
life, or such as impair its value for manufacturing purposes.[69]

Here we find, it would seem, three sufficient conditions for legal action: danger, sensory disruption, and disgust about primary objects,
where, at least in the view of this authority, this last might be separa-
ble from both danger and sensory impact. The idea is puzzling because both privies and animal corpses actually *do* create danger and,
eventually, strong sensory impact. But apparently Wood argued, and
the court agrees, that even if they don't, the mere thought of their
being there is disgusting and thus actionable. Similarly, in another
water-rights case, the fact that "a considerable quantity of impure
and objectionable and decayed and decomposing matter, filth and
various excreta of the human body, is from day to day deposited in
the water of the lake" is taken to be sufficient to constitute a nuisance, even though "such deposit has not been, and is not at present,
in sufficient quantities to be appreciable in its effect upon the water,"
because knowledge that the stuff is there "produces disgust and tends
to prevent the use of the water by the public for domestic purposes."[70]

Does the extension of nuisance to these cases admit "merely constructive" disgust of the type that we have criticized in earlier sec-
tions? It seems highly significant that the disgust that is admissible as
a ground of legal action is disgust at the thought of something that
would, present over time in sufficient quantities, suffice to occasion
strong sensory disgust. Moreover, its current presence is already dangerous. Such cases look very different from a case alleging that a lake
is contaminated by the fact that an African-American swam in it,
even though many, if not most, white Americans would at one time
have held that view. The cases in which an extension is permitted are
cases squarely within the primary-objects limitation: corpses and feces
are paradigmatic of the primary objects of disgust. So the small ex-

tension does not seem to be a major theoretical shift in the direction of admitting "merely constructive" nuisances.

But of course people do not like living in proximity to groups whom they find disgusting. Many laws in the Jim Crow South were ultimately fueled by disgust at the thought of sharing toilets, drinking fountains, or other public facilities with African-Americans, and by the magical thinking about contamination that accompanied racist disgust. And people will always try to use zoning or other residential restrictions to screen out groups whom they find polluting. Sometimes these pollution ideas masquerade as legitimate concerns about nuisance. Let us consider the case of *Cleburne v. Cleburne Living Center*.[71] (This case will be discussed in more detail in chapter 5). Following a city zoning law that required permits for "homes for the insane or feeble-minded or alcoholics or drug addicts," the Texas city in question had denied a permit for a group home for the mentally retarded. (Permits were not required for convalescent homes, homes for the elderly, and sanitariums.) The mentally retarded are typically viewed with both fear and disgust, and the denial of the permit appeared to reflect these attitudes, despite the city's attempt to claim that the area was on a "five-hundred–year flood plain," and that the mentally retarded might not be able to escape in case of a flood. In one of the rare cases where a law is found not to have a rational basis, the Supreme Court held that the permit denial violated the Equal Protection clause because it rested only on "invidious discrimination," "an irrational prejudice against the mentally retarded," and "vague, undifferentiated fears."

Cleburne gives us a benchmark to follow in thinking about the extension of disgust in areas of residential law, zoning, and nuisance law. Irrational prejudice may not be the basis of the denial to a person or group of a right to live and enjoy property on a basis of equality with others. The traditional category of nuisance is rightly understood as an extremely small and precise one, narrowly focused on sensory disruption, danger to health, and a few cases of powerful ideational disgust directed at primary objects and in ways that lie very close to both distaste and danger. All use of disgust based on group prejudice or magical thinking must be utterly rejected as a basis for legal regulation or legal action, even in the areas of zoning and housing.

Let us consider just two more cases, which illuminate this boundary line in an interesting way. As Mill points out, people whose religion tells them not to eat pork often develop an intense and very physical disgust at pork. (He cites Muslims as his example, but the phenomenon is also well known among Jews.) Their bodily experience, when in the presence of people eating pork, may be very intense and perfectly comparable to disgust at feces and corpses. Would it then be right to prohibit the eating of pork in any community in which Muslims or Jews are sufficiently numerous? Or even, following the paradigms considered in this section, to give Muslims and Jews a cause of action against neighbors who cook pork and waft the odors thereof onto their property?

The case is complicated because the disgust in question cannot easily be distinguished from disgust at primary objects, and food is prominent among disgust's primary objects. Nonetheless, Mill argues, the origins of the disgust lie in a religious prohibition that tells them they should not eat pork, and that eating it is wrong. Respect for people who have different religious beliefs should prevent them from imposing the sentiments that grow out of this teaching on other people. I agree: the disgust at pork is ideationally inseparable from a religious identification and a projection onto another group of disgust-attributes: uncleanness, revolting habits, et cetera. While it would surely be courteous for a neighbor of such a sensitive Jew or Muslim to try to arrange that the smells not be wafted onto the adjacent property, it does not rise to the level of a cause of action, in a religiously plural society.

Let us now consider, by contrast, the disgust of a vegetarian at the eating of meat. To make the contrast sharper, let us suppose that the neighbors in question are eating meat from animals that have been raised, as most animals in the food industry are, in cruel and revolting conditions. At this point, in our own society, vegetarianism is treated as similar to religion: it is but one of the many comprehensive doctrines of the good that citizens rightly hold. At this point, then, the vegetarian's disgust at the veal roast next door gets treatment that is no different from the Jewish neighbor's disgust at a pork roast next door. It seems to me, however, that the cases are actually different, and may come to be recognized as such. The vegetarian's disgust grows out of a moral principle, which recognizes the needless suffering of animals as a very bad thing, or even a thing that violates rights that these animals have. Were this moral principle to be generally recognized in society, it would be the sort of thing that would form part of the society's political core, since it concerns basic rights. In that case, the vegetarian's disgust would be honored in law, and there would be a variety of laws restricting the practices of factory farming and the use of meat illegally so produced. Notice, however, that these would be ordinary harm-based criminal laws, and that the disgust of vegetarians would not itself be legally salient. If we ever agreed that it is intolerable to raise animals for food in the way that is currently done (leaving aside, for the sake of argument, whether any humane way of raising animals for meat might be found), then the bad practices would be illegal directly, and the neighbor would simply not have a veal roast in his oven—or, at any rate, not a roast from a calf raised in a pen of the sort that is now used.

The contrast between these two cases shows us something instructive: in neither is disgust of the "constructive" sort, resting on a person's moral or religious doctrine, a legally salient factor. Either it is the sort of moral tenet that is fit to be recognized by society as a whole, as part of the core of doctrines that are basic for political purposes, in which case it is that recognition, and not disgust, that will drive legislation; or else it is among those doctrines concerning which citizens permissibly differ, in which case it is wrong for one citizen to use his disgust as a reason to limit another citizen's liberty.

VI. Disgust and the Jury: "Horrible and Inhuman" Homicides

We have now considered most of the common legal appeals to disgust. But one significant category remains: a class of cases especially pertinent to the type of progressive pro-disgust argument advanced by Dan M. Kahan, and a linchpin of his analysis. These are cases in which a jury is asked to consult reactions of disgust in order to determine whether a homicide is "especially heinous, atrocious, or cruel," a determination that many state statutes make relevant to the potential applicability of the death penalty.[72] A salient example is a Georgia statute that permitted a person to be sentenced to death if the offense "was outrageously or wantonly vile, horrible and inhuman."[73] We can easily see that this sort of language, while not explicitly mentioning the term "disgust," invites jurors to consult their disgust-reactions when considering aggravating circumstances. It is plausible enough to think that here disgust plays a central and also a valuable role in identifying an especially heinous class of homicides.

The first and most obvious problem with this use of disgust, repeatedly noted by the Court, is that the language of the requirement is so vague that it virtually ensures that the death penalty will be applied in "an arbitrary and capricious manner." Such was the holding in *Godfrey* concerning the Georgia language. "There is nothing in these few words, standing alone," the Court wrote, "that implies any inherent restraint on the arbitrary and capricious infliction of the death sentence. A person of ordinary sensibility could fairly characterize almost every murder as 'outrageously or wantonly vile, horrible and inhuman.'"[74] Similar was the finding in the Oklahoma case, in which a unanimous Court found the wording "especially heinous, atrocious, and cruel" to be unconstitutionally vague, offering insufficient guidance to the jury. What has emerged as constitutional is a "limiting construction," or set of such constructions, that give jurors far more concrete description of aggravating circumstances: murder during the commission of a felony, for example, and murder with torture. [75]

If we have such descriptions, however, we can leave disgust to one side; we really don't need it to tell us whether torture was used. And the emotion clearly does not track very well the class of murders that are typically understood to involve aggravating circumstances. Many murders committed during a felony will not typically elicit the reaction of disgust: for example, the shooting of a bank officer during a holdup will ordinarily be found very bad, but rarely disgusting. On the other hand, some murders that seem disgusting to at least many jurors may not involve constitutionally defined aggravating circumstances: the Court is surely right that many jurors will react with disgust to many, if not all, murders, when bloody or gory circumstances are precisely described. Bloodiness and goriness are the usual elicitors of disgust, but many especially vile murders lack these features, and many murders that have these features are vile only in the sense that any murder is vile.

Such distortions may be magnified if the jury is for some reason unsympathetic to the defendant: for example, if a black male defendant appears before a predominantly white jury for a crime committed against a white woman. Thus the appeal to disgust would appear to raise serious equal-protection issues, above and beyond those that are raised in any case by the uneven racial record of the death penalty.[76] More generally, appeals to the monstrousness and disgustingness of the criminal's offense distance the jury from the defendant, asking them to regard him as utterly "other." Such appeals can collude with antecedent prejudice in an unfortunate way, fueling the demand for extreme punishment.[77]

Disgust also may raise serious issues about mental capacity. If the prosecution appeals to a type of disgust that places the murderer in a class of heinous monsters more or less outside the boundaries of the jury's moral universe, such line-drawing inevitably raises questions about sanity. The further we place the murderer at a distance from us, the less obvious it is that this is a moral agent at all, and the less obvious it consequently is that this person deserves the penalty we reserve for fully responsible agents. No matter how we define insanity for legal purposes, when we turn someone into a monster we immediately raise the issue of sanity. Aristotle already held that certain individuals (for example the mythical king Phalaris, who boiled people in cauldrons) were so weird that they were not even vicious because such extreme and bizarre pathology shows that someone is not really a chooser of ends at all.[78] No matter what psychological concepts we use, we have a hard time not getting into a similar difficulty when we try to combine a strong ascription of moral responsibility with an account appealing to disgust at the alleged monstrousness and inhumanity of the person's deeds. Perhaps this difficulty can be solved, but it needs to be squarely faced. Disgust, far from shoring up the moral borders of our community, may actually make them harder to police.[79]

Notice that this problem is directly linked to the cognitive content of disgust in a way that it is not associated with the cognitive content of indignation. Disgust is all about putting the object at a distance and drawing boundaries. It imputes to the object properties that make it no longer a member of the subject's own community or world, a kind of alien species of thing. Indignation works in the opposite direction: by imputing blame to its object, and by focusing on the wrongful nature of the person's act, it presupposes the ascription of humanity and responsibility.[80] It presupposes, indeed, something very close to the legal definition of sanity: that the person was aware of the difference between right and wrong when he acted. Disgust seems tailor-made, then, for a diminished-capacity defense, and we may often have disgust for the acts of a mentally deranged murderer. But Kahan's suggestion that disgust helps us get tough on deliberate and fully sane murderers here encounters another problem.

There is a deeper point that we should now consider. Frequently, I have argued, our disgust at a group signals a desire to cordon ourselves off from something about ourselves that this group represents to us. This diagnosis is especially clear in the areas of misogynistic and homophobic disgust, but I believe that it applies to our response to evil as well. We very often tell ourselves that the doers of heinous wrongs are monsters, in no way like ourselves. This tendency plays a strong role, for example, in writing and reading about the Nazis and the Holocaust. The tremendous enthusiasm for Daniel Jonah Goldhagen's *Hitler's Willing Executioners,* both in Germany and the United States, cannot easily be explained either by its novelty or by its quality.[81] What does explain it, I believe, is the desire of many people (including present-day Germans, who are carefully exonerated by Goldhagen) to believe that the culture that gave birth to the horrors of Nazism was a monstrosity, an aberration. Unlike other books that stressed the commonness of the evil deeds of Nazi perpetrators (in different ways, Hannah Arendt, Christopher Browning[82]), or books that stressed the role of cultural ideology in building a Nazi mentality (in different ways Raul Hilberg,[83] Omer Bartov[84]), Goldhagen's book argues that the Germany that produced the Nazis was sui generis, a "radically different culture" to be viewed "with the critical eye of an anthropologist disembarking on unknown shores."[85] These people were not made by factors that can easily be replicated in other times and places, and they are not acting out deeply shared human capacities for destruction. They are unique disgusting monsters. We are nothing like this, and we could not possibly create anything like this.[86]

When we see Nazis in this "anthropological" way, whether in works of history or in films and novels, we are comforted: evil is outside, alien, has nothing to do with us. Our disgust creates the boundary: it says, this contamination is and must remain far from our pure bodies. We might even say, in this case again, that we call disgust to our aid: by allowing ourselves to see evil people as disgusting, we conveniently distance them from ourselves.

By contrast, when we see Nazis depicted without disgust, as human beings who share common characteristics with us—whether the emphasis is on the capacity of all human beings for evil, or on the universal role of peer pressure in producing moral depravity, or on a universal submissiveness to authority, including that of distorting ideologies—this is alarming because it requires self-scrutiny, warning us that we might well have done the same under comparable circumstances. It alerts us to the presence of evil (whether active or passively collaborative) in ourselves, and requires us to ask how we might prevent similar phenomena from materializing in our own society.[87] We have to confront the fact that we might become them, but this means that, in a significant sense, we already are them—with the fearfulness, weakness, and moral blindness that cause such evils. Because this response to evil is so much more psychologically troubling and politically challenging than the response elicited by Goldhagen, it is not surprising that his book has been embraced with warm approval. It permits us to forget the atrocities U.S. military officers perpetrated in Vietnam, the atrocities perpetrated against slaves and Native Americans (not to mention Jews, who were hardly well treated, even if they were not exterminated) in our own history. No, monsters cause evil, and that sort of evil could only happen over there.[88]

I believe that a similar thing happens when, as jurors or as spectators, we are urged to react with disgust at the criminal acts of a murderer. We are urged to see that person as a monster, outside the boundaries of our moral universe. We are urged precisely *not* to have the thought, "there, but for . . . go I." But in reality, it seems likely that all human beings are capable of evil, and that many, if not most, of the hideous evildoers are warped by circumstances, both social and personal, which play a large and sometimes decisive role in explaining the evil that they do. If jurors are led to think that evil is done by monsters who just were born different, are freaky and inhuman, they will be prevented from having thoughts about themselves and their own society that are highly pertinent, not only to the equal and principled application of the law, but also to the construction of a society in which less evil will exist. (This problem may be especially pressing in liberal democracies, since citizens are aware that demonization of other minorities is in general unacceptable, so criminals may more readily become the vehicle for the need to demonize.) If we classify murders as involving "aggravating circumstances" by some reasoned account—for example, by enumerating aggravating conditions such as torture and felony murder—we permit such useful thoughts to come forth and not to be stifled, for such a classification requires us to ask why we think torture bad, and to reflect about the strong social reasons we have for seeking to deter it. (Emotions of indignation will frequently be connected with such a reflective process.) If we classify by disgust, I would argue, we stifle such thoughts and comfort ourselves where comfort is not due.

We must now consider one more specific case, since it figures prominently in Kahan's pro-disgust argument.[89] A murderer named Beldotti apparently killed in order to gratify sadistic sexual desires.[90] He strangled his female victim, cut off her nipples, and stuffed her into trash bags. Police recovered from his home numerous postmortem photographs of the deceased, posed with dildoes penetrating her vagina and anus. The jury found that Beldotti's crime showed "extreme atrocity and cruelty" and sentenced him to life in prison without parole. While in prison, Beldotti requested that the dildoes, photos of the victim, the trash bags in which she had been placed, and other sexual paraphernalia be returned to his representatives outside prison. The state opposed this request, arguing that giving these items back, even if not to Beldotti himself, would "justifiably spark outrage, disgust, and incredulity on the part of the general public." They urged that the property be put in the trash, and

the Massachusetts Court of Appeals agreed, concluding that returning the property would be "offensive to basic concepts of decency
treasured in a civilized society."

According to Kahan, the Beldotti case shows that disgust plays an
ineliminable role in criminal law by shoring up community morality:
the result in the case, and what is good about it, cannot be explained
without giving disgust a central role. Kahan argues that no concern
with rehabilitation or specific deterrence could explain the result
(given Beldotti's life sentence), and that a concern with general deterrence would not explain the state's refusal to surrender these particular items. The only remaining explanation, Kahan concludes, is
disgust. If it had granted Beldotti's request, the state itself would be
"tainted" by the contamination his relics would impart. The request
to put the items "in the trash can where they belong" is an unmistakable expression of disgust, and the case shows that this emotion is
central to protecting society's moral boundaries.

First of all, I am not persuaded by Kahan's arguments about general deterrence. Obviously enough, to surrender to a murderer the
paraphernalia he used in a murder would be a treatment so indulgent that it could well lessen the deterrent effect of his life sentence.
The message is that he can have a good time in jail, indulging his
sadistic fantasies, knowing that all his paraphernalia is safely in the
hands of his agents. By contrast, giving his relatives back his keys or
his wallet would have little tendency to make other sex murderers
think that Beldotti had gotten away lightly; that would be a perfectly
unremarkable thing to do with a prisoner's effects, and it probably
would never be publicly commented on or reach the ears of other
sex murderers.

But the heart of the issue surely is that Kahan has forgotten about
retribution. The most natural way to view the state's refusal is as a retributive quid pro quo: you took a woman's life with these sex toys, so
to punish you we are going to refuse you the things that give you sexual pleasure.[91] The state mentioned not one reaction, but three:
"outrage, disgust, and incredulity." Kahan focuses only on disgust
and contamination. But surely the first and third responses are also
highly significant, and they go closely together. Outrage expresses
the idea that it is unreasonable and wrong to reward Beldotti in just

that area where he should be most severely punished. Such a reward would not only be astonishing—the response of "incredulity"—it would be a profound injury and disrespect to the dead, to anyone who cares about her, and to society itself. This sense of outrage is highly cognitive, expressing a reasoned judgment that can be publicly shared.[92] Its cognitions are not focused, as are those of disgust, on contamination to the self; they focus on the harm or wrong that has occurred. Outrage is thus closely linked to the idea of retributive punishment, to the thought that (instead of rewarding this guy by returning his murder weapons) we should be punishing him by denying him access to the tools he used to commit his hideous crime.[93]

Disgust is clearly in the picture; no doubt the state is right that the public would react with disgust (expressing a sense of contamination and defilement), as well as with outrage and incredulity, were it to grant the request. But outrage is sufficient to explain the result and why it is correct; we do not need to rely on disgust, as Kahan suggests. And outrage, as I have argued, is a moral sentiment far more pertinent to legal judgment, and far more reliable, than disgust. It contains reasoning that can be publicly shared, and it does not make the questionable move of treating the criminal like an insect or a slug, outside of our moral community. Instead, it firmly includes him within the moral community and judges his actions on a moral basis. Thus it avoids any tendency to portray the criminal as a monster, one whom none of us can possibly be.

Indeed, I believe it is clear that in the actual case outrage is not only the sounder response to Beldotti, but also more explanatory of the outcome and the opinions. For neither the state nor the court does treat Beldotti as an alien or a monster, with the eye of an "anthropologist disembarking on unknown shores." They treat him as a perfectly sane person who has made an absolutely outrageous request. They react with "incredulity" because they assume that Beldotti is not a monster, but a sane human being, and must know that his request is outrageous. Were they thinking of him as like a slug or a heap of vomit, they would not be so outraged by the request, they would just see it as lunatic pathology. But they don't: they know he is a human being with recognizable rationality, and that is why the right response to the request is anger. Disgust is there, but it is in considerable tension with outrage and incredulity. I suggest that the judgment in the case followed, rightly, the moral sentiment of outrage and indignation, which is much easier to square with treating Beldotti as a sane and responsible agent.

Disgust is a deeply embedded response. All adult human beings acquire it in some form, and all known societies teach it in some form. It may even be that many, or even most, human beings need some of it in order to live, because we cannot endure too much daily confrontation with our own decay and with the oozy stuffs of which our bodies are made. And although disgust does not do very well tracking genuine danger, it is a reasonably useful device for steering us away from danger when we are too young or too inattentive or ill-informed to ponder the merits of the case. We should not, however, conclude from these facts that disgust is a valuable response for legal and political purposes. Many responses that are deeply embedded in human life are morally questionable and unworthy of guiding public action. Disgust, I have argued, offers limited guidance in a narrow set of laws concerned with physical distaste and danger. But when it becomes a constructive criterion of legally regulable conduct, and especially when it conduces to the political subordination and marginalization of vulnerable groups and people, disgust is a dangerous social sentiment. We should be working to contain it, rather than building our legal world on the vision of human beings that it contains.

Chapter 4
Inscribing the Face:
Shame and Stigma

If someone has been condemned to a gladiatorial school or to the mines for the crimes he has been caught committing, let him not be marked on his face, since the penalty of his condemnation can be expressed both on his hands and on his calves, and so that his face, which has been fashioned in the likeness of the divine beauty, may not be disgraced.

— Edict of the Emperor Constantine, CE 316

Before her disfigurement [amputation of the distal half of her nose] Mrs. Dover, who lived with one of her two married daughters, had been an independent, warm and friendly woman who enjoyed traveling, shopping, and visiting her many relatives. The disfigurement of her face, however, resulted in a definite alteration in her way of living. The first two or three years she seldom left her daughter's home, preferring to remain in her room or to sit in the backyard.

— Cited in Erving Goffman, *Stigma*

Thus, by being born we have made the step from an absolutely self-sufficient narcissism to the perception of a changing external world and the beginnings of the discovery of objects. And with this is associated the fact that we cannot endure the new state of things for long, that we periodically revert from it, in our sleep, to our former condition of absence of stimulation and avoidance of objects.

— Sigmund Freud, *Group Psychology and the Analysis of the Ego*

I. The Blushing Face

Like disgust, shame is a ubiquitous emotion in social life. When I was a child one of my relatives, fond of advice giving, used to say to all children, "Soar with your strengths and learn to cover your weaknesses." And of course we all do learn to cover our weaknesses as we go through life, whether by compensating for them with other strengths, by training to overcome them, or by avoiding situations in which they will inevitably manifest themselves. Most of us, most of the time, try to appear "normal," a notion whose strangeness I shall later discuss, but whose allure is undeniably strong in all modern democratic societies. Sometimes, however, our "abnormal" weaknesses are uncovered anyway, and then we blush, we cover ourselves, we turn away our eyes. Shame is the painful emotion that responds to that uncovering. It brands the face with its unmistakable signs.

Because we all have weaknesses that, if known, would mark us off as in some ways "abnormal," shame is a permanent possibility in our lives, our daily companion. As Erving Goffman memorably wrote in his classic book *Stigma:* "[I]n an important sense there is only one complete unblushing male in America: a young, married, white, urban, northern, heterosexual Protestant father of college education, fully employed, of good complexion, weight and height, and a recent record in sports."[1] But of course few are ever like that, and nobody is like that for long. Shame, therefore, dogs our footsteps. As Goffman says, "the issue becomes not whether a person has experience with a stigma of his own, because he has, but rather how many varieties he has had his own experience with. . . . The stigmatized and the normal are part of each other."[2]

I shall argue, indeed, that shame is on the scene already even before we are aware of the "normal" perspective of the particular social value-system within which we dwell. For it is present for all of us in the infantile demand for omnipotence, for fullness and comfort—accompanied, as it increasingly is as the infant matures, by the awareness of finitude, partiality, and frequent helplessness. Shame therefore cuts beneath any specific social orientation to norms, and serves as a highly volatile way in which human beings negotiate some tensions inherent in their humanness—in, that is, their awareness of themselves as beings both finite and marked by exorbitant demands and expectations. (To that extent, though not in other ways, I shall be agreeing with Max Scheler's classic account of the emotion.)[3]

Some people, however, are more marked out for shame than others. Indeed, with shame as with disgust, societies ubiquitously select certain groups and individuals for shaming, marking them off as "abnormal" and demanding that they blush at what and who they are. People who look different from others—people with visible diseases or so-called deformities, the mentally and physically handicapped—wear their shame on their faces, so to speak: social behavior tells them every day that they ought to blush to show themselves in the company of the "normal." When there is no visible brand, societies have been quick to inflict one, whether by tattooing and branding or by other visible signs of social ostracism and disapproval. The branding of criminals—frequently, as Constantine's edict observes, applied to the face—is a practice that keeps reappearing in one or another form, and thus shame has been throughout history a pervasive part of practices of punishment.

Today we find two diametrically opposed views about the role shame should play in the law. On one view, the shaming of those who are different is a pernicious aspect of social custom, which should not be sanctified by building it into our legal practices. According to this view, law should protect the equal dignity of all citizens, both by devising ways in which those already stigmatized as different can enjoy lives of greater dignity and by refusing to make law a partner to the social infliction of shame. This view has deep roots in the history of European law, as my passage from Justinian records: even the Romans, who meted out many extreme punishments, were loath to brand the part of the human being in which human dignity primarily is thought to reside. So too today, some prominent legal thinkers hold that law should seek to inhibit the stigmatization of vulnerable minorities. Even where malefactors are concerned, these thinkers typically hold that, while punishments must be meted out for reasons including both the deterrent and the retributive, a concern with the dignity of the offender should always be solidly built into the system of punishment, and, with it, the idea of eventual reintegration of the offender into society. This first view is supported by numerous writers about the legal rights of people with disabilities, including Michael Bérubé and Martha Minow.[4] We also find it in some recent writings on punishment, including studies of European punishment by James Whitman and more general writings about shaming by Toni Massaro and about reintegration by John Braithwaite.[5]

On the second view—not unrelated to Lord Devlin's views about disgust—what is wrong with modern societies is that they don't make a large enough place for shame. We are adrift without a moral compass, in large part because we have lost our sense of shame. For the late Christopher Lasch, for example, America is in trouble precisely to the extent that we have lost "the shared social and legal boundaries that shame once policed."[6] Similarly, communitarian political thinker Amitai Etzioni recommends the revival of shaming punishments as a way of expressing and reinforcing shared moral values.[7]

The pedigree of this view about shame is conservative, and it does end up defending entrenched social norms as good sources of both behavior and law. But, as with disgust, the apparently conservative position has also been endorsed by some thinkers who consider themselves progressive (as perhaps Lasch once was), ostensibly in order to mobilize opposition to callous behavior on the part of the dominant classes. Once again, as with disgust, Dan M. Kahan of Yale Law School has led this part of the campaign, arguing that shame penalties ought to be favored over other alternatives to imprisonment, such as fines and community service.[8] In a wide range of legal areas, ranging from sex offenses to drunken driving to public urination, Kahan, like Etzioni, favors bringing back the brand on the face: offenders should be forced to wear signs on their property, or car, or to perform some clearly humiliating ritual before the public gaze. Kahan likes shaming because of its expressive power: no other mode of punishment as vividly and surely expresses society's disapproval of the offender. He thinks of the view as a progressive view, and is able to sell it that way to some extent, in part because he dwells on examples in which the humiliated person is a powerful person. (He particularly likes a punishment ordered by the city of Hoboken, New Jersey, in which businessmen who urinate in public have to scrub the street clean with a toothbrush.)[9]

As readers of my chapters on disgust will by now suspect, I shall be supporting the first position and criticizing the second. I think, however, that we gain a new understanding of our reasons for so doing if we investigate the natural history of shame and shaming, and the deeper reasons why human societies again and again seek to brand the faces of some of their members with what Erving Goffman perceptively calls a "spoiled identity." Only then will we be in a position to understand what forms of shame might be pernicious in human life and what forms might actually be connected with valuable forms of aspiration. For I shall argue that the normative situation of shame is a good deal more complicated than that of disgust: some forms of shame indeed have a positive ethical value; thus, if we do criticize many roles shame plays in the law, as I think we should, it must be because those roles make appeal to a primitive or bad form of shame, or are at risk of doing so.

I shall, then, spend a good deal of this chapter developing an account of shame and its roots in infancy that is closely linked to object-relations psychoanalysis, and in particular to the work of Donald Winnicott.[10] I shall show that this account has by now been confirmed by a good deal of clinical work by practitioners such as Andrew Morrison and Otto Kernberg.[11] I shall then examine in detail the relationship between shame and several related emotions, including disgust, guilt, anger, and depression. I shall then use that account of shame and pathological narcissism to begin analyzing social shaming and its pathologies.

In chapters 5 and 6, I shall apply my general model to some concrete issues that face us as we think about the role of shame in the law: the role of shame in punishment; the phenomenon of "moral panics" and their relationship to differential legal treatment of minorities; the protection of personal privacy; and, finally, legal treatment of people with disabilities, particularly in the area of education. As I confront these issues, I will argue that modern liberal societies can make an adequate response to the phenomena of shame only if they shift away from a very common intuitive idea of the normal citizen that has been bequeathed to us by the social-contract tradition so influential in the history of European thought: the image of the citizen as a productive worker, able to pay for the benefits he receives by the contributions he makes.

II. Primitive Shame, Narcissism, and the "Golden Age"

Human beings are born into in a world that they have not made and do not control.[12] After a time in the womb, during which needs were automatically met, they enter the world, thus making, as Freud put it in the epigraph to this chapter, "the step from an absolutely self-sufficient narcissism to the perception of a changing external world and the beginnings of the discovery of objects."[13] Human infants arrive in the world in a condition of needy helplessness more or less unparalleled in any other animal species. What they encounter is both alarming and delightful. In a passage that lies at the origins of European thought about infancy, Roman poet Lucretius writes that the infant, helpless and weeping from the disturbance of birth, "like a sailor cast forth from the fierce waves, lies naked on the ground, without speech, in need of every sort of life-sustaining help, when first nature casts it forth with birth contractions from its mother's womb into the shores of light. And it fills the whole place with mournful weeping, as is right for someone to whom such troubles remain in life" (5.222–27).

A "gentle nurse" now calms the child with calm talk and caresses, as well as nourishment. The poet bleakly remarks that the rougher, better-equipped wild animals have no need of such soothing (5.229–30). The prolonged helplessness of the human infant marks its history; and the early drama of its infancy is the drama of helplessness before a world of objects—a world that contains both threat and promise of good things, the things it wants and needs. The infant's central perception of itself, Lucretius suggests profoundly, is as an entity very weak and very powerless toward things of the greatest importance. Freud, noting the same facts, comments that "we cannot endure the new state of things for long, [so] that we periodically revert from it, in our sleep, to our former condition of absence of stimulation and avoidance of objects."[14]

But the infant is not altogether helpless. For from the first there are agencies in the environment that minister to its needs, supplying what it cannot supply for itself. These agencies therefore take on an intense importance in the infant's inchoate, and as yet undemarcated, awareness of the world. Its relationship to them focuses, from the first, on its passionate wish to secure what the world of nature does not supply by itself: comfort, nourishment, protection.

Lucretius presents a picture, not a theoretical account, but we may extrapolate an account from it. Unlike some psychoanalytic accounts, but like those developed in the object-relations tradition, the Lucretian picture makes the drama of infancy focus on what the ancient world called "external goods"—uncontrolled external objects of high importance. From the first the infant feels a need for the removal of painful or invasive stimuli, and for the restoration of a blissful or undisturbed condition. This need gives a central importance in the infant's "object world" to that or those object(s) who are perceived as the agents of this restoration. Whether it is mother, father, nurse, or some other caretaker or caretakers who plays or play the primary role here, this restorative agency will at first be experienced by the infant not so much as a distinct object, but as a process of transformation through which the infant's own state of being is altered. For this reason analyst Christopher Bollas speaks of the caretaker as a "transformational object," and perceptively remarks that much of a human being's subsequent history bears the imprint of early longing for this object, in the form of a desire for a "second coming" of that shift toward bliss, and for an object that can be its vehicle.[15] Still in a state of utter helplessness, the infant can do little to control the arrival of the transformational process, and its sudden arrivals and disappearances mark the infant's world as a chancy and unpredictable one, in which the best things arrive as if by lightning, in sudden penetrations of light and joy.

Consider a myth that plays a central role in ancient accounts of emotion. It is, I think, best seen as an imaginative attempt to recreate this world of infancy. This is the well-known story of the Golden Age—an age in which people do not have to do anything for themselves, to labor, to act, to move here and there. For the earth itself brings forth nourishment exactly where they are. Rivers of milk and honey spring up out of the ground; the mild climate gives no need for shelter. The people of this age, Hesiod remarks, lack prudential rationality—presumably because they have no need of thought. They live in a state of blissful totality. Stoics who repeat the story add that in this age "crime is far off": there is no aggression because everything is complete.[16] What this myth describes is the omnipotence of the infant, its sense that the world revolves around its needs, and is fully arranged to meet its needs.

But of course, as our Lucretian image lets us see, the infant's experiential world is from the very start unlike the world of the Golden Age. Perhaps, as Freud observes in the epigraph, rudimentary prebirth experiences give the infant a true Golden Age: hooked up securely to the sources of nourishment and comfort, the infant is indeed in a state of blissful totality. But birth disrupts all that, as Freud says, bringing the infant into a world of objects, in which it must depend on those external things and persons for its survival. Thus, although at times the infant's world is a Golden Age world, these times alternate with times when the world is hungry, distressed, and in discomfort.[17] The earth does not give everything automatically, and the infant's world of sudden transformations is felt from the start as chancy, porous, full of uncertainty and danger.

It is always somewhat speculative to reconstruct the inner world of preverbal infants, although we should remember that adults equipped with language are not always able to verbalize the most important features of their inner world, and may not even fully know their own inner world; thus excessive reliance upon verbal cues may be a source of error in the adult case as well. No doubt early psychoanalysts were often too inattentive to experimental evidence about infant behavior. They were more like great imaginative artists than like clinicians or experimentalists, although such artists can illuminate the world of childhood with enormous insight, as Proust most surely does. More recently, however, there has been a valuable interchange between experimentalists and analysts, and some of the leading theorists of infancy today, such as Daniel Stern and Margaret Mahler, are both.[18] (Moreover, like Winnicott, who was a pediatrician as well as an analyst, Mahler and Stern study a wide range of children, not all afflicted with obvious disturbances; thus their work, like Winnicott's, has a clearer relevance to common familial and social issues.) John Bowlby's work was an early example of the fruitful combination of experimental evidence with object-relations theory; his views have now received additional experimental confirmation.[19] And the clinical work of thinkers in the object-relations tradition, such as W.R.D. Fairbairn, Winnicott, Otto Kernberg, and Christopher Bollas,[20] and of Andrew Morrison in a closely related tradition,[21] provides a kind of depth in the study of individual patients that the experimental literature often lacks. The picture I shall present from now on derives, then, from the part of the object-relations tradition that is consistent with experimental evidence and that receives most support from detailed clinical studies.

In the first months of life, then, the infant is not aware of itself as a distinct object, or of its caretakers as distinct objects. But it does experience the sense of an alternation between fullness and comfort,[22] as well as a state of emptiness and torment.[23] Fullness and comfort are what its being demands, and yet they arrive by chance in a way quite ungoverned by the infant's own actions. Its relationship with the caretaker is at times one of blissful symbiosis—and yet at times there is a void.[24]

As the infant's perceptual capacities mature, it is soon able to distinguish parts of itself from parts of the environment—by six months or so, it is now believed. Its early inchoate identification of its caretaker (even at a few weeks of age, infants can distinguish the smell of their own mother's breast milk on a pad from the smell of another mother's breast milk) becomes more definite, and it begins to see the mother as somewhat separate from itself. It begins to learn that it can wiggle its own toes, but it cannot make its mother's breast arrive. And yet, the infant's whole conception of the mother, at this time, is still totally centered on its own needs; the mother is basically a feeding breast and a comforting body, not a being with her own desires and activities.[25]

At this point in an infant's development it begins to be plausible to ascribe to it some rudimentary emotions: of fear when hunger strikes and relief is not in sight; of love for the source of food and comfort. These emotions, unlike adult emotions, are not addressed to a fully distinct object, and thus the emotion itself is fuzzy and indistinct. It may, however, still be extremely powerful. As the infant begins to recognize a routine of regularities in its feeding and holding, it also develops a rudimentary conception of itself as the center of these routines, and a set of expectations that its needs should be met. These conceptions, as both Freud and object-relations theorists emphasize, are fully egocentric. Freud's famous phrase "His Majesty the baby" describes a world of thought and feeling in which there is basically just one center, and everything revolves around that. The good mother is a breast that turns up at the right moment.[26]

But of course the breast does not always turn up at the right moment. The primary caretaker has projects of his or her own, and may even seek deliberately to get the infant to tolerate at least some frustration. For frustration is an important part of the developmental process, prompting the infant to make efforts at movement.[27] So the infant, increasingly aware of itself as a definite center of need and longing, is also increasingly aware of the caretaker as a part of the world that does not always minister to its needs. And we should remember that the cognitive capacities of the human infant develop very rapidly during the first year of life, a time when the physical ability of the infant to meet its own needs is basically nonexistent. A dependent being who sees itself as such will have rudimentary forms of both love and anger toward the agencies on which it depends. The infant loves the caretaker as the source of its comfort and nourishment. But it also has anger toward the caretaker as the source of a damage, when need is not met and pain ensues. To some extent, an infant may even have the Aristotelian sense that the damage was wrong, should not have occurred: to the extent that an infant has come to expect to be the center of the world, it will react to the situation as a withholding of something that is rightfully its own.[28]

Such reactions, obviously, become sharper and more developed as awareness matures. Indeed, the very recognition that both good things and their absence have an external source guarantees the presence of both love and anger, and guarantees their close interrelationship. Thus, Bowlby argues, on the basis of both experimental and clinical work, that all attachment-love is fundamentally ambivalent. In a way that is reminiscent of Spinoza's perceptive philosophical account of emotions, he argues that love and anger always occur together in the child because love involves the recognition of an external agency that benefits us, and anger involves the recognition of an external agency that harms us.[29] Of course, from the point of view of infantile egotism, not to gratify is to harm, and all external agencies are thus, in their very separateness and uncontrollability, sources of harm.

Where in this history should we locate shame? I can approach this topic by introducing yet one more classical myth, the story of the origins of love told by Aristophanes in Plato's *Symposium,* which builds on the classic Golden Age story. Human beings were once whole and round, says Aristophanes. Our spherical shape was the outward image of our totality and our power. We were "awe-inspiring in force and strength," and "had great ambitions" (190B). Humans, in consequence, assailed the gods, with the aim of establishing their control over the universe as a whole (190B). Instead of wiping us out completely, Zeus simply, making us "weaker," made us humans—creating for us the condition of need, insecurity, and incompleteness that sets an unbridgeable gulf between us and the gods. He accomplished the change by cutting the spherical beings in two, so that they walked on two legs—and then he turned their faces around so that they would always have to look at the cut part of themselves. Incompleteness is revealed to us, then, by the very form of our bodies, with their pointy jutting limbs, their oddly naked front parts, their genitalia that betray our need for one another. The navel represents the gods' sewing together of what they have cut, and is thus a "memorial of our former suffering" (*mnêmeion tou palaiou pathous*) (191A). The people in the myth are ashamed of the way they now are. (Indeed, the Greek term for genitalia, *aidoia,* contains an allusion to shame, *aidôs.*)[30] Aristophanes' small detail about the navel suggests that the myth is not about sexuality per se, but is intended to capture the traumatic character of birth into a world of objects: for of course what the navel really reminds us of is our separation from the sources of nutrition and comfort and the beginning of a needy life.

Thus Aristophanes portrays shame as a painful emotion grounded in the recognition of our own non-omnipotence and lack of control, and he suggests that a memory or vestigial sense of an original omnipotence and completeness underlies the painful emotion as it manifests itself in life. We sense that we ought to be whole, and maybe once were whole—and we know that we now are not. We sense that we ought to be round, and we see that we are jagged and pointy, and soft and wrinkled. The way in which the speech connects sex and shame seems deeply perceptive: primitive shame is not about sex per se, but about sexual need as one sign of a more general neediness and vulnerability. It seems plausible that Aristophanes is right: a kind of primitive shame at the very fact of being human and nonwhole underlies the more specific types of shame that we later feel about handicaps and inadequacies.

To put it another way: all infant omnipotence is coupled with helplessness. When an infant realizes that it is dependent on others, and is by this time aware of itself as a definite being who is and ought to be the center of the world, we can therefore expect a primitive and rudimentary emotion of shame to ensue. For shame involves the realization that one is weak and inadequate in some way in which one expects oneself to be adequate.[31] Its reflex is to hide from the eyes of those who will see one's deficiency, to cover it.

How early does shame begin? Silvan Tomkins, whose important theory of affect remains the major contribution to the literature on shame in the area of cognitive psychology, named shame as one of the primary affects, and suggested that it begins almost immediately after birth.[32] He defined shame as a painful affect resulting from any interruption of pleasure and expectation, as when the infant expects a pleasurable feeding, and that does not take place. Because Tomkins's theory is an affect-based theory, he does not require any particular cognitive content in order to say that shame is present, and thus he is not troubled by questions about what thoughts infants may be said to have. Since my account, along with accounts in the object-relations tradition, holds that shame requires certain thoughts, I do have to confront such questions, and I do not find it plausible that the thoughts characteristic of shame (on my analysis) exist this early. Emotions, of course, may involve thoughts that are primitive or archaic. One may have a kind of rudimentary fear, for example, even before being securely aware of the distinctness of one's own body from the caretaker's body, and I have suggested that young infants do have such rudimentary emotions. Nonetheless, shame does require at least an incipient sense of one's own being, and an incipient sense of the distinctness of the helpless being that one is from the sources of comfort and nourishment. Francis Broucek has argued that shame emerges as soon as one is aware of this distinction and ceases to live in the blissful womblike world of symbiosis with the mother.[33] I would add, however (with Stern, Bollas, and others) that the world was never really blissful at any time after birth: infants experience an alternating absence and presence of good things as soon as they have experience, and gradually develop awareness of their power-lessness to control those good things. Thus I would suggest that shame emerges gradually over the course of the first year of life, per-haps becoming the full-fledged emotion only after a sense of one's own separateness is achieved.

Notice, then, that shame is far from requiring diminished self-regard in any very simple way. In a sense, it requires self-regard as its essen-tial backdrop.[34] It is only because one expects oneself to have worth or even perfection in some respect that one will shrink from or cover the evidence of one's nonworth or imperfection.

To put things very generally, shame, as I shall understand it here, is a painful emotion responding to a sense of failure to attain some ideal state. Shame, as is generally agreed by those who analyze it, per-tains to the whole self, rather than to a specific act of the self. (Guilt, as we shall see later, takes an act, rather than the whole person, as its primary object.) In shame, one feels inadequate, lacking some de-sired type of completeness or perfection. But of course one must then have already judged that this is a type of completeness or per-fection that one rightly ought to have. There are many types of shame in human life, as people come to value and aspire to many dif-ferent types of ideal traits. (Analysts typically express this idea by con-necting shame to the Ego-Ideal.) There is also general agreement, however, that the primary narcissism of a typical human infant gives rise to a particularly primitive and pervasive type of shame, as the in-fant encounters inevitable narcissistic defeats. From now on, I shall call this "primitive shame."

Andrew Morrison emphasizes the continuous influence of this in-fantile type of shame, even in later life:

[T]he essence of narcissistic concern is a yearning for absolute uniqueness and sole importance to someone else, a "significant other." This
yearning . . . is signalled in patients by such statements as, "If I am not
the only person important to [therapist or another], I feel like I am
nothing." Such a feeling reverberates with primitive fantasies of symbiotic merger, omnipotence, and grandiosity, what Freud referred to
as primary narcissism. Its emphasis is on the state and status of the
self, and yet, paradoxically, it implies as well the presence of an object
for whom the self is uniquely special or who offers no competition or
barriers to the self in meeting needs for sustenance. . . . Inevitably,
shame follows narcissistic defeat. Patients have described the torment
they have suffered from a perceived lack of specialness: "This humiliation is the most painful feeling I have ever experienced." . . . [S]uch
a yearning for uniqueness—by its very nature—can never be satisfied
fully or for long.[35]

In other words: the primitive shame that is connected to infantile
omnipotence and (inevitable) narcissistic failure lurks around in
our lives, only partially overcome by the later development of the
child's own separateness and autonomy.

Shame, in this picture, is an awareness of inadequacy that precedes any particular learning of social norms, although in later life it
will become inflected with social learning. Nor does it crucially focus
on the presence of a more general audience. The sense of emptiness
and defeat that accompanies it requires only the dyadic, and initially
symbiotic, relationship between infant and caretaker. As Gerhard
Piers argues in his classic treatment of shame,[36] shame is connected
to a fear of abandonment by the source of good;[37] its pain is felt primarily in relation to an ideal state that one fantasizes oneself, not, at
least in primitive shame, in relation to the group as such.[38] (Later,
even in relation to the social group, it is often felt in connection with
a fear of abandonment or ostracism.)[39]

As with disgust, so too with shame: societies have a good deal of
room to shape the experience differently, both by teaching different
views of what is an appropriate occasion for shame and by linking
shame differently with other emotions. Once again, Robert Kaster's
study of Roman *pudor* shows that it is subtly different, both with respect

to its objects and with respect to its links to other emotions, from similar emotion-types in other cultures.[40] In fact, however, the similarities across cultures seem to be great in this case, greater perhaps than in the case of disgust, perhaps because shame arrives on the scene so early in the infant's experience of life.

Why has shame been so often connected to the sexual and to a desire to cover our bodily organs from view? Aristophanes' speech suggests, as I have said, that our sexual nature is a sign of mortality and neediness. And Max Scheler's influential account argues that shame, as a painful awareness of inadequacy, is focused on the sexual because our sexual organs are symbols of our animality and mortality, states that we are striving to transcend, always vainly.[41] He thus connects shame very closely to disgust, as both he and I understand it. But infants obviously do not feel shame about their sexual organs, at least not until they are first taught to feel disgust at their feces. In general, shame at the sexual organs is highly variable culturally. I am inclined, with Aristophanes, to see shame as connected primarily to the more primitive longing for wholeness and the sense that one ought rightly to be whole.[42] The sexual organs at some point in life draw attention to themselves as painful aspects of our incompleteness, and the demand for an ideal sexual object becomes (as with the patients Morrison describes) an aspect of infantile narcissism in a person who has not surmounted primitive shame.[43] I do not, however, see any reason to think that shame is above all or primarily sexual in nature; it seems likely to be connected to pervasive themes about narcissism and abandonment, of which the sexual is just one manifestation.[44]

We can already see that this primitive shame is closely connected to aggressive wishes toward those people who fail to minister to the infant's needs; thus we can look down the road to see that some difficulties for social interactions may arise if primitive shame is not adequately dealt with. We can now observe that the behavior of caretakers or parents makes a great difference in setting the trajectory that this primitive shame will take. The subsequent chapters of this history are described in somewhat different ways by Fairbairn, Winnicott, Mahler, and Stern, but it seems possible to describe the common ground in all these accounts. Between one and three years of age, a child ventures out increasingly into the world, experiment-ing with separation and individuation.[45] Often it relies, in crucial parts of this period, on "transitional objects"—toys, blankets, other objects that substitute for the periodically absent caretaker, and per-mit the child to learn to comfort itself.[46] At some point, having ex-perimented with an anxious to and fro between its caretaker and the larger world, it develops a crucial ability: the ability to play alone in the presence of its parent.[47] A child who has had sufficiently stable care typically comes to feel that it is all right not to have the caretaker around all the time. Even when the caretaker is present, it is possible to focus with pleasure on one's own activities. At this point, to an ex-tent not present before, the child has a robust sense of itself as a dis-tinct being with a distinct world of experience, and also of the caretaker as a distinct person with distinct needs and activities. The parents' (or other caregivers') ability to meet the child's omnipo-tence with suitably responsive and stable care creates a framework within which trust and interdependence may thus gradually grow: the child will gradually relax its omnipotence, its demand to be at-tended to constantly, once it understands that others can be relied on and it will not be left in a state of utter helplessness.

Given the ambivalence of a child's early emotions, such a state is not likely to be attained without struggle. For around this same time, the child is likely to become aware that its emotions of love and rage, which it previously experiences as directed toward different aspects of the world (as Melanie Klein puts it, the good breast and the bad breast) are in fact directed to a whole person who is one and the same. The ideal completing parent who dotes only on me is also the bad frustrating parent whom I wish to annihilate. Given that the child (of two to three years) is aware that it loves the parent, this is likely to occasion an emotional crisis.

There is much to be said about this crisis that would take us rather far from shame.[48] Since, however, it is also an important part of our theme to see how narcissism is overcome in the direction of a rela-tionship of genuine mutuality, we must say at least something about it. The best account of this particular part of the child's life seems to me to be W.R.D. Fairbairn's account of what he calls the "moral de-fense." The idea is that the child who recognizes that it wishes to destroy the parent whom it loves feels threatened with a sense of limitless blackness in itself. It sees that it has badness in itself, and feels that perhaps it is all bad. But by now the child is capable, in a rudimentary way, of understanding the distinction between the self and its deeds. It can seek atonement for bad acts without feeling altogether lost. Morality comes to the rescue, in the sense that it is able (with help from others) to understand that doing bad, and even wanting bad, are not the same as being bad through and through.

What ought to happen at this point is that the child should become gradually able to renounce her demands for complete control over the caretaker, seeing these as inappropriate. This renunciation will be attended by grief and mourning for a time of bliss that in a sense never fully was, and also for a time of innocence in which the child was not yet aware of its own capacity for destruction. But it will also be attended by creativity, as the child learns that it can atone for bad wishes and deeds with good wishes and good deeds. Melanie Klein perceptively argues that a great deal of human love and creativity can be traced to the moment when the child realizes that its very demand to be the center of the world has projected injury toward another. It now sets about doing things for others, showing that it recognizes that other people too have a right to live and have their own plans.[49] In general, the child learns to live in a world of individuals, in which others have legitimate claims and separate purposes, and in which respect for those claims limits the inordinate demands of the self. Love is increasingly understood in terms of interchange and reciprocity, rather than in terms of narcissistic fusion and the rage for control; the self is increasingly understood, and accepted, as human, incomplete, and partial, rather than as grandiose and demanding completeness.

That is the ideal story; and it sometimes happens that way. I shall say more about these developments later in contrasting shame with guilt. And yet, the mark of early narcissism on human life is deep. Proust holds that it can never be overcome, and that all later love is essentially an attempt to control the mother who refused to be controlled. This is too pessimistic, but the idea that reciprocity is the stable human norm and that most people come to accept their incompleteness, lack of control, and mortality is much too optimistic. After all, it is just bad not to be able to have what one wants and thinks one ought to have, especially immortality; much of human life is caught up in this painful state of affairs. To get a sense of where shame and narcissism may go wrong, and how they derail development, it will be useful at this point to turn to some case histories.

III. The Refusal of Imperfection: The Case of B

The circumstances under which what I have called "primitive shame" may deform an adult personality receive a fascinating exploration in the fragment of a lengthy analysis by Winnicott posthumously published under the title *Holding and Interpretation*.[50] The patient B, a young male medical student, suffered from an inability to be spontaneous or to express any personal thought. In the presence of others, he could not initiate either conversation or activity, and he was found extremely boring. The petrified and lifeless persona he presented to others was an attempt to maintain omnipotent control over his inner world, by constant vigilance of language and thought.

During the analysis, it emerged that B had suffered from rigidly anxious and unresponsive parenting in early life.[51] His mother required perfection of herself, and interpreted any neediness on the part of the infant as a signal that she had not achieved the desired perfection (which she saw as commanded by a quasi-paternal idealized husband).[52] (Winnicott notes that the mother's tendency to idealize her husband implied that she did not love him: "not being concerned with a real person, she emphasized the quality of perfection.") As B makes contact with these memories of a holding that was stifling, the patient gradually becomes aware of his own demand for perfection in everything—as the corollary of his inability to permit himself to be a needy child. Because his mother wanted perfection (which he felt as a demand for immobility and even death), he could not allow himself to be dependent on, or to trust, anyone. "Imperfect for me means being rejected," he finally tells Winnicott. And then: "I feel that you are introducing a big problem. I never became

human. I have missed it."⁵³ Signs of humanness were rejected by his
mother, who, because of her own anxiety, was pleased only by a
quiet, perfect baby. Already in the first months, then, the character
of parental care and "holding" shapes the child's attitude to its own
human neediness—either creating the sense that human neediness
is all right, and that its helpless body is a source of pleasure and concern—or, on the other hand, sending the message that perfection is
the only tolerable state and that anything else will be repudiated.⁵⁴

   In terms of my earlier analysis, what has happened to the early
emotions of this unfortunate man? First, the dynamics of both love-
gratitude and anger have been thrown off by his inability to trust that
he is being held, that his mother wants to hold and care for a dependent needy baby. A feeling of "infinitely falling" lurks in the background. This feeling gives rise to an especially intense anger and a
possessive love that brooks no human reality. The patient so fears his
own anger that he frequently makes himself fall asleep. As Winnicott
says to him, "there is very great hostility wrapped up in this sleepi-
ness."⁵⁵ Second, for this reason the play of a normal human child's
imaginative capacity has been arrested: the creativity that grows in a
context of trust and holding has never matured, and the patient's
way of presenting himself is stilted, rigid, entirely impersonal. In a
personal relationship imperfect things might happen, but the patient's way "makes it all impersonal, and there is no excitement or
anger or elation, and I do not want to get up and hit you."⁵⁶ This
rigid impersonality, in turn, marks his relations to persons: one constant feature in the analysis is the patient's inability to describe his
wife or any other person, and his frequent inability to use people's
Christian names.⁵⁷ Winnicott tells the patient that in a real personal
relationship there is an element of "subtle interchange": this was
lacking in his early relationship with his mother, and that his sleepi-
ness expresses hopelessness about finding such a relationship anywhere. The patient responds with real excitement: "I must have been
aware of the idea of a subtle interchange because I recognize that I
have been looking for just something like that, without really knowing it." Winnicott points out that he has just been achieving it: "We
are both engaged in this matter of subtle interplay. I think that the
experience of subtle interplay is pleasurable to you because you are

so vividly aware of hopelessness in this respect." The patient responds: "I would go so far as to say that it is exciting." Love, concludes Winnicott, means many things, "but it has to include this experience of subtle interplay, and we could say that you are experiencing love and loving in this situation."

Finally, we notice that there is another primitive emotion that dominates this patient's entire existence: it is what I have called "primitive shame," connected to the very fact of his own humanness. As I have argued, this shame is far from requiring diminished self-regard in any very simple way. It is only because one expects oneself to have control or even perfection in some respect that one will shrink from or cover the evidence of one's lack of control and imperfection. A good development, we have suggested, will allow the gradual relaxing of omnipotence and transcendence in favor of trust, as the infant learns not to be ashamed of neediness and to take a positive delight in the playful and creative "subtle interplay" of two imperfect beings. B's mother, instead, understood that all that was not perfect was worthless, and that her child was worthless just by virtue of being a child and wanting to be held and comforted: "imperfect for me means being rejected." His crying, his demands to be fed, all these signs of his human nakedness were so many signs of worthlessness in her eyes. The good feeding, as he understood, would be one that blotted him out completely. (Thus he dreams of being smothered by his mother's hair.) "There is only one way of achieving anything," he concludes, "and that is by perfection."[58]

B therefore becomes obsessed with the way in which others will look at him, wanting them to see him as perfect, and knowing that if they see the real him they will not see perfection.[59] We see here how the audience enters the account of shame: not as an essential feature of the painful experience, since B's shame is generated already by his sense of his relationship with his caregivers, but as an intensification of the painful experience and as a surrogate for the critical way in which the omnipotent self looks at the pathetic childish self.[60] B's rigidity, his unwillingness to express himself, are attempts to maintain omnipotent control over his inner reality, so that he need not feel the shame of allowing his needy dependent self to manifest itself, even when no others are present. Sleep was a defense against anger, but it was also the reflex chosen by his shame lest some human part of himself be revealed. A baby asleep is a good and perfect baby, and this is what his mother had wanted. Shame, then, causes the real vulnerable self to hide, the robotic and inauthentic "False Self" to come to the fore.[61] Recognizing that he had also expected perfection in Winnicott, and prompted by the analyst's gentle reminder that this idea is a defense against anxiety, the patient remarkably states, "The alarming thing about equality is that we are then both children and the question is, where is father?"[62] Here he arrives momentarily at a position of trust and playful holding that many children attain in infancy.[63]

This case shows us the extent to which the infant's ambivalent relation to its own lack of omnipotence can be shaped for better or worse by interactions that either exacerbate primitive shame or reduce it. A primitive shame at one's weakness and impotence is probably a basic and universal feature of emotional life. But a parent who takes delight in having a child who is a child, and who reveals in interacting with the child that it is all right to be human, eases the ambivalence of later object relations; B's mother so exacerbated primitive shame that the real man was obliged to go underground, his place to be taken by a simulacrum, or by prudent sleep. "A feature of excitement," says B, "is irritation that it is not private . . . I have always had a difficulty that in a sexual relationship with a girl there is no privacy, because there are two people. It is undesirable."[64]

Shame, of course, comes in many forms. Any ideal to which one holds oneself has shame as its permanent possibility. What I have termed "primitive shame"—the demand for perfection and the consequent inability to tolerate any lack of control or imperfection—is a specific type of shame, closely connected with narcissism, or infantile omnipotence. Later I shall discuss possible cases of constructive shame. What my account suggests, however, is that the primitive type of shame is very likely to be an ongoing danger in the moral and social life, especially for someone whose development, like B's, has been skewed in the direction of pathological narcissism, but to some extent for us all. Thus primitive shame and the aggression that accompanies its narcissism may lurk behind a more acceptable form of shame, and may manifest itself in many forms, among them being the shaming of others.

The immediate family is one very powerful agent of shame-development, whether healthy or unhealthy. But the surrounding society is another. In B's case, the explanation for his hypertrophy of shame lay primarily in his parents' behavior. But societies vary also in the type of developmental pattern they hold up as normal. What Winnicott prescribes is a form of life in which parents understand and present themselves as imperfect, and nourish in the child a sense of delight in the sort of "subtle interplay" that two equally incomplete figures can have. This can be done, for example, by showing delight in the child's playfulness and creative efforts.[65] Such a familial or social culture requires giving up a certain type of safety, namely that to be found in a rigid system in which a perfect and merciless father prescribes all duties from on high.

B's is an extreme case. We might therefore think that it is too rare to illuminate general social issues. We should recognize, however, that many familial and cultural norms contain elements of the demand made by B's mother, the demand to be without need, the demand not to be a needy child. Such a demand, Nancy Chodorow argues, is implicit in the developmental history of males in many cultures of the world.[66] Taught that dependence on mother is bad and that maturity requires separation and self-sufficiency, males frequently learn to have shame about their own human capacities for receptivity and play, whereas females are more likely to get the message from their parents that maturity involves a continued relation of interdependence, and that emotions expressing need are appropriate.

In the light of our discussion of B, we can now see that the males Chodorow describes will frequently, like B, though less extremely, both hide their need for others and avert their own gaze from their inner world, not mapping it with care. This can become a vicious cycle as unscrutinized and undeveloped emotions remain at an infantile level and are therefore felt to be all the more shameful, all the more out of step with the controlling adult self who appears. "Thus," as Andrew Morrison puts it, "shame and narcissism inform each other, as the self is experienced, first, alone, separate, and small, and, again, grandiosely, striving to be perfect and reunited with its ideal."[67]

The clinical literature is rich with examples of patients—predominantly, though far from exclusively, male—who create for themselves a false veneer of competence and normalcy that they present to the world, while the needy inner aspects of the person are successfully hidden, fail to develop, and thus are felt to be all the more shameful. Winnicott's concept of the "False Self" and Christopher Bollas's concept of the "normotic personality" are variants on this theme.[68] The "normotic" personality, a type frequently encountered in treatment, is an externally "normal" and competent person who may get along very well in a career, and who often deploys to good effect an intellectual approach to life. And yet the person is in a crucial sense "unborn": in a way "normal," but in a way "robotic." The emotional personality, and subjective awareness of the self, are developed only to a rudimentary degree. Such a person may have friends of a sort; he may be cheerful and good at superficial social engagements. Real intimacy that requires the exchange of subjective feeling and trust in another eludes him, however, because he has not learned to attend to and communicate his inner needs and is averse to trusting any other person. For the same reason, such patients typically take no pleasure in literature or poetry, at least insofar as the works revolve around the inner world and its strivings. At the bottom of this syndrome, argues Bollas, is "[t]he drive *not to be* (human) but to master being." Because mastery never really works, and all human beings are persistently reminded by life of their incompleteness, such patients often end up in treatment for depression or a sense of emptiness.

Winnicott's concept of the "False Self" is slightly different, because for Winnicott having a false self is not necessarily a pathological condition. Winnicott emphasizes that all of us cover things about ourselves in some contexts, and all of us therefore need, and use, a false self that we will present to the world. That is in no way pathological, and is in fact compatible with psychological health. In a healthy person, however, the false self plays only a limited role: it is "the polite and mannered social attitude, a 'not wearing the heart on the sleeve,'" a kind of protection we wear when we don't want the general public to see all our fears, needs, and vulnerabilities. In other words, it is a defense against a reasonable and limited type of social shame. The person is well aware that there is a vulnerable non-omnipotent self within, and is able to take pleasure in that self, and manifest it to intimates.

In many patients, however, there is such primitive shame about the very existence of the vulnerable self that the false self takes over completely and the person becomes unable to get access to the inner world, or to manifest it to others. Winnicott describes one such patient, a middle-aged woman, as reporting that she "had the feeling all her life that she had not started to exist."[69] She operated competently, but, like B, lacked a sense of her own human reality, because her needs were so completely hidden that, like B, she had missed being human.

A remarkable example of the dialectic between false and true selves, and of their connection with the role of poetry, is given by Otto Kernberg.[70] A patient of his, incapable of any curiosity about either his own inner life or anyone else's, always depreciated poetry on that account: he accepted only "strong, cold, useful facts." One day he remembered the Andersen fairy tale of "The Nightingale," and the story came to fascinate him for days. The story, recall, is that of an Emperor who rejects the live nightingale in favor of a jewel-covered mechanical substitute. Becoming ill, he longs for the nightingale's song, but the mechanical nightingale is broken and offers no comfort. When he is about to die, in a state of bleak despair about himself and his life, the real nightingale comes back at last and saves his life. The patient, deeply moved by this memory, saw himself as the Emperor who had preferred a mechanical lifeless self to the real self, and who desperately wants to get access to the real live self that is still inside. "The Emperor was saved," he concludes, "because he had kept inside himself such a good and forgiving object." Evidently he was recognizing that he himself had not died completely, because, like the Emperor, he still had a living spirit within himself, capable of forgiving the neglect imposed by the demand for jewel-like perfection. Kernberg notes the importance of the fact that these insights came to the patient via a previously scorned form of writing. Apparently what was important about the story was both its form—appealing to the inner world of imagination and activating powerful emotions—and its specific content, addressing issues of need, emotional deadness, and inner vitality in a way that supported the patient's own search for his inner life.

Such examples indicate the prominent role that issues of shame and narcissism play in the treatment of a large number of patients. Both Kernberg and Morrison discuss these phenomena at great length, with numerous case histories, arguing that pathological shame is a very underused diagnosis, and that it is actually a ubiquitous category, particularly in patients whose initial symptoms are those of either depression or inappropriate rage, or both.[71]

The clinical literature repeatedly emphasizes that intellectual gifts create a particular danger for people at risk for hypertrophy of the false self. A good intellect can create a very powerful and competent false self, which takes people quite far in life and is then further reinforced by its own successes. Increasingly as life goes on, it produces a dissociation between intellectual activity and a sense of one's emotions and weaknesses.[72] The clinical literature emphasizes, by contrast, the importance of an education that includes poetry and that cultivates pleasure in the inner world. I therefore cannot resist adding to the list of cases one more of particular interest to me, especially in this book: for these themes are central to John Stuart Mill's account of his own mental crisis in the *Autobiography*. Mill's views about liberty inform my argument at many points, as chapter 1 has made clear. It is therefore of interest to see that these views issued from a struggle, remarkably honest and self-aware, with some of the very problems we have been discussing. I believe that much is to be gained by seeing Mill's whole development in the light of the psychological concepts we have just been considering.

Mill, as he famously records, and as much other evidence demonstrates, was brought up by his father to be hypercompetent, and to share his father's shame at powerful emotions.[73] Gradually, as a result of this education, he came to feel himself rather robotic and passive, lacking in any inner sense of agency.[74] All this he tells us with much insight.

What we also find in the evidence for Mill's childhood, and in parts of the *Autobiography* that he was persuaded not to publish, is that he never received very successful or stable care for the vulnerable and needy parts of his personality. Mill's mother was evidently a woman of no marked intellectual interests or accomplishments, and she soon became very exhausted by bearing so many children. For both of these reasons, James Mill seems to have treated her with contempt. He certainly did not encourage her to have much contact with his prize pupil. She evidently spent time with the younger children, but in the company of her husband and elder son, she retreated into a kind of generalized and pallid geniality, which John certainly experienced as a lack of warmth.[75] In a passage from an early draft of the *Autobiography* (deleted prior to publication at the urging of his wife, Harriet) Mill speaks of her with remarkable harshness:

> That rarity in England, a really warm-hearted mother, would in the first place have made my father a totally different being, and in the second would have made his children grow up loving and being loved. But my mother, with the very best of intentions, only knew how to pass her life in drudging for them. Whatever she could do for them she did, and they liked her, because she was kind to them, but to make herself loved, looked up to, or even obeyed, required qualities which she unfortunately did not possess. I thus grew up in the absence of love and in the presence of fear; and many and indelible are the effects of this bringing up in the stunting of my moral growth.[76]

As with B, so with Mill: in his early twenties he encountered a crisis of depression, which he vainly sought to relieve by thought of the general social welfare, and by the habits of analysis he had learned from his father. The crucial turning point is a very mysterious incident that has been much discussed:

> I was reading, accidentally, Marmontel's *Memoirs*, and came to the passage which relates his father's death, the distressed position of the family, and the sudden inspiration by which he, then a mere boy, felt and made them feel that he would be everything to them—would supply the place of all that they had lost. A vivid conception of the scene and its feelings came over me, and I was moved to tears. From this moment my burthen grew lighter. The oppression of the thought that all feeling was dead within me, was gone. I was no longer hopeless: I was not a stock or a stone.[77]

The crisis gradually lifts, and Mill finds great sustenance in Words-worth's poetry. He returns to society. Several years later, after several unproductive infatuations with women of artistic and poetic tastes, he meets Harriet Taylor at a dinner party.

The Marmontel episode has typically been analyzed in terms of an alleged death wish by Mill toward his father. The assumption of such interpreters is that Mill is identifying himself with Marmontel, and expressing the desire to care for his family, displacing the father he feared. No doubt this is not altogether misguided, for hostility toward his father is a palpable emotion in the narrative, if counterbalanced by a great deal of love and admiration. The problem with this ac-count, however, is that Mill does not seem particularly keen on car-ing for others, either before or after this episode. Indeed, he tells us that he tried to lift his depression by active concern with the well-being of others, but that this effort did no good. Instead, the focus of his search is all on finding care for himself, and in particular for the emotions and subjective feelings that his father's education had treated as shameful. It seems to me much more likely that Mill above all identified with the orphaned family who were now going to re-ceive the care that they needed. He imagines someone saying to him, your needs will be recognized and fulfilled, you will have the care that you need. Your distress will be seen with love, and you will find someone who will be everything to you.

If we now examine the original Marmontel passage, as inter-preters of the *Autobiography* usually do not bother to do, it strongly confirms this reading. Marmontel makes it clear that his consolation of his family was accomplished through the aid of a difficult control over his own emotions, as he delivered the speech "without a single tear." At his words of comfort, however, streams of tears are suddenly released *in his mother and younger siblings:* tears no longer of bitter mourning, he says, but of relief at receiving comfort.[78] So Mill is clearly in the emotional position not of the self-contained son, but of the weeping mother and children, as they are relieved to find a comfort that assuages sorrow.

In part, as the *Autobiography* makes clear, Mill's wish for care is ful-filled by a new relation to himself: he becomes able to accept, care for, nourish, and value the previously hidden aspects of himself.[79] He turns to Wordsworth's poetry as his ally in the enterprise of further cultivating the needy parts of himself. (Not very long after this, in his wonderful essay on Bentham, he characterizes Bentham as a child who had never learned how to cultivate his human feelings or appreciate poetry.)[80] In part, too, he shortly discovers in Harriet Taylor—as her letters show, an extremely emotional person and very skilled at circumnavigating John's intellectual defenses—the person who would care for him as his mother (he felt) did not.[81] And his strong statements of preference for French over British culture also show how much he prized freedom of emotional expression, which seems to release his own imprisoned emotions. (Perhaps another aspect of the Marmontel episode is the language in which the releasing text was written.) Throughout his philosophical career, Mill attached great importance to the recognition and nourishment of the inner world, and to the climate of political liberty that alone, he felt, could produce an emotionally robust culture.[82] (To this point I shall return in chapters 6 and 7.)

This range of examples shows us that infantile narcissism, shame, and the weakness of the vulnerable "true self" are common human problems, presenting themselves in many different forms in people who frequently live "normal" lives, and even lives of outstanding achievement. Negotiating the tensions inherent in the structure of human life is a delicate and perilous matter. Probably no human life is completely free of such tensions. But the delicate balance embodied in Winnicott's idea of "subtle interplay" requires nurturing, both familial and social. In families in which there is an inordinate emphasis on perfection, and in societies where need and vulnerability are viewed as shameful for dominant social actors, there is a particular danger that this balance will be thrown off, and that a sense of emptiness will give rise to rage, to depression, or to both.

It is worth emphasizing that families and societies may nourish primitive shame in many ways, some of them very subtle. Not just parents who are in obvious ways defective, as B's mother and Mill's father in different ways were, but normal, affectionate parents may overstimulate their children's narcissism, reliving in their children narcissistic fantasies of their own:

> The child shall have a better time than his parents; he shall not be subject to the necessities which they have recognized as paramount in

life. Illness, death, renunciation of enjoyment, restrictions on his own will, shall not touch him; the laws of nature and of society shall be abrogated in his favour; he shall once more really be the centre and core of creation—"His Majesty the Baby", as we once fancied ourselves. . . . At the most touchy point in the narcissistic system, the immortality of the ego, which is so hard pressed by reality, security is achieved by taking refuge in the child.[83]

As parents we at some level believe, and transmit the belief, that our children will not die, that they will never know pain or painful limitation. This seems particularly likely to be true in America, where the sense of the omnipotence of the will is especially sharp, the acceptance of mortality and failure especially shaky, and in which illness and death are all imagined as potentially eliminable by the right kind of scientific and technical effort. Combine these fantasies with the equally prevalent American fantasy that a real man is a self-sufficient being without deep needs for others, and we have the ingredients of some painful social tensions.[84]

These tensions are especially evident, at present, in the lives of boys. In recent years, there has been an explosion of work on the special developmental problems of boys, after many years when the focus was more likely to be on the difficulties girls encounter in a male-dominated environment. In their outstanding book *Raising Cain: Protecting the Emotional Life of Boys,* Dan Kindlon and Michael Thompson, clinical psychologists who have both been treating school-age boys for thirty-five years, analyze the predicament of boys in American culture in ways that are strongly reminiscent of the argument I have presented.[85] They are cautious about biological accounts of sex difference. While they believe that there probably are such differences, they argue convincingly that there are no good reasons to think that the excess aggressiveness of boys can be traced to the effects of testosterone. For one thing, girls and boys have similar levels of testosterone before puberty, while aggression levels differ greatly. For another, the boys who are most problematically aggressive are often the "losers," not the dominant group, and tend to have a lower level of testosterone than those in the dominant group. The differences that seem to them most likely to come from biology are two: boys on the whole learn language skills somewhat later than girls, and (young) boys have a greater need to burn off energy in intense physical activity before they can focus on a task.

Far more problematic, however, are differences that upbringing and culture impose. Above all, boys are never encouraged to explore and articulate their inner world. They are emotionally illiterate— because adults don't expect more of them. Experiments cited by Kindlon and Thompson show that when little boys ask their mother questions about feelings ("Why is Johnny crying?"), they tend to get a brief and dismissive answer, whereas little girls will get a much longer answer. Mothers expect girls to take an interest in such things, and they just don't expect that of boys. By the time boys get to school, they are clueless about their own feelings of sadness and have great difficulty empathizing with the emotions of others. They already learn that sadness and need are shameful—the message constantly given to them is to bear up, be stoical, be a man. At school, many boys then encounter shame again: if, as often happens, they cannot read right away, or have difficulty sitting still, they are stigmatized by the dominant organization of the school world and made to feel bad about themselves. They don't understand how they feel, and they become depressed and/or filled with rage.

Later on, a "culture of cruelty" reinforces this painful dynamic, stigmatizing boys who are not leaders or athletes. One feature of boy-culture that Kindlon and Thompson find especially problematic is its tendency to denigrate all parts of the personality that are viewed as female: emotions, especially need, sadness, and compassion. It's all right to be hostile and contemptuous, but not all right to be "soft." Indeed, the account Kindlon and Thompson give of typical American boy-culture sounds ominously like Theweleit's account of the young officers of the Freikorps, and is similarly connected to denigration of the female. So the multiple experiences of shame that mark many boys' lives are channeled into hostility: toward women, toward the vulnerable part of themselves, and, often, toward dominant members of their own culture. Because they have not developed the inner resources that would enable them to handle such conflicts, they often cannot even name their problem. Repeatedly, Kindlon and Thompson find that boys who are having problems, whether as bullies or as the bullied, cannot answer simple questions about how someone else may be feeling. Often they react as if the question comes from Mars—and in a sense it does, for it has not been a part of their culture. It is no surprise that many young men have difficulty in relationships with women, they argue—for they have no ability to conceive of what intimacy is like, and their masturbatory fantasies equate pleasure with control and invulnerability.

Of course this narrative about boys already contains a bad scenario for women, who are all too often the victims of male inability to accept the characteristics they denigrate as "feminine." But the female side of shame-inducing cultural ideals contains other destructive elements, in particular the continual emphasis on an inflexible ideal of female beauty that emphasizes thinness as a key to desirability. Much has been written about the connection between these ideals and eating disorders, increasingly prevalent in adolescent and even preadolescent girls. These problems have been closely connected to the hypertrophy of shame by Andrew Morrison, who argues that shame at imagined bodily imperfections frequently becomes the vehicle for earlier and more general feelings of infantile shame: the cultural norm interacts in a pernicious way with infantile distress, further feeding the tendency to a destructive type of narcissism.[86] This shame about the body then often produces a vicious cycle, in which feelings of inadequacy produce an eating disorder, initially aimed at restoring control over the body and achieving the desired perfection. But the eating disorder itself (especially if it is bulimia, with its messy and hidden vomiting and purging) becomes a new source of shame. The disorder is concealed, giving rise to still further shame.[87]

These ominous cultural pictures show us something important about shame and its dynamics: namely, how much power society has over the damage shame does. In one sense, primitive shame is necessary and inevitable. But the social argument presented by Kindlon and Thompson about boys, and by Morrison, Pipher, and others about girls, is constructive. These authors identify a set of cultural problems, and propose ways of dealing with them. Their proposals are not unlike those of Mill—more cultivation of the emotions, more attention to the world of imagination and to the goal of genuine empathy and understanding, more care for the vulnerable portions of the self, ideals that are flexible and individualized rather than inflexible and general. In educational terms, Mill's own prescription is confirmed: education needs to focus constantly on the needs and anxieties of the inner self, at the same time developing the capacity to perceive need in others. Narrative literature and the other arts can frequently tap emotions that might remain uncultivated if education neglected these materials. Education should nourish the sense of life's difficulty, and also the sense that, through cooperation and empathy, human beings can to some extent address these difficulties, that we can achieve a limited conquest over helplessness through "subtle interplay." The choice of literary, artistic, and musical works should be made with these aims (among others) in view, devoting particular attention to the experiences of the most vulnerable and stigmatized groups in one's society.[88]

Thus, deep though the problems are that human life presents to all human beings, society can create a "facilitating environment" for its young people, where emotion is concerned, or it can do just the opposite. (I shall return to this point in chapter 5.)

IV. Shame and Its Relatives:
Humiliation, Embarrassment

Before we turn to social issues, we need to investigate some distinctions. Shame seems closely related to humiliation and to embarrassment. Although the taxonomy of the shame-family of emotions is somewhat differently understood in different languages and cultures, and although our remarks in this section begin from an Anglo-American understanding, the distinctions in question probably occur in some form in many, if not most, cultures. Humiliation I understand to be the active, public face of shame. To humiliate someone is to expose them to shame; and to shame someone is, in most cases, to humiliate them (at least if the shaming is severe enough).[89] Of course humiliation does not always lead to actual shame, but that is its intent. We may also speak of feelings of humiliation, which will be very closely related to feelings of shame, but with the added idea that something has been *done to* the person who feels it.

William Miller draws a contrast between humiliation and active shaming, arguing that humiliation is in the universe of the comic, and involves mockery and the deflation of grandiose pretensions, whereas shame is a much more serious matter: contemplating humiliation, one laughs, while when contemplating shaming one is more likely to be moved to pity.[90] I do not find these distinctions convincing: people do not react to prospective humiliation with laughter. Humiliation is an especially serious sort of being-shamed, and is feared as such. I know of no other writer who opposes the terms in Miller's way. Investigating the comic use of shame and humiliation is indeed an interesting project, but I do not believe that the comic-tragic distinction tracks the shame-humiliation distinction. It is natural for writers on social norms to speak of a good society as one that protects its members from humiliation, where humiliation is understood as a particularly damaging insult to the person's human dignity.[91]

Insofar as shaming and humiliating differ, shaming seems a broader concept, potentially including some instances of justified moral critique (to be discussed in section VI, below), and also including some lighter instances that do not seem to insult the person's very humanity. Humiliation typically makes the statement that the person in question is low, not on a par with others in terms of human dignity.

Embarrassment, by contrast, is usually a lighter matter than shame. Like the emotion of shame, it is a subjective emotional state. Unlike most cases of shame, it may be momentary, temporary, and inconsequential. One reason for this difference seems to be that shame is typically connected with ideals or serious norms, and thus is always moral in a broad sense of that term. Embarrassment typically deals with a feature of one's social situation, which may be, and often is, relatively short-lived, and not closely connected to important personal values. Thus, as Gabriele Taylor puts it, shame is "weightier and more shattering," insofar as it pertains to elements of one's aspirations that lie deep.[92] Embarrassment, indeed, may not involve a sense of defect at all: it may only involve a perception that something is socially out of place, or that one is, without wishing or expecting it, suddenly the object of social scrutiny. Thus one may be embarrassed by farting in public, even if one thinks farting perfectly normal and even enjoyable. One may be embarrassed at the discovery that one's slip is hanging down below one's dress, although there is no serious violation of propriety or modesty involved, and thus no occasion for shame. Young teenage girls typically feel embarrassment about their developing breasts, although they certainly do not feel shame about them, and usually feel pride. Embarrassment records their unease about their new social presentation. All of a sudden they are being seen as women, and they haven't learned how to handle that; it feels out of place to them, used as they are to being viewed as little girls. People often feel embarrassment at being publicly praised. Their embarrassment does not record any sense that the praise is not due them, but they may just feel uncomfortable being described in glowing terms before others, feeling it socially awkward and out of place.

This brings out another difference between embarrassment and shame: embarrassment is always social and contextual, in a way that shame need not be. Because shame concerns matters that lie deep, it can be an emotion of self-assessment whether the world is looking on or not. There is no embarrassment without an audience, however, and embarrassment responds to one's awareness of the nature of that audience, shifting with one's perception of a shift in the nature of the audience. Thus I do not feel embarrassment urinating in public among other runners any more than I feel embarrassment, in that context, at a sweaty body odor; I would feel embarrassment at both of these things in most other social contexts. (I do not think I feel shame about either, anywhere.) I am embarrassed if a stranger walks in when I am using the toilet, but not if it is my daughter or my partner. I am embarrassed about forgetting someone's name if I am talking to that person, but not (usually) if I am telling a third party something about that person. I will feel shame in this case only if I feel that the forgetfulness manifests a relatively serious personal defect, such as an absence of due attentiveness or the beginning of mental decay.[93]

Finally, embarrassment usually comes by surprise and is rarely deliberately inflicted. If we imagine the deliberate infliction of embarrassment, we are moving toward the universe of humiliation. To be seen by strangers while urinating in a public park is usually merely embarrassing; to be forced to urinate in public before strangers is shaming and humiliating because it denies one choice over the exercise of intimate functions, something that goes to the essence of humanity. To wear a shirt with holes in it may not be embarrassing at all, since it can be a deliberately cultivated expression of one's personality. To find that one has, without realizing it, walked around all day with a hole in one's shirt is embarrassing; to be forced by others, whether through economic impoverishment or some sort of punishment, to walk around in clothing that contains holes is humiliating, depriving one of a kind of self-respect that is due to one's status as a dignified citizen.

V. Shame and Its Relatives: Disgust, Guilt, Depression, Rage

Shame's conceptual and causal relationship to some emotions that are not its immediate relatives must also be analyzed, since they also bear on the issues of public policy that we shall shortly examine. Shame, as I have analyzed it, is distinct from disgust, and is in many respects a more productive and potentially creative emotion. Disgust, as I argued in chapter 2, focuses on reminders of our mortality and embodiment as sources of contamination for the self. It thus functions to distance us from something that we actually are. Although it may have some practical value in steering us away from sources of genuine danger, Rozin's research has shown that it is conceptually distinct from the fear of danger and does not always track it well. In general, it is a deeply and, I have argued, an inherently self-deceptive emotion, whose function, for better or worse, is above all to conceal from us, on a daily basis, facts about ourselves that are difficult to face.

Shame is more subtle: for it goads us onward with regard to many different types of goal and ideals, some of them valuable. In that sense, it is not inherently self-deceptive, nor does it always express a desire to be a sort of being one is not. It often tells us the truth: certain goals are valuable and we have failed to live up to them. And it often expresses a desire to be a type of being that one can be: a good human being doing fine things. In that sense, shame should not be thought of as a nonmoral emotion, connected only with social approval or disapproval. Here I agree with Bernard Williams: it often has a moral content.[94]

Nonetheless, because shame has its origins in a primitive desire to be complete and completely in control, it is potentially linked to denigration of others and to a type of aggression that lashes out at any obstacle to the self's narcissistic projects. Narcissism, and its associated aggressions, are dangers that always lurk around the corner of even a rightly motivated shame, and indeed it will be a wise person and society that can always keep the two distinct.

Because it is standard to contrast shame with guilt, I must now pause to give my own view on this perpetual question. My analysis is closely related to my analysis, in chapter 2, of the contrast between disgust and anger. Recall that I said that anger responds to a harm or damage; it aims at the righting of the wrong. So too, I shall now suggest, does guilt, in the particular case where the wrongdoer is oneself. Guilt is a type of self-punishing anger, reacting to the perception that one has done a wrong or a harm. Thus, whereas shame focuses on defect or imperfection, and thus on some aspect of the very being of the person who feels it, guilt focuses on an action (or a wish to act), but need not extend to the entirety of the agent, seeing the agent as utterly inadequate.[95] In developmental terms, as I suggested in section II, guilt originates in the child's perception that her aggressive wishes have harmed, or have projected harm toward, another person who does not deserve to be harmed. It is a reaction to perceived ambivalence toward parental caretakers, but at a stage at which the child already acknowledges that these caretakers are separate people who have the right to exist and go their own way. In and of itself, guilt recognizes the rights of others. In that way, its very aggression is more mature, more potentially creative, than the aggression involved in shaming, which aims at a narcissistic restoration of the world of omnipotence. Guilt aims, instead, at a restoration of the wholeness of the separate object or person. As Fairbairn eloquently argued in his writing on "the moral defense," guilt is thus connected to the acceptance of moral demands, and to the limiting of one's own demands in favor of the rights of others. And as Melanie Klein argues, it is also, for that reason, linked to projects of reparation, in which the child tries to atone for the wrong that it has either done or wished.[96]

One way of getting at this difference is to return to Winnicott's patient, B. Because B had to be perfect, he could not see himself as someone whose aggression was a bad *deed* that he had *done*. As yet incapable of guilt, because he had not renounced his narcissism, he saw his own aggression, instead, as an inexorable badness covering his whole self. Shame, not guilt, was thus his primitive response: hiding, and shutting down. He had no way of coping with his own anger, and so he simply refused to go through the struggle most children fight with their anger and envy. "I see now," B concludes, "that there can be value in a struggle later when things have gone well at the beginning. . . . To sum up, my own problem is how to find a struggle that never was."[97] Winnicott says he is "cluttered up with reparation capacity" because he has not yet found the anger "that would indicate the use of the reparation phenomenon."[98] In consequence, he of course became utterly incapable of morality, since morality involves the use of reparation capacities, respect for the humanity of another person, and regard for the other's neediness.

Thus in my account guilt is potentially creative, connected with reparation, forgiveness, and the acceptance of limits to aggression. Shame of the primitive type is a threat to all possibility of morality and community, and indeed to a creative inner life. Guilt can, of course, be excessive and oppressive, and there can be a corresponding excessive focus on reparation, one that is unhealthily self-tormenting. On the other side, shame of a specific and limited sort can be constructive, motivating a pursuit of valuable ideals, within a context where one already renounces the demands of narcissism.[99] But in their role at a pivotal stage of a child's life, shame, with its connection to narcissism, would appear to be the emotion, of these two, that poses the bigger danger to development. I connect this suggestion with the idea that one of development's central tasks is the renunciation of infantile omnipotence and the willingness to live in a world of objects. Guilt is an aid in this task because it contains the great lesson that other people are separate beings with rights, who ought not to be harmed; whereas shame threatens to undermine the developmental task entirely, by subordinating others to the needs of the self. This account, if correct, suggests that the law might be well advised both to express society's feelings of guilt about crime and to rely on guilt as a social motive; shame will be a more slippery and unreliable tool.

In discussing the "False Self" and the "normotic" personality, I have already suggested a strong link between primitive shame and depression. This link is amply documented in the clinical literature. The shamed person feels a pervasive sense of inadequacy, and no clear steps suggest themselves to remove that inadequacy. The tendency may often be simply to retreat and shut down. More generally, if what the self deeply wants is a kind of ideal symbiosis and completeness that is unattainable, the unattainability of this object, together with shame at one's incomplete human existence, produces a global sense of emptiness and meaninglessness. Alice Miller's extensive clinical study of the relationship between depression and narcissism-shame argues (in a way reminiscent of B's case) that the patient whose depression is linked to primitive narcissism is unlikely to improve without acquiring the ability to mourn: that is, to give up the illusion of perfect wholeness and perfect fusion with the caretaking object.[100]

Miller emphasizes that the alternative to depression in such patients should not be understood as mere cheerfulness and absence of pain. That would be just another version of the fantasy of wholeness. What one "gets" as a result of becoming healthy is "the whole scale of human experience, including envy, jealousy, rage, disgust, greed, despair, and mourning." In other words, one comes to experience oneself, rather than the robotic false self.[101]

Finally, the link between shame and narcissistic rage has also been amply documented. On my analysis, there is inherently a strong link between primitive shame and rage at the source of lack in the self. The self, aware of its inadequacy, seeks to blame someone for this condition. In the case of infants, a culprit is usually ready at hand: the caretaker, who is not doing his or her "job" of making the self feel powerful and utterly complete. Such attitudes can very easily lead to rage in later life since these narcissistic demands are difficult to give up, and are rarely given up completely. As Kernberg puts it, behind all the strategies of the narcissistic adult lies "the image of a hungry, enraged, empty self, full of impotent anger at being frustrated, and fearful of a world which seems as hateful and revengeful as the patient himself."[102] Accordingly, minor slights are often the object of inordinate rage in patients who feel humiliated by any obstacle.[103]

This shame-driven rage often constructs its own object—whatever the most plausible surrogate in the surrounding environment might be for the original source of frustration. Let us return to Klaus Theweleit's study of the Freikorps, which we have already discussed in chapter 2. In the aftermath of the humiliating defeat the Germans suffered in World War I, there was a need for an image of a male who could not be shamed.[104] Theweleit demonstrates in detail the remarkable ideal image of the German male such officers had internalized, and the pathologies of rage to which it led. The goal, as we have seen, was to be hard, a man of steel and metal, capable of anything, susceptible to nothing.[105] This ideal self-image had to define itself against something, however. Studying these officers' descriptions of their mothers and other women in their environment, Theweleit shows that this ideal male self-image is closely connected to a hatred and denigration of the female, as a threat to the steely self-sufficiency of such a nonhuman person. Females were depicted as both shameful and disgusting. By contrast, the "men of steel" have transcended the dependency on females characteristic of the men of old, with their merely human bodies, born out of women's bodies.[106] This shame-driven rage was hardly confined to females alone; other threatening social groups were portrayed as extensions of the hated feminine: communists, Jews, the poor. Only by the strictest insistence on a gulf between the German male and these other groups could they maintain the fantasy of restored omnipotence.

Such examples, once again, seem extreme. And yet, all societies know the demand for invulnerability, and all societies know rage against minorities that can be plausibly connected to this idea. The point brought home again and again in the clinical literature is that individuals whose developmental process has not led them out of narcissism and into a willingness to accept the equal rights of others are highly susceptible to such rages, whether individually or in groups. Such rages are a danger for any society based on the idea of equal rights.

VI. Constructive Shame?

I have insisted that shame can at times be a morally valuable emotion, playing a constructive role in development and moral change. We now need to assess that claim more fully, since it will affect our assessment of public policy alternatives. Let us think about the claim, then, by thinking first about adults, and then about child development. (Since children are in general more labile than adults, and closer to the roots of primary narcissism, special care needs to be taken over the use of shame in their case.) So, when would it be good for adults to feel shame, and when would it be good for acquaintances and fellow citizens to encourage them to feel shame?

We can begin with an astute observation at the end of Barbara Ehrenreich's book *Nickel and Dimed.* In the book, Ehrenreich describes how she lived while posing as a woman without credentials, in need of a job. She describes the arduous and health-threatening working lives that she was forced to live in three different states, concluding that the failure to ensure adequate housing and employment options to the working poor is a major social problem in America. Summarizing, she says that it is not enough for Americans to feel guilt about this problem. "[G]uilt doesn't go anywhere near far enough; the appropriate emotion is shame."[107] What does she mean, and what might be appropriate or good about the shame she has in mind?

What Ehrenreich presumably means is that the predicament of the working poor in our society, and the fact that we more prosperous people live in a way that depends on the "underpaid labor of others," is not the result of this or that bad act by this or that individual. It results from deeply rooted and long-standing patterns of thought and commitment in American society: the love of luxury, the common resentment of redistributive taxation, the belief that the poor cause their poverty, and a lot more. What we need to do is not simply to apologize for this or that harmful action, but rather search into ourselves and reexamine our habits and our national character. It is too easy to say, "Let's not do A again." We need to say, "Let's not be that way any longer (greedy, materialistic, hostile to equality, etc.)."

Now obviously this is sometimes a very good sort of thing to say, when one has developed bad character traits, as an individual or as a society. And it seems good that Ehrenreich has issued her public invitation to Americans to examine their characters and to feel shame for what they find there. The question that I must face is, how can this productive kind of shame be distinguished from the dangerous kind that either is primitive shame or strengthens it? And can this distinction be made without special pleading, without taking account of the fact that I happen to find the politics of this example attractive and the politics of other instances of shame not so attractive?

First, let us consider the emotion itself. The shame that one might feel on reading Ehrenreich's book and then examining one's life— shame at individual complicity or collaboration with a bad communal norm—is connected, let us stipulate, to valuable moral and public norms, norms to which it seems good for all human beings and societies to aspire. Shame expresses the idea that one has had too much greed and insufficient compassion, and that the inequalities that result from this inattentiveness to others subvert the very ideas of equality and democracy on which this country is based. Shame may also be felt at one's lack of attentiveness to the problem and one's lack of political involvement to change it. Now of course some readers may feel that Ehrenreich's book is all wrong, that the poor do cause their poverty, and so forth; but those readers will not feel shame. Insofar as readers do feel shame, they feel shame because of a perceived discrepancy between their current character and ideals that are broadly shared across political lines. That is why the appeal to Americans to feel shame can be expected to work, if, that is, the reader accepts the book's analysis as correct.

Moreover, accepting these ideals and feeling shame at their non-realization in oneself does not reinforce primitive shame; it actively works against it. For the person who feels shame is moving out of a comfortable narcissistic conviction that all is well with her world, and is acknowledging the rightful claims of others on her time, her efforts, her money. Instead of going her own way undisturbed, she is acknowledging the fact that she has been out of touch with the reality of other peoples' lives, and she is making halting steps to exit from narcissism and to cultivate "subtle interplay."

At the same time, and importantly, she is acknowledging a common vulnerability that all human beings share. The strategy of Ehrenreich's book is precisely to produce this sense of common humanity: for it takes a person whom the reader knows to be intelligent, hard-working, attractive, physically fit, and successful—a kind of good case of human effort—and then, by simply stripping away degrees and credentials, shows how that same person plunges into a world of misery from which she cannot extricate herself. Readers either identify with Ehrenreich, or think themselves inferior to her. (I myself can't imagine how I could have endured such a life without physical collapse.) So this means that readers are brought close to the lives of those among whom Ehrenreich lives, and they see that what makes the difference between those lives and their own more privileged life (in the case of most readers) is not so much difference of talent as difference of circumstance. Their subsequent shame includes shame about their (former) tendency to think themselves above working-class people and to underestimate the commonality between themselves and poor workers.

So we can say two related things in defense of the Ehrenreich example. First, we can note that the norms in connection with which shame is felt are morally good norms, indeed norms that are very basic to the shared political conception of the United States, and shared by people who otherwise differ politically about goals and ends. And, second, the shame inspired by Ehrenreich's book is not only non-narcissistic but actually antinarcissistic, reinforcing a sense of common human vulnerability, a sense of the inclusion of all human beings in the community, and related ideas of interdependence and mutual responsibility. Those two conditions seem, if not necessary, at least sufficient for an experience of adult shame to be a valuable one. To invite another adult to feel such shame seems unexceptionable, so long as the invitation, as here, is noninsulting, nonhumiliating, and noncoercive. (Often the invitation will be best issued by oneself.) This sort of moral shame seems likely to be connected, like guilt, with projects of reintegration and reparation, as members of different classes in society draw closer to and support one another.[108]

Let us now consider the raising of children. My analysis suggests that any appeal to shame in connection with the child's human weaknesses, whether bodily or mental, would be a very dangerous and potentially debilitating strategy. And since the child is always so vulnerable to the parent's power, and can so easily interpret even a limited moral shaming as a painful humiliation, I am inclined to say that shame is always dangerous in the child-rearing process. Even if one is dealing with a persistent habit, a focus on guilt about bad acts, accompanied by an expression of love for the child, seems to be a wiser strategy than an appeal to shame, which can too easily seem debasing. On the other hand, there may be Ehrenreich-type cases here as well. If a child has a habit of being inattentive to the needs of others and persistently behaves in a grandiose, insensitive, or manipulative manner, guilt may not be enough. Shame, focused on a trait or pattern of behavior, seems morally appropriate. Whether it is appropriate for the parent to encourage the child to feel shame is, however, another question; as I said, the danger of damaging humiliation is great, and a focus on guilt about single bad acts may therefore be the wisest and most loving strategy. Grandiosity often hides fear and weakness, and the parent needs to show love for the hidden weak parts of the child that the rejection of grandiosity exposes in an uncomfortable way.

What about cases where shame neither reinforces nor undermines narcissism? Shame over laziness, lack of dedication, and other failure to pursue valuable personal ideals? For adults, such aspirational shame may be constructive, although it seems most appropriate that the invitation to feel shame come from oneself. Strangers have no business telling a person that he or she is not living up to some personal ideal, where that ideal is not part of the shared political culture. Friends may possibly issue such an invitation, although there are always dangers in telling a friend that you think a part of him is defective. Again, it seems wiser to focus on acts, even if they do form a pattern that is generally defective.

In the context of a shared enterprise, one might feel shame about a pattern of underachievement, which "lets the team down." This shame might be constructive, motivating more dedication and hard work, particularly if the invitation to feel shame is issued by oneself. Shame can also be paralyzing, however, particularly if the invitation to shame is issued by another. Should the manager of a team encourage his players to feel shame when their play is disgracefully sloppy? Well, shame is often appropriate in such cases, and it might be constructive. On the other hand, we know all too well that this sort of shame can fatally undermine self-confidence, making things a lot worse. I find it interesting that good managers, in public at least, instead focus on expressions of confidence and hope, trying to relax people.[109] Although a manager may get short-term results through shaming, it seems unlikely to be a productive long-term course.

Where children are concerned, aspirational shame seems very dangerous, especially when the invitation to shame is issued by the parent. Parents may think that they are endorsing valuable ideals (hard work, excellence) and encouraging their children to live up to them. But so often there is really something else going on: the parent is rigidly imposing personal ideals and expectations on a child who has different talents and wishes. Or the parent may be expressing a lack of love and acceptance for the child. Whether that is the parent's agenda (conscious or unconscious) or not, there is a high likelihood that a child will hear such shaming as unloving and retentive, as expressing the idea that only perfection is lovable. Again, a focus on acts, in the context of expressing love for the child, seems a more constructive and clearer message.

Does this mean that people should be "shameless," steeled against others' invitations to feel shame? It seems to me that this does not follow. Whether one is young or old, it seems appropriate to be sensitive to an invitation to shame, and related self-examination, issued by people one loves and respects. Indeed, if one were "shameless" toward people whose ideals one shares and on whose good will one has learned to rely, that would be a dangerous sign, itself, of narcissism. Part of being a mature person is to accept one's own *moral* imperfection, and to recognize that one's efforts toward valuable personal ideals (including moral ideals) can always be improved by the insights of others. That is one aspect of what "subtle interplay" requires: the thought that one might actually stand to gain morally from one's interaction with a friend. And part of trusting friends and people one loves is learning to have regard for their opinion of oneself and one's character.[110] To put oneself in a position, in a personal relationship, in which one would not feel shame at the other person's critique of one's character is to insulate oneself from that person in a way that impedes intimacy. The vulnerability to shame is part of the exposure of self that is involved in intimacy.

Of course this shows why it is so problematic to invite another to feel shame: there is great exposure and vulnerability in intimacy, and the potential for damage is very great. For this reason too it is obviously dangerous to become intimate with people whose values one does not share and respect. Many women, for example, have incurred great psychological damage from the shame to which they open themselves in relationships of intimacy that are not founded on mutual respect.

So shame can indeed be constructive. The person who is utterly shame-free is not a good friend, lover, or citizen, and there are instances in which the invitation to feel shame is a good thing—most often when the invitation is issued by the self, but at least sometimes when another person issues it. At the same time, however, these constructive instances show us the dangers inherent in any invitation to another person to feel shame. Such invitations may be non-narcissistic or even antinarcissistic, but they may also bear a concealed narcissism at their core—as when a parent, under the guise of encouraging a child to work harder, tries to control the child and make him just like the parent's ideal self-image. And they may be expressions of respectful criticism in a relationship of love or friendship, but since love and friendship are hardly immune to the dangers of narcissism, even here they may bear subtle messages of narcissistic control that belittle the very humanity of the person shamed. As we turn to the role of shame in social interaction, we will see reasons to beware these pathologies.

VII. Stigma and Brand:
Shame in Social Life

All societies mark some people as normal. As Goffman trenchantly observed, all deviations from the normal are marked as occasions for shame. Each person in a society looks out at the world from the perspective of its norm of normalcy. And if what he or she sees when looking in the mirror does not conform to that norm, shame is the likely result. Many occasions for social shame are straightforwardly physical: handicaps and disabilities of various kinds, but also obesity, ugliness, awkwardness, lack of skill in sports, lack of some desirable secondary sexual characteristic. Some are features of the person's form of life: sexual minorities, criminals, and the unemployed are major recipients of stigma.

These latter types of deviation from the normal are not branded on the face. Societies have, in consequence, found it convenient to inflict a visible mark. The word "stigma" is in fact the Greek term for this mark.[111] In the ancient Greek world the word-group (noun *stigma*, verb *stizô*) referred to tattooing, not to branding,[112] and tattoos were widely used for penal purposes. As the edict of Constantine records, the mark was frequently applied to the face, in order to shame the offender in a publicly visible way.[113] Similar practices are found in many societies, some involving branding as well as tattooing. And the evidence shows, time and again, that those singled out for branding include not just those convicted of a particular offense, but various other undesirables: slaves, the poor, members of sexual and religious minorities.

What is going on when societies stigmatize minorities? How might this behavior be connected to the dynamics of human development I sketched out above? At this point any account is bound to be highly conjectural, but with shame as with disgust, we are dealing with phenomena of such ubiquity that we ought at least to try to understand them. At the heart of the matter is the strange notion of the "normal," with its way of linking what might seem to be two altogether distinct ideas.[114] On the one hand, there is the idea of statistical frequency: the normal is the usual, that which most people are or do. The opposite of "normal" in that sense is "unusual." On the other hand there is the notion of the good or normative: the normal is the proper. The opposite of "normal" in this sense is "inappropriate," "bad," "disgraceful." Social notions of stigma and shame typically link the two rather closely together: whoever does not do what most people do is treated as disgraceful or bad. The puzzle is why people should ever have drawn this peculiar connection. For, obviously enough, what is typical may or may not be very good. Bad backs, bad eyes, and bad judgment are all very typical, and Senator Roman Hruska's claim in the 1970 Senate debate that intellectual mediocrity should be represented on the U.S. Supreme Court met the widespread mockery it deserved. As Mill observed, much progress in human affairs comes from people who are unusual and who live lives that the majority does not live or even like. So why, in more or less all societies, has the notion of the normal as the usual also served a normative function, setting the different up for stigmatizing treatment?

The puzzle becomes more complex when we recall Goffman's observation about the normal in the sense of the usual: that, as a composite picture of a person, it is actually a fictional construct. Almost nobody is, in every aspect, the "normal" man. Even if with regard to each single attribute that attribute is widespread, when we combine the whole list of such attributes, there is almost nobody who has them all. Protestants, people under fifty, and heterosexuals may all be "usual" categories, but when you begin to combine them the intersection is much smaller; by the time we go all the way down Goffman's list, we get a person who is rare indeed, and highly temporary, given that we all move too rapidly into the stigmatized category of the aging. So why should a category this elusive and in a sense contradictory have such power to mar human lives?

I believe the use of the category "normal" to stigmatize deviant behavior should be understood as the outgrowth of the primitive shame that to some degree affects us all. Because we are all aware that there are many ways in which we fail to measure up to the exorbitant demand of infancy for complete control over the sources of good, because we retain our nostalgic longing for the bliss of infantile oneness with the womb or the breast, we need a surrogate kind of safety or completeness. And those who call themselves "normals" find this safety in the idea of a group that is both widespread, surrounding them on all sides, and good, lacking in nothing. By defining a certain sort of person as complete and good, and by surrounding themselves with such people, normals gain comfort and the illusion of safety. The idea of normalcy is like a surrogate womb, blotting out intrusive stimuli from the world of difference.

But of course, this stratagem requires stigmatizing some other group of persons. Normals know that their bodies are frail and vulnerable, but when they can stigmatize the physically disabled they feel a lot better about their own human weaknesses.[115] They feel really all right, almost immortal. Normals know that their intellects are flawed in many ways; all human beings have many deficiencies in knowledge, judgment, and understanding. With the mentally disabled around them, however, and stigmatized as "morons," "idiots," "Mongoloid idiots," or "crazy people," normals feel positively sage and brilliant. Normals know, again, that their relations with other people are vulnerable and that loss and betrayal may affect anyone, but when they stigmatize another group as morally depraved, they feel positively virtuous. In sexual relations all human beings feel deeply exposed, and sex is a particular site of both physical and emotional vulnerability, but if normals can brand a certain group as sexually deviant, this helps them avoid the shame that they are prone to feel. In short, by casting shame outwards, by branding the faces and the bodies of others, normals achieve a type of surrogate bliss; they satisfy their infantile wish for control and invulnerability. Goffman revealingly refers to the stigmatized person, therefore, as "the person he [the normal] is normal against."[116]

In short, I am suggesting that the stigmatizing behavior in which all societies engage is typically an aggressive reaction to infantile narcissism and to the shame born of our own incompleteness. Even if in many respects many human beings overcome infantile narcissism, learning to form relationships of mutual interdependence with other people and to recognize their separate reality, there is an instability to that recognition given that people still don't want to be mortal and weak; in consequence there is a powerful tendency to revert to self-protective aggression when weakness makes itself felt. We might even say that the presence of disabled people functioning in our midst reminds normals too much of their own weakness, so that they feel an urge to reject from their sight through public shaming those who wear their weakness on their face. Thus shame in the self often leads to the wish that others feel shame, and to practices of humiliating or active shaming that inflict stigma on vulnerable people and groups.[117]

This suggestion is amply borne out in the clinical literature. Repeatedly, patients troubled by a pathological degree of primitive shame show an interest in representing themselves as "normal" according to the norms of their society: because, says Kernberg, "they are afraid of the attacks to which they would be subjected if they do not conform."[118] Morrison, similarly, reports that part of the experience of primitive shame is often a feeling of being "weird," not "normal." Normalcy is thus a good way of hiding.[119] This aim to be seen as normal looks at first inconsistent with the aim of most such patients to be seen as grandiose or invulnerable. But we should insist, with Goffman, that social norms of the normal usually have little to do with the weaknesses of the average man: the normal is a thoroughly normative notion, and a kind of surrogate perfection or invulnerability.

This analysis does not mean that when society holds out certain norms and asks people to live up to them, shaming them when they do not, those norms are never valuable and good. I have already said that shame can serve a valuable moral function in connection with good ideals. But thinking about the infantile roots of shame does inform us that society's shaming behavior is not to be easily trusted, or taken at face value. It can easily get out of control, and it will be difficult both to keep it tethered to genuinely valuable norms and to calibrate it properly. Behind the parade of moralism and high ideals, there is often likely to be something much more primitive going on to which the precise content of the ideals in question, and their normative value, is basically irrelevant. Such reflections should make us more skeptical about even the moralizing type of shaming, more determined to sift and analyze the ideals in question to see if they have more going for them than their sheer ubiquity.

Central to the operation of stigma is a dehumanization of the victim. The urge to brand the face keeps on recurring in the history of this topic, not only because the face is visible, as hands and calves may not be, but precisely because it does, as Constantine says, bear the mark of our humanity and individuality. Accordingly, Romans were particularly keen on shame penalties that tattooed the name of the offense, or of its punishment, on the forehead of the offender.[120] In this way, the penalty inflicted a permanent mark of what Goffman calls "spoiled identity." It was also a mark of loss of uniqueness: the offender becomes a member of a degraded class,[121] and it is that, rather than his distinctive personality, that is written on his face.[122]

Recall that one remarkable reflex of B's shame was the inability to recognize individual people or to call them by their Christian names. In his desire to control and to shut off sources of need, he saw other people only as vague looming threats to his projects; their qualitative distinctness could not be seen, and their separateness could not be acknowledged. So too with the narcissistic aggression that underlies much social stigmatizing: its urge is to efface the human individuality of the other, whether by a literal brand or simply by classifying the person as a member of a shamed class rather than as an individual person. By classifying a person as "a cripple," "a mongoloid idiot," "a homosexual," we deny both the humanity we share with the person and the person's individuality. As Goffman says, "He is thus reduced in our minds from a whole and usual person to a tainted, discounted one. . . . By definition, of course, we believe the person with a stigma is not quite human. On this assumption we exercise varieties of discrimination."[123]

An advantage of an approach to public policy issues through issues of infant development is that it alerts us to the dynamics frequently involved in shaming and gives us reason to suppose that its dehumanizing tendency is no accident, nothing we might easily remove while keeping shame's expressive and deterrent potential. It is part of the logic of infantile narcissism itself. Let us now turn to issues of law and public policy with these problems in mind.

Chapter 5
Shaming Citizens?

Quamdiu vixerit, habebit stigmam.
[He will have the penal tattoo as long as he lives.]
—Petronius, *Satyricon* 45.9

Sit denique inscriptum in fronte unius cuiusque quid de re publica sentiat.
[Let each man's opinions about our state be tattooed, at long last, on his forehead.][1]
—Cicero, *Against Catiline* 1.32

I. Shame and the
"Facilitating Environment"

Societies inflict shame on their citizens. They also provide bulwarks that protect citizens from shame. Law plays a significant role in both parts of this process. A decent society, one might think, would treat its citizens with respect for their human dignity, rather than degrading or humiliating them. A decent society would also protect its citizens from at least some types of degradation or humiliation. In this chapter we shall investigate public shaming, asking whether the law should ever use shame as a device to bolster public morality. In the next chapter we shall study a few of the ways in which law can protect citizens from humiliation. The two topics are closely linked, since one of the types of humiliation from which citizens might most want protection is law-based or law-administered humiliation.

By examining these aspects of the role of a legal system, we are asking, in effect, how law can provide what Donald Winnicott called a "facilitating environment" for lives of trust and reciprocity. We are thus investigating the psychological underpinnings of some cherished liberal norms. Let us now return, then, to our argument about child development. Although my ensuing account of law will be supported by a variety of arguments, many of them independent of that particular psychological account, the account provides the political argument with additional depth and force.

Having described the dangers and excesses of narcissism, Winnicott and Fairbairn go on to describe a norm of emotional health, a condition in which emotional development is said to culminate in a person who has not suffered some unusually disturbing blow. Fairbairn revealingly uses the term "mature dependence," rather than "independence," and contrasts this with the young child's "infantile dependence."[2] In infantile dependence a child perceives itself as terribly needy and helpless, and its desire is to control and incorporate the sources of good. In mature dependence, by contrast, which from now on I shall call "mature interdependence," children are able to accept the fact that those whom they love and continue to need are separate individuals and not mere instruments of their will. They allow themselves to depend upon caretakers in some ways, but they do not insist on omnipotence; they also allow the caretakers, in return, to depend in certain ways upon them.

Although this acceptance is never achieved without anger, jealousy, and envy, the story of maturity is that at a certain point children will be able to renounce envy and jealousy along with other attempts to control. They will use the resources of gratitude and generosity that they have by now developed—and developed in part on account of their guilt and sorrow—to establish the relationship on a footing of equality and mutuality. They acknowledge that they will always need love and security, but they see that this can be pursued without a jealous attempt to possess and control. It is only at this point, Fairbairn stresses, that adult love is achieved, since love requires not only the recognition of its object's separateness, but also the wish that this separateness be protected.

This state of health is a precarious achievement, however, and highly prone to destabilization by forces both personal and social. Behind the increasing competence and maturity—and, indeed, the mature and generous love—of such an adult lurk immature wishes that are never altogether displaced: seething jealousy, a demand to be the center of the world, a longing for bliss and comfort, a consequent desire to surround oneself with "normals" and to stigmatize vulnerable people and groups. The form these demands take will be influenced by each individual's familial and personal history; but it will also be influenced by the surrounding society, which can create to varying degrees what Winnicott calls a "facilitating environment" for the emotional health of its citizens.

What, then, should these issues of stigma, shame, and narcissism mean for public policy? If the only issue we had to deal with were the emotional health of those who stigmatize others, some liberals might insist that law and public policy have no business promoting emotional health by moderating the influence of stigmatizing and branding in citizens' lives. If those "normals" are acting out an infantile type of shame, and failing to form relationships of mature interdependency, so much the worse for them, such a liberal might say, but that is part of their choice of a way of life, and the law has no business intervening. I think that even such a liberal might be answered, because surely the capacities for emotional health, self-respect, and mutually respectful relationships with other citizens are "primary goods" that it seems reasonable to think any liberal society should make available to its citizens.[3] It is clear, however, that the stigmatizers and their mental health are not our only concern. The stigmatized suffer tremendous damage from the stigmatizing behavior of others. Sometimes they suffer legal and civil disabilities through no fault of their own, as when a minority religion or a minority lifestyle that does no harm to nonconsenting third parties is discriminated against under law. Still more frequently, they suffer from pervasive discrimination in housing, employment, and other social functions, with no legal recourse, as has long been the situation of gays and lesbians in most modern societies, along with the short, the fat, the HIV positive, and many others. Almost always, too, individual members of stigmatized groups suffer pain from mockery, taunting, and the assault on their human dignity and individuality that is so intrinsic a part of shaming.

This being the case, any society built on norms of mutual respect and reciprocity has very strong reasons to consider how the harmful impact of stigma can be minimized. Although political liberals and communitarians differ on many questions, they presumably can agree that mutual respect and reciprocity are extremely important social goods, goods that lie at the heart of the political conception of a liberal democracy such as the United States.[4] Thus, up to a point at least, we may advance an argument that has some hope of persuading communitarian proponents of greater social homogeneity, as well as political liberals who hold that reasonable disagreement about values is a hallmark of a liberal society.

One point should be strongly emphasized from the start: the impact of institutions on child development goes deep. It is crucial not to think of children as if their development takes place in the "private sphere" until they are adult citizens. At every stage, it is affected, for better or worse, by laws and institutions. A society's public norms regarding matters of gender, sexuality, and discrimination affect the lives of parents, hence those of their children, in many different ways. As children mature, these norms affect children more directly. Thus, for example, the norms of masculinity that I have discussed with reference to Chodorow and to Kindlon and Thompson are transmitted by parents and peers to children against the background of social norms and institutions. There are many ways in which laws and institutions can affect these norms: for example, through public education, formal and informal; through policies that give men incentives to participate more fully in child care; and through parental leave and through incentives to employers to create more flexible work policies.[5] The creation of a norm of maleness that emphasizes interdependence rather than self-sufficiency is a complex task, involving the participation of institutions in many different aspects of children's and parents' lives, and at many different levels. Thus the specific areas of law that I shall henceforth investigate are but a small and especially obvious part of the terrain to be considered.

Our first question concerns the active participation of law in inflicting shame: when, if ever, is this a good thing? It may look pretty obvious that the law should not cause citizens degradation or humiliation any more than it should participate in slavery. Even if a citizen wants to be humiliated (and even if the preference for humiliation is one that, within certain limits of bodily safety, the law typically respects among consenting adults in personal relationships), for the state to dole out humiliation to the willing customer seems subversive of the very ideas of dignity and equality on which liberal democracy is based. Suppose the law said to its citizens: "Here is a penny. If you give back the penny we will treat you with respect; but you may keep the penny, in which case we will subject you to humiliating treatment." This offer seems unacceptable, even in a democracy that attaches great value to freedom of choice.[6] We do not want to live in a democracy in which people have to pay to be treated with respect—even if the money is trivial and is given to them by the state. Respect is a sine qua non of the relationship between the state and its citizens, all of its citizens.

Those who propose that the state participate in shaming citizens do not directly question this conception of the liberal state. Instead, they appear to rely on two distinctions that we will need to examine: a distinction between criminal offenders and other citizens; and a distinction between shaming that merely humiliates and shaming that performs a constructive social function. Thus we cannot rule out their proposals from the beginning on the basis of a general conception of liberal democracy. We must investigate the proposals in their detail.

II. Shame Penalties: Dignity
and Narcissistic Rage

Shame penalties have recently attracted a great deal of interest. In part, this interest stems from a more general conservative desire to revive the blush of shame. Communitarian theorists claim that citizens today have lost inhibitions and that social disorder and decay have been the result. We can best promote social order and give support to important values connected with family and social life if we do stigmatize people who behave in a deviant way: alcohol and drug offenders, single mothers, people living on welfare, and so forth.[7] Kahan and other proponents of shame penalties in the law are in part motivated by something like this general idea.

For Dan M. Kahan, the basic purpose of punishment is expressive: by punishing certain sorts of offenders, society expresses its most basic values.[8] This being the case, he argues, shame penalties have a particular power. Humiliating someone in public makes a definite statement.[9] The person cannot hide: his offense is exposed to the gaze of others. By contrast, even imprisonment, humiliating though it is, is too anonymous: the person is shut away behind closed doors rather than being hung up for public viewing. And Kahan commends shaming particularly strongly as an alternative itself to other "alternative sanctions," that is, sanctions not involving imprisonment. Paying a fine, he argues, is just not humiliating; thus fining really does not involve a statement by society that a given form of conduct is disgraceful. We think nothing much about paying a parking or even a speeding ticket; we think we have got off, and we don't feel disgraced. (We may note that he ignores the burden fines impose on poor people.) And the alternative of community service, Kahan argues, is even worse, because it rewards a person for disgraceful conduct. Instead of being humiliated, the person is given something good to do, something about which he can feel good himself, and something that will make others think well of him.

In addition, Kahan and Etzioni add, shame is likely to have a very powerful deterrent effect.[10] People who pick up prostitutes will be far less likely to do so if they know that part of their penalty will be unpleasant publicity in the newspapers. People will think twice about driving while intoxicated if they know they may have to drive around for a year with a license plate saying DUI. And those New York businessmen who went to Hoboken to eat lunch and then peed in the street would probably have thought twice had they known that the penalty would be not a quiet, hidden fine, but rather the public act of scrubbing the streets with a toothbrush.

These are plausible claims. Shame does have powerful expressive and deterrent effects. So we need to have more to say against these punishments than the simple fact that they seem unpleasant. Let us, then, grant to Kahan that one thing punishments do is to express social values. If the primary function of shame penalties were to express certain valuable, concrete social norms and to give people (both the offenders and the general public) very strong incentives to live up to those norms, then there would be a strong expressivist case to be made for them.

Even in this imagined situation, where shame penalties are securely tethered to specific concrete norms, political liberals would still have reason to inquire whether the norms being enforced in this way are norms that law is really entitled to enforce. Are they central to the political conception of a liberal democracy, or are they the sort of thing about which citizens reasonably disagree, and whose enforcement is therefore, according to the political liberal, not the business of law? I have argued in chapter 1 that such a liberal, while not strictly committed to accepting Mill's harm principle as a necessary condition of the legal regulation of conduct, is likely to be quite sympathetic to that principle. Thus, the political liberal will still object to many shaming penalties on the grounds that they are penalties for offenses that really should not be offenses because they involve "self-regarding" conduct, that is, conduct that does no harm to nonconsenting third parties. Many laws dealing with drugs and sexual behavior, for example, fall in this category.

This objection, however, is not an objection to shaming penalties as such: it is an objection to all forms of punishment for offenses that fall in the category of the "self-regarding." And it is clear that one objection we often have to certain shaming penalties—for example, to newspaper publication of the names of men who solicit prostitutes— is that we are uneasy with the criminalization of prostitution and soliciting, and become even more uneasy when a harsh punishment ensues. We need to separate that objection from reasons we might have for objecting to shaming penalties as such. So from now on let us consider only offenses that involve harm to nonconsenting parties: they meet Mill's test. Kahan's failure to separate these two categories of offense seems to me unfortunate, but we need not follow him. Let us, then, consider offenses such as drunk driving, theft, fraud, harmful sexual conduct (e.g., child molestation), and other related offenses.[11] These are really bad things that deserve to be punished.

Notice that the nature of our system of criminal justice makes it impossible to institutionalize a pure shaming punishment, as we have articulated the distinction between shame and guilt. Shame, I argued, pertains to a trait or feature of the person, whereas guilt pertains to an act. Our system of justice is based on the idea of a guilty act. In order to get to the point of punishment at all, an offender must have been indicted and convicted of a criminal act, and the punishment, strictly speaking, is a punishment for the commission of that act. Thus the use of shame comes along after guilt has already determined the structure of indictment, trial, and conviction. In other times and places, things were not so: religious minorities, heretics, people with "deviant sexuality" were punished by public shaming without a conviction for any criminal act.[12] What we are assessing, then, is a mixed proposal: that shaming come along at the penalty phase, for a person convicted of a criminal act, after guilt has already shaped the trial. The fact that many consider shame penalties acceptable can in part be traced to the mixed character they inevitably take on in our legal system.

Five arguments against shaming penalties have been advanced in the recent literature. I shall now argue that each of them receives a deeper rationale by being connected to the account of shame and stigma I advanced in chapter 4. We might oppose shaming penalties without endorsing that account, but the account gives more power and flesh to the arguments, and thus gives us new reasons to accept them.

The first argument that has been advanced is that shame penalties humiliate, and thus constitute an offense against human dignity.[13] This argument, rightly understood, does not require us to hold that people who receive these punishments actually *feel* humiliated; thus it is not undermined by the phenomenon (known in the ancient Roman world as well as in subcultures today) that groups targeted for shaming may come to feel pride in the marks inflicted upon them.[14] Rightly understood, the argument focuses on what the penalty itself expresses: the intent to degrade and humiliate. Thus it is incompatible with a political commitment to giving all citizens the social conditions of self-respect, even if, for some contingent reason, the person happens not to feel humiliation.

Why is shaming supposed to be an offense against human dignity in a way that fines and imprisonment are not? The claim is that those punishments are meted out for acts; they do not constitute a humiliation or degradation of the whole person (though the punishment itself may come to have such features, as I shall discuss at the end of this section). Thus they track guilt, and indeed are predicated on a finding of guilt. Shame punishments, historically, are ways of marking a person, often for life, with a degraded identity. Shame, I have argued, is an emotion that focuses on a trait, whereas guilt focuses on an act. Guilt punishments make the statement, "You committed a bad act." Shame punishments make the statement, "You are a defective type of person." The two statements may be difficult to distinguish in our current legal situation, since shame piggybacks on guilt, and is a mode of punishing a person who has been convicted of a guilty act. But tattoos, brands, signs—these mark a person as having a deviant identity, and their role historically has been to announce that spoiled identity to the world. In many times and places no finding of a guilty act was required; the identity was targeted directly, often in ways that persisted through life—the tattoo, the scarlet letter. And even in our inevitably mixed case, shame announces to the world that this is a person of a certain (degraded) sort: a "drunk," a "bad woman," et cetera. When the public laughs at someone in the pillory, they are not invited to focus on any particular act: they are invited to scoff at the person's spoiled identity. The first argument against penalties that shame is that this message, administered by the state, is incompatible with the proper public regard for the equal dignity of all citizens.

A variant of this argument, which does deal with the offender's actual feelings, has been recently advanced by Julia Annas.[15] Using evidence from literature and history, she argues that shame, because it targets the whole person, is particularly likely to be linked to "a broken spirit"—a long-term inability to recover self-respect and a sense of one's own worth. These psychological claims, which are plausible, would give additional impetus to the contention that shaming penalties rob people of a central "primary good."

At this point I would like to inject a personal observation. As the child of an alcoholic mother, I contemplate the prospect that she might have had to drive around with a "DUI" license plate on her car. (In fact, she was never arrested, although no doubt she often drove while somewhat intoxicated.) Instead of quietly settling her score with the state through driving school, license suspension, and the other guilt penalties that are in common use, she would in that case have a public mark that would stain her identity permanently. Long after the license plate came off, she would be sullied in the community. She would be permanently marked as a "drunk mother." Moreover, my father, sister and I would also be marked as having a substandard identity (after all, it's a family car, and people would know her family connections even if it weren't). The difference between that penalty and the guilt-based alternatives seems to me enormous. I know that such a penalty would indeed have broken her spirit. It would be a cruel state, with deficient respect for human dignity, that would string up someone for public viewing in that way rather than offering treatment for the underlying problem, together with protection for privacy and dignity.

But let us consider the dignity argument in light of the account of shaming that I have presented. As I have suggested, one thing that shaming of subgroups typically expresses is a denigration of the very humanity of the people being shamed. They are somehow, in Goffman's terms, subhuman, not distinct human beings with individuality and dignity. More generally, in shaming people as deviant, the shamers set themselves up as a "normal" class above the shamed, and thus divide society into ranks and hierarchies. Such statements do have expressive power: they give voice to something many people deeply feel. Nonetheless, there is surely something indecent about the idea that a liberal society, one built upon ideas of human dignity and equality, and respect for the individual, would express that particular meaning *through its public system of law*. The fact that the state is complicit in the shaming makes a large difference. People will continue to stigmatize other people, and criminals are bound to be among those stigmatized. For the state to participate in this humiliation, however, is profoundly subversive of the ideas of equality and dignity on which liberal society is based.

Some proponents of penalties that (seem to) involve shame deny that their proposed penalties humiliate. I shall turn to a few such proposals below. At this point I am only confronting the proposals of Kahan and Etzioni, who never deny that humiliation is a goal of the sort of shaming they favor. The dignity argument seems powerful against their view. Public humiliation by the state does appear profoundly at odds with norms inherent in liberalism. The basic attitude animating Kahan's policy is one that divides people into two groups, the frail and the above-it-all, and that scoffs at those disgraceful wretches down below us. Such forms of hierarchy may, and probably will, continue in human life. The liberal state, however, cannot become their agent without deeply compromising its role as guardian of equality.

In developing the dignity argument, I have so far relied only on my analysis of stigma and what it expresses, not on my underlying causal thesis about "primitive shame." And we could stop here. We have said enough to make the dignity argument a powerful one. If, however, we believe something like the developmental story I have given, we have further reasons to accept it. For on that account, people who inflict shame are very often not expressing virtuous motives or high ideals, but rather a shrinking from their own human weakness and a rage against the very limits of human life. Their anger is not really, or at least not only, anger at immorality and vice. Behind the moralism is something much more primitive, something that inherently involves the humiliation and dehumanization of others, because it is only in that way that the self can defend its fragile narcissism. Thus we can show that it will not be easy, if indeed it is possible, to remove from even the most morally tethered shame penalties the quality of insult and humiliation to which the proponents of the dignity argument rightly object. Primitive shame is only satisfied by humiliation: thus it is not easily removable from shame punishments, so long as primitive shame remains on the scene. Kahan does not seek to remove humiliation from shame penalties; indeed he seems strongly to favor it. So his proposal is vulnerable to the dignity objection directly. A different type of communitarian might, however, try to maintain that morally tethered shame penalties can avoid humiliating. Here our developmental story proves valuable, indicating that the link between shaming and humiliating is no accident. So if we have even a suspicion that this developmental story, or something like it, is correct, we should at least be more skeptical of some likely retorts to the dignity argument. The social conditions of self-respect for all citizens may indeed be jeopardized by the widespread use of punishments based upon shame, even if they claim that humiliation is not involved. I shall return to this point later, when we study some apparently constructive shame penalties.

Guilt, and punishments predicated upon guilt, do not suffer from a similar problem. For guilt contains within itself a separation between the person and the person's act, and is thus fully compatible with respect for the dignity of the person. Punishments may treat the act very harshly, while still expressing the sense that the person is worthy of regard and of ultimate reintegration into society. Indeed, Kant's view was that retributive harshness was a *way* of expressing respect for the person, by holding him fully responsible for his acts. By both holding people responsible for their crimes and then offering them ways through which to make reparation and to reintegrate themselves into society, we strengthen the reparative capacities, in the process treating the offender as someone from whom good things may come. Community service, for certain crimes, would be one way of promoting reparation and reintegration.

Let us now turn to a second argument against shaming penalties advanced by James Whitman.[16] Whitman argues that shaming penalties typically involve a type of mob justice and are problematic for that reason alone. In shaming, the state does not simply mete out punishment through its own established institutions. It invites the public to punish the offender. This is not only an unreliable way to punish, but one that is intrinsically problematic, for it invites the "mob" to tyrannize over whoever they happen not to like. Justice by the mob is not the impartial, deliberative, neutral justice that a liberal-democratic society typically prizes.[17]

This argument, like the dignity argument, can be strengthened by thinking back to our account of stigmatization in chapter 4. If fears of inadequacy typically lead people to form groups and to define themselves as "normals" over against some less powerful group, and if the infliction of stigma and shame is typically connected with this process of group formation, as Goffman has powerfully argued, then we can see more clearly just what is likely to prove objectionable about it. These mechanisms of group self-protection look very different from the type of balanced and impartial administration of justice we rightly demand from a system of law.

Adding to Goffman's account of stigma the causal account of "primitive shame," we can go still further: often, the reasons why people form such groups and target others is a kind of deeply irrational fear of defect that is part of a more general shrinking from something troubling about human life, a search for an impossible type of hardness, safety, and self-sufficiency. Appreciating the irrational roots of the desire to shame makes us see even more clearly why a system of law ought not to build on this motive. As with disgust, the claim is not that all emotions are unreliable as a basis for legal rules. The claim is a specific claim about the etiology and operations of this particular emotion.

A third argument, distinct from Whitman's though closely related to it, is Eric Posner's historical argument that shame penalties are simply unreliable.[18] History shows that they very often end up targeting the wrong people, and/or calibrating inaccurately the magnitude of the penalty. They therefore fail to fulfill well the deterrent function of punishment: they may deter behavior that is not bad, but rather simply unpopular, while failing to deter other, far worse behavior. To the ample evidence from Europe presented by Posner (and also Whitman), I can add the ancient Roman evidence, which shows the same thing very clearly. Although shaming penalties in late antiquity were introduced with a clear class of real offenses in view (theft, fraud, et cetera), they very quickly ended up being used to stigmatize whatever group happened to be unpopular at the time: sexual minorities, Christians, and, in the era of Christian domination, heretics.[19]

We can understand why shaming is likely to be unreliable by connecting this historical argument to Whitman's argument about mob justice. Shaming is unreliable in part because it is administered not by neutral and impartial agencies of government but by the mob. When government invites the mob to punish, it can expect targeting of people who are regarded as unsavory, even if they have done nothing, or nothing much, wrong.

Once again, the historical evidence by itself makes a very strong case for Posner's point. But history is slippery. Our data are always going to remain incomplete, and it is hard to know how representative recorded cases are. It would be good to have a causal hypothesis, in addition, showing us some reasons why shaming can be expected to be unreliable and uneasily tethered to the nature and magnitude of actual offenses. My story about shame and stigma provides such a causal hypothesis. It is no accident that shame shifts rather rapidly from real offense to mere dissident identity, because shame is not about a bad act in the first place. It is addressed to a person or group of persons, and to a person seen as embodying some deviant identity (perhaps even an identity seen as disgusting), against which a dominant group seeks to define, and thus protect, itself. When we add that the mechanism behind the protection is a search for invulnerability and narcissistic triumph, we can see that the people who are likely to be targets of the shamer's rage are not particularly likely to be real malefactors but, instead, anyone who reminds the "normal" of his weakness, anyone who can become, as it were, the scapegoat of these weaknesses, carrying them out of the community. Narcissistic rage is inherently irrational (in the normative sense) and unbalanced, and so it is no surprise that it goes after Christians as well as thieves, disabled people as well as forgers.

A fourth argument addresses the claim that shame-based penalties have strong deterrent potential. Psychologist James Gilligan argues that the evidence supports a very different conclusion: people who are humiliated become more alienated and troubled than before.[20]

Especially for alcoholics, child molesters, and others whom Kahan's shame penalties would target, shame is a large part of their problem in the first place. To expose that person to humiliation may often shatter the all-too-fragile defenses of the person's ego. The result might be utter collapse. Short of that, it is likely to be a sense of great alienation from society and its norms, which may well lead to greater violence if the offender is prone to violence. Using shame to control crime is, in that sense, like using gasoline to put out a fire. An additional, related consideration is that the shamed person may have no available source of respect in the community other than criminals or other stigmatized people; thus shame can reinforce a tendency to identify oneself with antisocial groups. These claims have been strongly supported by recent empirical research conducted by criminologist John Braithwaite, showing "stigmatization to increase law-breaking."[21]

Once again, this argument, expressed in terms of general ideas of shaming and stigmatization, derives new force and depth from the psychological account of shame that we explored in chapter 4. In a person with an already fragile ego, as I argued, the experience of shame is closely connected with both depression (the broken spirit) and aggression. Then to reinforce the sense of shame may well lead to more, rather than less, violence. Recall Theweleit's German officers: it was precisely because they felt publicly humiliated by the defeat in World War I that they focused obsessively on violent imagery and projects of revenge. Kindlon and Thompson's research on boys—and our experience with violence in incidents such as Columbine—tell the same story. The infliction of shame, far from containing crime, is likely to lead to more violent outbursts.

Finally, we have an argument proposed by Steven Schulhofer, which appeals to the well-known phenomenon of "net-widening."[22] The basic idea is that shame penalties are likely to lead to an ever-widening attempt to put more people under social control. With shame as with some other initially promising reform proposals, the argument goes, the reform (such as early parole, juvenile courts, et cetera) is initially packaged as a way to divert low-level, less dangerous offenders to a regime that is less harsh than prison. They are then proposed, however, to a public that is in no mood to take chances, especially with people who might otherwise have been sent to prison. So a shift occurs: the allegedly "lighter" penalty is not used for people who would otherwise go to prison after all. It is used, instead, for people who would probably have gotten light probation or would not have been prosecuted at all, in a regime of limited resources. So instead of being diverted out of prison the shamed person is diverted into social control and penalties they otherwise would have escaped. This argument suggests that shaming will not function as a progressive reform, but rather as an agent of increased social homogeneity and social control.

This argument reveals a tension in Kahan's pro-shame argument, for he shifts his ground between two conceptions. When he faces opponents who criticize shaming as harsh, he portrays his proposal as an alternative to prison. In other contexts, however, he embraces the goal of increased social control, focusing on offenses that are usually not prosecuted at all, and/or treating shaming as an alternative to fines and community service. Unlike our other arguments, this is not a direct argument against shame penalties since we would need to combine it with a normative assessment of increased social control. It does, however, raise some serious worries about the claim that shaming will be "light" and "progressive." Combined with the dignity argument and the argument of Eric Posner, it becomes a very serious worry about the extent and reach of these penalties.

This worry is exacerbated when we think about the psychology of shame. People are all too ready to project shame outward, dealing with their own uncertainties in ways that stigmatize others. The "net-widening" involved in shaming can easily be imagined as an instance of this baneful social dynamic. This suspicion will be reinforced when we study "moral panics" in our next section.

We have, then, five arguments against shaming penalties. All of them have independent force, and any one of them might be sufficient to convince us that these penalties are a bad idea. I have argued that we get additional support for these arguments from the account of shame I have presented, and a much deeper understanding of why shaming penalties should be thought to threaten key values of a liberal society.

Defenders of shame penalties frequently reply by insisting that these penalties well serve four primary purposes of punishment: retribution, deterrence, expression, and reform or reintegration. I have already argued that, though shame penalties are powerfully expressive, what they express is deeply problematic in a society based on ideas of dignity and equal worth. Their deterrent potential has also been called into question by Posner's and Gilligan's convincing arguments. But we need to consider further the claims about retribution and reform.

James Whitman has written that shame penalties are "beautifully retributive."[23] Toni Massaro, another leading analyst of such penalties, concurs.[24] And of course there is something quite striking about punishments like the Hoboken toothbrush cleanup—they have a Dantesque flavor, and seem exquisitely tailored to the crime. Similarly Dantesque is the Kahan example of a slumlord who was sentenced to live for a period of time in one of his own rat-infested tenements. Some of these examples appear not to be about shame at all. The slumlord's punishment was not apt on account of the way it shamed him in front of others. In fact we have no reason to suppose that he was shamed at all, as in the cases where people wear special signs or marks. The public did not administer the punishment; he was not held up for public viewing, and, so far as we know, his ordinary dealings with people were not affected by marks of a "spoiled identity." In fact this punishment seems like a perfectly ordinary retributive guilt punishment: in retribution for his bad act, he is being assigned a penalty that seems more nearly apposite and proportional than simply going to prison.

If we consider the core group of shame penalties, however, it is not clear that they really do serve the purpose of retribution, as that notion is best understood. In an excellent recent article,[25] Dan Markel has argued (drawing on Herbert Morris's classic discussion)[26] that the best way to make sense of retributivism in the theory of punishment is to think of it as a view about free riding and equal liberty. We believe that all citizens are equal and should enjoy an equal liberty of action. The criminal offends against this basic social understanding, claiming for himself an unequal terrain of liberty. He implicitly says, I will steal, and you will continue to obey the law. I will rape, and nobody will rape me. As Kant argued, people who in this way make an exception of themselves are treating humanity as a mere means, rather than respecting it as an end. (This is the best way of connecting the Formula of Universal Law with the Formula of Humanity: the way we can tell whether we are using other people as a means is to test our conduct by seeing whether it could be made into a Universal Law of Nature.)[27] Retributive punishment brings the offender to book for that claim of unequal liberty: it says, no, you are not entitled to an unequal liberty, you will have to accept the limits that are compatible with a like liberty for others.[28] It is thus very different from revenge, which is typically based on personal motives and has little concern with general social equality.

If we understand retributivism in this way, we see, as Markel argues, that shame penalties are not at all retributive. They do not express a sense of the equal worth of persons and their liberty, but something very different, something connected to hierarchy and degradation. Returning to my account, we see this very clearly: for defining a top group against deviant groups is what shaming penalties seem to be all about. They certainly may and often do express the desire for revenge—and as I have argued there is often a powerful connection between primitive shame and vindictive rage.[29] They are not, however, "beautifully retributive" in anything like Kant's sense, the sense in which retributivism is a defensible and powerful theory of punishment for a liberal democratic society.

What about reform? John Braithwaite has argued influentially that shaming penalties serve very well the purpose of confronting the offender with his offense and the toll it has taken on others, and, ultimately, of reintegrating the offender into the society.[30] He practices, a type of "reintegrative conferencing" between victims and offenders that promotes these goals.[31] Such efforts are becoming increasingly common in a variety of liberal democracies.

It is important to understand Braithwaite's argument correctly because his views have sometimes been assimilated to those of Kahan and Etzioni, who cite his work as if there is agreement. He insists that he does not favor "shaming penalties," and writes, "This is a term I have never used in my writing unless it has been to disagree in passing with shaming penalties in response to the U.S. law review debates of the late 1990s."[32] Moreover, Braithwaite's overall theory of punishment is "utterly opposed to retribution," and focused instead on prospective questions of reform and reintegration. Normatively,

Braithwaite is not a communitarian, valuing social homogeneity as a central goal, but a republican, valuing both strong communities and strong individuals.[33] He uses the term "communitarian" in a descriptive sense only, as a variable indicating the strength of social bonds in a society. And while he admires some aspects of a strongly "communitarian" society such as Japan, where social bonds are very strong, he finds fault with Japan in other respects, for its insufficient protection of individuals against pressure to conform.[34] The type of consensus he values is the type a political liberal also values: consensus about society's core political values. And respect for each person is a core value of the society he would favor. "[F]undamental human rights should set legal limits on what restorative processes are allowed to do."[35] It is against this general background that we must situate Braithwaite's argument on behalf of a limited use of shame in punishment.

Not surprisingly, Braithwaite's normative proposal is very different from those of Kahan and Etzioni. First of all, he makes it clear that he considers shaming appropriate only for crime that involves harm to a victim: "predatory crime" is his characteristic phrase. Thus he operates from the start within the limits of Mill's principle. Second, he draws a very strong distinction between shaming that stigmatizes and shaming that promotes reintegration. He is critical of the former (although at times he suggests that it might be better than no shaming at all), and supportive of the latter. The proposal with which he has experimented over the years is one that confronts victims and aggressors, arranging a type of "reintegrative conferencing." He makes it abundantly clear that humiliation is entirely unacceptable in the context of this endeavor.

There are certainly aspects of Braithwaite's book that have contributed to the mistaken assimilation of his position to those of Kahan and Etzioni: one example is his unusual use of the term "communitarian," which can easily be misread as expressing a sympathy for normative communitarianism as a political philosophy.[36] From the point of view of my argument here, however, the central problem with Braithwaite's account is his failure to make any clear distinction between shame and guilt. He favors punishments that focus on the act rather than the person, and that ask the person to make atonement for an act, as a prelude to being forgiven and reintegrated into the community. He insists that these punishments must be meted out without stigmatization, and in an atmosphere of mutual respect for humanity. All of this is very appealing, and I am inclined to have much sympathy with the proposals he advances.[37] What is totally unclear is whether this has anything at all to do with shame. He insists that malefactors are not to be humiliated, and that we are to separate the act from the person. All this is characteristic of guilt rather than shame. Similarly, notions of forgiveness and atonement are at home in the world of guilt rather than shame. In fact, there would appear to be no important difference between Dan Markel's confrontational conception of retributivism, which focuses on expressing to the wrongdoer the badness of an act that claims an unequal liberty and violates the rights of others, as a prelude to atonement and forgiveness, and Braithwaite's so-called shaming penalties. But Markel, it seems to me correctly, situates his conception in the Kantian world of respect, guilt for an act, and subsequent apology and atonement. (Kant is not enamored of forgiveness, but that is a feature of Kant, not of the type of conception he advances.) So I conclude, tentatively, that Braithwaite's ideas are not only very far removed from those of Kahan and Etzioni—as he himself stresses—but also quite unconnected to traditional notions of shaming punishment, and rather part of the universe of guilt punishments. Braithwaite himself acknowledges this point, when, in recent writings, he uses the term "Shame-Guilt" in place of the simple "shame" for the emotion that (within limits) he favors, and when he describes the spectatorial emotion he seeks as a "just and loving gaze."[38]

What, then, of constructive shaming? In chapter 4 I have said that there are instances in which guilt is an insufficient response and shame is appropriate. I have mentioned Barbara Ehrenreich's account of working-class poverty in America as one instance of a public invitation to shame that seems legitimate. Americans should examine their ways of life and their commitments, and, so doing, realize with shame that we have failed to live up to ideals of equal respect that are central in our society. This sort of shame, as a result of critical self-examination, seems likely to promote reform. Is there a way in which the law could devise shame penalties (as distinct from Braithwaite's basically guilt-based penalties) that focus on this constructive sort of shame, which involves an acknowledgement of one's common human weakness and is thus not only not narcissistic, but actually antinarcissistic? What might such shame penalties (as distinct from guilt-based penalties) look like, and for what crimes would they be meted out?

The minute the law starts shaming individual citizens, there are always issues of degradation and humiliation to be worried about. Even when that individual is extremely powerful, and guilty of a kind of narcissism and a pretension to invulnerability that seems rightly addressed by Ehrenreich's sort of invitation to shame, the idea that the law should assail the fragile individual with a ritual of public humiliation seems unpleasant. Let us consider two recent examples, where public shaming seems initially attractive for the type of reason that Ehrenreich gives. Martha Stewart stands accused of insider trading. (She has not been indicted for that criminal offense, but rather for a related civil offense for which the burden of proof is lower.) Her whole career has been one long paean to narcissism. The idea purveyed in her magazine and her television appearances, that women and their homes should be perfect, is a narcissistic fantasy of a baneful type, which has diverted attention from the real burdens (such as elder care and child care) facing women in our society. Indeed, Stewart's success can be attributed in large part to the shame she induces in messy ordinary women, whose homes are far from perfect. So it seems delicious that Stewart would be publicly shamed by being shown up as nothing but a common criminal. Well, of course, one will say, if she is guilty she should be punished. But that is too quick a response: for any prosecutor must choose among many possible crimes, and Stewart is being singled out for prosecutorial attention, on the basis of what looks to be a very mild and questionable case, while other much more serious probable offenders have not been indicted. Worse still, however, is the punishment of public shame that is a large part of Stewart's situation: she has suffered significant reputational losses through shame, even before her case is heard.

One of the downsides of fame is that one is strung up for public humiliation willy-nilly, and nothing a judge could do would equal what has happened to her already. It seems to me, however, that what is happening is quite morally unpleasant, and that the relationship between the legal assault on Stewart and the public shaming is most problematic. For example, the indictment was issued on the next working day following a television special on her life that was nothing but food for the public desire to see her shamed. People are gleeful about her "downfall" because they like to see her alleged perfection sullied, but that is no excuse for parading intimate aspects of her life across network television in a tasteless and humiliating manner. Indeed, the pleasure the television drama solicits is itself narcissistic: for it says to the viewer, "She told you that she was perfect, and that you are a mess. Well, she is a mess, and you (because you no doubt are not guilty of insider trading) are, by contrast, perfect." Suppose a judge had ordered the making of that NBC special as a punishment: I think that would have been an egregious abuse of the legal system. But it is almost as bad that the drama and the indictment were so closely linked together, as though life imitated art.

Even when the law does not participate, public shaming that might initially look constructive often has a deeply unpleasant aspect. Let us now consider another recent recipient of shame, William Bennett. Bennett stands revealed as a heavy gambler. Even though he has not harmed his family or even violated the norms of his own religion, people find hypocrisy in the juxtaposition of this reality with the public pretense of virtue. I am quite unsure of the charge of hypocrisy, but at any rate there probably is something narcissistic about Bennett's use of his vast wealth for his own private amusement. And Bennett has long been in the habit of casting shame upon the imperfect. So, is it right to shame him publicly? And, were there an occasion, would it be right for the legal system to join in?

Here we are confronted with the inconvenient problem that Bennett has not broken any law: so the public will have to step in without the law's assistance. I have to say that I find the spectacle distasteful, indeed distastefully narcissistic. Many of the people who are shaming Bennett are guilty of what seems to me to be exactly the same moral error: namely, they are spending their money on their own personal pleasure, rather than on the needs of the poor. That is what most well-off Americans do. Is there really a great moral difference between gambling and ski vacations? So the shaming is not as antinarcissistic as it seems; it is in many respects an anxious defense-from-scrutiny of people's own narcissism. Even if Bennett had violated some law in the course of his gambling, it seems to me that it would be quite inappropriate for the judge to join in the public chorus of shame, for example, by ordering the making of a prime time television special (which we will shortly have, no doubt), documenting Bennett's allegedly shameful behavior. In general, public intrusion into people's private conduct, where that conduct is not relevant to their performance of their public duties, is often an unpleasant form of narcissistic self-defense.

By considering these individual cases, we come to see that part of what makes Ehrenreich's invitation to shame constructive is its utterly general character, and, importantly, its self-inclusiveness. The public shaming of Stewart and Bennett is oppositional: people line up against them, taking pleasure in their downfall. In this way, shaming others reinforces narcissism, buttressing people's false belief in their own invulnerability. Ehrenreich's proposal, by contrast, is inclusive: issued to all relatively well-off Americans, including herself. Moreover, it is informal, and in that sense gentle: readers are urged to reflect, rather than forced into some ritual of public confession. And it is, so to speak, silent: each person is invited to reflect in the privacy of that person's conscience, and to join in public discussion only as chosen. Could we imagine a compulsory public penalty that would be constructive in a similar way? These features seem difficult to capture in a system of law.

The closest that I can come in thinking about this issue would be to imagine shame-based penalties for powerful organizations—corporations, law firms—who have committed crimes of a sort that reveals the very kind of hubris and narcissism that Ehrenreich attacks. And in fact both Julia Annas and Deborah Rhode have suggested that shaming penalties might be appropriate for organizations that do harm, where they would be inappropriate as applied to individuals.[39] Annas argues that organizations cannot suffer the deep harms that individuals suffer, and that they have, as such, no dignity to protect: thus it may be appropriate to humiliate them by bad publicity. Rhode, thinking particularly of law firms that violate norms of professional conduct, suggests that bad publicity for offending firms, for example, would not be objectionable in the way that shaming would be outside this institutional context.

Of course there is informal public shaming of sleazy corporations and sleazy law firms. And possibly there should be more of it, both in the press and in public discussion. Certainly the narcissistic pretension to invulnerability has been a major source of criminal activity on the part of corporations and their officers, and antinarcissistic shaming of a sort that reinforces common human vulnerability is much to be desired in an America all too hooked on myths of invulnerability. As to whether shame should be meted out by the legal system, however, I have no clear view. Annas and Rhode certainly make a strong argument with respect to issues of dignity and certainly bad publicity among one's peers is not the type of mob justice about which Whitman is most concerned. The worry that shame will produce more bad behavior, not less, probably does not apply in such cases as it does to people with alcohol or drug problems. Whether Posner's worries about uneven deterrence apply here remains unclear. It seems to me that deterrence is likely to be most appropriate if the focus is on the acts of which the organization has been guilty, rather than on a simple shaming of the whole organization. To that extent, the punishment would be on the borderline between shame and guilt.

Etzioni raises another interesting question: should shame penalties be used for acts that it makes no sense to render illegal? A red flag goes up immediately. One good thing about the penalties he and Kahan favor is that they are not pure shame penalties because they are securely tethered to a finding of guilt for an act. We know that in other times and places people have been publicly shamed for the sort of people they are and that this has caused great damage. Etzioni's example is initially more attractive, however: he focuses on failures to aid, arguing that "bad Samaritan" laws are probably not workable and that a much more feasible way of punishing people who do not intervene to help someone who is being assaulted, for example, is to give them bad publicity, thus promoting norms that encourage people to take risks for others. He recognizes that liberals will ask, Why not focus on good publicity for people who help? His answer is that people, as he sees it, are more likely to be motivated by fear of bad publicity than by desire for good publicity. We could say that this sort of shaming has many of the features that make

Ehrenreich's example attractive, even if not all: it is antinarcissistic and aimed at jolting obtuse people out of their complacency.

Etzioni's psychological claim is speculative, and he offers no evidence for it. More important, he avoids the key question: who does the publicizing? Obviously there can be no objection to citizens getting together to disseminate information of this sort, or to journalists making a practice of reporting on such failures. But that, of course, is not a shaming punishment. If, however, the state is really going to get involved, then what will be the basis for this involvement? If there is no bad Samaritan law, what is the state saying, exactly, when it metes out a shame punishment for these bad acts? We are punishing you for something that is not illegal, and which we have no intention of rendering illegal? That would be a rather peculiar statement. And how will the punishment be determined? Will there be a trial, and evidence? If not, then the idea is obviously unacceptable. If so, we require a totally new institutional framework for trials concerning acts that are not illegal. Etzioni is so unclear about what he is actually proposing that we really do not yet have a position to assess.

The right direction, in thinking about nonimprisonment sanctions, seems to me to be Braithwaite's: whatever penalties we choose, our focus should be on the future, on reform and reintegration. Community service is often valuable in this effort, precisely for the reason for which Kahan does not like it: it gives people something good to do, and a good new relationship to the community, strengthening the sense of self as good and constructive rather than bad and antisocial. Also of the first importance are programs aimed at treatment for drug and alcohol problems, and therapy for sex-based offenses. Such treatments are generally most effective precisely to the extent that shaming is kept carefully out of them. Thus Alcoholics Anonymous, by far the most effective treatment program for alcoholism, practices what its name preaches. Members are never able to use publicly the full name of any other member. Even when they have come to know a person as a friend, they may not mention that person's name in connection with A.A. (Alcoholics Anonymous) membership. So strict is this prohibition that it was for a time unclear whether quite a few of my mother's friends would be allowed to allude to her A.A. service, and their personal experience with it, at her funeral. They did speak, but it was understood to be a rare breach of decorum.

Admittedly, there are numerous crimes for which community service and other types of restorative justice are not appropriate alternatives. Usually for these crimes shame penalties are not appropriate either, and prison is chosen. Nonetheless, defenders of shame penalties point to the humiliating character of imprisonment in order to convict the opponent of inconsistency: either reject prisons, Kahan's argument goes, or accept signs and placards and other types of public shaming.

We should admit that as they operate in many societies, and certainly in the United States, prisons are profoundly humiliating. The question is whether this must of necessity be so. James Whitman's extensive comparative study of punishment in the United States, France, and Germany establishes that the trend in Europe has been toward mildness in punishments and toward an acute concern with respect for human dignity.[40] Because in Europe's history penal practice was strongly class-divided, with harsh punishments going to the lower classes, modern European democracies focus anxiously on respect for the equal dignity of each individual, and punishments are always attentive to this respect. That focus has led to lighter punishments generally, to improved prison conditions, and to an emphasis on the fact that prisoners retain most of the rights of citizens. Maria Archimandritou's new book *The Open Prison,* a study of penal practices in the Nordic countries, Germany, and several others parts of Europe, comes to a similar conclusion; she documents in detail the trend toward extending to prisoners all the basic rights of citizens, including rights to health care.[41] The United States is the outlier, and we should not allow the deplorable state of our prisons to make us believe humiliation and prison must always go together.

Even in the United States, defenders of the rights of prisoners have long waged a campaign to establish in the courts and in the public mind the fact that prisoners are not just animals, that they have certain rights of privacy and rights to personal property.[42] We recall that issues of human dignity were central in leading a Pennsylvania court to rule that disgusting toilet facilities were a "cruel and unusual punishment." Judge Richard Posner recently wrote a very

interesting opinion that came to the same conclusion in the area of
shame: he held that it is cruel and unusual punishment for a male
prisoner to be forced to undress, shower, and use the toilet while
being watched by a female prison guard.[43] In the process, he made
some very significant observations about the status of prisoners:

> There are different ways to look upon the inmates of prisons and jails
> in the United States in 1995. One way is to look upon them as mem-
> bers of a different species, indeed as a type of vermin, devoid of human
> dignity and entitled to no respect; and then no issue concerning the
> degrading or brutalizing treatment of prisoners would arise. In par-
> ticular there would be no inhibitions about using prisoners as the sub-
> ject of experiments. . . . I do not myself consider the 1.5 million inmates
> of American prisons and jails in that light. This is a non-negligible
> fraction of the American population. And it is only the current inmate
> population. . . . A substantial number of these prison and jail inmates,
> including the plaintiff in this case, have not been convicted of a crime.
> They are merely charged with crime, and awaiting trial. Some of them
> may actually be innocent. Of the guilty, many are guilty of . . . victim-
> less crimes uncannily similar to lawful activity (gambling offenses are
> an example). . . . It is wrong to break even foolish laws . . . [b]ut we
> should have a realistic conception of the composition of the prison
> and jail population before deciding that they are a scum entitled to
> nothing better than what a vengeful populace and a resource-starved
> penal system choose to give them. We must not exaggerate the distance
> between "us," the lawful ones, the respectable ones, and the prison and
> jail population; for such exaggeration will make it too easy for us to
> deny that population the rudiments of humane consideration.

Posner now goes on to argue that the plaintiff in the case deserved
the right to protect his personal modesty from the gaze of strangers,
given that the right to cover oneself is an essential element of human
dignity.[44] Posner is not just issuing an opinion in a single case.[45] He
is issuing a fundamental critique of American prisons. He clearly
thinks that too many people are in prison in the first place, and that
the treatment of prisoners as vermin is widespread and incompatible
with the acknowledgment that they are human and, indeed, citizens.
His reference to the Nazi practice of medical experimentation on

Jewish prisoners makes this point forcefully. We abhor that history, and yet we behave in similar ways.

There is no reason to think that the whole institution of imprisonment is incompatible with basic human dignity and respect. The very fact of limiting a person's freedom for a period of time does not express the view that this person is not fully human. The right direction to go in order to respond to Kahan is to pursue the humanization of prisons and the protection of certain basic rights of inmates. One essential first step in this process would be to rethink the grotesque policy current in ten U.S. states that denies convicted felons the right to vote for life.[46] Approximately 510,000 African-American men alive today in the United States are unable to vote for this reason; that is to say, one-seventh of the African-American men in the United States, and one-third of the African-American men in Florida and Alabama. In addition, 950,000 more African-American men are temporarily ineligible because of incarceration. One-third of the 4.2 million Americans disenfranchised for such reasons are African-American, although African-Americans comprise only 12 percent of the population.[47]

Such a policy surely does shame and stigmatize for life. European nations have never endorsed such an idea; indeed, in the nations where voting is compulsory, prisoners are required to vote like everyone else. Whitman has drawn attention to a very important difference between European and U.S. penal practices, although he may somewhat underestimate the importance of race as an explanatory factor.[48] Denying African-Americans equal dignity as citizens was not easy to do after the Voting Rights Act, until, that is, this expedient was found (and the timing of the laws chimes in ominously with that act). It is obvious that this "Southern strategy" worked, deciding at least one national election. In any case our situation is not like that of the European democracies, eager to live down the legacy of a class-divided society. Indeed, many people in the United States are eager to maintain a race-divided society, and a focus on harsh incarceration, and concomitant deprivation of rights, is a powerful weapon in the service of this goal.

Rethinking imprisonment along European lines (if the public will to do so could be created) would establish that prison is not a form of lifelong stigmatization, but, rather, a basically respectful form of deterrence and/or retribution, preferably coupled with programs aimed at reform and reintegration. The public will to support such programs does not exist because in the United States we have not yet acknowledged the full and equal humanity of our racial minorities.

III. Shame and "Moral Panics":
Gay Sex and "Animus"

Shame at oneself can all too quickly become stigmatization of a deviant group. We have seen some examples of this dynamic in chapter 4, section V, examining the connection between shame and aggression. And Theweleit's study of the Freikorps (discussed in chapters 2 and 4) shows how shame at weakness, which is identified with the feminine, converts itself into aggression against groups (communists, Jews, sexual minorities) who come to symbolize a threat to a controlling male identity. The officers in question came to believe sincerely that these groups were threatening their health, their values, their very being, and their panic at the "red flood," et cetera, turned into a campaign of aggression whose ultimate results are all too well known.

These phenomena are hardly sui generis. Indeed, there is by now a burgeoning literature in sociology on the phenomenon of "moral panics"—situations in which deviant groups become targeted for aggressive treatment at the hands of police and other authorities because they are believed to pose a grave and immediate danger to society—but the danger is in large measure constructed, as are the danger-bearing characteristics of the targeted group. The classic work that coined the term "moral panic" and elaborated the key concepts is Stanley Cohen's *Folk Devils and Moral Panics: The Creation of the Mods and Rockers* (1972). Cohen's account, which can be closely connected to Goffman's work on stigma, has implications for some controversial contemporary issues, so it is worth summarizing in some detail.

Clacton, a small holiday resort on the east coast of England, was the scene of the event that began the "panic." Easter Sunday was cold and wet. Many shops were closed. Irritated and bored, some young people roared up and down the street on bikes and scooters, broke some windows, and wrecked some beach huts. One boy fired a gun into the air. The young people wore clothing that popular lore began to distinguish into two groups, one called the Mods, and the other the Rockers.

These events were, by themselves, not very alarming. The news media, however, having little else to distract them at the time, sensationalized the incident. All national newspapers but one bore headlines such as "Day of Terror by Scooter Groups," "Wild Ones Invade Seaside." This type of coverage spread across Europe and on to the United States, Australia, and South Africa. The news stories that accompanied these headlines exaggerated the number of people involved and the extent of the damage, primarily through the use of suggestive language such as "orgy of destructon," "battle," "beat up the town," and "screaming mob." They alluded to "deserted beaches" and to "elderly holidaymakers" trying to escape the violence—all without mentioning that on the day in question the beaches were deserted anyway because the weather was so bad.

Similar overreporting greeted later minor incidents. Typical was a paragraph in the *Daily Express;* "There was Dad asleep in a deckchair and Mum making sandcastles with the children, when the 1964 boys took over the beaches at Margate and Brighton yesterday and smeared the traditional postcard scene with blood and violence." Papers continued to publish rumors as fact, and even to publish already discredited stories. Over time, the public got a picture of events that was in all key respects false: instead of loosely organized and disparate gatherings of mostly working-class youths looking for something to do, they got a picture of tightly organized gangs of affluent young men from London who swooped down on holiday resorts with the express intent of terrorizing and inflicting violence.

Although the initial culprits were the media, at this point public perception begins to take off on its own. Folk mythology constructed images of the two "gangs," Mods and Rockers, and of their characteristic clothing. "Symbols and labels," writes Cohen, "eventually acquire their own descriptive and explanatory potential" (41). In all parts of British society, the danger was discussed, and the inventory of the characteristics of the allegedly dangerous group further refined. Summarizing the errors that were thus further perpetuated, Cohen concludes that here, as in other inventories of characteristics of deviant groups, "are elements of fantasy, selective misperception and the deliberate creation of news. The inventory is not reflective stock taking but manufactured news" (44). Rapidly the inventory is connected to the idea of a crisis of values: all that we hold dear is threatened by the group, and the group becomes of interest less in its own right than as a symbol of what is wrong with modern society. As in the case of Theweleit's Freikorps, so here: the key idea is that of civilization under threat from something amoral and atavistic, as "restraint normal to civilized society was thrown aside."[49] Terms such as "wild ones" and "hooligans" enter the account of the situation, serving, as Cohen argues, "to provide a composite stigma attributable to persons performing certain acts, wearing certain clothes or belonging to a certain social status, that of the adolescent" (55).

The next stage in the process is an attempt at social control. Not surprisingly, given the widespread misreporting and misattribution, and the public hysteria about civilization under threat, the reaction was poorly calibrated to the nature and severity of particular offenses. Discussing the roles played by the police, the courts, and local civic bodies, Cohen demonstrates that there were all too many cases in which individual rights were violated. Many juveniles accused of relatively minor offenses were held in custody for up to three weeks, as the refusal of bail came to be seen as a tough measure to restore societal boundaries. In one case two juveniles, eventually fined five pounds each for obstruction, spent eleven days in Lewes Prison. Tough sentencing was another way in which the legal system tried to respond to public fear. A young student, a first offender with a good school record, was sentenced to three months in a detention center for "using threatening behavior": he had thrown a make-up case at a group of Rockers. In Margate, a magistrate gave fines of fifty to seventy-five pounds to youths arrested for "threatening behaviour," and to one of them a three-month prison sentence. He accompanied these remarkably tough sentences with a speech designed for the gallery and the news media:

> It is not likely that the air of this town has ever been polluted by the hordes of hooligans, male and female, such as we have seen this weekend and of whom you are an example.

These long-haired, mentally unstable, petty little hoodlums, these sawdust Caesars who can only find courage like rats, in hunting in packs, came to Margate with the avowed intent of interfering with the life and property of its inhabitants.

Insofar as the law gives us power, this court will not fail to use the prescribed penalties. It will, perhaps, discourage you and others of your kidney who are infected with this vicious virus, that you will go to prison for three months. (109)

The imagery of this speech, in which youths are compared to vermin, to a virus, and to air pollution, is uncannily similar to imagery of German anti-Semitism and anticommunism, as Theweleit and others document these diseases. Notice that it evokes disgust at the same time as it shames.

Panic was not satisfied by mere toughness. The demand was for public humiliation of the offenders. "Deviants must not only be labelled but also be seen to be labelled; they must be involved in some sort of ceremony of public degradation" (95). These shaming ceremonies ranged from the requirement that offenders' fathers take time off work to appear publicly in court with their sons to the practice of removing the belts from suspicious young people's pants before they had done anything wrong. "They complain that they cannot keep their trousers up, but that is their problem entirely." Interestingly enough, that last comment, reporting on the crisis in Britain, was made by a British constable, but then admiringly cited by Judge J. Edward Lumbard, then chief judge of the U.S. Court of Appeals for the Second Circuit, in a speech addressing the Chicago Crime Commission on the need for U.S. police to seek broader powers of search and seizure.[50] Notice that the penalty (or deterrent, since no offense preceded it) is exactly the same one that Amitai Etzioni has recommended for first-time young African-American drug offenders.

Cohen's analysis shows graphically that many wrongs were done to individual young people through the regime of panic. Interestingly enough, even the proponents of harsh measures do not deny this. They justify the inappropriately harsh sentences they impose by pointing to the gravity of the social danger they have been facing. A crime is not just a crime, it is *part* of a dreadful social threat. As the chief judge at Hastings puts it:

In considering the penalties to be imposed, we must take into account *the overall effect* on the innocent citizens of and visitors to the Borough. Though some of the offences committed by individuals may not *in themselves* seem all that serious, they form *part and parcel* of a *cumulative series* of events which ruined the pleasure of thousands and adversely affected the business of traders. The Hastings Bench has always taken a stern view of violent and disorderly conduct and we do not propose to alter that attitude. In pursuance of that policy we shall impose in these cases penalties—in many cases the maximum—which will punish the offenders and will effectively deter other law breakers.[51]

This response would not exactly be consoling to individuals who have been singled out for a sentence wildly disproportionate to other sentences typically meted out for that type of offense. Nor does it even touch on the (obviously widespread) phenomenon of railroading the innocent, or the even more widespread phenomenon of targeting and harassing youths who were pursuing perfectly lawful activities (as with the belt-removal scheme, so much admired in Chicago).

The concept of the moral panic has been used to analyze a number of different social issues. Nachman Ben-Yehudah has put it to work analyzing the reaction to youthful drug offenders in Israel.[52] Philip Jenkins's *Moral Panic* focuses on the fear of psychopathic sexual predators.[53] In *Policing the Crisis,* Stuart Hall and his coauthors study the creation of the term "mugging" and related issues about the fear of urban crime in Britain.[54]

Cohen's concepts are fruitful in themselves, but we can take them further if we combine them with Goffman's work on stigma and with our causal hypotheses about the roots of shame. Goffman's work helps us to see the moral panic phenomenon as an instance of a more general pattern in which unpopular and "deviant" groups are stigmatized. And our causal hypothesis helps us to understand why such panics tend to recur. Indeed, Theweleit's material about German aggression against communists and Jews, which he analyzed convincingly in terms of narcissism and misogyny, is, as I have already suggested, an instance of the phenomenon Cohen identifies, since the stigmatized groups were believed to be dangerous sources of cultural decay, subverters of cherished social values.

My analysis of primitive shame and narcissism suggests that narcissistic anxiety and aggression are very likely to produce a herd mentality in which "normals" find a surrogate safety by bonding together over against a stigmatized group. What Cohen's analysis helpfully adds to this picture is the fact that this bonding often takes a moralized form. The category of the "normal," as we have seen, is already heavily normative. In many circumstances, this normativity is *moral* normativity. Condemnation of the "deviant" group is particularly effective if it takes the form of invoking cherished moral values, to which the deviant group is allegedly a threat. Portraying one's normal group as under siege from a menacing group of devils is, as Cohen shows, one very potent way of organizing hostility and energizing the struggle to preserve one's own safety.

In contemporary American society, few issues are as fraught as our struggles to come to terms with the presence of same-sex attraction and conduct in our communities. Such struggles exist in many societies, but the United States has had a particularly difficult time with this issue—more so, in almost all respects, than the nations of Europe. In chapters 2 and 3, I have already suggested that gays and lesbians are, to many Americans, a revolting source of contamination, a threat to the safety of (male) American bodies, but those chapters, focused on revulsion, left a lot of the terrain of contemporary antigay feeling uncharted. Animosity to gays and lesbians does not always take the form of disgust. In chapter 2, indeed, I suggested that disgust is most likely to be a male reaction to gay men. Lesbian sexuality is greeted with a rather different range of emotions, and women typically do not respond with disgust to the sexuality of gay men. But the absence of disgust does not mean the absence of intense hostility, however. We can now fill in another piece of the picture by seeing the operations of primitive shame at work, in converting the encounter with homosexual men and women into a classic moral panic.

Moral judgment about homosexuality is ubiquitous in American society, and much of it takes the form suggested by Cohen's analysis: gays are seen as a threat to all that Americans hold dear. In particular, as the trial of Amendment 2 in Colorado showed, they are routinely portrayed as enemies of the family and dangers to children. The state, defending the amendment, argued that it had six different "compelling interests" in maintaining the law in question. These included an alleged compelling state interest in protecting family privacy, and a separate alleged compelling interest in "promoting the physical and psychological well-being of children." Furthermore, the state alleged that a compelling interest in "public morality" pervaded all the other compelling interests: thus, for example, the interest in protecting the family was to be understood as pervaded by an interest in public morality.[55]

More recently, the "Defense of Marriage" Act, passed by an overwhelming majority in Congress, defines marriage (for purposes of federal law) as the union of a man and a woman, and tries to ensure that no state will be under pressure to recognize same-sex unions celebrated in states that might decide to legalize them. This law suggests in its very title the idea that the institution of heterosexual marriage is under threat from the possibility of same-sex unions and their public recognition. The debate surrounding the law contained a high level of rhetorically expressed anxiety about the alleged dire threat to cherished values and to the very survival of American society. Consider, for example, a speech made in the floor debate regarding this act by Senator Robert Byrd of West Virginia:

> Mr. President, the time is now, the place is here, to debate this issue. It confronts us now. It comes ever nearer . . . Mr. President, throughout the annals of human experience, in dozens of civilizations and cultures of varying value systems, humanity has discovered that the permanent relationship between men and women is a keystone to the stability, strength, and health of human society—a relationship worthy of legal recognition and judicial protection. . . .
>
> [*After reading a long list of Biblical passages mentioning marriage*] Woe betide that society, Mr. President, that fails to honor that heritage and begins to blur that tradition which was laid down by the Creator in the beginning. . . .
>
> [*After describing a trip to the ancient city of Babylon*] I stood on the site, or at least I was told I was standing on the site of where Belshazzar, the son of Nebuchadnezzar, held a great feast for 1,000 of his lords. Belshazzar took the cups that had been stolen from the temple by Nebuchadnezzar. He and his wife and concubines and his col-

leagues drank from those vessels, and Belshazzar saw the hand of a man writing on the plaster of the wall, over near the candlestick, and the hand wrote "me'ne, me'ne, te'kel, uphar'sin" and the countenance of Belshazzar changed, his knees buckled, and his legs trembled beneath him. He called in his astrologers and soothsayers and magicians and said, "Tell me what that writing means," but they were mystified. They could not interpret the writing. . . . Daniel interpreted the writing:

> God hath numbered thy kingdom and finished it. Thou art weighed in the balances and art found wanting. Thy kingdom is divided and given to the Medes and Persians.

That night Belshazzar was slain by Darius the Median, and his kingdom was divided.

Mr. President, America is being weighed in the balances. If same-sex marriage is accepted, the announcement will be official—America will have said that children do not need a mother and a father; two mothers or two fathers will be just as good.

This would be a catastrophe. Much of America has lost its moorings. Norms no longer exist. We have lost our way with a speed that is awesome. What took thousands of years to build is being dismantled in a generation.

I say to my colleagues, let us take our stand. The time is now. The subject is relevant. Let us defend the oldest institution, the institution of marriage between male and female, as set forth in the Holy Bible. Else we, too, will be weighed in the balances and found wanting.

Many other speeches, if less colorfully, referred to a grave threat to America's survival, to the very existence of family as its oldest and most important unit, to "homosexual groups" bent on carrying out a subversion of traditional standards. Representative Asa Hutchinson of Arizona said, for example, that "I am convinced that our country can survive many things, but one thing it cannot survive is the destruction of the family unit which forms the foundation of our society." Representative Tom Coburn of Oklahoma stated that "the fact is, no society . . . has lived through the transition to homosexuality and the perversion which it lives and what it brought forth." Speaking very near to a national election, many politicians seemed eager to whip up a storm of fear around the issue of same-sex marriage.

We must move cautiously here because many people of religious conviction sincerely hold that homosexual acts are immoral. We should not suggest that in and of themselves such beliefs are an instance of moral panic. What does hook up with the phenomena investigated by Cohen, however, is the special urgency and salience given to this judgment and to dire threats rhetorically associated with it, especially when we inspect the whole range of the moral values of the religions in question. One sentence in Leviticus condemns some (male) homosexual acts. Hundreds of sentences in both Testaments condemn greed. And yet we do not hear that the greedy, or those who perform greedy acts, are an infestation in our community, that they are subverting our cherished values, and that a compelling interest in public morality leads us to deny them equal civil rights.

Nor does the condemnation of same-sex relationships and even unions seem to be an issue peculiar to religious believers. Indeed, the largest single body in the United States today that officially recognizes same-sex marriage is a religious body, the Reform Jews; and every major religious denomination in the United States contains a wide range of positions on this and related issues, as do secular groups.[56] All this being so, the highly rhetorical and aggressive singling out of same-sex conduct and same-sex unions for condemnation in the name of values and Judaeo-Christian religion does seem problematic, especially when the nature of the threat posed by these instances of alleged immorality is left so vague.[57]

Why, in fact, should it be thought by anyone that the presence of gay men and lesbians living openly without discrimination in our communities is a threat to families or to children? As Judge Bayless said in his opinion in the bench trial of Colorado's Amendment 2, it seems logical that a "compelling interest" in the family would be pursued by action that was profamily: "Seemingly, if one wished to promote family values, action would be taken that is profamily rather than anti some other group." And in particular, why should it be thought that recognition of same-sex marriage would ruin heterosexual marriages? It is difficult even to identify the logic behind this thought. Is the idea that heterosexuals are so unhappy with the institution of marriage that they will all rush out and choose same-sex unions if they are made available? Surely that is highly unlikely. Or is the idea that in some nebulous way the institution will be degraded or demeaned, made shameful, by contact with that which is shameful? This seems the more likely reading of the "defense of marriage" idea, and yet the mechanism by which something "good" becomes shameful by proximity to something allegedly shameful is reminiscent of the magical thinking involved in disgust, with its core ideas of contamination and contagion. Similar thinking is often at work with stigmatization and moral panics.

If the public debate about gay marriage sometimes seems like a case of moral panic, we still need to ask what the panic is really about. Cohen's research suggested that at a time of social change, people fear for the stability of their lives; the immediate occasion becomes a way of expressing a more personal and general unease. We may conjecture, similarly, that if gay marriage seems threatening to so many heterosexuals, it is likely to be because of some anxiety about changes in their own lives that is somehow associated with the growing toleration of same-sex relationships. The debate focused on this connection: something is going wrong with heterosexual marriage, and gays and lesbians are somehow to blame. What, then, is this connection likely to be about?

If there is a connection between same-sex relationships and trouble for the institution of heterosexual marriage, it appears to be the indirect connection that is described by legal thinkers Andrew Koppelman, Sylvia Law, and Cass Sunstein. Discrimination against gays and lesbians, they argue, is a form of sex discrimination, because what it is all about is shoring up traditional heterosexuality, including the patriarchial nature of traditional marriage. Gays and lesbians are a symbol, in much of the public imagination, for sex without reproduction, for the decoupling of marriage from commitment to raising a family in the traditional way, which has certainly been a male-dominated way.[58] (Never mind that many gay and lesbian couples do in fact have and raise children, whether their own from previous marriages, or conceived within the relationship through artificial insemination, or adopted; many more do not and would like to in the future.) The connection between recognition of gay unions and the erosion of traditional marriage is that if sex is thought to be available outside of the marriage bond, women will have fewer incentives to embark upon marriage and child rearing, and may not wish to do so if marriage continues to be a largely patriarchal and unequal institution. In much of Europe, the birth rate has been falling alarmingly, largely, it is thought, because women have other opportunities in life and are unwilling to enter unions that will work to their disadvantage. For many Americans, gay marriage is scary because it is a symbol of sex, and therefore women, eluding patriarchal control. This sort of anxiety about change that eludes control, and the loss of control over cherished values, can easily awaken narcissistic fear and aggression. We may tentatively conjecture that the panic about gay marriage is at least in part a panic about women eluding male control.

If the institution of marriage is indeed in trouble, as divorce statistics in many modern democracies suggest, there are many things that could be done to come to its assistance, many of which would involve making marriage more attractive for women who have other options. As Senator John Kerry said during the Senate debate on the Defense of Marriage Act:

> The truth that we know, which today's exercise ignores, is that marriages fall apart in the United States, not because men and women are under siege by a mass movement of men marrying men or women marrying women. Marriages fall apart because men and women don't stay married. The real threat comes from the attitudes of many men and women married to each other and from the relationships of people in the opposite sex, not the same sex. . . . If this were truly a defense of marriage act, it would expand the learning experience for would-be husbands and wives. It would provide for counseling for all troubled marriages, not just for those who can afford it. It would provide treatment on demand for those with alcohol and substance abuse, or with the pernicious and endless invasions of their own abuse as children that they never break away from. It would expand the Violence against Women Act. It would guarantee day care for every family that struggles and needs it. It would expand the curriculum in schools to expose high school students to a greater set of practical life

choices. It would guarantee that our children would be able to read when they left high school. It would expand the opportunity for adoptions. It would expand the protection of abused children. It would help children do things after school other than to go out and perhaps have unwanted teenage pregnancies. It would help augment Boys Clubs and Girls Clubs, YMCAs and YWCAs, school-to-work, and other alternatives so young people can grow into healthy, productive adults and have healthy adult relationships. But we all know the truth. The truth is that mistakes will be made and marriages will fail. But these are ways that we could truly defend marriage in America.

Such practical steps to support marriage were not even on the table. The law was entirely negative in orientation, aimed at injuring an unpopular group rather than at giving real support to traditional values. So even if we bracket the deep moral issues involved for many people when they think about issues of same-sex conduct, we have strong reasons to think that the panic surrounding the debate over this particular law is not just about morality and family—that it expresses, at least in part, the more primitive aggressive feelings we have been exploring.

Sex, as I argued in chapter 4, is an area of great human vulnerability and anxiety. It is thus a likely locus for shame, even if, as I have argued, it is not *the* (only or even primary) locus. People are extremely anxious about their sexuality, and feel threatened with shame in that area, especially in an America in which ideas of sexual perfection suffuse the popular culture, promoting unrealistic and inflexible norms for all. Because sex is both intimate and in its very nature not susceptible of full control, it is likely that in this area people who experience difficulties with lack of control and with the very idea of intimacy (which entails lack of control) will feel particularly threatened. All this leads us to expect that "moral panics" will crop up with particular frequency in the area of sex.[59] Freud long ago observed that Americans appear to be particularly fearful and shame-ridden about their sexual lives; he added that they convert their libido into moneymaking, which is easier to manage. A similar observation was made by philosopher Theodor Adorno, an emigré to the United States from Germany, who observed that Americans are preoccupied with norms of health in the area of sex, and spoke often of a "healthy sex life." "Sexuality is disarmed as *sex*," he continued, "as though it were a kind of sport, and whatever is different about it still causes allergic reactions."[60]

The family is also an area of great anxiety and lack of control. Families often contain our most intimate relationships, through which we search for the meaning of life. And yet there is much hostility, ambivalence, and anxiety involved in many, if not most, family relationships. Thus shame once again enters the picture: the roles we assign ourselves in the family, as "the good father," "the good mother," are cherished and comforting norms, and precious aspects of people's attempts to define themselves as normal, precisely because there is so much at stake when control is lost and something unexpected happens. People are typically aware of deficiency in their family roles, and thus they need all the more anxiously to shore up their purity.

We have many reasons to suppose, then, that a good deal in the aggressive public campaign against same-sex marriage and nondiscrimination laws for gays and lesbians is not about religion at all, but contains elements of a primitive narcissistic type of aggression, desirous of reasserting control over family and sex by stigmatizing gays and lesbians. In the debate over the "Defense of Marriage" Act, several participants referred usefully to the climate of panic and hatred that once surrounded interracial marriage, which was legal in some states and illegal in others until the U.S. Supreme Court declared the state bans unconstitutional in 1967. The possibility of interracial marriage was a related, deeply upsetting challenge to the structure of the "normal" family, which made white men, in particular, sense a potential for shame about their masculinity. The need to draw boundaries rigidly expressed the desire to keep this threat of shame at bay.

As evidence of the sort of thinking involved in our "moral panic" over gay marriage, let me mention one more rather alarming example. In July 2001, a letter came to my home. Although I usually throw away most mass mailings unopened, this one caught my eye because the envelope announced, in red letters, a "National Campaign to Stop the American Civil Liberties Union" (ACLU): I looked again, and saw that, unlike most commercial solicitations, it was addressed to me as "Professor Martha Nussbaum," which seemed to indicate some personal acquaintance. So I opened it. The letter inside, signed by a coalition of Christian groups and leaders called the Alliance Defense Fund, and backed by a warm testimonial from former U.S. Attorney General Edwin Meese, addressed me as "Dear Christian Friend"—a double irony. The letter described a legal challenge by the ACLU to a referendum recently passed in Nebraska that amended the state constitution to bar legal recognition of same-sex "marriages" and "civil unions" (scare quotes as in letter). First, the letter accused the ACLU of hypocrisy, on the grounds that the organization had insisted, apropos of the Florida election recount, that it was extremely important that each person's vote should be counted. And yet, here they are holding, at the same time, that the votes of the citizens of Nebraska, who had passed the referendum by 70 percent to 30 percent, ought not to count. This use of clever rhetoric to obscure the distinction between fundamental constitutional rights, which cannot be overturned by a majority vote, and the election of a president, where a state's electoral votes are determined by a majority vote, was just one instance of a Cohen-like rhetoric of distortion that filled the letter.[61]

The letter then continued by documenting all the bad things that would allegedly happen in our communities if the ACLU were successful in its campaign. The catalogue of horrors began with imagery reminiscent of descriptions in both Cohen and Theweleit: "*If the ACLU wins in Nebraska, it will set a dangerous national precedent. The floodgates will be opened for extremists to overturn marriage laws in every state.* If that happens, you won't recognize America." One of the alleged horrible consequences was that "pastors" would be "forced" to perform same-sex unions, as if the existence of a civil marriage right could ever force a religious leader to perform a religious ceremony. (Has the Alliance forgotten that First Amendment rights of nonestablishment and free exercise do not currently force Catholic priests to marry Jews, or indeed to marry anyone whose commitment and background they do not approve of?) The culmination of all the horrors, however, was especially revealing: it was that "activists will be given immense power and boldness to pursue the rest of their agenda, including so-called 'hate crime' and other laws that could actually criminalize much public opposition to homosexual behavior."

This remarkable sentence looks like a slip. For the people who address me as "Christian Friend" surely don't want to admit that they support forms of "public opposition to homosexual behavior" that would be targeted by hate crimes legislation. Or do they? The scare quotes around "hate crime" are ominous. It would appear that the sentence is not careless, but a canny appeal to people who think that violence against gays and lesbians is a legitimate form of resistance, and that the very term "hate crime" for this conduct should be rejected. Now we are not dealing with religion at all, and certainly not Christian religion, which, even in its conservative form, typically stresses love for the sinner. We are dealing with a primitive, and dangerous, form of narcissistic aggression.

What is the appropriate remedy for this violent animosity? Above all, it must be to ensure that members of stigmatized subcultures receive the equal protection of the laws. In our next chapter we will discuss affirmative ways of protecting minorities from shame. But one necessary part of guaranteeing citizens the equal protection of the laws, pertinent to our inquiry in the present chapter, is to guarantee the equal protection of the laws to all citizens by invalidating laws that are based on mere prejudice and inflict stigma. I believe that it would be right to oppose the Defense of Marriage Act on these grounds, given the nature of the debate surrounding it.

That law did not garner much opposition, and passed overwhelmingly. In another related area, however, the principle I advocate was recognized. In responding to the case concerning Colorado's Amendment 2, the U.S. Supreme Court found (highly unusually) that the law lacked a "rational basis" because it was based merely on "animus." Despite the moralizing rhetoric of the proponents of Amendment 2, the Court argued that the motivating force behind the amendment was "animus." The majority opinion argued that to disqualify gays and lesbians from seeking and winning nondiscrimination laws at a local level was in conflict with the basic idea involved in the notion of equal protection of the laws:

> The resulting disqualification of a class of persons from the right to seek specific protection from the law is unprecedented in our jurisprudence. . . . It is not within our constitutional traditions to enact

laws of this sort. Central both to the idea of the rule of law and to our
own Constitution's guarantee of equal protection is the principle that
government and each of its parts remain open on impartial terms to
all who seek its assistance. . . . A law declaring that in general it shall
be more difficult for one group of citizens than for all others to seek
aid from the government is itself a denial of equal protection of the
laws in the most literal sense.[62]

The law was held to have no "rational relationship to a legitimate
government purpose," and, further, to have been "born of animosity
toward the class that it affects."[63]

A closely connected earlier case, indeed one of the very few cases
in which the Supreme Court has held that a law duly passed by Congress or by state voters lacks a "rational basis," dealt with a similar
issue of stigma and panic, establishing a precedent that the Court
followed in *Romer*.[64] *City of Cleburne v. Cleburne Living Center* (also discussed in chapter 3) concerns a Texas city that denied a permit for a
group home for people with mental retardation, following a city zoning law that requires special permits for such group homes.[65] (Permits were not required for convalescent homes, homes for the
elderly, and sanatoriums: only for "homes for the insane or feeble-
minded or alcoholics or drug addicts.") The denial of the permit was
plainly prompted by fear and other negative attitudes expressed by
nearby property owners. The city further alleged that people with
mental disabilities might be in danger by being located on a "five-
hundred–year flood plain," since, in the event of a flood, they might
be slow to escape from the building. The Supreme Court held that
the permit denial had no rational basis, resting only on "invidious
discrimination," "an irrational prejudice against the mentally retarded," and "vague, undifferentiated fears." Here the Court refuses
to allow plainly pretextual arguments to parade as rationality: they
know a panic when they see it, and they name it plainly.

In *Romer*, then, the Court pursues the same strategy, insisting that
even the weak rational-basis standard is not satisfied by a law born of
bare animosity.[66] In terms of our analysis of moral panics, they were
entirely right to do so. If public rationality and the equal protection
of the laws mean anything, they must mean that bare fear and dislike

are insufficient grounds for a law that withholds basic privileges.[67] A vigilant defense of equal protection of the laws is a minimal commitment for a decent society to make in protecting unpopular groups from the damaging effects of stigma and associated fears.

Let us now return to the topic of same-sex marriage: does the Defense of Marriage Act itself threaten the equal dignity of all citizens? The right to marry the person of one's choice is an extremely basic right. In *Loving v. Virginia*, the case in which the Supreme Court declared Virginia's ban on miscegenation unconstitutional, the Court stated that "[t]he freedom to marry has long been recognized as one of the vital personal rights essential to the orderly pursuit of happiness by free men."[68] Arguing against the ban on grounds of both due process and equal protection, the Court also found that the only purpose of the statute was to uphold "white supremacy." The fact that the prohibition was worded neutrally—blacks could not marry whites, and whites could not marry blacks—did not prevent the statute from reinforcing a social hierarchy that, in the view of the Court, was incompatible with the basic meaning of equal protection.

Although it would take us too far afield to investigate the legal issues that would have to be faced in applying these two lines of reasoning to the question of same-sex marriage, it seems likely that they do apply to it, as the Hawaii Supreme Court argued in *Baehr v. Lewin*,[69] and that a ban on gay marriage is just as unconstitutional as the ban on interracial marriage.[70] This does not mean that judges will say so any time soon. It does not even mean that they ought to say so, for one legitimate concern will be not to create a panic reaction and thus energize the resistance to gay marriage still further.[71] It does mean, however, that the logic of the ban on same-sex marriage is constitutionally unacceptable. It enforces a hierarchy, defining some people's intimate choices as less worthwhile than those of others. Very likely, it also enforces a traditional notion of marriage, and thus a conventional sexual hierarchy.

Other nations have seen these problems, and have subsequently moved to legalize gay marriage. As U.S. citizens observe developments in Europe, where several countries have legalized same-sex marriage and many others have legalized Vermont-style civil unions, and especially in Canada, where, in June 2003, an Ontario court declared the heterosexual definition of marriage to be unconstitutional, and Prime Minister Jean Chrétien said that he would move to legalize gay marriage across the nation, there may be occasion to note that society does not fall apart, or even greatly change at these developments.

It is, however, somewhat unfortunate that the public debate has focused on the sole question of whether same-sex marriage should be given the privileges afforded heterosexual marriage. This way of posing the issue forestalls a prior question, namely whether a single institution, marriage, ought to enjoy the large and heterogeneous bundle of privileges it currently does enjoy, privileges in areas ranging from immigration, adoption, and inheritance to the spousal privilege in testimony to decisions about burial and medical care. Should the United States actually continue with its binary approach to the status of marriage, or pursue a more flexible strategy such as the strategy that France has recently adopted, recognizing some groupings for some purposes, others for other purposes?[72] This larger debate has been greatly inhibited by the single-minded focusing on same-sex marriage rights.

The fact is that marriage as an institution has housed both love and violence, both the nurturing of children and their abuse and degradation. Women and female children, in particular, have not typically done well in that institution, which continues to burden women with a grossly disproportionate burden of child care, and, today, a growing burden of elder care. The world contains many examples of how these burdens may be shared: by extended families, by villages and other local groupings, and with the aid of sensible reforms in public policy and the structure of the workplace. We need to ponder all these alternatives as we chart our course for the future. Unfortunately, both the panic over gay marriage and the natural response to it—the focus on securing equal marriage rights for gays and lesbians—postpone this urgently needed public debate.

One more area in which gays are targeted by law now demands our attention. In the light of *Cleburne*, we are invited to think about the issue of zoning for adult establishments. Zoning would appear to be a gray area where communities may in some instances be free to exercise judgment that certain nonharmful practices are nonetheless to be restricted. Thus zoning restrictions for establishments offering sexually explicit materials are not off the table in my view, as restrictions on publication would surely be. General concerns about freedom of association suggest that residents should have at least some latitude in deciding what to permit in their communities. *Cleburne* shows, however, that a community is not free to enact into zoning law any prejudices against a group it may happen to hold. To refuse a permit to a home for mentally retarded persons, when similar permits had been given to homes for the aged and physically disabled, was an unconstitutional denial of the equal protection of the laws. Even in this area of law, moral panic has legal limits.

When we consider *Cleburne,* the recent debate about zoning regulations for gay bookstores and clubs in New York City raises very interesting issues. Michael Warner and other gay activists have already used the language of moral panic to describe the reaction of the Giuliani administration, calling it a "Sex Panic" and rallying against it. The group, called Sex Panic!, focuses on six recent trends: (1) the closing of gay video stores and sex clubs in the name of the health code; (2) the fencing off and patrolling of traditional gay meeting places on the piers along the Hudson River; (3) the upturn in arrests of gay men for cruising, often on public lewdness charges; (4) the general decline of available public space in the city; (5) the harassment of bars, dance clubs, and other sites of nightlife, often on technicalities of cabaret license violations; and (6) the 1995 zoning amendment that further restricts "adult businesses" by defining them in a broader and vaguer way and permitting them only in certain areas that are both poor and dangerous; there are other burdensome restrictions pertaining to size of establishment, location, signage, and inspection. All six changes are part of a policy aimed at making "sex less noticeable in the course of everyday urban life and more difficult to find for those who want sexual materials."[73]

These trends seem unfortunate to me, as they do to Warner. It is certainly legitimate to try to prevent behavior that offends many members of the community from being inflicted on children, for example; thus there is some legitimacy to laws against "public lewdness" and to zoning regulations for adult materials. (I shall return to this topic in chapter 6.) Yet of course most behavior penalized under the rubric of "public" lewdness takes place in seclusion—a washroom stall being the classic case, and secluded wooded areas. Massachusetts has recently issued a state police policy, to be included in the state police policy manual, stating that sex in public places such as beaches, rest areas, and parks will not be considered illegal if the activity is adequately hidden from view.[74] This is a reasonable policy, which strikes the right balance between the disparate values involved. "This is major," said Captain Robert Bird, a state police spokesman. "The State Police don't want to infringe upon anybody's rights and I think this order will help clarify exactly what those rights are." By contrast, the current New York situation is both unnecessarily restrictive and implicitly discriminatory in its application and impact: for it was clearly implemented in a way that targeted gay men.

As for adult materials, it is one thing to restrict them to a particular zone and still another to restrict them to areas that are (already) undesirable and dangerous. And again, it is plain that at least part of that Giuliani policy targets gay men. The policy is, in effect, a shame punishment: it stigmatizes gay meeting places and gay bookstores, requiring them to hide themselves as if everything they signify is shameful.

These examples show that the familiar distinction between the public and the private frequently offers bad guidance when we think about the regulation of conduct. Space that is "public," in the sense that it is part of publicly owned facilities and/or open to those who wish to enter (many privately owned establishments are "public accommodations in that sense), is not necessarily "public" in the sense that behavior in it necessarily affects nonconsenting parties. "Public" behavior may be quite secluded and free from impact on nonconsenting parties, as the Massachusetts police policy recognizes. I shall return to this issue in chapter 6, arguing that the "public-private" distinction is vague and offers bad guidance; good guidance, by contrast, is offered by John Stuart Mill's distinction between conduct that is "self-regarding," affecting only the interests of the doer and other consenting parties, and conduct that is "other-regarding," affecting the interests of nonconsenting others.

Is any of these policies unconstitutional? The legal issues are much less clear than in *Cleburne* because the regulations are discriminatory in effect while being neutrally written. Moreover, the regulation of clubs and adult stores is generally understood to be an area in which city officials have broad discretion; in that way as well, the case looks quite unlike *Cleburne*, where the plaintiffs wanted a permit for a group home of a type for which permits had frequently been given. For these reasons and others, it seems unlikely that a constitutional challenge to the Giuliani zoning regulations based on *Cleburne*-type arguments would succeed. My argument suggests, however, that the issues involved in the two cases are actually very similar. Both are about the desire of the majority to hide away aspects of human behavior that trouble them. Shame and stigma is what they are both about. And the fact that gay men bore the effects disproportionately, that heterosexual men were not required to the same extent to conceal their sexual behavior (as, really, they never are), makes the issue look like the type of invidious stigmatization of an unpopular group against which I have been arguing throughout this chapter. The gay community will, and should continue to, debate the moral issues involved in the culture surrounding bathhouses and adult establishments. It is one thing, however, to hold that moral controversy is appropriate, quite another to hold that conduct may be regulated by law. It seems a good idea to continue emphasizing issues of shame and stigmatization, and criticizing the effort to regulate consensual gay sex by law.[75]

Same-sex conduct and relationships cause a lot of anxiety in our society. In part, I have argued, the anxiety is occasioned by issues about the body and its boundaries that we discussed in chapters 2 and 3. In part, as I have argued in this chapter, the anxiety is also a more general one about loss of control over cherished patterns of family relationship, including patriarchal control over women. In response to anxiety, people often try to use the law to shield themselves from what they fear. Sodomy laws, discussed in chapter 3, and the various laws dealing with gay life that we have discussed in this section—the Defense of Marriage Act, Colorado's Amendment 2, and a variety of zoning laws for adult establishments—seem inspired by the desire to stigmatize an unpopular group. Law is not going to solve all social problems, and yet it gives an important signal as to who is regarded as fully equal and who is not. I have argued that a decent society will not permit the desire to stigmatize to hijack the legal process and will insist on giving all citizens the equal protection of the laws, no matter how unpopular they, and their practices, are. The desire to stigmatize is not a rational basis for law.

IV. Moral Panics and Crime: The Gang Loitering Law

If Americans fear sexual degeneracy and the breakup of the family, they fear crime even more. Sex and crime, indeed, are the two focal points of contemporary panic about the subversion of core moral values. Cohen's study made clear that moral panic can easily be generated by the thought of young criminals, imagined as physically powerful and amoral. The panic so generated can lead to the adoption of remedies that show deficient respect for individual rights. It seems appropriate, then, to apply these insights to one of the most controversial issues in recent criminal law, namely laws and policies that target juvenile offenders. There are many such tactics, including curfews and informal police policies of detaining and harassing young men on the street. But a particularly interesting and controversial such tactic has been the passage of antiloitering laws targeted at members of inner-city gangs.

In 1992 the city council of Chicago held public hearings to explore problems caused in the city by street gangs involved in criminal activity. Testimony showed that such gangs are involved in a wide range of criminal activities, including drug dealing, drive-by shootings, and vandalism. One problem mentioned by many witnesses was the problem gang members cause by simply loitering in public, as part of their strategy to recruit new members, establish territorial supremacy, and intimidate rival gangs and ordinary members of the community. In response to these concerns, the city council passed the Gang Congregation Ordinance, commonly known as the gang loitering ordinance. The law states that "[w]henever a police officer observes a person whom he reasonably believes to be a criminal street gang member loitering in any public place with one or more other persons, he shall order all such persons to disperse and remove themselves from the area. Any person who does not promptly obey such an order is in violation of this section." "Loiter" is defined as "to remain in any one place with no apparent purpose." The law, and the police guidelines accompanying it, soon became a subject of controversy. In October 1997, the Illinois Supreme Court found the law unconstitutional on the grounds that it is impermissibly vague and an arbitrary restriction on personal liberties.[76] In June 1999, the U.S. Supreme Court upheld this judgment, holding the ordinance unconstitutionally vague and thus in violation of the due process clause of the Fourteenth Amendment.[77]

The primary arguments against the ordinance are fairly obvious. "Loitering" is very vaguely defined. Many people pursuing innocent activities remain in a place "with no apparent purpose"—resting after a run, getting out of the rain, waiting for a friend, and so forth. Indeed, the non-innocent purposes of drug dealing and intimidation would apparently not be covered by the law. The fact that one might be in the proximity of a person concerning whom a policeman has a "reasonable belief" that this person is a gang member is hardly easy to ascertain, since it depends on the subjective state of mind of the police officer. The order to disperse is itself vague, since it does not make clear how far away one must go, or for how long. In short, a criminal statute "must be sufficiently definite so that it gives persons of ordinary intelligence a reasonable opportunity to distinguish between lawful and unlawful conduct," and the gang loitering law fails to pass this test.[78]

The history of loitering laws, moreover, shows us that such vague laws invite arbitrary and discriminatory enforcement. Police officers are given absolute discretion concerning which persons are reasonably believed to be gang members and as to what "no apparent purpose" shall mean.[79] The police guidelines that accompany the ordinance do not solve this problem, for they are rather vague as well and have been inconsistently applied. For example, the guidelines state that gang "membership may not be established solely because an individual is wearing clothing available for sale to the general public." Nonetheless, the officer who arrested plaintiff Jesus Morales testified that his only reason for believing Morales to be a gang member was that he wore black and blue clothing, which are the colors of the Gangster Disciples criminal street gang.

Street gangs raise a very different set of problems from Cohen's Mods and Rockers. They are much more dangerous, and have been demonstrated to cause both more and worse criminal activity. They are a dire threat to life and safety in many inner-city neighborhoods, and they do use loitering to recruit and intimidate. Some of this conduct is already illegal, but one can sympathize with the city's feeling that it needed a further weapon to protect life in inner-city neighborhoods. In that sense, panic about gangs is rational, in a way that panic about the Mods and Rockers never was.

On the other hand, a fear may be both rational and irrational. That is, elements of legitimate fear may become complexly mixed with elements of stigmatization based on race and age. And there is little doubt that the fear of gangs on the part of both inner-city residents and the general public contains elements of panic, along with legitimate fears based on experience and evidence. As a society, we have a guilty history of violence against African-American men, fueled by irrational fears that they are dangerous predators. These irrational fears can become complexly intertwined with legitimate fears, and both can underwrite a general tendency to abuse of power that is a standing danger in all police departments. It is all too easy to imagine police officers targeting idle young African-American men unfairly under cover of such an ordinance. Even officers with completely honorable and nonracist motivations might let their anxieties run away with them when they form a "reasonable belief" that a given young man is a gang member, as the arresting officer in Jesus Morales's case evidently did.

In this situation, knowing what we know about social tendencies to moral panic, and knowing that moral panic often operates on the basis of flimsy stereotypes and stigma, we ought to respond by making very certain that there is clarity about what harmful behavior is being targeted and clear standards that distinguish the harmful behavior from innocent loafing around. When arbitrariness and discriminatory stigmatization threaten, the natural defense would appear to be an emphasis on clarity in the formulation of legal standards and on the protection of individual rights in their implementation. Reflection on shame and moral panics, then, seems to support the wisdom of the Illinois and U.S. Supreme Court decisions.

The decisions have been strongly challenged, however, in the name of communitarian values. Once again, Dan M. Kahan, defender of shame-based penalties, has been a central figure, coauthoring his work, in this instance, with African-American legal scholar Tracey Meares. The Meares-Kahan argument goes as follows. In the 1960s, when law enforcement was highly racist and African-Americans were under-represented in the political process, it was important to focus on an individualistic conception of rights and to uphold these strongly against government intrusion. Now, however, things are different: African-Americans play a large and influential role in politics, and the police are far less racist than they used to be. At the same time, inner-city communities themselves feel threatened by the behavior of gangs. The impetus to pass the gang loitering ordinance came from within the poor and African-American communities most sorely af-fected by the problem of gangs, and these local communities ought to play a role in deciding what rights their members do and do not have. When a community is politically effective, and when it is pre-pared to shoulder within itself the burden that its proposals impose, such a community should be entitled to redefine rights in ways that seem limiting in the perspective of the 1960s. Judges are paternalis-tic if they insist on this older conception of rights when the commu-nities themselves want rights to look different. Meares and Kahan apply their analysis not only to the gang loitering ordinance but also to so-called sweeps—unwarranted police searches for weapons in the housing projects, which are typically opposed by defenders of tradi-tional individual liberties, but supported, they argue, by a majority of the members of the housing projects under discussion.[80]

There are a number of empirical questions to be raised about the Meares-Kahan argument. How broad, for example, is the support for the loitering law in the inner-city communities most affected by it? (Solid evidence is hard to come by, and the relevant aldermen and community leaders were actually quite split.) How much has the racist behavior of the police really changed? Who is it who comes to meetings in the housing projects at which votes on the sweeps are taken?[81]

These questions are important, but let us put them to one side for our purposes in order to focus on a deeper conceptual issue. This issue is, what is the relevant "community"? The Achilles heel of all communitarian arguments is their disregard of this all-important question. No group is fully homogeneous. Even in the case of small religious or ethnic communities that are renowned for their homogeneity of values, that renown is typically based on a false and romanticized notion of the group in question, as Fred Kniss has eloquently shown in his important study of American Mennonite communities.[82] All communities contain differences about norms and values, and also differences of power. Frequently these two types of difference are connected: what gets to parade as the "values" of the "group" are, frequently, the values of the group's most dominant members. Thus, for example, most of what we think we know about the "values" of most ethnic and religious groups in history really represents the views of male members of those groups, rather than the views of women, which may be impossible to recover from the silence of history. Other dissident and relatively powerless groups—the young, the elderly, those who hold unpopular religious, political, or moral views—may not win recognition as part of what the "group" stands for. Differences of power also affect who is permitted to count as a group member and who is not. Groups frequently define their boundaries in ways that stigmatize and exclude; thus, rather than acknowledging the presence of a dissident or minority subgroup, they may simply refuse to recognize these people as members of their body at all.[83]

Communitarians, moreover, typically focus on groups that are united by ethnicity, location, or the history of a common culture or language. There are, however, other groups to consider: groups united, for example, by shared tastes or occupations, by shared problems, by a shared history of oppression. In this sense, women are a group, and share many common interests all over the world, though one will not find communitarians thinking of women as one of the "communities" whose values ought to be upheld. Other dispersed groups include the elderly, members of sexual minorities, children, adolescents, music lovers, defenders of the rights of animals, lovers of nature. All these people have common interests and values, but they are not counted as "communities" for purposes of arguments like those of Meares and Kahan.

These conceptual questions cause problems for the Meares-Kahan argument about the gang loitering ordinance and the sweeps. Throughout their argument there is much unclarity even about what they think the relevant community is: all African-Americans in Chicago? Poor inner-city African-Americans? All poor inner-city people?[84] Whatever the relevant characterization is, however, there is clear evidence of internal disagreement about the merits of the ordinance. More African-American aldermen voted against the ordinance than for it; the African-American press was divided; many prominent African-American leaders harshly criticized the measure. Most pertinently, it may be presumed (though nobody seems to have thought to ask them) that adolescent African-American men, whether gang members or not, would strongly oppose an ordinance that gives the police license to harass and disperse them. So what we seem to be dealing with, under the attractive language of "burden sharing," is a situation in which some adult members of the African-American community inflict a burden on other members. Clearly the aldermen and other community leaders who support the policy will not be bearing its burdens, which will be borne almost exclusively by adolescent males. If Meares and Kahan should reply by saying that these adolescents aren't really members of the group because the group only includes those who suffer from the criminal behavior of gangs, then they are conceding that their burden-sharing argument is mistaken: those who bear the burden of the policy are not members of the same group that supports it.

The sweeps raise the same issues in an even more troubling way. For the group consenting to the burden sharing was the group of people who showed up at a meeting in the projects to discuss the issue. As anyone who lives in a housing project, condominium community, coop apartment building, or other group dwelling knows, people who show up for meetings are not necessarily representative of all the relevant types and opinions that exist. People who are likely not to be present are not only the criminal elements such a policy targets; they also include people who work at night, people who work two jobs, people with child-care responsibilities, people who don't like meetings, young people who prefer to go on a date, people who don't like the people who usually show up at meetings.

Again, the people who are likely to bear the burden of the policy are extremely unlikely to be the same ones who support it. Indeed the whole idea of the sweeps presupposes the existence of a nonconsenting minority: for a search is always legal if the person gives consent, so the new contribution of the proposed policy is to inflict searches on those who do not consent. Some of the nonconsenting may have something to hide; others may just like to walk around home in their pajamas out of the gaze of the police officer.

Indeed, both the sweeps and the gang loitering law create two tiers of people with two tiers of rights. Those who don't live in the inner city, whether they are good people or bad people, have the old rights that Meares and Kahan calls "1960s-style" rights: rights against arbitrary arrest, rights against unwarranted search and seizure. Those who happen to live in the inner city, and in the projects, have weaker and fewer rights: they may be harassed by the police because they happen to stand next to the wrong person; their dwelling may be invaded with no cause in the middle of the night.

Meares and Kahan rely on the premise that our society has become more fair-minded and less prone to harass people on arbitrary and racially biased grounds. This is where our analysis of shame and stigma enters the picture. We can, of course, point to particular evidence that the police are not as well behaved as this argument suggests: the use of racial profiling in traffic arrests is a clear example. More deeply, though, our argument suggests that "normals" are never likely to behave reliably toward minorities, because there is something deep in the logic of human psychology that drives stigmatizing behavior and the moral panics to which it is so closely linked. I have suggested, moreover, that issues of narcissistic aggression are particularly acute in today's America because of our culture's peculiar attachment to ideas of control and (especially male) invulnerability. These problems don't go away quickly, to the extent that they go away at all. Thus the rejection of 1960s-style rights seems premature. We can and should deal sternly with criminal behavior. But we have the resources to do this through laws already in place, including laws against harassment and intimidation. We need not sweep so broadly as to take in innocents who may simply want to loaf around, whether on the streets or in their own dwelling.

V. Mill's Conclusion
by Another Route

Considerations of stigma and moral panic have led us, by a slightly different route, to a conclusion that Mill long ago defended in *On Liberty*. The dignity and freedom of the individual person need constant and vigilant protection against the tyranny of majorities who define their own ways of doing things as right and normal, and who then set about inflicting damage on others. What Meares and Kahan call 1960s-style rights are always a good idea, as our constitutional tradition has wisely seen, because people have a tendency to band together in groups and to tyrannize over vulnerable minorities. What our analysis in terms of shame and stigma has added is a deeper account of why we should expect this to be a permanent feature of most or all human societies.

Mill simply observes the operations of stigma in England. He argued well for his conclusions, up to a point, but he did not have a sufficiently detailed or deep psychological understanding of the forces that lead to stigmatization and shaming. He therefore was forced to rest much of his argument on other considerations, which were in many ways less persuasive, as I shall argue in chapter 7. We have now advanced an account—sociological on one plane (Goffman, Cohen), psychological on another (Winnicott, Morrison)—that will help us defend Mill's policies in the face of opposition from optimistic communitarians who believe that the problems Mill talked about have gone away.

The first and most essential antidote to the operation of stigma is a firm insistence on individual-liberty rights and a firm guarantee to all citizens of the equal protection of the laws. The law should offer strong protections to individuals against the arbitrary intrusions, both of state power and of social pressures to conform. Thinking about the dynamics of group narcissism and shaming help us to see why the individual is always at risk in society, and therefore why vigilant protection for Millian liberties and for the equal dignity of all citizens is so important. So far, however, I have advocated only a minimal policy of refusal: the law should not use shaming as a part of the public system of punishment, and we should refuse to make, or invalidate if made, laws whose primary or only purpose is to inflict stigma on vulnerable minorities. These are essentials of a decent society, but they are far from sufficient. In chapter 6 we must therefore consider more positive remedies.

Chapter 6

Protecting Citizens from Shame

By necessaries I understand, not only the commodities which are indispensably necessary for the support of life, but whatever the custom of the country renders it indecent for creditable people . . . to be without. A linen shirt, for example, is, strictly speaking, not a necessary of life. The Greeks and Romans lived, I suppose, very comfortably, though they had no linen. But in the present times, through the greatest part of Europe, a creditable day-labourer would be ashamed to appear in publick without a linen shirt. . . . Custom, in the same manner, has rendered leather shoes a necessary of life in England. The poorest creditable person of either sex would be ashamed to appear in publick without them.

—Adam Smith, *The Wealth of Nations*, V.ii.k.3

How hard and humiliating it is to bear the name of an unemployed man. When I go out, I cast down my eyes because I feel myself wholly inferior. When I go along the street, it seems to me that I can't be compared with an average citizen, that everybody is pointing at me with his finger. I instinctively avoid meeting anyone.

—Quoted in Goffman, *Stigma*[1]

No courts have held or even darkly hinted that a blind man may rise in the morning, help get the children off to school, bid his wife goodby, and proceed along the streets and bus lines to his daily work, without dog, cane, or guide, if such is his habit or preference, now and then brushing a tree or kicking a curb, but, notwithstanding, proceeding with firm step and sure air, knowing that he is part of the public for whom the streets are built and maintained in reasonable safety, by the help of his taxes, and that he shares with others this part of the world in which he, too, has a right to live.

—Jacobus tenBroek, "The Right to Live in the World: The Disabled and the Law of Torts"[2]

I. Creating a Facilitating Environment

So far, I have argued that the law must refuse to take part in active stigmatizing of vulnerable people and groups. But of course a decent society needs to go further, finding ways to protect the dignity of its members against shame and stigma through law. This is such a fundamental goal of any decent society that it might lead us in many different directions. Laws protecting the freedom of religion and conscience; laws protecting citizens against arbitary search and seizure (touched upon in chapter 5); laws against cruel and degrading punishments (partially treated in chapter 5); laws against the sexual harassment of women in the workplace; laws against rape, together with enforcement procedures that show respect for women's dignity; laws against libel and slander—all these, and many more, play a role in making a society the sort of place that protects human dignity, creating a "facilitating environment" in which citizens can live lives free from shame and stigma. In this chapter I shall consider only a sampling of the pertinent issues. First, I shall briefly address the role of a society's system of social welfare in providing the opportunity for a shame-free life with others. Second, I shall turn to the area of antidiscrimination law and law against crimes based on hatred and bias. Third, I shall consider some aspects of the legal protection of personal privacy. And finally, I shall turn to a central locus of stigma in contemporary American society, disability, and to some recent legal reforms that attempt to protect citizens with disabilities from shame.

II. Shame and a Decent
Living-Standard

One of the most stigmatized life-conditions, in all societies, is poverty. The poor are routinely shunned and shamed, treated as idle, vicious, of low worth. Perhaps this is especially likely to be true in America, where it is widely believed that poverty is evidence of laziness or lack of will power. Goffman's research reminds us that this general stigmatization of poverty is compounded if the poor person is unemployed, or has little education. And stigma runs in the family. As soon as children go to school, their wealth or poverty is marked in countless ways, by their clothing, the food in their lunch boxes, their accents, the homes to which they bring friends after school. As Adam Smith cogently argued, poverty has an absolute aspect: one may lack the necessities of life, such as food, shelter, healthcare. But it also has a comparative and social aspect: one may, while being adequately nourished and sheltered, lack items that are part of the social definition of a decent living-standard in one's society, such as a linen shirt and leather shoes in Smith's society, a personal computer, perhaps, in our own.

Although this vast topic can at most be mentioned in the present book, not to mention it would be a failing, since the failure to address it adequately is perhaps the major cause of shame and stigma in today's America.

There are many reasons for societies to concern themselves with securing a decent living-standard for all citizens, since life, health, educational opportunity, meaningful work, and a decent opportunity to develop one's mental faculties all have intrinsic importance. I address these questions elsewhere, arguing that a minimally just and decent society would provide all its citizens with a minimum threshold amount of certain key opportunities or "capabilities." For the purposes of my argument in this chapter, however, I shall focus on just one of my list of capabilities: "Having the social bases of self-respect and nonhumiliation; being able to be treated as a dignified being whose worth is equal to that of others."[3] How is this capability to be secured, and what role, in securing it, must be played by general policies in the area of social and economic entitlements?

When children grow up without adequate nutrition, health care, or shelter, the minimum level of this capability has not been secured. These are necessities of life in every society. In America today, several further requirements play the role of Smith's linen shirt: they are necessary in order to take one's place in society without stigma. Among these requirements, particularly important is free and compulsory primary and secondary education, plus access on a basis of equal opportunity to higher education. So too, in our society, is employment—at least for adult males. Although some societies (for example ancient Greece) have ranked the unemployed above the employed, thinking it base to work for a living, our society has the reaction that Goffman's example depicts: the unemployed feel shame in their own eyes, and are forced to hide from the shaming gaze of others.[4]

Stigma also has a more localized comparative aspect: one may be stigmatized in a particular school, for example, simply for not having the same expensive clothes that the rich and popular students in that school have.[5] For the purposes of my argument here, however, I shall leave the upper levels of comparative shame to one side, focusing on the level of support that Smith is talking about: the minimum needed to appear in public without shame, as a citizen whose worth is equal to that of others.

Growing economic and educational inequalities in the United States contribute to a situation in which many Americans live stigmatized lives for reasons of poverty alone. Aspects of their poverty include lack of suitable health care, lack of adequate educational opportunity, unemployment, and lack of suitable housing. Indeed, the challenge of creating low-cost housing that does not stigmatize is a huge and fascinating topic, which could easily occupy an entire book on its own. Most cities and towns in America have not adequately met that challenge. Barbara Ehrenreich's *Nickel and Dimed,* to which I have referred in chapter 5, shows that many poor workers are forced to pay for sleazy and stigmatizing housing, such as cheap motel rooms, simply because they are unable to come up with a deposit for a rental.[6] Meanwhile, public housing projects that once were intended to give adequate and respectable shelter to poor residents now stigmatize all those who live in them.[7] Access to shame-free housing is among the major challenges our society must face in the next decades.

The connection between human dignity and some degree of public support for basic needs has been made in quite a few modern constitutional traditions, including those of South Africa and India. India, for example, has understood the constitutional requirement that no citizen may be deprived of life or liberty without due process (their analogue of our Fourteenth Amendment) to mean not mere life, but life with human dignity; removing the belongings of the homeless has been held to violate this constitutional requirement. South Africa has gone further, recognizing affirmative rights to decent housing in severe cases. Both have constitutionalized as a fundamental right the right to free and suitable primary and secondary education. More generally, the international human rights movement has now recognized that social and economic rights are human rights comparable in importance to political and civil rights. Indeed, the very distinction between the two groups of rights probably cannot be maintained, for political and civil rights have necessary social and economic preconditions. A person who is in a bad way through lack of nutrition or health care cannot participate as an equal in politics. An illiterate person is unlikely to be able to go to the police or to the courts for enforcement of other political and civil rights.

The idea that human dignity has economic requirements is not alien to the tradition of thought in the United States. Franklin Delano Roosevelt's "Second Bill of Rights" focused on the provision to all citizens of essential aspects of material well-being, as did Lyndon Johnson's "Great Society."[8] In the Johnson era, moreover, courts were beginning to take the line that some of these rights enjoyed constitutional protection. In 1970, Justice William Brennan wrote a memorable opinion in *Goldberg v. Kelly*, a case that established that welfare rights could not be abridged without a hearing:[9]

> From its founding the Nation's basic commitment has been to foster the dignity and well-being of all persons within its borders. We have come to recognize that forces not within the control of the poor contribute to their poverty. . . . Welfare, by meeting the basic demands of subsistence, can help bring within the reach of the poor the same opportunities that are available to others to participate meaningfully in the life of the community. . . . Public assistance, then, is not mere charity, but a means to "promote the general Welfare, and secure the Blessings of Liberty to ourselves and our Posterity."[10]

It is significant that Brennan makes his argument with reference to the idea of human dignity as well as that of well-being. He recognizes that poverty is not just deprivation, but also degradation. In this period, it seemed possible that the Supreme Court would gradually move in the direction of recognizing that our Constitution protects a range of economic rights for the poor.[11] Justice Brennan clearly was interested in giving constitutional protection to at least some of these entitlements, which were, of course, widely, if unevenly, protected by popularly supported legislation.[12]

The move to full constitutional recognition of economic entitlements as inherent in the idea of human dignity did not take place. The "Reagan Revolution" changed the direction of constitutional jurisprudence. Meanwhile, legislative protection of welfare rights has also been gradually rolled back. It is certainly legitimate, and even desirable, for states to experiment with different welfare strategies, but something more troubling is currently in the air, a backing away from the "basic commitment" to dignity and well-being that Brennan finds, plausibly, at the heart of our traditions. Unlike Brennan, we seem to have come to the conclusion that the poor cause their poverty.[13]

Unemployment, growing at the time of this writing, is a problem closely linked to but distinct from poverty. Some societies that have an ample social safety net cannot guarantee full employment. (This is true, for example, of Finland, where the economy does well, but the available employment—for example, in the telephone-technology sector—is not labor-intensive.) Exactly how large a problem this is depends to some degree on the social context: if unemployment is not stigmatized, unemployed men and women can use the social benefits they have to continue their education and still function as fully equal citizens. In most modern societies, however, unemployment is stigmatized. So too, moreover, are many varieties of employment open to poor people, such as domestic service and many other types of low-income employment. Even when a type of employment is not stigmatized as such, as Ehrenreich's book makes clear, it may involve debasing and dehumanizing treatment, together with dangers to health and well-being that undermine generally the worker's attempt to live a life with human dignity. So the provision of employment and the humanization of work are also issues of the greatest urgency for any society that wants to call itself a decent one.

As I have said, these issues are too vast for policy-oriented treatment in this book, but to omit them would be absurd. It would be equally absurd to omit the question of our own responsibility, as a rich nation, to the poor in other nations. Countless people all over the world suffer from hunger, malnutrition, lack of education, and lack of medical care when there would be a great deal that the United States, and its wealthy corporations, could do to relieve that misery. The present book has approached the issue of shame and stigma with a domestic focus, largely because of its legal emphasis. But the question of justice across national boundaries, a major topic of my work elsewhere, cannot fail to be mentioned when we consider how our public policy can protect human beings from stigmatized lives.

It will be said that it is absurd to think about the poor in other nations when we do not do enough for our own citizens. But it seems counterproductive to address the problems in a lexical order, trying to produce a perfect society internally before dealing at all with our responsibilities to our fellow world citizens. American corporations are doing business daily in other nations in a way that greatly affects well-being, opportunity, and access to medical care. It would be grossly culpable to fail to address the global AIDS crisis, for example, a major cause of stigmatized lives, until we had perfect health care in our own nation. The two problems are in large measure independent, and it is not the case that money spent (for example, by pharmaceutical companies) to address the former will be deducted from the latter. Moreover, other nations, not as prosperous as our own, are managing to devote a good deal more of their budget to foreign aid than we are without failing to address domestic problems of inequality. All these questions need to be on the table together, as we think about a world in which the goal ought to be that all people have the opportunity to lead lives with human dignity.

III. Antidiscrimination, Hate Crimes

Let us now return, however, to the more narrowly demarcated issues on which we have been focusing: how might we use specific types of legal change to protect vulnerable minorities from stigma? In chapter 5, I argued that we should not enact, and should invalidate if enacted, laws whose primary purpose or effect is the stigmatization of unpopular minorities. How much further should the social commitment to protect such groups extend? This is itself a vast question, raising complex issues, both legal and moral, that lie beyond the limits of the present book. Let me, then, show the direction in which my argument takes us by returning to the two issues that concerned us in chapter 5: the protection of suspected lawbreakers from the invasion of their individual rights, and the protection of gays and lesbians from shame.

About the first of these two issues, raised in my discussion of loitering laws in chapter 5, I have little to add to my defense, in that chapter, of the familiar battery of rights of criminal defendants. As I mentioned in that discussion, criminals and suspected criminals have slowly won a range of protections against the abuse of police power that should not be eroded, whether by new laws like the Chicago loitering law or by the slow undermining of guarantees such as the *Miranda* warning, the right to effective assistance of counsel, and so forth. Strong insistence on these protections is a crucial way to protect racial minorities from the damage that social stigma inflicts, linking race with criminal behavior.

An issue of intense current public concern in this area is racial profiling. Of course law enforcement officers use profiling in many ways when searching for criminals: for example, a serial killer's modus operandi is profiled by psychological experts in order to narrow the segment of the population within which police will search. That sort of profiling is unobjectionable, because it begins from a committed crime and works backward. Far more troubling is a kind of profiling that precedes crime, or at least discovered crime, using other traits as proxies for (alleged) criminal intent or activity. There may be some instances in which national-security interests strongly support these policies. Thus, there are at least some cogent arguments supporting the recent profiling of Arab and Arab-American men, given the shortage of time and money for comprehensive airport searches, et cetera. Even then, this policy unfairly stigmatizes all members of a group, and probably encourages police and airport-security officers to behave badly toward these people, sending the message that they are not fully equal citizens (or visitors). So I am opposed to profiling even in such cases. Far more clearly, it is both intrinsically objectionable and unwise policy to use race as a proxy for crime, as when traffic stops and searches of vehicles are triggered by the race of the suspect. No doubt in order to use resources wisely police must engage in some types of profiling in searching for drugs. Searches of the vehicles of elderly motorists, for example, are likely to prove wasteful. Profiling by age and by type of vehicle probably does not raise a serious issue of fairness. But when profiling tracks existing social stigma, a grave issue of fairness is raised.

The stigmatizing of African-American men as criminals is one of the ugliest and most invidious aspects of American racism, closely linked to the racially skewed disenfranchisement of convicted felons that I discussed in chapter 5. Leading African-American intellectuals, from Cornel West to Brent Staples, have written eloquently about the pain and isolation inflicted by society's immediate perception of the black man as criminal, as when West, dressed in a suit and standing on Park Avenue, could not get a taxi to pick him up. Historically, this stigmatization was linked with gross harms: with lynching, unfair trials, discrimination in employment. If our society wants to pursue a course of racial reconciliation, as seems both just and prudent, racial profiling is a very stupid policy, even if it were efficient in terms of police resources, which has not been convincingly demonstrated by the evidence.[14] Profiling is probably also intrinsically unfair, since it denies people an important sort of equality before the law on grounds of race.

Let us now consider the protection of gays and lesbians from public stigma. In considering this issue, our society has recently turned to two remedies: antidiscrimination laws and hate crimes laws. In these two areas, the issue confronting a liberal society is how to safeguard the vulnerable without infringing on the expressive rights of those who hold views that offend liberals. Communitarians of various types can favor laws that express a commitment to protecting the vulnerable without encountering a countervailing tug, to the extent that they lack the liberal's deep commitment to the liberty of the individual, and, in particular, to a range of liberties in the area of thought, speech, and expression. The liberal, by contrast, is committed to protecting those who say something hate-filled as well as those who are targeted by hate—within certain limits.

Nobody is really an absolutist about free speech. There is broad agreement about criminalizing many forms of speech, such as blackmail, threats, perjury, bribery, unlicensed medical advice, misleading advertising. In a gray area is most commercial speech and much artistic speech: there is a good deal of debate about whether and when these forms of speech are covered by the protection of the First Amendment. Even concerning political speech our society has not always agreed in giving it broad First Amendment protection. Only as recently as 1918, when Eugene Debs went to jail for urging people to refuse military service in World War I, the Supreme Court held that the political speech of dissidents during wartime was not protected by the First Amendment. By now, we have come to a different view: such speech is paradigmatic of what the First Amendment is taken to protect. However much people differ about the precise account of First Amendment liberties and their rationale, however much they differ about the precise protections to be afforded to various types of commercial and artistic speech, there is little disagreement that objectionable and unpopular political speech lies at the very core of what the First Amendment protects. Liberals today, however, are likely to hold that strong First Amendment protections apply very broadly—to all political speech and much artistic speech, at any rate. Liberals also ascribe considerable importance to freedom of association, which may also be at issue in dealing with discrimination, when claims of nondiscrimination clash with the wish of a club or group to exclude individuals whose practices or views it does not like.

With respect to these two important values, free speech and freedom of association, nondiscrimination laws seem unproblematic, at least up to a point. To protect gays and lesbians against discrimination in employment and public housing, in ways similar to the protections our country has already offered to racial minorities and women, does not, as such, prevent the expression of racist, or sexist, or homophobic political opinions. Thus the Employment Discrimination Act introduced by Senator Edward Kennedy at the same time that the Defense of Marriage Act was debated, which would have added sexual orientation to the list of prohibited grounds of discrimination, seems a logical and indeed a required step, and it is a national scandal that this law has still not been passed some years later.

Nondiscrimination is a very complex issue, and there will continue to be disputed zones, particularly in the area of religion: how far should religions be exempt from general prohibitions on discrimination on grounds of race, sex, or sexual orientation? (The Employment Discrimination Act exempted religious organizations and educational institutions controlled by them, small businesses, private-membership clubs, and the military. Religious exemptions were also allowed in Denver's nondiscrimination law, challenged by Colorado's Amendment 2.) As a country we have not fully sorted out the issue of exemptions from nondiscrimination laws; our policies are not consistent. (For example, Bob Jones University lost its tax-exempt status for its policy opposing interracial dating, but religious universities that have statutory requirements that the university president be a male member of a particular religious order retain their tax exemptions.) Where sexual orientation is concerned, it is clear that our public debate is still at a much more primitive level than it is in the case of race and gender. We have not even resolved such obvious questions as whether private landlords can exclude gay tenants because of their sexual orientation, much less questions about how far religious institutions would be permitted to discriminate in hiring and benefits on such grounds.

The recent Supreme Court case regarding the Boy Scouts showed clearly the deep tension between the liberal value of freedom of association and the liberal value of nondiscrimination.[15] In this instance, freedom of association won out, although, in part, because the Boy Scouts were understood to be a private club, rather than a public accommodation, perhaps a mistaken judgment. These remain difficult areas and we will need to grapple with them. On the whole, however, it seems clear that a general policy of nondiscrimination on the basis of sexual orientation in employment and public accommodation, at least, is morally required (perhaps constitutionally required)[16] by the very notion of equal protection, and that lesbians and gays should get the same types of protection that are currently extended to racial minorities, women, and people with disabilities.[17]

Discrimination against gays and lesbians has strong links to discrimination against women, as I argued in chapter 5. It also has close links to gender-based discrimination, a topic too little explored. People may be stigmatized and discriminated against for gender-deviant behavior: a woman who dresses in too "manly" a way, a man who is too "effeminate." One persistent problem in our legal culture is precisely how to deal with discrimination that, while evidently based on gender stereotypes, looks different from discrimination based upon sex all by itself. It seems clear that this type of discrimination is somehow connected to the two other types of discrimination. To fire a man because he acts in a feminine way is to denigrate female attributes, as well as, possibly, to impugn his sexual orientation. To tell a woman to behave in a more feminine way is to reify aspects of gender in a way that seems connected to the inferior and denigrated status of women, although the connection remains elusive. Finally, to tell a woman to behave in a more masculine way is also to signal that only the traits of the dominant are valuable—it is rather like telling an African-American employee to behave in a more "white" manner.[18]

There is something wrong with all these demands where not justified by a job-related necessity. So much is widely acknowledged, as we can see from the well-known case *Price Waterhouse v. Hopkins,* in which the Supreme Court held that it was impermissible sex stereotyping to advise a female candidate for an accounting partnership to walk and dress "more femininely."[19] What remains disputed is precisely how far these forms of discrimination are covered under existing laws, and whether a new law governing discrimination on the basis of gender is needed to address them. In an excellent recent analysis, legal scholar Mary Anne Case argues that in fact all are covered by existing law. The requirement that employees conform their gender to their sex merely for reasons of conformity is "already outlawed by the plain language of Title VII as well as by the prohibitions on sex stereotyping outlined by the Supreme Court. It is impermissible disparate treatment."[20] So too, she argues, is "categorical" discrimination on the basis of gendered characteristics: the requirement, for example, that all workers in a given job, regardless of sex, display conventionally masculine traits.

Another problem closely related to discrimination on the basis of sexual orientation is a problem that Goffman calls "covering," and recently discussed in a detailed legal article by Kenji Yoshino.[21] Even when gays and lesbians are hired with knowledge of their sexual orientation, they may face a subtle battery of demands not to "flaunt" their orientation. These demands are usually asymmetric to similar demands made of heterosexuals, and are analogous to demands sometimes informally made of African-Americans that they imitate the behavior of the dominant race, playing down traits that are linked in the popular mind with their race. These demands are aspects of stigma: they are enforced upon a vulnerable group in a way that inflicts shame. A lesbian mother may find that she cannot mention her partner, or bring her to school functions, without jeopardizing her child's standing in school, even though the school knows that she is lesbian. A gay man, widely known to be gay, can attain a high position, but at the price of never bringing his partner to public functions or alluding to him as a partner. Goffman compares such cases to the way in which blind people learn to wear dark glasses, because they know that people don't want to look at their eyes.[22] Clearly not all forms of insensitivity and callousness should be regulated by law, but if employment is really conditional on this sort of "covering," asymmetrically applied to gays and not to "straights," that is a form of discrimination that probably should be regulated by antidiscrimination law.

In chapter 5 I analyzed a fund-raising letter that expressed anxiety about the growing popularity of laws against hate-based crimes, which mandate enhanced penalties for crimes based on racial bias, gender bias, or, in some cases, bias as to sexual orientation. Such laws raise complicated issues. On the one hand, there is no doubt that gays and lesbians urgently need protection from violence, which menaces them continually. [23] Police are often reluctant to enforce the laws that exist; all too often, they share the homophobic sentiments of the perpetrators of violence. On the other hand, one might argue that treating a hate crime based on race or sex or sexual orientation more severely than a similar crime motivated, say, by hatred of one's brother is a way of penalizing unpopular political opinions. The only difference between the two acts is the nature of the motivation, and the significant difference in the motivation, in this case, is that a political opinion is part of it.[24]

I am not convinced by this retort. In all kinds of ways, the law already expresses a commitment to protecting vulnerable citizens and to penalizing especially severely those who prey on the vulnerable. Blackmailers, for example, get a higher sentence under the Federal Sentencing Guidelines if they prey on an "unusually vulnerable victim." In a very interesting opinion, Judge Richard Posner argued forcefully that gay men in America are in that category.[25] The behavior of a person who commits an assault or a homicide motivated by hatred of a vulnerable group is relevantly similar: he chooses to prey, in a criminal manner, on an unusually vulnerable type of victim. A hate crimes statute would simply arrange that he, like the blackmailer under the federal guidelines, would receive an upward departure in sentencing.

Nor, I think, should we accept the contention that the penalized motivation is protected political speech. The wish to eradicate someone from the earth does have a cognitive content, to be sure: that this person ought not to exist, or ought to suffer pain. We should not evade the issue by denying that emotions can and do have cognitive content. But there is a huge difference between a person who writes a pamphlet saying that gays ought to suffer, or even that hate crimes should not be curbed (as in the letter I received), and a person who goes out and perpetrates such an offense. This difference informs the cognitive content of the two people's emotional motivations. The person who wrote my fund-raising letter expresses hatred, but there is no evidence of criminal intent. So that person's speech is protected speech, and there is nothing else to penalize. The perpetrator of a hate crime has, in addition to his political opinions, a criminal intent, a specific type of hate-based mens rea, intrinsically directed toward conduct, that goes well beyond the content of the protected opinions expressed in the pamphlet. What is being penalized is a specific type of criminal intent, not just a specific type of opinion. Using similar reasoning, the U.S. Supreme Court has upheld enhanced penalties for hate crimes.[26]

To be sure, this distinction is not, and should not be, easy to make. Many nations do regulate hate speech that is clearly political: in Germany, for example, one may not circulate anti-Semitic materials, and political parties organized along hate-based lines are illegal. Given Germany's past, it seems sensible for it to adopt a somewhat more restrictive attitude to political speech than the United States has (only recently) seen fit to adopt. Even Germany, however, does not propose to criminalize the writing of anti-Semitic pamphlets; it is enough to prevent them from circulating. We can agree, then, that a necessary condition of criminal conviction is a criminal act, understood in a traditional way. What the proponent of hate crimes laws asks is that the intent to harm a person as a member of a stigmatized group be singled out and treated more severely than the intent to harm a person for money, or jealousy, or a range of other motives. This demand does not seem to penalize speech in an unacceptable way.

One might ask what hate crimes laws actually accomplish. If the real problem is underenforcement of current laws, such an objector might say, it is not clear that making the laws tougher is the right way to solve the problem. That objection, of course, is very different from the free-speech criticism I have just rejected. But I think that it probably fails as well. We cannot tell until we experiment with such laws, but it seems to me that attaching especially severe penalties to hate crimes is likely to prove an effective deterrent. The criminals who prey on gays and lesbians are not, on the whole, a bunch of committed desperadoes who would go to their death for their principled opposition to the "gay agenda." As Gary David Comstock showed in his comprehensive study of antigay violence, they are for the most part young male troublemakers who don't have a particular political aim, but just want to beat up on someone whom the police probably won't protect.[27] They choose gays because they are gay, and commit hate crimes in that sense, but they aren't deeply committed to eradicating gays, and they probably would go do something else—many of them, at least—if they got the signal that this is something society was going to take really seriously. Moreover, a social statement that these offenses are intolerable in our society has wider consequences: it is a way of affirming the equal dignity of gay and lesbian citizens, and the commitment to rendering them fully equal under the law. To make that statement, in the wake of our long indifference to such crimes, seems the decent thing to do.

IV. Shame and Personal Privacy

Shame causes hiding; it is also a way in which people hide aspects of their humanity from themselves. In shaming others, people often, I have argued, project onto vulnerable people and groups the demand that they conceal something about themselves that occasions shame for the shamer. Thus, people's insecurity about sex and the lack of control involved in sex leads them to constitute themselves as a dominant group of sexual "normals," and to ask sexual minorities to conceal themselves. People's insecurity about bodily vulnerability leads them to demand that "the disabled" hide from the public gaze.

My argument so far has emphasized the importance, for a liberal society, of resisting these demands. People whose actions are threatening only in the sense that they occasion anxiety in the dominant group should not be punished by being hidden away. That type of scapegoating, in which some vulnerable minority bears the burden of the fears of the majority, is an unacceptable form of discrimination. Thus my argument has stressed the importance of protecting the right of minorities who are doing no harm to others to inhabit the public world alongside others. In my next section, discussing the disabled, I shall take this argument further.

At the same time, however, my argument suggests that we need to protect the spaces within which people explore and confront aspects of their humanity that are problematic and may occasion shame, whether to themselves or to others. I have suggested that imagination and fantasy, often in connection with art and literature, are ways in which people may learn to explore the problematic aspects of their humanity without undue anxiety, thus developing a richer sense of themselves. This self-exploration enhances the ability to imagine the experiences of others; both abilities are crucial not only to good personal relationships, but also to the functioning of a healthy liberal society.

All this suggests that societies need to protect the spaces within which people imagine and explore themselves, even when their imaginings are perceived as shameful, whether by themselves or by others.[28] Thus my argument also suggests the importance of giving legal protection to areas of personal privacy, and in particular to privacy for activities and imaginings that some may regard as shameful.

Thus, although in chapter 5 I criticized certain ways in which vulnerable groups are forced to hide—and thus criticized a particular way of using the familiar public-private distinction, namely, one that forces unpopular people underground—it is now necessary to turn to the other side of the issue: a liberal society must also provide citizens with certain protected spaces within which they can hide from the shaming gaze of others if they choose to do so. Social groups will continue to inflict shame on others with or without the cooperation of the law, so the law needs to do more than simply refuse to join in this behavior. It should actively protect the individual who may want a place of retreat from the shame that inevitably will continue to attach to unusual people and behavior.

This is a vast topic. It has implications for the law of the press, the law of slander and defamation, the law of cyberspace, limits to surveillance by law enforcement agencies, the freedom of artistic expression, and much else. It seems best, in the context of the present argument, to approach it somewhat abstractly, considering a proposal that has recently been made by philosopher Thomas Nagel.

In an extremely interesting article entitled "Concealment and Exposure," Nagel speaks, in ways that are congenial to my argument, of the importance, for most people, of having spaces within which to pursue fantasies that others may find shameful or repulsive. Much sexual behavior, he plausibly argues, is bound up with such fantasies. Nagel then defends certain strict limits to intrusion on personal privacy by others, calling this one face of the public-private distinction. But this distinction, he then argues, has another "face": it is the importance of keeping disruptive material behind concealing barriers.

The public-private boundary faces in two directions—keeping disruptive material out of the public arena and protecting private life from the crippling effects of the external gaze. . . . It is the other face of the coin. The public-private boundary keeps the public domain free of disruptive material; but it also keeps the private domain free of insupportable controls. The more we are subjected to public inspection and asked to expose our inner lives, the more the resources available to us in leading those lives will be constrained by the collective norms of the common milieu.[29]

Nagel explicitly endorses the idea of the "normal" as a construction through which we protect ourselves from disruption. Thus he endorses an asymmetry in the way in which the public-private boundary is likely to operate: as the price we (all) pay for (all) getting protection for our private fantasies, when we want to protect and conceal those, we must support a regime that forces *some* (the "abnormals") to conceal themselves from public view, even when they don't want to conceal themselves.

One feels that something has gone wrong at this point. Two crucial issues have been lost from view: the issue of liberty of choice and that of equality. The appearance of symmetry that Nagel creates by his use of the metaphor of the two "faces" is illusory. The public-private boundary does not function symmetrically on both sides because it protects "normals" both in their choice to conceal and in their choice to make public, whereas "abnormals" are required to conceal.[30] Thus "normals" may choose to conceal their kisses, or they may kiss in the public street. "Abnormals," beginning from an unequal social position, are protected only when they conceal themselves, even if they would quite like to kiss in the public street. Nagel seems to be saying that "normals" just can't take too much disruption, so the price our society will have to pay for a system of personal liberty is a set of unequal demands for concealment applied to vulnerable minorities.

If this were advanced as a predictive claim, we would test it by looking to history. I believe that we would find it false. Not too long ago, women were forced to hide their sexuality behind clothing that concealed legs and sometimes arms, and that surrounded the lower body with a large screen of fabric. They were also forced to conduct themselves in ways that dissimulated desires they had and activities that they performed or at least wanted. Society told women: we can't tolerate too much disruption. We can't stand to have those legs in the world, and so we make you pretend that you don't have legs. As art historian Anne Hollander comments, the customary norm of female dress prior to the twentieth century

> corresponds to one very tenacious myth about women, the same one that gave rise to the image of the mermaid, the perniciously divided female monster. . . . Her voice and face, her bosom and hair, her neck and arms are all entrancing, offering only what is benign among the pleasures afforded by women . . . but it is a trap. Below, under the foam, the swirling waves of lovely skirt, her hidden body repels, its shapeliness armed in scaly refusal, its oceanic interior stinking of uncleanness.
>
> It is really no wonder that women seeking a definitive costume in which to enact their definitive escape from such mythology should choose trousers.[31]

Now women may show their legs, with or without trousers, and democracy has not collapsed. Indeed, Hollander plausibly argues that a precondition of genuine democracy was the recognition of women's equally human bodies; and that this, in turn, required the overturning of puritanical conventions in dress, allowing women to show their legs. Our system of personal liberty does not in fact say that we will protect women's fantasies on the inside only at the price of making them hide their bodies on the outside. These days, however, we do make that demand of gays and lesbians—that is, when we even go so far as to protect their consensual acts in private. Yet it seems wrong to think that society will collapse if gays and lesbians openly announce their sexuality, or even hold hands on the street in ways now acceptable among heterosexuals. One even knows places in which these things happen, and yet personal liberty has not altogether vanished. One might think that, as with female trousers, so here: what genuine democracy requires is that all citizens should be able to demonstrate their full and equal humanity.

But of course Nagel is not advancing a descriptive or predictive claim: he is advancing a normative claim about how society ought to be: it *ought* to protect certain areas of liberty-in-seclusion for all actors, and, as the alleged price of this system of liberty, it *ought* to require of minorities that they refrain from "disruption," that is, of conduct offensive to "normals." For the idea that the resulting society would be either just or good, no support is offered, except the scare-predictive maneuver that says that we would lose our personal liberty without such restrictions on minorities. This is Mill turned upside down: Nagel wants to say that we can't have a subset of the liberties that Mill prized without supporting and protecting forms of social tyranny by the majority that Mill abhorred.

Nagel's argument is led in this unfortunate direction, I believe, because he uses the slippery notion of privacy, and the equally slippery notion of the public-private distinction. The concept of privacy has long been the target of criticism for several reasons; one is its unclarity.[32] In some arguments, "privacy" is used as equivalent to "liberty" or "autonomy." Thus, the right to privacy, in the areas of contraception and abortion, is really best understood as a right to certain forms of liberty of choice. Abortion and contraception are not particularly secret or secluded; in fact the right in question protects one whether one takes one's contraceptive pill in the public square or at home. In other discussions, "privacy" means seclusion or solitude: rights against intrusion by the media, for example, are rights that create a sphere of seclusion around the person. Seclusion, however, is quite a different matter from liberty, and, as we have seen, sometimes one may be forced to seclude or conceal some aspects of oneself that one might wish not to seclude: seclusion may be linked to a denial of liberty.

One key notion, in analyzing these areas of law, is that of liberty: what should people be at liberty to conceal, and what should they be at liberty to reveal or enact publicly? And the contrast we really need to think well about this question of liberty, in turn, is not the elusive contrast between the public and the private, but the contrast that John Stuart Mill advanced, between actions that are self-regarding, implicating the interests only of the agent and consenting others, and actions that are other-regarding, implicating the interests of nonconsenting others. I have already argued that this is the pertinent distinction to ponder in thinking about the regulation of gay sexual conduct, no matter where it occurs. The pertinent question is not whether the conduct occurs in a place denominated "public," but rather if nonconsenting others are present, and, if so, how they may be affected. It seems to me that what Nagel's powerful argument about fantasy really shows is that we all ought to have areas of personal liberty in which we may pursue self-regarding acts, with or without consenting others. The rightful sphere of such liberty should be limited by the potentially harmful impact of this behavior on nonconsenting others who are, or may be, present.

To consider this distinction, think about nude dancing. Let us agree for the sake of argument that it would be permissible to ban nude dancing in a public park, on the ground that children and other nonconsenting parties are present. (I shall return to this issue later.) On the other hand, nobody disputes that nude dancing in one's living room with the blinds pulled down is not regulable by law (although many laws targeting sex acts do not observe this restriction). What, then, about a club that admits only those who choose to enter and pay a fee? Indiana restricted nude dancing in such clubs. The Seventh Circuit Court of Appeals declared that law an impermissible restriction on the freedom of expression.[33] The Supreme Court overruled this decision; Justice Rehnquist (joined by three others) cited the importance of "public morals."[34] The dissenting opinion, (written by Justice White and joined by Justices Marshall, Stevens, and Blackmun) made the Millian point well:

> The purpose of forbidding people from appearing nude in parks, beaches, hot dog stands, and like public places is to protect others from offense. But that could not possibly be the purpose of preventing nude dancing in theaters and barrooms since the viewers are exclusively consenting adults who pay money to see these dances. The purpose of the proscription in these contexts is to protect the viewers from what the State believes is the harmful message that nude dancing communicates. [This] being the case, it cannot be that the statutory prohibition is unrelated to expressive conduct.[35]

In other words, the important distinction is one between conduct that affects only those who consent and conduct that affects (in a potentially harmful way) those who do not consent.

This argument parallels our argument about disgust in chapter 3. The fact that people who merely imagine what is going on inside the club feel that the dancing is shameful is insufficient to restrict conduct that does not inflict or threaten harm. Once we put the issue in terms of Mill's distinction, however, the picture of a public-private distinction that has two faces necessarily interrelated, as two sides of a single coin, collapses. Liberty of choice in one sphere has not been shown to entail forced concealment in another sphere. There seems to be no reason to think that protection of spheres of liberty for self-regarding conduct entails, as its other face, the consequence that unpopular minorities *must* hide their conduct even when they don't want to. Protecting the liberty of heterosexual men and women to have sex without intrusion, when that is what they want and seek to do, obviously does not entail the requirement that women cover their legs when they don't want to. Protecting the liberty of gays and lesbians to have consensual sex away from the public gaze, when that is what they want to do, does not entail, as its other face, the requirement that they refrain from kissing and holding hands in public, when that is what they want to do. Nor, as the Massachusetts police have recognized (see chap. 5), is there any good liberty-based argument for requiring them not to have sex "in public," so long as they take steps to seclude themselves and thus to preserve the self-regarding nature of their acts.

The public-private distinction, as applied by Nagel to sexual expression, is inherently discriminatory: it asks minorities to conceal themselves in ways that it does not ask of the majority, and it excuses these restrictions by alleging that a system of personal privacy demands this as its other face. We have been given no good reason to believe in this connection. What we really need to sort out is the crucial question of impact on others: what forms of impact on nonconsenting others do we really worry about, and what limits on our conduct are we willing to tolerate in order to protect others from these harms, or putative harms? And we need to sort out the question of personal liberty: what choices do we want to protect for all citizens, and how do seclusion and informational privacy figure in the analysis of these liberties? In the process, we may decide that the home deserves special protection, but it is unlikely that the sphere of protected liberty will coincide entirely with the boundaries of the home. Thus it was wise of the Supreme Court, in *Lawrence v. Texas,* while focusing on the protection of consensual sexual conduct in the home, to state in the very opening of the opinion that "there are other spheres of our lives and existence, outside the home, where the State should not be a dominant presence. Freedom extends beyond spatial bounds."

One issue that clearly must be faced is the more general issue of public nudity. I have conceded for the sake of argument that it is legitimate to restrict nudity in public places, on the ground that nonconsenting parties, including children, may be present. But elsewhere I have insisted that people do not have a right to restrict conduct, where that conduct does no harm, simply because they are repelled by it. In chapter 3, for example, I argued that nuisance law should be narrowly tailored (as it typically is) to regulate disgusting conduct that actually causes either danger or sensory offense serious enough to count as harm. The disgust someone feels when looking at unpopular conduct (for example, a gay couple holding hands) should not be grounds for legal regulation. It seems clear that there is a similar distinction in the area of shame: not all conduct that is widely viewed as shameful can legitimately be regulated when it occurs in places where nonconsenting parties are present. It is not at all clear, however, how to draw the boundary.

On one side is sexual conduct that has a clear potential for harm: a person who masturbates in public in the presence of children may threaten them and cause psychological harm. On the other side is conduct that is clearly innocuous, although once it would not have seemed so: a person walks down the street in shorts and a halter top, a lesbian couple hold hands in public, a mother nurses her infant on a public bus (something for which women have indeed been arrested). But what about public nudity, just walking around without clothes, without any sex acts or other behavior of a sort that might be thought to frighten and threaten children? It seems pretty innocuous; in many countries it is routine beach behavior. And by all accounts, nudity quickly becomes unremarkable when generally practiced; bodies in

a nudist colony are not regarded as sexually charged in daily interactions. So isn't this just like the question of women showing their
legs? People may think it is a disruptive invitation to sex, but that is
their problem. And if people mention their religious convictions, we
can always point out that we do not allow religious objections to
women in bathing suits to prevail in law, or religious objections to
same-sex public hand-holding.

I am inclined to think that this is correct: the reasons supporting
laws against public nudity are weak. But many people really do believe that premature exposure to the sight of adult genitals harms
children, and the intrusion on personal liberty that is involved in restricting public nudity is probably not great enough to worry about,
so long as zoning creates at least some beaches and park spaces in
which nudists may congregate.

One area in which the pendulum is swinging toward greater toleration is that of women baring their breasts. Of course standard
bathing suits cover very little. But in Europe there is widespread toleration for toplessness on beaches, and in some other contexts as
well. In 1996, the Ontario Appeals Court reversed the conviction of
university student Gwen Jacobs for indecency: she had walked
through the streets of Guelph topless to protest the fact that on a hot
day men can remove their shirts and women cannot. At trial she
maintained that breasts are just fatty tissue, no different from the
male analogue. While the court did not accept this reasoning, they
did use Millian reasoning in finding that her conduct was not regulable: "No one who was offended was forced to continue looking at
her." This ruling seems utterly rational, and one may hope that at
least some parts of the United States will experiment with liberty in
this area.

These are large questions, and we continue to wrestle with them
in many areas. The fiction that a unitary concept of privacy, and a
unitary and clearly understood contrast between the public and the
private, gives us good guidance in these matters should be abandoned.

V. Shame and People
with Disabilities

No group in society has been so painfully stigmatized as people with physical and mental disabilities. Moreover, many people who would wholeheartedly oppose all stigmatization based on race or sex or sexual orientation feel that some sort of differential treatment is appropriate for those who are different "by nature."[36] Mrs. Dover, who hid herself in her house after the amputation of one side of her nose (see epigraph, chap. 4), is not atypical in feeling that she had better not emerge into society, for if she does she will be treated as a nonperson. People do not want to look at someone with half a nose. Far less, often, are they willing to look at a child with Down syndrome; such children used to be summarily tossed into institutions and treated as "Mongoloid idiots," without individual personalities, without individual names, without genuine humanity. As Goffman says, the entire interaction with such a person is articulated in terms of the stigmatized trait, which means that the person's full humanity cannot come into focus.[37]

Now that people with disabilities are increasingly writing scholarship about their social situation, it is becoming possible to take the measure of the isolation and marginalization imposed upon them, and the extent of their routine humiliations. Thus legal scholar Jacobus tenBroek, who is blind, opens his classic account of the restrictions people with disabilities face as they try to move around in public space with a footnote stating that his study has been illuminated by his personal experience more than by all cited academic sources.[38] Jenny Morris, a politician and activist who lost the ability to walk as the result of an accident at the age of thirty-three, explains how her former associates treated her entirely differently as a result, behaving as if she had lost competence and the ability to sustain personal relationships.[39] Philosopher Anita Silvers, a wheelchair-user, begins the volume *Disability, Difference, Discrimination* with an account of a more or less typical day in which she and another philosopher, also a wheelchair-user, were kept waiting outside a grocery store in the rain because the handicapped entrance had been locked by a manager eager to prevent people from taking shopping carts out into the parking lot. And of course the lot of people with severe cognitive disabilities is even worse: they have frequently been denied humanity itself, and the right to live in the world, at all, with other human beings. Parents are reproved for allowing such a child to come into existence; the whole life of such children has been regarded as an ugly mistake. New scholarship is making these facts evident as well—in writings by parents of children with cognitive disabilities,[40] but also in writings by the people cognitively disabled themselves, such as Mitchell Levitz's and Jason Kingsley's account of their life with Down syndrome.[41] Such writing is an important part of countering the pervasive effect of shame and stigma, which forces the stigmatized to conceal themselves from our gaze.

The first point to be made in confronting this issue is a familiar one, and yet it evidently needs repeating, since one hears so many arguments that ignore it. This is, that a handicap does not exist simply "by nature," if that means independently of human action. We might say that an impairment in some area or areas of human functioning may exist without human intervention, but it only becomes a handicap when society treats it in certain ways. Human beings are in general disabled: mortal, weak-eyed, weak-kneed, with terrible backs and necks, short memories, and so forth. But when a majority (or the most powerful group) has such disabilities, society will adjust itself to cater for them. Thus we do not find staircases built with step levels so high that only the giants of Brobdingnag can climb them, nor do we find our orchestras playing instruments at frequencies inaudible to the human ear and audible only to dog ears. Even when a particular achievement is possible for some humans with great difficulty and extensive training, we typically do not demand it of all "normal" citizens. Thus we do not design the world so that only those who can run a mile in four minutes can manage to get to work. We develop prostheses—cars, trains, buses—to help us cover a mile in under four minutes.[42]

The problem of many people in our society is that their disabilities have not been catered for, because their impairments are atypical and perceived as "abnormal." There is no intrinsic "natural" difference between a person who uses a wheelchair to move at the same speed as a person walking or running and a person who uses a car to accomplish something of which her own legs are incapable.[43] In each case, human ingenuity is supplying something that the body of the individual does not. The difference is that cars are typical and wheelchairs are atypical. Our society caters for the one, and, until recently, has neglected the other. We build roads, but not (until very recently) wheelchair ramps. Again, blindness is surely an impairment that gives the blind person fewer ways of dealing with the world than are available to the sighted person (who also has the "normal" use of the other senses). And yet, how much of a handicap blindness really is depends on many social decisions. Will the primary mode of communication be auditory or visual? Will makers of computer software design them with voice-operated options for users who are blind? Will communities invest in tactile signage in addition to visual signage? Will the streets be maintained with attention to the pitfalls a person who is blind may encounter, or will it be presumed that such people have no real right to use the streets?[44] Often the fortunes of a group of people with impairments fluctuate wildly through the sheer chance of a shift in technology: thus, the growing use of email has greatly helped people with hearing impairments, though the technology was not developed for the sake of their well-being. In general, until recently, the well-being of people with minority impairments has rarely been considered in the design of buildings, communications facilities, and public accommodations.

Put it that way and it does not sound very nice: why should mere atypicality give one a life of hardship? Typically, however, "normals" think of themselves as perfectly in order, and of people with unusual disabilities as the only ones with flaws: they are the bad apples in the lot, the spoiled food amid the healthy food. What does one do with spoiled food? Put it to the side (or throw it out), lest it contaminate the good. And the peculiar reluctance of most modern societies to tolerate the presence of people with disabilities—especially mental disabilities—in schools and public places betrays this same uneasy sense that their very presence will spoil the lives of others. The fact that our own lives are also frail and disabled lives is thus the more effectively screened from view.[45] Politician Jenny Morris, a wheelchair-user, aptly refers to these policies as "tyrannies of perfection."[46]

In order to make this point one need not accept the radical thesis that there is nothing bad about the classic disabilities, such as blindness, deafness, and mental retardation.[47] We may grant that many people with disabilities have extremely valuable lives, as rich in value as those of most "normals," without taking the implausible position that when we can prevent or cure blindness, loss of hearing, loss of motor ability, et cetera, we should make no particular attempt to do so. (Similarly, we may grant that many poor people have lives rich in value without taking the position that money is irrelevant to happiness.) We may grant that some central functional capabilities are not just typical, but also very useful—good things to have in pursuing a variety of different human plans of life. In so judging, we need take no stand on the contested question of whether these abilities are "natural" in any value-free sense.[48] Without any such controversial claim, we may say that seeing, hearing, locomotion of the limbs, et cetera, are valuable instruments of human functioning, and thus reasonable things to shoot for in thinking about what a system of health care should promote.[49] They are thus political goods, whether or not they have any particular metaphysical or "natural" status.[50]

This same way of thinking also implies, however, that if an individual is not able to achieve mobility, communication, and so forth, in the most common ways because of an impairment, society has a particularly urgent set of reasons to (re)design things in the social, educational, and political environments so that those capabilities will be available to that individual. All too often, however, fictions of normalcy block us from understanding that institutions such as staircases, visual (rather than tactile) signage, and telephones are in no sense inevitable or natural, and that they have vast consequences for people who are in wheelchairs, blind, deaf, et cetera.

Such false ideas of perfection and defect have had as their consequence the creation of two worlds: the public world of the ordinary citizen and the hidden world of people with disabilities, who are implicitly held to have no right to inhabit the public world. And we might say, therefore, that the most basic right to which these people are entitled, as human beings and citizens of equal worth, is what Jacobus tenBroek called the "right to live in the world." This means many things at a concrete level, including wheelchair-access on public transportation, permission for guide dogs in places that are usually closed to dogs, tactile signage, et cetera. Most generally, however, it means the right to be treated as a citizen, one for whom the public space is designed and in whose interests it is maintained. Among the rights most at stake in this more general right are the right to work and the right to the necessary means to participate effectively in political and social life.[51]

As I argued in section III, a basic strategy to counter public shaming of a group is the traditional civil rights strategy of nondiscrimination legislation. The Americans with Disabilities Act (ADA) of 1990 has in many respects extended the civil rights movement to people with disabilities, institutionalizing the idea of the openness of the world of work and public activity to those with serious impairments. The act constructs people with disabilities as a protected class whose equality as citizens has long been impeded by injurious social arrangements and artificial fictions of incompetence, and requires employers to make a "reasonable accommodation" for the needs of such workers. Thus a central strategy of the civil rights movement has been extended to at least some disabled citizens.

There are many ambiguities in the ADA and the legal tradition surrounding it. The account of impairment limits the protections of the act to those impairments that "substantially limi[t] one or more of the major life activities of such [an] individual." (Individuals are also protected if they have a history of or are "regarded" as having such an impairment, but the impairment in question, in these clauses, must again be one of those that substantially limits a major life activity.) This categorization leaves out some pervasive sources of stigma: obesity, for example, is not covered unless the person is 100 percent above desirable weight. In this way, the ADA's medicalized understanding of serious impairments is in tension with its civil rights purpose, which should be to counteract irrational stigma, whether grounded in a definite biological condition or not. (We do not need to grant that race has biological salience, which it does not, in order to grant that race-based discrimination should be illegal.) Moreover, people who function well by virtue of epilepsy medications and other corrective treatments are not clearly included in the protected class, even though they are vulnerable to stigmatization and discrimination.

This, again, leaves a gap because such people may still be targets of irrational stigmatization and discrimination. (This gap can to some extent be filled by arguing that they are "regarded as" having a disability that affects a major life activity, despite the correction.)[52] Furthermore, the very notion of "major life activities" is amorphous and leaves a great deal of room for courts to arrive at untheorized, and in some cases ad hoc, specifications.[53] Diseases—diabetes and arthritis, for example—that leave large numbers of people vulnerable and in need of special workplace conditions are not clearly covered, especially where treatment has kept the disease from greatly affecting functioning.

Finally, the act's notion of the "reasonable accommodation" that must be made by employers is both unclear and itself contestable: for, after all, employers are not let off the hook with regard to racial discrimination if they can show that accommodating racial minorities would be very costly. In short, the act still permits the world of work to be arranged around the needs of the "normal," and treats the special changes required to accommodate people with disabilities as costs against that baseline, which may not have to be borne if they are too great.

These conceptual difficulties should be noted, and should be the object of further reflection and concern. And yet it seems clear that it is highly desirable to give strong and definite protections to a large proportion of disabled people, even if the protections do not reach as far as the existence of social stigma itself. The problem is that on the analysis I have favored, stigma is indeed a very extensive notion. As Goffman suggests, the stigmatized and the "normal" are part of one another. This analysis entails that any demarcation of a protected class will be to some extent arbitrary, and will leave other relevantly similar cases without special protection. On the other hand, a protected class defined so broadly as to include the moderately overweight, the short, and the unattractive would be legally unworkable and would bring the entire idea of the protected class into disrepute.[54] We all know that antidiscrimination law is a blunt instrument, protecting some individuals who are not disproportionately vulnerable and failing to protect many who are. But the value of protecting even a subclass of people with disabilities seems great. One may hope that such protections will lead to a generally beneficial shift in social attitudes. In informal practices of moral education and social debate we may reach more broadly, opposing the stigmatization of the obese, the short, and other groups who do not receive protection under the ADA.

As we debate these issues, we ought to ask ourselves whether there are any more general features of our political culture that conduce to the stigmatization of people with disabilities. I have suggested that one such general feature is the American emphasis on "perfection"—self-sufficiency, competence, and (the fiction of) invulnerability. But we may now go further. Closely linked to that fiction is another, which has had and continues to have a profound influence on our very theories of social justice. It has major implications, I now want to suggest, for our attitudes toward the disabled in general, but particularly toward the cognitively disabled, who are not likely to seem "productive" even in changed social circumstances. This is the myth of the citizen as a competent independent adult, as that idea has been used in the social-contract theories that have deeply shaped the history of Western political thought. Although I shall have more to say about this issue in my concluding chapter, it must be introduced now, so that we can understand some deep sources of the stigma against the mentally handicapped.

The parties to the social contract are assumed by John Locke to be "free, equal, and independent."[55] Contemporary contractarians explicitly adopt such an hypothesis. For David Gauthier, people of unusual need are "not party to the moral relationships grounded by a contractarian theory."[56] Similarly, although in a very different and morally much richer theory, the citizens in John Rawls's "Well Ordered Society" are "fully cooperating members of society over a complete life."[57] And since the partnership envisaged is for the mutual advantage of the contracting parties, provisions for people who aren't part of the bargain will be an afterthought, not part of the basic institutional structure to which they agree.[58]

Most forms of social-contract doctrine do, of course, make provision for "normal" human needs, but they do screen from view, in the initial design of basic political principles, all the times of asymmetrical or unusual dependency, even those that result from childhood or old age, stages of life through which all citizens pass. In that way, as Goffman observes, there is a public fiction that a sharp line divides the "normal" from the stigmatized; in reality, the normal and the stigmatized are a part of one another. Thus the fiction of the independent adult becomes a version of the fiction of perfection, and is itself a vehicle through which those with atypical needs are regarded as dependent, lacking in competence, et cetera.

To some extent we can insist that these perceptions are in error: people with physical impairments can be highly competent and productive citizens, given a supportive social environment. And it is very important that advocates for people with disabilities insist on this response, refusing the idea that special treatment is a handout for pathetic victims. Nonetheless, the social changes required to create a supportive environment for people with physical disabilities are very expensive, and a drag on social productivity; thus a society based on notions of independence and productivity can all too easily be seduced into disparaging such changes.

We find an even more tenacious problem when we consider the situation of people with severe mental disabilities, who typically do not count as parties to the social contract at all, as the major such thinkers define those parties. The basic structure of society is mapped out without including them, and their needs are left as an afterthought. Indeed, the fiction of independence, a type of fiction of perfection, effectively screens their asymmetrical needs from view.

As I shall argue more generally in chapter 7, any productive approach to the social situation of people with atypical disabilities must begin, then, by recognizing that we all have many impairments, and that life includes not only "normal" needs but also periods, more or less prolonged, of unusual and asymmetrical dependency, during which the situation of the "normal" approximates to that of a person with an unusual disability in one or more respects. This means that if we are to give even "normals" the social conditions of self-respect we must at the same time think about the self-respect of the lifelong disabled and try to devise ways to recognize and support their full humanity and individuality. Thinking about them is thinking about us. But then, good thought about both requires revising the idea of the citizen as independent bargainer and replacing it with a more complex image of a being both capable and needy, who moves from helplessness to "mutual interdependence," and, unfortunately, often back to helplessness again.

There is a great deal to say about where these ideas might take us in thinking about public policy toward people with disabilities and more generally about theories of justice.[59] I shall suggest in chapter 7 that these issues give us strong reasons for preferring an account of social justice based on the "capabilities approach" to those based on the social-contract doctrine.[60] My present concern, however, is not to commend one particular form of liberal political theory, but, instead, to talk about ways in which issues of shame affect the very possibility of a liberal society based on ideas of equal respect and the worth of the person. At this point, then, I shall focus on one issue only, the education of children with severe mental disabilities. And I shall approach the issue by considering the history of one American law, the Individuals with Disabilities Education Act (IDEA).

Our treatment of children with unusual mental disabilities has had many inequities. Often, such children do not get the medical care and the therapy they need. (Often, indeed, assumptions of cognitive incompetence have prevented people from recognizing that they need forms of physical therapy that can greatly augment their cognitive potential. For example, muscle therapy for children with Down syndrome can make it possible for these children to negotiate their world in a way that promotes active learning.) More, even, than people with many physical disabilities, children with cognitive impairments have been shunned and stigmatized. Many of them have been relegated to institutions that make no effort to develop their potential. And they are persistently treated as if they have no right to "live in the world." In the congressional hearings prior to the passage of the ADA, many examples of this shunning were cited, including that of children with Down syndrome who were denied admission to a zoo so as not to upset the chimpanzee.[61]

The most egregious gap, however, has been, perhaps, in the area of education. Stigmatized as either uneducable or not worth the expense, children with mental disabilities have been denied access to suitable education. Adults of my generation can recall the classrooms for "special" children that were typically hidden away in basements of schools, so that "normal" children did not have to look at these children. And in many cases children with mental disabilities were turned away from the public schools altogether. Early court cases upheld these exclusions. For example, in 1892 the Massachusetts Supreme Court upheld the exclusion of John Watson, diagnosed as mentally retarded, from the Cambridge public schools, citing the disruptive effect of his appearance and unusual behavior (which, they admitted, was not harmful or disobedient) on the experience of the other children.[62]

In the early 1970s, advocates for people with mental disabilities began a systematic attempt to challenge this situation, achieving two influential victories. In *Pennsylvania Association for Retarded Children v. Pennsylvania,* a federal district court issued a consent decree compelling Pennsylvania public schools to provide "free appropriate education" to children with mental disabilities.[63] The plaintiffs alleged that the right to education is a fundamental right, and that the school system therefore needed to show a "compelling state interest" in order lawfully to exclude children with mental retardation. The court, however, lightened the plaintiffs' burden, holding that they had established a constitutional claim even under the less stringent rational-basis test: in other words, they did not need to show that education is a fundamental right in order to make their equal protection claim. (Thus, the decision anticipates the Supreme Court's 1985 decision in *Cleburne:* exclusions of children with mental disabilities lack a rational basis.) The plaintiffs' contention that the exclusions violate both due process and equal protection prevailed.

In the same year, in *Mills v. Board of Education,* the U.S. District Court for the District of Columbia ruled in favor of a group of children with mental disabilities who challenged their exclusions from the District of Columbia public schools. This group was broader than the group of plaintiffs in the Pennsylvania case: it included children with a wide range of learning disabilities. In an analysis that self-consciously set out to apply *Brown v. Board of Education* to the situation of children with disabilities, the court held that the denial of free suitable public education is an equal protection violation.[64] Moreover, they held that this equal protection violation could not be reasoned away by saying that the system had insufficient funds: "The inadequacies of the District of Columbia Public School System, whether occasioned by insufficient funding or administrative inefficiency, certainly cannot be permitted to bear more heavily on the 'exceptional' or handicapped child than on the normal child." Significantly, the court cites *Goldberg v. Kelly,* the case concerning welfare rights that I discussed in section II, where the Supreme Court held that "the State's interest that [the welfare recipient's] payments not be erroneously terminated, clearly outweighs the State's competing concern to prevent any increase in its fiscal and administrative burdens." "Similarly," reasons the D.C. court, "the District of Columbia's interest in educating the excluded children clearly must outweigh its interest in preserving its financial resources."

These two cases sparked a national debate, focused on both guaranteed access and funding. In 1975, Congress passed the Education for All Handicapped Children Act (EAHCA), which turned the *Mills* decision into federal law, giving a wide range of children with mental disabilities enforceable rights to free suitable public education, and making funds available to the states to help them meet their constitutional obligation.[65] This law was slightly modified and elaborated in 1997 in the form of IDEA.

IDEA begins from a simple yet profound conception: that of human individuality. Rather than regarding the various types of disabled persons as faceless classes of persons, the act assumes that they are in fact individuals, with varying needs, and that therefore all prescription for groups of them would be inappropriate. The guiding idea of the act is thus that of the Individualized Education Program (IEP), defined as "a written statement for each child with a disability that is developed, reviewed, and revised." The act requires that states affirmatively undertake to identify and locate all unserved children with disablities. It also requires that districts establish extensive procedural safeguards to give parents input in decisions regarding the evaluation and placement of their children, as well as access to records and rights to participation in due process hearings and judicial review.

In general the act obliges states to educate children with disabilities in the "least restrictive environment" appropriate to meet their needs. It thus urges "mainstreaming" of these children—a practice defended by advocates for people with disabilities by pointing to benefits both to the newly included child and to other children, who learn about humanity and its diversity by being in a classroom with a child who has unusual disabilities. But the underlying recognition of individuality is paramount: thus, when a child seems to profit more from special education than from mainstreaming, the state is required to support such a special placement.

Two contrasting cases show how the IEP can work when parents and schools work well together. Michael Bérubé's son Jamie, who has Down syndrome, has been successfully "mainstreamed" in an Illinois public elementary school. He finds the classroom stimulating and is making cognitive progress; teachers and students respond well to his sweet personality, and the teacher emphasizes that they have all learned a great deal about human beings from Jamie's presence. By contrast, my nephew Arthur, who has Asperger syndrome (a type of high-functioning autism), is being educated at a private school with state funds, because his disability makes it difficult for him to develop as a person in a class with other children. He doesn't look different, but he acts different, and thus is easily mistaken for a "bad kid," and teased by "normal" children, whereas in a school with other children with Asperger's he can both realize his high cognitive potential and find real friends for the first time in his life.[66]

Such a law goes a long way toward undermining stigma, for it tells society that children with mental and physical disabilities have rights and are individuals, and that their rights include access to the same classroom with "normals." Teachers and parents have to play their part as well, but it is by now clear that the very fact of state recognition and attention, together with pressure applied to schools and teachers, has greatly changed the climate for stigmatized children. In his eloquent account of his son's life, Bérubé writes about the achievement of raising a child who sees himself and is seen by others as Jamie, a particular child with particular tastes and a quirky sense of humor, not a member of some faceless class of "mongoloid idiots." Since individuality is so often what stigma denies the stigmatized, it is fitting that the remedy should itself be one focused on recognition of individuality.

IDEA is far from being a perfect law, in theory or in practice. In practice, it suffers, first of all, from lack of funding: for although the statute refers to federal funding, the amount envisaged has never actually been appropriated. Furthermore, its practical implementation is rarely as individualized as it ought to be: formulae are typically found for common disorders. Arthur has profited from the fact that Asperger's is a recently recognized condition without much of a track record: in such a case, educators are willing to look and see what seems to work for a particular child. Finally, the practical implementation of the law is often unequal, giving better results to parents who are well-read about their child's disorder and energetic in prodding the local school system. Thus it is no accident that the Bérubés, both college professors, and my sister, a professional musician with a graduate degree, have succeeded in using the system to their advantage, while many other parents have not. The internet is a very valuable source of information and exchange for parents of disabled children; thus the "digital divide" also raises legitimate concerns about inequality of outcome.

Theoretically, there is also a serious problem with IDEA. It reaches out to embrace not only the pervasive cognitive disabilities we have been discussing, but also a wide variety of "specific learning disabilities" whose aetiology and nature is poorly understood. Specific learning disabilities are very different from mental retardation and autism, in that they are conceptualized as specific impediments that typically conceal the student's true ability: thus a diagnosis of "learning disabled" (LD) is made on the basis of evidence of a discrepancy between "true ability" (measured, often, on an IQ test) and school achievement in one or more subject areas. It is very hard in practice to distinguish a child with a learning disability from a child who is simply slow or less talented than many. Nor is the conceptual framework of LDs secure: the theory suggests an organic cause of a specific impediment, and yet it is not clear that such causes exist for the wide range of impediments recognized. Nonetheless, the financial incentives created by IDEA give school districts reasons to rush toward classifying children as LD in order to qualify for federal funding. Such classifications may not always help the child: they can be stigmatizing in their own right, and they do not always point to a useful course of treatment. Moreover, they tend to be unfair to children who have problems in school but who cannot be plausibly classified as LD. One feels that all children should be helped to reach their cognitive potential, but the system promotes some children over others in a way that is more than a little arbitrary.[67] In practice, this defect has been somewhat mitigated by the looseness of the classificatory system, as school districts seek to include as many children as possible in the funding-eligible pool.[68]

These are all difficulties. In reality, what would be best is that each and every child would, in effect, have an IEP, an education focused on an understanding of that child's individual needs. On the other hand, it seems legitimate to focus on individualizing the education of children with mental disabilities because these children have so often been denied individuality entirely.

Despite its imperfections, IDEA is an achievement of which our society should be proud. Along with the ADA, it represents a major assault on the structure of shame and stigma that has for so long enclosed people with disabilities, both children and adults, and makes available to them, often for the first time, the right to live in the world as equal citizens and to develop their potential. This law, like other expensive programs of social restructuring, is currently under threat in a time when many modern societies, in both Europe and America, increasingly push the fiction of competent adulthood and deplore the expense of caring for those who do not, as the saying goes, "pay their own way."

We should remember, once again, that the cost of the special support structures required by IDEA and the ADA is not "natural," entailed by a presocial difference between the person with a disability and other allegedly nondisabled people. It is a cost entailed by the fact that we have designed society to cater for the average person, a person whom we misleadingly call "normal." We should not let the narcissistic fiction of a surrogate perfection or invulnerability serve as a justification for denying the right to be in the world to large numbers of people whose heightened vulnerability is the result of social arrangements organized around the needs of a dominant group.

Perhaps the greatest insight of the classical-liberal tradition is the insight that each human individual is profoundly valuable, spacious and deep, capable of separate life and imagination, of being more than just the continuer of a tradition or a family style. This insight has been inconstantly and imperfectly implemented in liberal societies, insofar as they permit infantile narcissism to exercise political power, stigmatizing those who have weaknesses that make "normals" uncomfortable. But liberal societies can inhibit infantile narcissism and create "facilitating environments" in which people differently disabled can live lives of "subtle interplay." Liberalism is frightening. As B says: "The alarming thing about equality is that we are then both children, and the question is, where is father? We know where we are if one of us is the father." Similarly, we know where we are if some of us are "normal," independent, productive citizens, and others have their eyes downcast in shame. What liberalism requires of us, however, is something more chancy and fearful, some combination of adulthood and childhood, and aspiration without the fiction of perfection.

Chapter 7
Liberalism without Hiding?

The permanent shortening of skirts was the most necessary step in furthering the modernization of women.

—Anne Hollander, *Sex and Suits*

There are many who consider as an injury to themselves any conduct which they have a distaste for, and resent it as an outrage to their feelings; as a religious bigot, when charged with disregarding the religious feelings of others, has been known to retort that they disregard his feelings by persisting in their abominable worship or creed. But there is no parity between the feeling of a person for his own opinion and the feeling of another who is offended at his holding it, no more than between the desire of a thief to take a purse and the desire of the right owner to keep it.

—John Stuart Mill, *On Liberty*

As Adam early in the morning,
Walking forth from the bower refresh'd with sleep,
Behold me where I pass, hear my voice, approach,
Touch me, touch the palm of your hand to my body as I pass,
Be not afraid of my body.

—Walt Whitman, "As Adam, Early in the Morning"

I. Political Liberalism,
Disgust, and Shame

Throughout this book we have been connecting the analysis of disgust and shame to the idea of political liberalism: the idea, that is, of a social order based on the idea of human dignity and on social relations characterized by reciprocity and mutual respect, including respect for differing conceptions of the ultimate good in human life. The analysis of emotion and the political conception illuminate one another. Thinking about the ideals inherent in the political conception helps us identify clearly some dangers we face if we give disgust and shame a prominent role in the foundations of the law. For both emotions, when used as the basis for legal regulation, seem, in different ways, to threaten mutual respect. At the same time, thinking about the two emotions gives us a fuller understanding of the political ideal. When we see how often our ideals of reciprocity and respect for dignity are undermined by the narcissism, the shrinking from animality and mortality, and the anxious obsession with the "normal" that are such ubiquitous features of human societies, we see afresh why these ideals matter, and why it is no small task to make them the core of a political conception.

Indeed, we can see that the dangers posed by disgust and shame are in many respects especially antithetical to the values of a liberal society. For these emotions typically express themselves through the subordination of both individuals and groups based on features of their way of life. Although there are many political conceptions in which the subordination of minority religious, sexual, and other identities is affirmed, for political liberalism all such subordination is deeply problematic, since the guiding commitment of such liberalism is equal respect for persons, understood as entailing respect for their comprehensive conceptions of what has worth or value. For such a political order, then, the subordination of women, or Jews, or people with mental and physical disabilities is especially problematic, threatening its very core commitments. Subordination causes pain to vulnerable individuals in all societies; in a liberal society it also threatens core political values. So thinking about the operations of disgust and shame should put us on our guard against giving those emotions free rein, even in ways that might initially seem promising.

Creating a liberal society is not simply a matter of making a commitment to mutual respect and then going out and acting upon it. Things would be this simple if human psychology was simple, if there were no forces within it militating continually against mutual respect. But the analysis of disgust and shame—only a part, clearly, of a larger analysis that could be offered—shows us that human beings typically have a problematic relationship to their mortality and animality, and that this problematic relationship causes not just inner tension, but also aggression toward others. If ideals of respect and reciprocity are to have a chance of prevailing, they must contend against the forces of narcissism and misanthropy that these emotions so frequently involve. So we gain insight not only into some specific reasons for limiting the operations of these two emotions in the law, but also into a more general task that a liberal democracy must undertake if equal respect is really to prevail, informing both institutions and the conduct of individual actors.

II. Mill's Defense of
Liberty Reconsidered

My argument has many times crossed the path of John Stuart Mill's famous arguments for liberty of speech and association, and his defense of the "harm principle" as a necessary condition for the legal regulation of conduct. I have attempted not to presuppose the correctness of Mill's view while examining the difficulties of disgust-based and shame-based lawmaking. But my conclusions coincide to a large degree with those of Mill. Now, therefore, it is time to examine the different routes by which Mill and I have arrived at our conclusions. I shall suggest that Mill himself does not provide the most compelling defense for his own principle. A defense based on liberal norms of mutual respect and reciprocity carries us much further than do Mill's Utilitarian arguments. But the argument from mutual respect and reciprocity derives illumination, as I have said, from our analysis of disgust and shame. I shall now argue that this analysis has put us in a position to defend at least some aspects of Mill's idea in a more convincing and consistently liberal manner than he was able to defend them.

Mill was a Utilitarian philosopher. Though in many ways critical of Bentham's version of Utilitarianism, he remained convinced that the best way to defend a social principle was to show that it conduced to the greatest happiness of the greatest number. He understood happiness in a much richer way than did Bentham. He recognized qualitative distinctions among pleasures, and, in effect, espoused an Aristotelian conception of happiness as a plurality of functionings in accordance with excellence, pleasure being either identical with those activities or something that supervenes upon them.[1] He also appears to discount some pleasures altogether when arriving at the social calculus: thus, in both *On Liberty* and *The Subjection of Women* Mill does not weigh against the reforms he proposes the fact that many people (including, in the latter case, most men) will be very displeased with them. Thus he anticipates one of the primary criticisms modern Utilitarians have brought against classical Benthamite Utilitarianism when they argue that sadistic and malicious preferences should not be permitted to count at all in the social welfare function.[2]

In *On Liberty,* furthermore, Mill states that "I regard utility as the ultimate appeal on all ethical questions; but it must be utility in the largest sense, grounded on the permanent interests of man as a progressive being" (Introduction).[3] This tells us that not all interests and satisfactions are equal: some have a special claim to be consulted in defining social utility. Thus, although he is far from systematic in his account of these matters, it is clear that Mill's idea of social utility is more restrictive than Bentham's, excluding some satisfactions and giving special importance to others.

Mill further declares in the same paragraph of his essay that he will "forgo any advantage which could be derived to my argument from the idea of abstract right as a thing independent of utility." And yet, as is well known, Mill uses notions of rights prominently, both in chapter 5 of *Utilitarianism* and in *On Liberty* itself, where the harm principle is repeatedly defined in terms of harm that violates another person's "constituted rights." How to square the importance of rights with Mill's insistence that utility is the final arbiter in ethics is a question that continues to exercise interpreters, and we need not review all the alternative interpretations here. The most plausible account of the matter is that Mill means by "rights" certain very important interests, interests that at least form an important portion of the "permanent interests of man as a progressive being." Thus in *On Liberty*, defining the harm principle, he says that the fact of living in society imposes certain basic requirements on the conduct of individuals. The first such requirement is "not injuring the interests of one another, or rather certain interests which, either by express legal provision or by tacit understanding, ought to be considered as rights" (chap. 4). By calling these interests "rights" he accords them a certain centrality and indicates that they ought to be protected for all persons. Although, sadly, he never gives an exhaustive enumeration of these rights, chapter 5 of *Utilitarianism* makes it clear that security of the person and of property are central cases. Rights are not independent of utility: to defend a right one must first show the role that it plays in the happiness of the individual.[4] They appear, however, to be in some way non-negotiable: it is crucial to social utility that they be protected for all.

Mill is never terribly clear about how we form our conception of social utility out of the many individual utilities: is it by mere summing, or are there threshold conditions such that we could not secure the happiness of the whole by denying a small group their basic rights? Thus the place of rights and their protection in Mill's conception remains both unclear and insecure. Even if in the case of the individual we do not need to show that rights serve happiness, understood as an end altogether separate from rights—even, that is, if we do regard rights, or their fulfillment, as constituents of the individual's happiness—we still need to show that protecting the rights of each and every individual serves social utility. The only escape from this challenge would be to define social utility from the start as involving the protection of the rights of all. But such a definition of social utility would move very far from classical Utilitarianism and its focus on happiness or satisfaction; Mill shows no signs of making such a radical break. But to show that protection of rights always serves social utility, understood as the greatest happiness or satisfaction of the greatest number, is notoriously difficult. It is for this reason that many contemporary liberal thinkers, ranging from John Rawls to Richard Posner, have rejected Utilitarianism as a conception of social justice, arguing that it gives too insecure a position to fundamental rights and liberties.[5] The Utilitarian can always advance empirical arguments suggesting that the protection of rights will in fact serve social utility, but Rawls and others plausibly claim that we should not rest such important matters as the liberty of conscience on such a fragile basis.

If Mill's doctrine faces this problem concerning those rights (to security of the person and property) that are involved in his definition of harm to others, it faces the very same problem concerning those liberties (of speech and association) for which *On Liberty* provides the argument. It is with regard to these liberties that Mill forgoes the advantage that he thinks he might claim by a direct appeal to rights: he chooses, instead, as he tells us, to ground his case for liberty on social utility, understood as some kind of aggregate of individual utilities, in which the "permanent interests of man as a progressive being" play a central role. His argument for extensive individual liberty falls into two parts. In one part (chapter 2 of *On Liberty*), Mill defends liberty on the grounds of its relation to truth, and truth of a sort that is conducive to social utility. I shall refer to this as the "truth-based justification." In the other part (chapter 3 of *On Liberty*), Mill defends the role of liberty in promoting the self-development of individuals and (especially through outstanding individuals) the ennoblement of the human race. I shall call this the "person-based justification." Let us consider each of these arguments in turn, asking whether each is successful in giving liberty the secure place Mill wants it to have and whether, apart from that, each is the sort of argument that seems appropriate to the defense of political liberty in a liberal society.

The truth-based justification goes as follows. To inhibit the free expression of opinion is bad for society, for, first of all, the opinion suppressed may be true. Second, even if it is not wholly true, it may contain a part of the truth, and may help us to correct that part of received opinion that is in error. Third, even if it does not turn out to be true at all, it may help us get at the truth through the lively debate it provokes. Fourth, even if we already have the whole truth, we will be better off facing repeated debates and challenges: opinions that are held as mere prejudices lose their vigor, and over time we forget what they really mean.

All these are plausible contentions. But Mill's argument raises several problems that he does not appear to recognize. First, it does not grapple with some cases that would be especially difficult for such an argument, such as the role of hate speech, and related forms of political speech in a free society. Germany has decided that there is no social utility to be gained from anti-Semitic speech, including political speech. It is not clear that they are wrong, given their particular history. Even if the Millian were to make an exception for the case where there is an imminent danger of violence, the German opponent of anti-Semitism would not be satisfied. Does the truth of antiracism and human decency really need the stimulus of challenges of this sort? Thus Mill's truth-based justification may be too inclusive, defending forms of speech that really do not advance truth or social welfare.

In another area of life, allowing speech about medical and health matters to proceed without any constraints at all is something even the United States, with its uniquely generous protections of free speech, has decided that it cannot tolerate. Unlicensed medical advice and fraudulent commercial claims are regulated. Mill fails to distinguish between political speech and commercial speech, and suggests that the same high level of protection applies across the board. We may doubt, however, whether truth is served by allowing advertisers to make any claim they like about their projects, and for unlicensed quacks to offer medical advice without any restraint. Once again, Mill's justification appears too inclusive.

Thus, there are doubts about whether Mill's argument may not protect too much speech, or too much speech of low value. At any rate, Mill has not really confronted these troublesome cases. There are also doubts on the other side: in certain cases, the argument may actually be underprotective. Some core areas of human liberty are made hostage to contingent facts concerning what best promotes truth and progress. Mill points to the progress of science in Europe to bolster his general case for liberty. But suppose we discover that science can advance in a more restrictive climate: will that give us good reason to retreat from Mill's principle, even in the clearly central cases of political and expressive speech, and freedom of the press? It is here that Rawls and other anti-Utilitarians see the danger in a generally Utilitarian mode of justification. It makes important human interests hostage to some general social facts that seem to be only contingently and indirectly connected to those interests. But those interests seem important in their own right.

Furthermore, the issue of each person's rights causes trouble here again. Even if in general we are convinced that freedom of speech and press promote social well-being, it may well appear that we can get just as much or more total or average well-being if we restrict the speech of certain members of the society. Mill is worried about restrictions on exceptional individuals who have something unique to say. Suppose we concede for the sake of argument that such restrictions are unwise: we will impose restrictions only on mediocre and unpopular people who have nothing unusual to say. Such restrictions might advance social utility: we lose no new insights, and we make the majority happier, because they do not have to listen to people whom they dislike. The Millian might reply that freedom is not only instrumental to well-being, it is also a constituent of each person's well-being. Even so, we may be able to advance social well-being by some restrictions of unpopular minority speech. Again, something seems off about this: Utilitarianism treats the equality of citizens too lightly when it allows the rights of a small number to be sacrificed for the sake of the general happiness.

These issues, serious in their own right, lead us to a further issue, which I regard as the most serious argument against a Millian truth-based justification for liberty: that it is the *wrong sort* of justification, in the sense that it treats individual citizens as means to the general well-being, and, indeed, one generation as the means to the next generation's progress. If one starts from the idea that each human being has dignity and deserves respect, and that politics must be grounded in respect for the dignity of all citizens as equals, one will find that Mill has put things just the wrong way round. Instead of thinking truth good because of what it does for the self-respect and flourishing of individuals, he subordinates individual flourishing and dignity to truth, conceived as an abstraction. The Kantian intuition with which Rawls's *A Theory of Justice* begins is the idea that "each person possesses an inviolablity founded on justice that even the welfare of society as a whole cannot override."[6] This idea directs us to consider social arrangements in the light of that inviolability, and to treat each citizen as an end, never as a means to the ends of others. Claims to certain liberties and opportunities get their force directly from that idea, rather than having to issue from a highly indirect consideration of the overall welfare and progress of society. Operating in a political climate in which ideas of rights were often bandied around loosely as ways of advancing conservative and sectarian doctrines, Mill and Bentham feel that there is more to be gained from a focus on utility than from the vague notion of rights. Perhaps they would have the same qualms about the notion of inviolability. But really, politics must begin somewhere, with some moral ideas. And the Kantian-Rawlsian starting point seems in many ways more definite and helpful than Mill's idea of happiness, which is so unclear that even today commentators are very divided about what it really is.

Finally, there is one more objection that the Rawlsian political liberal will bring against Mill's argument. Political liberalism is grounded in reciprocity and mutual respect among citizens. But respecting citizens requires respecting their comprehensive doctrines, and the political-liberal society is based on the premise that there will remain a plurality of reasonable comprehensive doctrines of life, religious and secular, for which the state should show respect. So long as citizens can accept the moral principles that form the core of the political conception, they can be part of the social consensus, whatever the content of the rest of their religious or secular conception of value. The idea of basing society on such an "overlapping consensus," however, requires political liberalism to be cautious in the claims it advances as moral-political doctrines. In order to be acceptable to the contending doctrines, the political conception must not take sides in matters (metaphysical, religious, et cetera) on which citizens reasonably disagree. These matters include all claims about god and religion; other related metaphysical doctrines, such as the immortality of the person or the nature and existence of the soul; and ethical, aesthetic, and psychological doctrines that lie outside of the political core.

Because of these limitations, Rawls prefers not even to claim that the moral-political theses of the political conception are "true": they are simply reasonable, or even "most reasonable." This does not prevent them from enjoying objectivity of a certain sort, but political objectivity is carefully distinguished from ultimate truth. Some political liberals disagree with Rawls, holding that we can perfectly well say that the doctrines that shape the political conception are true, but they agree with him about the narrow scope within which claims to objectively valid status ought to be made.

Thus for all political liberals it is no good argument in favor of a political value that it promotes truth, certainly not if truth is taken to include metaphysical and ethical matters that lie outside the political conception itself. Scientific truth may be different, and I believe that there is no reason why a Rawlsian could not hold that at least one thing in favor of a policy is that it promotes scientific truth. Rawls himself, at any rate, appears to exempt science from his general hands-off attitude to truth-claims. But to claim that the freedom of speech promotes truth in metaphysics and morals would be to show disrespect for the idea of reasonable pluralism, and to venture onto a terrain where one is at high risk of showing disrespect to one's fellow citizens.

Mill is totally oblivious to all such considerations. He has none of the delicate regard for other people's religious doctrines that characterizes the political liberal. Instead, he simply wants society to figure out what is true—in science, in morals, and in religion. His arguments make no salient distinctions among these domains. Of course the ideas of reasonable pluralism have been most fully formulated in the post-Mill world, especially in nations that do contain great ethnic and religious pluralism. But one can find a sign of them as far back as Ashoka's edicts in third-century BCE India,[7] and in the West, probably in Cicero's letters to his friend Atticus (an Epicurean, who had a very different comprehensive doctrine of life from Cicero's own.)[8] Mill is just not very interested in such ideas, nor is he inclined to be very respectful of doctrines that differ from his own. In

On Liberty he does not hesitate to speak contemptuously of Calvinism as an "insidious" doctrine conducive to a "pinched and hidebound type of human character." And in essays such as "The Utility of Religion" his negative view of religion's social role becomes extremely plain. One may sympathize with the vehemence of his sentiments, given the many political disabilities encountered by atheists in his day, without feeling that he understands the type of mutual respect that is required in a pluralistic society. I agree with Rawls: such respect requires (in the public sphere at least) not showing up the metaphysical claims of religion as damaging, and not adopting a public conception of truth and objectivity according to which such claims are false.[9]

Mill, however, has a further argument for the protection of personal liberty, the argument I have called the person-based justification. So we must examine it to see whether it has the same flaws as the truth-based account. Put forward in chapter 3 of *On Liberty*, the person-based argument claims that conditions of liberty are necessary for the development of human potential. Restrictions on the legal regulation of conduct create a condition that "brings human beings . . . nearer to the best thing they can be" (chap. 3). So long as people act on the basis of authority, or prevailing opinion, Mill argues, they do not exercise their faculties of choice and discrimination. The person who goes by convention "has no need of any other faculty than the ape-like one of imitation." But "[t]he mental and moral, like the muscular, powers are improved only by being used." So there is a real loss in personal development if a society does not create spaces around individuals where they may develop their powers. As we shall see, this argument itself has two distinct strands. I shall call them the "perfectionist strand" and the "distributive strand."

As Mill acknowledges, even laws against conduct that harms others close off some spaces of choice from individuals. But he argues that the "means of development" such laws take away from the potential criminal are exercised at the expense of the development of other people. It is not terribly clear how such a consideration fits with the general Utilitarian framework of Mill's analysis. Mill seems to assume that everyone has an equal claim to the conditions of self-development, and that it is therefore unfair of some to claim a greater liberty at the expense of the liberty and development of others. This argument is plausible enough, but (as we shall shortly see) not easily reconciled with the ideas of Utilitarianism.[10] It has a Kantian flavor.

At various points in his argument, Mill shows a special interest in the person of genius, whose benefits to the human race may be lost through enforced adherence to conventional norms. This is the perfectionist strand in Mill's person-based justification. Geniuses, he argues, need freedom even more than others, because they are "more individual than any other people," and consequently less able to fit themselves comfortably into conventional modes of life. Mill argues that these geniuses are of use to others, and that the current condition of society cuts off those valuable contributions by making "mediocrity the ascendant power among mankind." Such remarks suggest that liberty is of use primarily because it fosters the development of a small number of outstanding people who make contributions that benefit others. Mill adds to this consideration the idea of the progress of the species over time. Through the contributions of outstanding people in time A, the human race becomes generally better at time B. Thus "human beings become a noble and beautiful object of contemplation; and . . . human life also becomes rich, diversified, and animating, . . . making the race infinitely better worth belonging to." Such perfectionist and inegalitarian considerations are clearly very dear to Mill, and often he seems to be asking his reader to tolerate some social disorder for the sake of the betterment of the species.

This perfectionistic strand in Mill's person-based argument sits very uneasily with the type of liberalism that I have been defending, which is based on ideas of mutual respect and equal worth. Nor is it easy to show that Mill's perfectionism actually justifies universal conditions of liberty rather than special exceptions for certain outstanding people. To defend the extension of liberty to the entire population on the basis of his perfectionist argument, Mill will need to argue that it would be impossible to recognize the outstanding individuals reliably or early enough to give them special treatment: they can develop only in conditions of general liberty, but whether this is true may be disputed. The ancient Greeks had many outstanding individuals who used the institution of slavery to their advantage.

Plenty of outstanding men, as Mill would be the first to grant, have developed their powers in conditions in which women had no liberty; often they found the nonliberty of women a distinct advantage in unfolding their powers. In general, no era prior to Mill's time had been an era of universal liberty, and yet geniuses emerged; in fact almost all the empirical evidence we have about geniuses comes from eras in which liberty has been considerably restricted.

Moreover, even if a convincing argument could be made to the conclusion that genuises require universal conditions of liberty, this hardly seems the right *sort* of argument to use in justifying the extension of liberty to all. Once again, some people are being used as means to the ends of others. The fact that indirectly they, or their descendants, may hope to profit from the discoveries made by the liberated genius does not do enough to show that Mill's argument respects them.

This is not the entirety of Mill's person-based argument, however. He also argues, apparently independently of the perfectionist strand in his argument, that all human beings need liberty for their self-development, and that all have a claim to the conditions that foster this development. This is what I shall call the distributive strand of the argument. After developing his perfectionist argument, he offers this more inclusive argument for liberty:

> But independence of action and disregard of custom are not solely deserving of encouragement for the chance they afford that better modes of action, and customs more worthy of general adoption, may be struck out; nor is it only persons of decided mental superiority who have a just claim to carry on their lives in their own way. There is no reason that all human existence should be constructed on some one or some small number of patterns. If a person possesses any tolerable amount of common sense and experience, his own mode of laying out his existence is the best, not because it is the best in itself, but because it is his own mode. . . . The same things which are helps to one person toward the cultivation of his higher nature are hindrances to another. . . . [U]nless there is a corresponding diversity in their modes of life, they neither obtain their fair share of happiness, nor grow up to the mental, moral, and aesthetic stature of which their nature is capable.

Mill evidently believes, then, that all citizens have a "just claim" to liberty of self-regarding conduct, as articulated by the harm principle. The reason for this is apparently to be found in the happiness and self-development of individuals. Liberty is necessary for each person's attainment of a flourishing life, because flourishing lives are so different from one another that any single pattern would fit some and misfit others, starving those others of the development that is their due.

Here Mill comes as close as he ever does in this work to a justification that a liberal could accept. For liberals, even political liberals in the Rawlsian mode, agree that a just society is a scheme for the distribution of certain benefits and burdens, and that the benefits (a small list of "primary goods") are thus part and parcel of what people of all different doctrines must agree to when signing on to the political consensus. Moreover, Rawls explicitly sees the "primary goods," liberty prominent among them, as necessary conditions for citizens' formation and development of their own plans of life.[11] Mill certainly has a much more perfectionistic way of expressing his idea of self-development than Rawls would countenance: he speaks not just of happiness but of "grow[ing] up to the mental, moral, and aesthetic stature of which their nature is capable." And the full development of this idea of "stature" would surely involve more in the way of a single and definite conception of ethical and aesthetic value than political liberalism would think appropriate.

Nonetheless, a modified version of this distributive strand in Mill's argument appears to be on the right track. Even the Rawlsian defender of liberty has to say something about why liberty is important, why it should be on a list of social primary goods.[12] A plausible answer to this question is given by citing the role liberty plays in enabling people to form and choose a plan of life that is their own. This is part of a conception of the person that we could agree to endorse for political purposes, while disagreeing about much else. To say that people need liberty in order to choose a plan of life is, in Rawls's conception and related liberal conceptions, simply another way of saying that they have a just claim to that liberty: there is something about a person, and a person's inviolability, that requires liberty. Thus, put in this way, the argument for liberty appeals not to the dubious notion of overall social good, but to the idea of what it is to treat each person as an end.

This is a promising argument. What is less clear (as I have already suggested) is that it is fully compatible with Mill's Utilitarianism. On the individual level it may well be compatible, because, as I have suggested, Mill's conception of individual happiness is (probably) very Aristotelian: it involves treating the development and unfolding of human faculties as an end in itself, at least one part of what happiness is. On the social level, however, a familiar problem again arises: why wouldn't it be admissible, on Utilitarian grounds, to deny some few people their fair chance for self-development, in order to give the greater number vastly increased opportunities for self-development? With women and men, Mill can plausibly say that society loses too much by denying self-development to fully half of its members. But he seems to have no clear way to rule out the permanent subordination of a small group (let's say, a group of enforced nurses and child-care workers) if that would be useful to the greater number. His own notion of the "just claim" to self-development rebels against such an idea, and, similarly, his arguments in favor of women's emancipation do not depend entirely upon Utilitarian considerations. Insofar as they depart from those, however, Mill is veering round to a different sort of theory, more Kantian in spirit, in which each person is inviolable, and an end.

To summarize: Mill's argument in *On Liberty* has great value for the way in which it shows how social conformity, peer pressure, and the legal realization of conventional morality all damage the self-development of individuals. Mill advances a plausible set of constraints on the legal regulation of conduct and gives a promising account of how laws that violate those constraints harm people. But when it comes to justifying his position on liberty, Mill's argument is not all that one might wish. The famous argument from truth is not especially helpful to a person interested in the core ideas of political liberalism— equal respect, reciprocity, and the inviolability of the person. First, it is underspecific, not considering the hard case of hate speech or the issue of possible low-value speech (commercial speech); to that extent it does not give detailed guidance even to those who agree with its basic spirit. Second, its contingent claims are fragile and set important areas of liberty on a dubious empirical foundation. Third, it seems to put the means before the end: instead of thinking of persons as ends and social conditions as means to their development, it treats truth as an end to which the liberty of individuals is a mere means. Finally, it takes a stand on contested metaphysical matters that a pluralistic liberal society should leave outside the core of the political conception.

The self-development strand of Mill's argument, however, fares much better. It is true that the perfectionistic strand of that argument suffers from problems similar to those of the truth argument: the general policy of liberty for all is but a means to the production of a few outstanding individuals; and even those individuals are, apparently, seen as a means to the general enhancement, over time, of the human species. But the distributive strand of the argument, according to which each and every individual has a "just claim" to the conditions of his or her self-development, has no such flaws, and can be developed in a nonperfectionistic way, using a political conception of the person, and of self-development—ideas that diverse citizens in a pluralistic society can all support. To develop it fully we will have to depart from Utilitarianism, even in Mill's modified form, but we would still be advancing an argument that is Millian in spirit.

Here we feel that we have arrived at the heart of what is troubling, for the liberal, in a policy like Devlin's, which willingly turns conventional morality into law even when the conduct in question causes no harm. Such intrusions of law into the "self-regarding" conduct of others deprive people of what they have a "just claim" to have, namely, a space within which to develop and unfold their own plans of life. Such considerations of respect for persons, rather than the considerations of social utility and species progress to which Mill is so drawn, are the right basis on which to justify a policy similar to Mill's.

III. The Case against
Disgust and Shame

How are the arguments about disgust and shame in the present book connected to the liberal case for liberty that I have sketched here? Or, to put it more poetically, what is the relationship of my epigraph

from Mill, in which Mill defends his harm principle, to my epigraph
from Anne Hollander, in which she connects a certain rejection of
shame and disgust about the female body to the possibility of
women's equality as citizens, and to Whitman's brief poem, in which
he invites Americans to accept the body (and its mortality) without
shrinking? I shall now argue that the psychological arguments advanced in this book help us make a stronger case than Mill himself
made for a political principle similar to his harm principle.

Human beings are deeply troubled about being human—about
being highly intelligent and resourceful, on the one hand, but weak
and vulnerable, helpless against death, on the other. We are ashamed
of this awkward condition and, in manifold ways, we try to hide from
it. In the process we develop and teach both shame at human frailty
and disgust at the signs of our animality and mortality. Both disgust
and primitive shame are probably in some measure inevitable parts
of human development. Disgust serves, in addition, a useful role in
steering us away from danger, and shame of the primitive kind is
closely linked, at least, to more productive and potentially creative
types of shame that spur people on to high achievements.

Both of these emotions may easily become problems, however,
both in the life of the individual and in the larger social life of which
it is a part. In particular, both emotions are associated with forms of
social behavior in which a dominant group subordinates and stigmatizes other groups. In the case of disgust, properties pertinent to
the subject's own fear of animality and mortality are projected onto
a less powerful group, and that group then becomes a vehicle for the
dominant group's anxiety about itself. Because they and their bodies
are found disgusting, members of the subordinated group typically
experience various forms of discrimination. In the case of shame, a
more general anxiety about helplessness and lack of control inspires
the pursuit of invulnerability (or the retrieval of that illusion, which
was very likely present in infancy). An appearance of control is then
frequently purchased by the creation of stigmatized subgroups who—
whether because they become the focus for social anxieties about
disorder and disruption, or because, quite simply, they are different
and not "normal," and the comforting fiction of the "normal" allows
the dominant group to hide all the more effectively—come to exem-

plify threats of various types to the secure control of the dominant group.

Given the ubiquity of this stigmatizing behavior and its very deep roots, it seems likely that disgust and shame provide bad guidance for law in a society committed to equal respect among persons. Shame in particular does come in less problematic and more admirable forms, but it is so hard to distinguish these forms from the bad forms, and so common to find a slippage from one to another, that the prominent use of shame in punishment and lawmaking seems tantamount to inviting people to discriminate and stigmatize.

Thus we arrive at some of the same problems that Mill diagnosed in *On Liberty*: the tyranny of the "normal" over the unusual, the crippling effect of dominant social norms, through law, on lives that do not conform. We have approached these problems by a different route from Mill's. Mill simply observed the operations of custom and did not spend much time asking why people behave this way. Nor, had he asked this question, could he easily have answered it with the psychology available to him. Despite his perceptiveness as a person, his official psychology was the rather impoverished form of empiricism bequeathed to him by his father, called "associationism," according to which all emotions and other attitudes are simply products of associations between one thing and another. Such a view probably would not have allowed him to arrive at an adequate account of the dynamics of disgust and primitive shame. I have argued in chapter 4 that it did not even permit him to grasp some crucial issues about his own mental crisis.

At the very least, then, our examination gives us a deeper account than Mill's own of the problems that preoccupy him in *On Liberty*. It shows why and to what extent the problems really are serious and pervasive problems, and it indicates that we cannot expect them to go away so long as human life has anything like its actual structure. Thus it also provides a deeper and more stable rationale for mistrusting laws based upon conventional norms and the emotions that so frequently enforce them. For all Mill says, his reader might feel free to conclude that English society of Mill's own time had the wrong norms, but that by now we have gotten things right and we may happily use shame and disgust to inform our own lawmaking.[13] Indeed, such a confidence in moral progress seems to inform Kahan's conception of disgust and shame as valuable and progressive sentiments.

Our account also provides a rationale for limits to the legal regulation of conduct that avoids the difficulties raised by Mill's truth-based justification and the perfectionist arm of his person-based justification. We have found fault with disgust and shame as bases for law simply by thinking about human dignity and the equal worth of persons. We did not need to invoke any notion of social utility, of progress toward the truth, or of the betterment of the human species, notions crucial to Mill's argument, but highly problematic in a contemporary liberal context.

Does our account support Mill's harm principle, or only a weaker principle, compatible with paternalistic prohibitions, for example, against various types of self-harm? I have said that it is one thing to require that laws target some type of harm and another thing to require that they regulate only conduct that harms others. In rendering problematic the pure appeal to disgust and shame, we have not yet answered paternalists, who may feel that some types of harm to self are just as severe as harms done to others, and that the severity of these harms justifies paternalistic laws against drug use, suicide, and so forth. I side with Mill here, but to make out the case requires much more in the way of a definite political theory than I have aimed to present in this book. One may even accept many of the proposals that I make in *Women and Human Development,* for a liberal state based on the recognition of a core list of human capabilities that are all linked to the idea of a life with human dignity, while differing about the role of paternalism in public policy.[14]

Certainly there are types of "self-harm" that are only called that because of phobic reactions based on disgust and shame of the sort that I have identified; without the backing of such emotions the claim of harm falls to the ground. At times we may have reason to feel that this is also true of reactions to drug use: the objector is not really focused on the danger that people will harm themselves, but on issues of disgust and stigmatization. For example, people who shrink from drug use do not always care to weigh its real dangers against those of other pursuits, for example, playing football or driving a car, to which no such objection is standardly raised. Smoking poses issues of harm to others (second-hand smoke), and also issues of disgust *as harm* in the sense that we endorsed in discussing nuisance law: smoke disgusts some people and damages their enjoyment of their surroundings. If we abstract from those issues, however, the public reaction against smoking may also contain elements of a more "constructive" disgust and of stigma and shame. Disgust and shame are often in the picture when some unpopular habits are singled out for condemnation and other practices that pose a similar risk of self-harm are ignored.

Despite these difficulties, though, we can at least agree that disgust and shame are not the only things driving people's interest in regulation of drugs, smoking, and dangerous sports (such as boxing). The liberal state admits the salience of life and health as basic goods on whose importance all citizens can agree. So even if we get rid of the malign influence of disgust and shame, there is still a good deal to argue about before we would be satisfied that Mill's principle is correct. I myself have defended the idea that the appropriate goal for political action is "capability," that is, opportunity to choose, and not "functionality": once the stage is fully set, in areas ranging from life and health to political participation, the choice to function or not to function should be left up to the individual. Thus, while I support paternalistic measures for children (for example compulsory schooling), I am opposed to paternalistic measures for adult citizens, such as compulsory voting, mandatory health measures, and so forth, with only a small number of exceptions.[15] But many people who agree with my general approach are prepared to be more paternalistic than I am about unhealthy and dangerous activities. This argument must continue, as we attempt to get clearer about what a sufficient respect for human freedom and choice requires.

To pursue that argument would obviously take us well beyond the limited agenda of this book. I have aimed to present a partial defense of Mill's principle by way of a critique of some of its more prominent opponents, but many matters remain to be further worked out, and reasonable differences will remain among those who are basically convinced by the argument I have made here.

My argument has not tried to deny that disgust and shame are powerful motives, and may at times play some of the good roles that

Kahan ascribes to them. But I have suggested that a liberal society has particular reason to be uneasy about them, because of the great importance such a society ascribes to the equal worth of persons, and to related notions of dignity, respect, and self-respect. These two emotions have an intimate connection to social hierarchy and to a public culture that expresses the belief that people are unequal in worth.

IV. Emotions and Forms of Liberalism

By exposing links between disgust and shame and pernicious forms of social hierarchy, an analysis of these emotions also helps us criticize some currently fashionable forms of liberalism. The new combination of a basically liberal state with communitarian moral sentiments, pioneered by both Kahan and Etzioni, seems attractive to many.[16] Our analysis has suggested, however, that in its reliance on shame and disgust as public motives it has a dangerous tendency to encourage stigmatizing and social hierarchy. Whether it is right even to call this view a form of liberalism ought to be questioned.[17] It certainly has much in common with the conservative moralism that Mill criticized as antithetical to liberty.

In quite a different way, chapter 6 has suggested, the older and highly influential idea of social relations as based on a social contract appears problematic from the point of view of our analysis. The commitment of major contractarian theorists to viewing society's basic structure as a contract among independent adults who are rough equals in power and ability has great strengths; this tradition has made a large contribution to deepening our understanding of liberal ideas of dignity and reciprocity. And yet, these theories' emphasis on equality and independence, and on mutual advantage as the goal of the social compact, encourages stigma, albeit in a much more subtle way than the views of Kahan and Etzioni. By representing the paradigmatic citizen as an independent adult, and by representing all adults as roughly similar in ability, such views may encourage the stigmatizing of those who are in asymmetrical ways disabled or dependent, whether for a part or the whole of life. Society's most basic political principles do not take account of such asymmetrical needs, nor do such theories encourage the thought that people who have such needs can take their place as citizens worthy of equal respect. The very fact that their needs are left as an afterthought, after society's basic institutions are already designed, encourages a sharp segmentation of the unusually disabled from the typically disabled (or, as "normals" like to call them, the "able-bodied").[18]

Both communitarian and contractarian liberalism, then, different though they are in other respects, leave troubling issues of stigma unresolved. My analysis suggests that both omissions may stem from a common problem. In both cases, the political conception of the person used by the theories is one that fails to confront certain deep tensions and difficulties inherent in humanity. Instead, these conceptions subtly encourage us to flee from these difficulties and allow us to go on pinning them on others. The Kahan-Etzioni conception divides citizens into bad disorderly children who need shame to keep them on the track, much in the way that one might toilet train a dog by rubbing its nose in its own shit, and good grown-ups who are totally in control. In that way, it encourages a repudiation of human weakness and imperfection, and a projection of one's own feared imperfections onto others who can be publicly controlled and disgraced. The social-contract tradition, though for different (and, to my mind, much more admirable) reasons, encourages a similar segmentation: "independent" citizens are marked off from those whose disabilities put them outside of the "normal" citizen category.

What we need, it seems, is a political conception of the person that makes sense of the fact that we all have mortal decaying bodies and are all needy and disabled, in varying ways and to varying degrees. At the same time, the political conception should be well aware of the dangers to social relations posed by the psychological facts we have outlined here and astute about addressing them. It should strive to create a "facilitating environment" within which citizens of many different kinds can live together with dignity and mutual respect.

Expressing agreement with Rawls's idea of political liberalism, I have argued that a liberal political conception should not be built on a metaphysical theory that is sectarian, belonging to one comprehensive view held by citizens rather than another. In general, political

liberalism seeks parsimony in its apparatus of principles and doctrines, because it wants to base its political construction on moral
doctrines that can be endorsed by all the major religions and other
comprehensive doctrines of human life citizens may hold. John Rawls
argued, plausibly, that this commitment to respect for comprehensive doctrines means that political liberalism must also be parsimo-
nious with regard to psychology: a "reasonable political psychology"
cannot include conceptions that are profoundly controversial among
citizens, or linked to one religious doctrine rather than another. Do
the ideas that I have advanced in this analysis meet that test?

I believe that, in a general way, they do. The findings regarding
disgust are very well supported by experimental research and by related theorizing from people who otherwise differ greatly in doctrine. Indeed, even William Miller, whose normative position on
disgust is diametrically opposed to mine, agrees with the basic analysis I have given. Nor is there anything about it that appears sectarian,
in the sense of favoring one religion rather than another.

My analysis of shame, though similarly based on experimental and
sociological data, also prominently invokes psychoanalytic materials,
and many people do not have a high regard for psychoanalysis. To
the extent that I use these materials here, however, I invoke them as
persuasive forms of humanistic interpretation that people with an interest in human life may accept without accepting the claim of psychoanalysis to be a science—a claim in which good practitioners
have increasingly little interest, and one that was of especially little
interest to Donald Winnicott, the pivotal figure in my account here.
Winnicott always saw analysis as closely linked to poetry and literature, a mode of imaginative understanding.[19] Guided by Winnicott's approach, I use psychoanalytic materials the way I use Plato
and Lucretius—as stories about the human condition by perceptive
and humanly wise people. Winnicott's wisdom has its source in the
treatment of patients, so to that extent he is different from a philosopher or a poet. But that seems to me to give him, if anything, a greater
claim to our attention.

Is the analysis of shame I propose on this basis at odds with major
religious ideas regarding shame? Certainly it is not at odds when it
emphasizes that perfection is an implausible and inappropriate goal
for a human being. Perhaps the normative idea of respect for human

dignity that runs through the analysis of shame and stigma is at odds with some religious ideas, insofar as there may be some religious conceptions that regard the human being as not worthy of respect. But the idea of human dignity, as a political idea, is pivotal to all known forms of political liberalism; it may reasonably be included within the core of moral ideas that form the basis for a political-liberal conception. Human dignity is affirmed as a moral part of the political doctrine, not as a metaphysical idea. A religion may accept it in this role while asserting that in some ultimate metaphysical sense human life is not very dignified. For the most part, however, I believe that the major religions already do accept the idea of human dignity, which lies at the core of modern notions of human rights.[20] Most of the major religions do support the ideas of human rights and do not view them as incompatible with their teachings regarding human frailty and inadequacy.

Thus it seems to me likely that the psychological conceptions advanced in this book are broadly acceptable to those who hold diverse religious doctrines, and that they can be accepted as part of a core of doctrines that forms a basic part of the underpinning of a political-liberal society. Obviously anything with any interesting content is also controversial in some way, and it cannot be a requirement of political liberalism that it say nothing that can be contested. But there must be some space between the utterly banal and the deeply divisive, and I hope and believe that the analyses proposed in this book occupy that space.

My analysis of disgust and shame suggests that certain forms of liberalism (or, in the case of Kahan-Etzioni, of purported liberalism) should be rejected, as in tension with liberal ideas of respect for human dignity. Does it suggest, by contrast, that there is any particular version of liberalism that we ought to favor? I believe it does. If we think, first, of the political conception of the person that the arguments of this book lead us to favor, we find that such a conception needs to combine an emphasis on human ability with an emphasis on imperfection, need, and also, at times, asymmetrical need. The Aristotelian idea of the citizen as "political animal" has great promise as we try to move beyond the problems diagnosed here because this conception emphasizes the continuity between the human being and other animal creatures, with their needy and mortal bodies, while not ignoring the fact that the human being has traits (and problems) that are different from those of any other animal creature, and a source of potential difficulty for society.[21] The Aristotelian conception sees the human being as a creature both needy and capable, whose capacities and whose dignity are thoroughly bound up with its animal nature, and whose capacities all require rich support from the material environment. This emphasis on materiality and need is conceptually helpful, because we learn not to think of our needs for material things as embarrassing and humiliating facts about us. Instead, materiality and need are themselves part of the specific form of dignity that a human being has.

Building on this political conception of the person, it will then be natural to conceive of the good things politics distributes not so much as simply stuffs or things, as if those had some goodness or worth in their own right, but rather as an interlocking set of human capabilities: states of people such that they are ready to select functioning of certain specified types, and those functionings are actually available to them. Seeing human beings as essentially material, mortal, and needy, we gravitate to a conception of politics that sees one of its primary tasks as that of providing support for human need so that human beings can choose to function. The aim of politics is seen as providing all citizens with a basic core of capabilities, which can be enumerated as basic entitlements of all citizens, whether through a constitutional list of entitlements or in some other way. Thus the "capabilities approach" to the foundations of liberalism that Amartya Sen and I have in different ways developed becomes attractive as a way of articulating the distributive task of such a society.

Capabilities have an *inner* aspect: the person herself has to be prepared to engage in the form of functioning in question (by education, health care, emotional support, and so on). They also have an *external* aspect: even someone who is all prepared, inwardly, to speak or think freely can be impeded from so doing by bad social and institutional arrangements. Thus the claim that politics should promote a set of central human capabilities is a demanding one: politics must distribute what I have elsewhere called *combined capabilities*— the inner aspect combined with external conditions suitable for the exercise of the requisite functions. This amounts to the claim that politics should make sure that people have whatever resources, training, and other material and institutional support is required for them to develop the wherewithal to function in that way, and actually to be in a position to do so.

Thus the "capabilities approach," which I have described at much greater length elsewhere, makes evident the complex forms of interdependence between human beings and their material, social, and political environments.[22] The approach is in this way particularly well suited to provide the core for a society that seeks to acknowledge humanness (including animality, mortality, and finitude) rather than to hide from it, calling shame and disgust to its aid. The capabilities approach may not be the only liberal approach that can do justice to these features of human life, but it does commend itself as among those that are in a strong position to do so.

What moral sentiments will be particularly important in such a political-liberal society, based on ideas of capability and functioning? In particular, on what sentiments will it rely as it makes laws? I have frequently suggested that anger and indignation will be such core sentiments because they react to harm or damage. A salient fact about the human being, from the point of view of liberalism, is its vulnerability to significant damage at the hands of others. Once again: not all instances of anger are reliable, based on correct views about what constitutes a significant damage, or whether such a damage has occurred. But it is a sentiment of the right *sort* on which to rely, once one evaluates critically all the concrete judgments contained within it. A liberal society, focused on the dignity, the self-development, and the freedom of action of the individual needs to inhibit harm; to the extent that anger tracks harm, it will be a reliable guide to lawmaking.

Similarly, a rightly focused fear and grief will be appropriate emotions for citizens who understand that human life is menaced by significant dangers and that loss of the most valuable things is always possible. Such sentiments will motivate citizens to care about the secure and fair distribution of resources to all, as also about the stability of the institutions that do the distributing. By the same token, positive emotions of gratitude and love prove important to citizens who depend upon one another, and upon social institutions, for many of the goods they experience in life. Once again: all such emotions may be well or poorly adjusted to their circumstances, and based on good or bad reasons. But they are the *types* of emotion that a citizen of the envisaged society will prominently experience, and that the society ought, in the appropriate ways, to foster.

Another crucial liberal sentiment, discussed prominently in chapter 1, is compassion. Compassion involves the thought that another person has suffered a significant hardship or loss, and it plays a prominent role in prompting helping behavior that addresses these losses. The classic occasions for compassion are also the cases of capability failure that are of particular interest to a liberal society, especially one that is built on the capabilities approach: illness, loss of mobility, loss of friends and family, loss of a sphere of work or activity. Compassion of the kind typically elicited by tragic dramas regards these losses as significant and judges that the suffering person herself is not (or not primarily) to blame for them.[23] To that extent it provides a valuable social motive to prevent or rectify such losses. In my 2001 book on the emotions I analyze the role of compassion in a liberal society in great detail, arguing that it is, if highly fallible, still a valuable sentiment for a liberal society to tap, and further to educate.[24] Chapter 1 gave us some examples of good roles that compassion can play in a legal system.

Yet compassion, like anger, can go wrong. Its sense of what losses are significant can go awry, as can its sense of when people are, and are not to be, blamed. Moreover, it usually gets the circle of pertinent people wrong, focusing on those close at hand to the exclusion of strangers and people at a distance. To that extent it is often at odds with impartial moral principles that teach the equal worth of all human lives. I argue, however, that the solution to this problem should be to educate compassion and extend it, not to jettison it. Well educated, it provides a good guide to aspects of the legal system, particularly those involving the articulation of fundamental entitlements. The argument of the present book suggests that this education should prominently include thought about human weakness, dependency, and disability. This thought need not conceive of the disabled as pathetic victims, any more than a tragic spectator sees the tragic hero as a pathetic victim. Part of the compassionate response itself can be, and frequently is, admiration for the courage and competence of people who encounter obstacles that give them a reduced sphere of functioning.[25]

In short, then, the analysis of this book has suggested that emotions are not all alike in their relation to different forms of political organization. A liberal state has an intimate relationship to both anger and compassion (along with fear, grief, love, and gratitude). It has a much more vexed and difficult relationship to shame and disgust. Disgust will remain a part of people's personal lives, and, almost inevitably, a part of their social lives. But its hierarchies of persons have no place in a liberal society. Shame of certain sorts can be a valuable moral sentiment in people's personal lives, goading them on to valuable forms of activity. But its use in punishment is deeply problematic and hard to square with equal regard for the dignity of all citizens. And the shame that society so often metes out to those who are different should be countered, in a liberal polity, by public action that focuses on promoting respect and empowerment for those groups of citizens who have traditionally been shamed.

We have arrived at a conclusion closely related to Mill's by a very non-Millian route, offering a complex analysis of emotions that Mill (appropriating his father's theory) saw as mechanical and determined mindlessly by behavioral conditioning. James Mill's simplistic view of emotion never fit very well with his son's thought, in other respects so nuanced, humanistic, and capable of acknowledging human complexity. But it was nonetheless the view J. S. Mill officially espoused, even while describing his own development in more complex terms, and while continually expressing his own emotions, particularly in correspondence with Harriet, in a manner that could not possibly have been explained by the simple view. Because Mill clung officially to the simple view, he was prevented from articulating some aspects of the problem of conformity and stigmatization that exercised him in *On Liberty*. And he was thrown back on a set of arguments in favor of liberty that are both seriously incomplete and, in some respects, unacceptable to a contemporary form of liberalism that respects religious pluralism.

My hope is that the present analysis has given support to Mill's general line from a new and unexpected quarter. Through the detailed analysis of the cognitive structure of sentiments that have sometimes been thought to lack all interesting cognitive structure, we arrive at a new understanding of the obstacles to equal respect for persons and their freedom, and thus we have a new set of reasons to be on our guard against moralistic versions of liberalism that rely on sentiments that appear to create these obstacles. To argue against trusting disgust and shame is hardly to advance a complete liberal theory of the moral limits of the law, as I have frequently pointed out. We need other arguments concerning paternalism, and a general positive understanding of the nature of punishment, before we would begin to have even the building blocks of a liberal theory of legal regulation. But since the opponents of liberalism, and even its so-called friends, so often rely on disgust and shame as their tools, we have done something if we have shown why this reliance is dangerous, insofar as human dignity is what we want to protect.

More generally, by reflecting on the deep difficulties in human life that prompt the reliance on disgust and shame as public sentiments, we have begun to see at least the outlines of some capacities that a liberal society should cherish and further develop: the ability to enjoy relations of interdependence, rather than domination; the ability to acknowledge incompleteness, animality, and mortality in oneself and in others. Through public education and the general crafting of public institutions and a public culture, a society can do much to encourage these capacities and discourage those that lead to unequal and hierarchical social relations.[26]

Nine months after the conclusion of his analysis, the patient B wrote a letter to Donald Winnicott. In his letter we see none of the rigidity, and also none of the shame, that characterized him earlier. Instead, he is willing to admit to uncertainty:

> Dear Dr Winnicott,
> . . . I am not at all sure what I will be doing after that. It is not yet possible for me to plan that far ahead. I am tempted at times to abandon analysis as I now feel so well. On the other hand, I do realise that the process is incomplete and I may then decide either to resume with you, or should that no longer be possible, to start with someone else. It seems to me to be a great step forward that I can accept that idea fairly easily.
>
> Should we not resume later, I would like to use this opportunity to express my gratitude for all that you have done.
>
> Yours sincerely,
> [*name*]

The phrase "should that no longer be possible" is particularly telling: for Winnicott, who had long had cardiac problems, was known to B to be severely ill; in fact he died a short time later. B is then accepting the mortality of the analyst and, by extension, his own. He shows his new understanding of human love by admitting that love itself (the "subtle interplay" he had enjoyed in his exchanges with Winnicott) is a relation between imperfect and mortal beings.

Such a frank admission of incompleteness and uncertainty is a good place to begin, perhaps, as people varyingly disabled work together to create a liberal society.

Notes

Introduction

1. These examples are taken from Kahan (1996) 632, with refs.
2. See Bérubé (1996), and discussion in Nussbaum (2000b).
3. *Commonwealth v. Carr,* 580 A.2d 1362, 1363–65 (Pa. Super. Ct. 1990). See generally Brenner (1995), and discussion in Kahan and Nussbaum (1996).
4. *Miller v. California,* 413 U.S. 15, 93 S. Ct. 2607 (1973).
5. Mison (1992); see further discussion in chap. 3.
6. Etzioni (2001, 37).
7. Cited by Sanders (1989, 183); his reference is to an article in the *Hartford Courant,* 19 April 1986, C6. Whether the intent of the proposal was to stigmatize or to warn prospective sexual partners, its effect is surely stigmatizing; nor does Buckley propose similar tattoos for women, or children, or "straight" men who are HIV-positive or carry some other infectious disease.
8. Massaro (1991, 1997), Markel (2001).
9. E. Posner (2000), Whitman (1998).
10. Rawls (1971), Bérubé (1996).
11. Whitman (1998), for example, argues that the liberal tradition gives us no good reasons not to punish by shaming. Kahan, in a very different way, appears to deny that shame penalties are illiberal (1996, 1998, 1999).
12. Devlin (1965), Miller (1987). Miller probably does not support Devlin's most famous recommendation, i.e., the prohibition of consensual homosexual acts. In general, he portrays himself as opposed to discrimination on grounds of sex and sexual orientation, though he makes few concrete legal judgments.
13. Kahan (1999).
14. Something like this would appear to be the position of Dworkin (1977), arguing against Devlin. Dworkin argues that Devlin's concept of a "moral position"

needs scrutiny: we accept, he says, as good grounds for law only judgments for which reasons can be given, and we make, in the process, a strong distinction between reason and emotion. "If I base my view about homosexuals on a personal emotional reaction . . . you would reject that reason as well. . . . Indeed, it is just this sort of position—a severe emotional reaction to a practice or a situation for which one cannot account—that we tend to describe, in lay terms, as a phobia or an obsession" (250). Now Dworkin does allow that if one can give reasons for one's emotional reaction they may be admitted; but he persistently treats the reasons as separate from the emotional reaction itself. What he calls "mere emotional reaction" (ibid.) by itself provides no reasons for anything. Later, he repeats the point: "I cannot settle the issue simply by reporting my feelings" (252). Devlin's mistake, he concludes, is to take a mere emotional reaction to be sufficient for a moral position. I admire a great deal in Dworkin's argument, but it sweeps much too broadly in treating all emotion as "mere emotion," and denying that emotions, in and of themselves, can ever contain good reasons, including moral reasons.

15. These ideas are developed at much greater length in Nussbaum (2001a), a systematic account of the relationship between emotion and belief, emotion and value. This shorter volume will inevitably make contact with that larger work at many points, and readers who wish a more extensive and detailed set of philosophical arguments on many points raised here should read the parallel discussions in that book.

16. See Nussbaum (1994, chaps. 10–12; 2001a, chap. 1).

17. A leading example of this approach is Posner (1990, chap. 5). Posner traces the view to Holmes: see his edition of Holmes (1992, 160–77, 237–64).

18. The same, I argue in Nussbaum (2001a), is true of many animals, though at different levels of complexity and sophistication.

19. See also Nussbaum (1997), for an account of higher education related to these arguments.

20. Winnicott (1986), discussed in chap. 4.

21. Of course here I am appropriating Plato's way of talking, in *Republic* IX, about his very illiberal state.

Chapter 1. Emotions and Law

1. *Small v. Commonwealth,* 91 Pa. 304, 306, 308 (1879).

2. *State v. Norman,* 378 S.E.2d 8, 9, 11, 13 (N.C. 1989); id. at 17, 21 (Martin, J., dissenting).

3. *Woodson v. North Carolina,* 428 U.S. 280, 303 (1976).

4. *California v. Brown,* 479 U.S. (1986), 538 ff.

5. Ibid., 538.

6. The majority opinion argues that jurors would easily understand this distinction. The dissenters argue that prosecutors are likely to confuse jurors, suggesting that they are in fact being asked to disregard all sympathy; numerous examples of such prosecutorial confusion are cited.

7. On outrage and its relation to punitive damages, see Sunstein, Kahnemann, and Schkade (1998) and Sunstein et al. (2002).

8. Today, "passion" usually designates an unusually strong subclass of emotions, but it used to be a more general term, as did French "passions." The ancient Greek term *pathē*, though having an extremely general meaning in which it designates any way of being affected by something else, came to have, as well, a narrower use in which it designated this family of experiences; subsequent thinkers basically follow this tradition, whatever term they use.

9. Typically the philosophical tradition attends closely to both ordinary ways of speaking and to literature. This was certainly true of the ancient Greek Stoics, who were much criticized by their contemporaries for this methodology (see Nussbaum [1994, chap. 10]).

10. See Nussbaum (2001a) for remarks about the theoretical traditions of India and China, and for anthropological material from a variety of cultures.

11. For example, surprise or "startle" is sometimes categorized as an emotion, sometimes not; the same is true of curiosity, wonder, and respect. "Love" is the name both of an emotion and of a complex relationship, and there are differences about how these aspects of love are to be connected.

12. See Nussbaum (2001a, chap. 2) for a detailed account.

13. Ibid. Anger requires causal thinking: the creature has to believe that it has been damaged *by* someone else. I write "usually" concerning the role of perspectival thinking in compassion, because I argue in Nussbaum (2001a) that this ability is not strictly necessary: we can have compassion for the sufferings of animals whose feelings we cannot in any adequate way imagine.

14. *Rhetoric* II.1–11.

15. See ibid., II.5.

16. See ibid., II.2–3.

17. I say much more about this in Nussbaum (2001a, chap. 1).

18. Smith, *The Theory of Moral Sentiments*, Section II, chap. 1.

19. A related phenomenon will be an anger that responds to a long chain of irritations, but where it takes the final one to cross the line between nonanger and anger.

20. See the subtle discussion in Graham (1990). I discuss these distinctions in more detail in Nussbaum (2001a, chap. 2).

21. *On Anger* III.36 ff.

22. *Nicomachean Ethics* VII.5, 1149a8. He says that such a person has "bestial cowardice," and contrasts with this the case of a person who fears a weasel because of the possibility of contracting a disease—this person's fear, apparently, is reasonable. My limited knowledge of weasels prevents me from commenting further on this contrast.

23. Someone who does not believe that evaluative judgments can be true or false may substitute at this point some weaker notion of correctness or aptness.

24. Thus when my daughter was in fourth grade (in a politically correct school in Cambridge, Mass.), she came home complaining about a boy named Jonathan who had allegedly insulted her in some way. "Which one is Jonathan?" I inquired. She gave lots of descriptions: he is loud, a fast runner, tall, likes to tease girls, et cetera. Only after quite a long discussion did I figure out that he was the only African-American in her class, the description that I would have used first thing. Kahan reports that in his son's kindergarten class in Hinsdale, Ill., a game was played in which people were asked to cross the room if

they had a given named color on their bodies (not clothes). Children interpreted this very literally, rejecting "white" as simply not one of the colors on
their bodies; many children answered to "peach," and the one African-American
girl did too, looking at her hands.

25. This process of moral transformation is wonderfully described by Iris Murdoch
in Murdoch (1970).

26. See Pohlmann (1999) for doubts; his analysis is further discussed in chap. 3.

27. See Sherman (1999) for one good account of this.

28. This is odd, when one considers his intense and highly accurate concern with
nonhuman animals, to whose anatomy and behavior he devoted a great part
of his career.

29. Not with perfect consistency: see Kahan and Nussbaum (1996) for evidence of
a more mechanistic conception of emotions as impulses.

30. See psychologist Richard Lazarus's summary in Lazarus (1991): "When we
react with an emotion . . . [t]he reaction tells us that an important value or
goal has been engaged and is being harmed, placed at risk, or advanced.
From an emotional reaction we can learn much about what a person has at
stake in the encounter with the environment or in life in general, how that
person interprets self and world, and how harms, threats, and challenges are
coped with. No other concept in psychology is as richly revealing of the
way an individual relates to life and to the specifics of the physical and social
environment" (6–7).

31. For an exception, see Kahan and Nussbaum (1996).

32. Compare Sir Michael Foster, Crown Cases 292 (1898) (ear-boxing) with *Stewart
v. State*, 78 Ala. 436, 440 (1885) (blow to face).

33. Compare *Regina v. Mawgridge*, 84 Eng. Rep. 1107, 1115 (1707) with *Rex v.
Palmer*, 2 K. B. 29, 30–31 (1913).

34. *Maher v. People*, 10 Mich. 212, 221–22 (1862).

35. *Commonwealth v. Carr*, 580 A.2d 1862, 1363–65 (Pa. Super. Ct. 1990).

36. Thus Dressler (2002) seems to me to pose the issue in the wrong way when he
suggests that we must make an all-or-nothing choice between seeing the defense as offering a justification and seeing it as offering an excuse. For
Dressler, if the act is not justified, the emotion itself is also unjustified. But we
can distinguish: the emotion itself (extreme anger) is justified by the situation, although, since a fully "reasonable man" would have other ways of dealing
with his extreme emotion, the crime itself is merely (partially) excused.

37. *Small v. Commonwealth*, 91 Pa. 308 (1879).

38. An alternative approach, endorsed by the Model Penal Code, does away with
the requirement of an aggressive act against the defendant; "extreme emotional disturbance" is enough. In a typical case applying the doctrine (*State v.
Elliott*, 411 A.2d 5 [Conn. 1979]), a man overwrought "by a combination of
child custody problems, the inability to maintain a recently purchased home
and an overwhelming fear of his brother" hunts his brother down and shoots
him without provocation, and then gets a reduction to manslaughter on account of his "disturbance." For a critique of this approach, and other such
cases, see Kahan and Nussbaum (1996, 322–23).

39. Given these facts, would it be more satisfactory to abolish the provocation defense entirely? Stephen Morse argues that it would be: "Reasonable people do not kill no matter how much they are provoked. . . . As virtually every human being knows because we have all been enraged, it is easy not to kill, even when one is enraged." Morse (1984) 33–34. Still, the case I have just described, the parent who discovers her child murdered, seems a compelling one (and does even to Morse, who urges that such a killer get a total defense based on diminished capacity). It would be a peculiar society that did not extend sympathy to a person who kills in such circumstances. The reasonable person in such a circumstance *would* lose normal self-control and be likely to act rashly. A different worry has been raised by feminist critics of the doctrine: it excuses a type of conduct that is part of male socialization: see Dressler (2002), Nourse (1997). This worry is certainly a reason to confine the defense, and not, for example, to treat as paradigmatic the case of the husband who murders a wife's lover. Nourse's proposal that the defense be confined to cases in which the provocation is a criminal offense is interesting, although, given the sex laws of this country, it does not exactly capture the distinction she is after.

40. *U.S. v. Peterson*, 483 F.2d 1222 (1973).

41. Blackstone, *Commentaries* IV, chap. 14. See also III, chap. 1: "[C]are must be taken that the resistance does not exceed the bounds of mere defence and prevention; for then the defender would himself become an aggressor."

42. Blackstone already analyzed self-defense in terms of both belief and emotion: see *Commentaries* III, chap. 1.

43. *People v. Goetz*, 68 N.Y.2d 96, 497 N.E.2d 41 (1986).

44. The court did, however, hold that in applying the reasonableness test one should take into account all the circumstances facing the defendant, which would include his physical attributes, and certain prior experiences that might provide a reasonable basis for his beliefs.

45. See, e.g., N. H. Rev. Stat. Ann. Para. 627.4 (II) (b) (c) (1986); N.Y. Penal Law para. 35.15 (McKinney 1987); Tex. Penal Code Ann. Para. 9.32 (West 1994).

46. *Beard v. U.S.*, 158 U.S. 550, 561 (1895) (Harlan, J.) (quoting *Erwin v. State*, 29 Ohio St. 186, 193, 199) (1876). Justice Harlan contrasts the English attitude, which accepts the idea that a man "retreats to the wall" before using deadly force, with prevailing American attitudes.

47. See the early criticism by Joseph H. Beale, Jr., in Beale (1903), who suggests that a "really honorable man, a man of truly refined and elevated feeling," would regret the cowardice of a retreat, but regret far more "the thought that he had the blood of a fellow-being on his hands."

48. *People v. Tomlins*, 107 N.E. 496, 497 (N. Y. 1914) (Cardozo, J.).

49. See the summary in Kadish and Schulhofer (1989), 874–75.

50. See Maguigan (1991).

51. *State v. Stewart*, 763 P.2d 572 (1988).

52. The most influential work in this area has been Walker (1980).

53. *State v. Kelly*, 478 A.2d 364 (1984).

54. See discussion in Kahan and Nussbaum (1996, 349–50); and compare the Goetz case, where Goetz was convicted only of a lesser weapons charge.

55. Sheridan Lyons, "Court Panel to Probe Judge in Sentencing," *Baltimore Sun*, 20 October 1994, 1B.
56. "She Strays, He Shoots, Judge Winks," *New York Times*, 22 October 1994, A22.
57. See documentation in Kahan and Nussbaum (1996, 346–47).
58. See Texas Penal Code art. 1220 (repealed 1973).
59. Correspondence from Albert Alschuler to Dan M. Kahan (May 1995, on file with the *Columbia Law Review*). Alschuler was one of the official reporters for the committee that proposed repeal of the "paramour statute" as part of the comprehensive reform of the Texas Penal Code.
60. *Regina v. Mawgridge*, 84 Eng. Rep. 1107, 1115 (1707).
61. Thus the provoking act need not always be a criminal act, nor is every criminal act a ground for reasonable provocation, but criminality certainly contributes to the idea that a reasonable man would be provoked by it.
62. See Kahan and Nussbaum (1995).
63. Here I follow the more detailed analysis in Nussbaum (2001a, chaps. 6–8).
64. Aristotle's term *eleos* is typically translated "pity," but for reasons given in Nussbaum (2001a, chap. 6), I prefer "compassion," which, like the Greek term, does not contain any suggestion of superiority or condescension, as English "pity" sometimes does.
65. Batson (1991).
66. See Nussbaum (2003b).
67. Clark (1997).
68. *California v. Brown*, 479 U.S. 540 (1987), quoting from the judgment of the California Supreme Court, which, in turn, cites *Woodson v. North Carolina*, the earlier case that clearly asserted the constitutional requirement, 428 U.S. 280 (1976).
69. *California v. Brown*, 538.
70. Ibid., 541–42.
71. Ibid., 553.
72. Ibid., 555.
73. See summary of the debate in Bandes (1999), who offers a cogent criticism of this position.
74. See Bandes (1997).
75. See Etzioni (2001) for the most recent statement.
76. See Rawls (1971, 1996) for this position.
77. I defend such a view of political life in Nussbaum (1999a, 2000, 2002).
78. This is the reply made in Kahan and Nussbaum (1996).
79. "Reasonable disagreement" is Larmore's phrase; Rawls tends to use the term "reasonable pluralism."
80. Rawls (1996), Larmore (1987, 1996). Although the view is most commonly associated with Rawls's book of the same name, the term "political liberalism," and the central ideas, were advanced earlier by Larmore; Rawls acknowledges his seminal role.
81. I have argued that the best way to conceive of such a list of primary goods is as a list of "capabilities" or opportunities for certain key types of functioning or activity. My list of the "central capabilities" includes items such as life, health, bodily integrity, and property rights that are obviously central to the criminal law.

82. See Mill (1861, chap. 5) for a similar approach.
83. See Nussbaum (2001a, chap. 8).
84. Mill (1859).
85. On the issue of ranking freedoms, see Nussbaum (2003a). My own approach insists on a special degree of protection for a core group of liberties associated with the "central human capabilities."
86. Mill (1859); the rights alluded to here should probably be understood to be those discussed in *Utilitarianism,* chap. 5: Mill (1861). These are basic rights to security of the person and of property. For further discussion of all the difficulties I have mentioned, see Nussbaum (2002a).
87. In using this phrase, which I have used to characterize political liberalism, I do not mean to imply that Mill was a political liberal. Usually he is understood to be a "comprehensive liberal," because he seems to believe that autonomy is a value that the state is entitled to promote across the board, even when it involves denigrating some religious traditions. Mill's attitudes to some forms of religion are not very respectful, as is clear from his disparaging remarks about Calvinism in chap. 3 of *On Liberty.* But given the very strong protections he would give to all forms of thought, expression, and "self-regarding" conduct, it is not clear to me that his views really are different from those of political liberals. The difference, if any, would show up in the way public education would be arranged, and the values that public officials would be entitled to express in their public capacity.
88. For further discussion of these points, see Nussbaum (2002). The Millian state par excellence is Kentucky, which embraced Mill's harm principle late in the nineteenth century in judging unconstitutional (under the *state* constitution) ordinances forbidding the private consumption of alcohol; more recently, the Kentucky Supreme Court used these cases as precedents in invalidating Kentucky's sodomy law.
89. *Barnes v. Glen Theatre, Inc.,* 501 U.S. 560 (1991). Although Rehnquist wrote for the Court, there was no majority opinion in the case, since there were two concurring opinions.

Chapter 2. **Digust and Our Animal Bodies**

1. I use the translation given in Dworkin (1987), which accurately renders the offensive connotation of the final work, usually softened.
2. See the masterful treatment of the topic in Miller (1997), to which I shall refer often in what follows.
3. Mr. Justice Wills, Sentence, quoted in Hyde (1956).
4. Devlin (1965, 17). Devlin's position about homosexual acts was actually complex: he favored the retention of the more serious offense of "buggery" (sodomy), but urged the abolition of the less serious offenses of "gross indecency" and "indecent assault," unless those offenses were committed toward "youths." His reasoning was that in this way it was likely that only "clear and flagrant cases" would be prosecuted. And he added that even where "buggery" was concerned, he himself did not favor heavy sentences (v–vi). He does reveal a very harsh attitude toward homosexuality, however: he refers to consenting adult actors

as "addicts," and says, "I agree with everyone who has written or spoken on the subject that homosexuality is usually a miserable way of life and that it is the duty of society, if it can, to save any youth from being led into it" (v). See the further discussion in section II of this chapter.

5. Miller (1997, chap. 7).

6. Kass (1998, 19).

7. *Miller v. California*, 413 U.S. 15, 93 S. Ct. 2607 (1973), n. 2, majority opinion written by Chief Justice Burger. The Court here corrects the definition of obscenity in *Roth v. U.S.*, 354 U.S. 15 487, S. Ct. at 1310 (1957), which mentions only appeal "to prurient interest." This definition, the Court argues, "does not reflect the precise meaning of 'obscene' as traditionally used in the English language." The dictionary definitions are further discussed in chap. 3.

8. See Mison (1992).

9. Devlin (1965, 13, 16).

10. Kass (1998, 19).

11. Miller (1997, 194). It is far from clear, in Miller's argument, why disgust alone should allegedly play this role, rather than indignation, or horror, or a sense of tragedy.

12. Kahan (1998, 1624). Kahan adds, concurring with Miller, that "the moral idiom of modern liberalism is not" (brazenly and uncompromisingly judgmental). This odd conclusion is supported only by the claim that liberalism values toleration and mutual respect, but aren't these definite moral judgments, which can be as uncompromising as any?

13. Kahan (1998, 1648).

14. Devlin (1965, 16).

15. See the response to Hart (1963) on 13 n. 1.

16. Devlin (1965, 13).

17. See Hart (1963) for a related reply.

18. Devlin (1965, 106), from an essay on Mill.

19. Ibid., 111.

20. Ironically, Devlin makes these claims in a lecture first delivered as the Ernst Freund Lecture at the University of Chicago Law School. Freund, a courageous advocate of the legal rights of dissidents of all sorts, himself the first Jewish law professor in the United States, was best known for advocating the freedom of speech of political dissidents during wartime, in particular Eugene Debs.

21. Falwell also alluded to the idea that God is angry at our permissiveness and has thus withdrawn protection.

22. Some of his remarks about prostitution do suggest this direction of thought (see 12), but it is certainly not developed, nor is it even suggested in regard to noncommercial sex acts of heterosexuals.

23. Devlin (1965, 15).

24. Ibid., 17.

25. Ibid.

26. Kass (1998, 19).

27. Kass goes on more controversially, speaking of the danger that we will regard "our bodies" as "mere instruments of our autonomous rational wills," a locution that suggests that bodies actually have an extrahuman purpose. Let us by-

pass that problematic locution, however, in order to focus on the argument about disgust.

28. Kass (1998, 19).
29. Ibid., 18.
30. Ibid., 18–19.
31. Ibid., 18.
32. Miller (1997, 9).
33. Kahan (1999a, 64). Kahan identifies a further thesis, the "conservation thesis": societies always make use of disgust to inform their judgments of high and low, changing only the specific rankings of acts and persons that they endorse. I bypass this thesis, since it does not give any support to the idea of using disgust as a basis for legal regulation.
34. Miller (1997), drawing on Judith Shklar.
35. In an article written after the book, Miller seems to abandon the moral thesis in favor of a position virtually identical with that of Leon Kass, holding that "there are certain large constraints on being human and we have certain emotions that tell us when we are pressing against those constraints in a dangerous way. This is part of the job that disgust, horror and the sense of the uncanny do." (Miller [1998, 87]).
36. Kahan (1998), a detailed review of Miller, and Kahan (1999a), a more synthetic article including discussion of Miller's ideas.
37. By "classic," Rozin and I mean both that these are ubiquitous occasions of disgust and also that these are the central paradigm cases to which people typically turn in explaining disgust or why a particular thing is disgusting.
38. Rozin has published many articles on aspects of disgust, but a comprehensive account of his views is in Rozin and Fallon (1987). See also, Rozin, Haidt, and McCauley (2000). An influential earlier treatment is Angyal (1941).
39. Menninghaus (1999, 7).
40. Rozin, Haidt, and McCauley (2000, 639).
41. Darwin (1872).
42. This contrast survives the convincing argument in Korsmeyer (1999) that taste itself is not altogether "brutish," but frequently involves a cognitive element.
43. Rozin and Fallon (1987, 24 n. 1). Unfortunately, however, the so-called "D-scale" introduced in Haidt, McCauley, and Rozin (1994), does not always observe these distinctions. Thus respondents get disgust points for answering "true" to "I probably would not go to my favorite restaurant if I found out that the cook had a cold," even though one might legitimately think that the cook's germs are a source of *danger*. Some questions were confusing in a different way. Subjects get a positive disgust score for an affirmative answer to, "I think it is immoral for people to seek sexual pleasure from animals," even though the grounds of the objection might be the harm that is done to the animal, not one's own disgust at the act. And one also gets positive disgust points for answering "false" to "I might be willing to try eating monkey meat, under some circumstances," even though one might be a vegetarian on moral grounds, and thus reject the meat for that reason, along with all meat, and not because of disgust.
44. See Rozin, Haidt, and McCauley (2000, 640).

45. Ibid. They note that, although this belief is sometimes thought to be characteristic of "traditional cultures," it actually has deep roots in common sense: if two things combine, the product will resemble both.
46. Angyal (1941), cf. Rozin, Haidt, and McCauley (2000, 640).
47. Miller (1997); Rozin, Haidt, and McCauley (2000).
48. Some people find okra disgusting; philosopher Jeffrie Murphy suggests that this may be because it has "what seems like a mucous membrane" and thus strikes him as animal-like. I recall having a similar reaction as a child, although now okra (a staple of Indian cuisine, where it typically loses its mucosity by being stir-fried) is one of my favorite dishes both to eat and to cook.
49. Rozin and Fallon (1987, 28), citing Ortner (1973). Mother's milk is another interesting case, but not in the end, I think, a counterexample to the Rozin claim. For Rozin, Miller, and others make it clear that even feces are not disgusting so long as we are dealing with our own children. And mother's milk, while it can be touched by mothers without disgust, seems to inspire disgust when the mother is asked to ingest it. Elizabeth McGarry, asked by an airport security officer to drink from the bottles of breast milk she was carrying in her carry-on luggage, said, "It was very uncomfortable and very embarrassing and very disgusting" (*U.S. News and World Report*, 19 August 2002, 4). Even more clearly, breast milk inspires both disgust and tremendous anxiety in nonrelatives, especially males—hence the prohibitions of public breastfeeding that make life so difficult for many nursing mothers. Nor is the prohibition simply about embarrassment. Consider a famous episode of the television series *Married with Children*, in which Marcie and her feminist friends claim the right to breastfeed in the shoestore where Al Bundy works. His response is to get the gross-looking men of the group "No Ma'am" to present their naked beer bellies to the women, as if one gross and disgusting display deserves another.
50. Rozin and Fallon (1987, 28), citing Angyal (1941).
51. Miller (1997, xiv).
52. Rozin and Fallon (1987), citing T. Despres.
53. *Masonoff v. DuBois*, 899 F. Supp. 782, D. Mass (1995).
54. Freud (1905, 1908, 1930, 1965). Good accounts of Freud's view can be found in Miller (1997), and especially Menninghaus (1999).
55. Becker (1973, 31).
56. Becker (1973, 33). See also Menninghaus (1999, 7): "Every book about disgust is not least a book about the rotting corpse." Although Becker tends to impute fear of death to very young children, we do not need to do so, for we may explain the disgust of young children as caused by the fear-inspired disgust of their parents.
57. Compare Rozin, Haidt, and McCauley (2000, 645): "Driving this desire to distinguish ourselves from animals may be our fear of animal mortality."
58. Douglas (1966).
59. See Kim (2001) for a first-rate critique of Douglas, to which I am much indebted. See also Miller (1997, 47).
60. Two other worries raised by Kim seem less significant: poor bodily hygiene fits squarely within Rozin's bodily waste theory; disgust at "unnatural" sexual acts is highly mediated by social teaching, and demonstrably not among the "primary" objects of disgust.

61. This law has a positive side as demonstrated by our eagerness to possess or even touch objects that have been the property of celebrities, to sleep where they have slept, et cetera.

62. Rozin, Haidt, and McCauley (1999, 435).

63. Rozin, Haidt, and McCauley (2000, 640).

64. See also ibid., 638.

65. Rozin, Haidt, and McCauley (2000) also stress the importance of "framing" in limiting the extension of disgust: we learn not to think about certain things, such as who prepared our food in the kitchen of a restaurant.

66. Rozin and Fallon (1987), Rozin, Haidt, and McCauley (2000, 641).

67. Rozin, Haidt, and McCauley (2000); compare Freud (1910).

68. See Rozin, Haidt, and McCauley (2000, 646).

69. Ibid.

70. See ibid., 647, and Rozin, Fallon, and Mandell (1984). Miller (1997) tells the following stories about his children. "One of my daughters felt such a revulsion to feces immediately following her toilet training that she refused to wipe herself for fear of contaminating her hand. And one of my boys at age three not only removed underpants but the pants over them if but one drop of urine dripped out after he went to the bathroom. This could mean several changes of clothing a day. . . . My son Louie, at age four, offered during his bath the observation that since one's insides never get washed they are very dirty. The hostile reader might discern a chip off the old block" (13, 270 n. 46).

71. *Republic* IV.

72. Kaster (2001).

73. Seneca, *De Ira*, 1.3.3, 1.2.3b; the first is Seneca's version of the Aristotelian view, the second is Posidonius's version; the third is in Diogenes Laertius and Stobaeus: see *Stoicorum Veterum Fragmenta* III.395–97.

74. Aristotle, *Rhetoric* II.2.1378a31–33. He adds that the desire is accompanied by pain, and he specifies the wrong as an inappropriate "slighting" toward oneself or one's own.

75. Thus Spinoza: "Indignation is hatred towards one who has injured another": *Ethics* III, *Definition of the Emotions*, 20.

76. See Lazarus (1991, 217–34), defending and developing Aristotle's account of anger and showing that it is supported by recent experimental work. See also Ortony, Clore, and Collins, (1988), defining anger as involving "disapproving of someone else's blameworthy action" (148); and Averill (1982), stressing the role of socially shaped norms in anger.

77. *Rhetoric* II.3.

78. Adam Smith, *The Theory of Moral Sentiments*, I.ii.2.1.

79. Smith connects this fact about love to the fact that most serious literature dealing with love focuses on the lovers' predicaments, not on their happy absorption in one another's idiosyncrasies. The latter, he argues, is typically comic. See "Steerforth's Arm" in Nussbaum (1990).

80. One day a baby bat stuck its head out of the drain in my kitchen sink in Cambridge, Massachusetts. (It had gotten in the apartment somehow, and had then retreated into the drain of the upstairs bathroom, and followed the pipe on down.) I recoiled in horror and disgust. I asked my cleaning woman if she could help me. She too recoiled in horror and disgust. Together we managed

to get the bat into a cooking pot, put the lid on, and took it outdoors. As we set the pot sideways on the grass and the bat crept out, a neighbor, working in the garden, exclaimed, "The sweet little thing! Are you sure it is all right?" Afterwards I was strongly tempted to throw away the cooking pot, but I did manage to convince myself to disinfect it and continue using it. I do not mention this to my dinner guests.

81. Amendment 2 was an amendment to the State constitution, approved by voters in a statewide referendum, that denied local communities the right to make nondiscrimination laws on grounds of sexual orientation. It was ultimately declared unconstitutional by the U.S. Supreme Court in *Romer v. Evans,* 116 S. Ct. 1620 (1996).

82. Testimony of Will Perkins, trial of Amendment 2, heard personally by me, October 1994.

83. Extreme Stoics would deny it: the only thing worth valuing is virtue, which is always within our control.

84. See also *LaReau v. MacDougall,* 473 F.2d 974, C.A. 2 (1972). The court found that forcing a prisoner to "live, eat and perhaps sleep in close confines with his own human waste" was too degrading and debasing to be permitted.

85. *On Liberty,* chap. 4.

86. Rozin, Haidt, and McCauley (2000).

87. See ibid.: this is a typical case in which the extension takes place.

88. Mahler, letter to Max Marschalk, cited in Deryck Cooke, *Gustav Mahler* (Cambridge: Cambridge University Press, 1980).

89. I discuss this movement of the symphony in Nussbaum (2001a), chap. 14.

90. For helpful discussion on this point I am indebted to Talbot Brewer.

91. Brewer mentions Nietzsche's appeal to disgust in *Zarathustra,* but this appeal, and the consequent image of an impossible "overman" who lacks typical human weaknesses, is just the danger that I have in mind.

92. See Kahan (1999). A problem in Kahan's argument is that he appears to assume that any society contains a fixed quantity of disgust, whose target may be shifted, but not its intensity or amount. He adduces no evidence for this claim.

93. See Weininger (1906, 306–22).

94. See Theweleit (1987; 1989, vol. 2, 160).

95. Ibid., 160–62.

96. See, for example, Glover (2000), Adorno et al. (1950).

97. See the remarkable exhibit of such children's books in the Historisches Museum in Berlin. Similarly, untouchables, in the traditional Indian caste system, were viewed as quasi-animals, soiled by the pollution of the animal aspects of their betters.

98. Proctor (1999, 46–48).

99. Boyarin (1997) suggests that there is an important kernel of reality in such perceptions, in the sense that Jews not only valued sedentary and scholarly occupations, but also cultivated a set of masculine norms to go with them. In at least some prominent and long-lasting parts of the Jewish tradition, the normative Jewish male is soft, contemplative, gentle, funny, very unlike the "man of steel." This feminized norm, he stresses, did not lead to greater support for the aspirations of real women or render the religion less patriarchal than others.

100. See, for example, Gilman (1991).

101. See Geller (1992). These popular views were aided and abetted not only by misogynists and anti-Semites but also by leading Jewish intellectuals: see Geller's discussion of the Freud-Fliess correspondence.

102. Miller (1997, 109–42).

103. This idea is evident, too, in the apparently widespread distaste of straight men for cunnilingus after ejaculation. Although it is difficult to find anything beyond anecdotal evidence on this point, the aversion seems to be connected to an idea of being made "womanly." A gay man who read this paper writes: "Interestingly, both in my own experience and that of my gay male friends, I have found no such aversion to semen whether one's own or that of others (apart from a reasonable concern with safe-sex practices and the transmission of HIV)."

104. For a valuable treatment of these aspects of disgust, see the essays "Repulsion" and "Dirt/Death" in Dworkin (1988), from which the first two epigraphs in this study were taken.

105. Weininger (n.d., 300). Like Tolstoy's killer-husband, Weininger advocates that males strive to overcome sexual desire and the whole idea of providing for the continuity of the human race. "Every form of fecundity is loathsome. . . . That the human race should persist is of no interest whatever to reason; he who would perpetuate humanity would perpetuate the problem and the guilt, the only problem and the only guilt" (346). He argues that only such a general renunciation will liberate women from their status as merely sexual, thus permitting them to be human. In that future, "Men will have to overcome their dislike for masculine women, for that is no more than a mere egoism. If women ever become masculine by becoming logical and ethical, they would no longer be such good material for man's projection; but that is not a sufficient reason for the present method of tying woman down to the needs of her husband and children and forbidding her certain things because they are masculine" (340).

106. Unpublished paper by Rachel Nussbaum, based on research on the Jewish woman in anti-Semitic novels of the 1920s and 1930s. Weininger also has this idea: if the Jew is a woman, the Jewish woman is accordingly the most sensual and bodily, the "odalisque." There are related stereotypes of black women.

107. Hollander (1994).

108. Thus it is not surprising that (to males) the thought of homosexual sex is even more disgusting than the thought of reproductive sex, despite the strong connection of the latter with mortality and the cycle of the generations. For in heterosexual sex the male imagines that not he but a lesser being (the woman, seen as animal) received the pollution of bodily fluids; in imagining homosexual sex he is forced to imagine that he himself might be so polluted. This inspires a stronger need for boundary drawing.

109. See Nussbaum (2003c) for a longer treatment.

110. Golwalkar, founder of Hindu nationalism, admired and praised National Socialism in Germany, so the affinity between his imagery and that of Germans for Jews is no accident, though it is not easy to say whether he was influenced by Nazism or drawn to it by a preexisting affinity.

111. See Sarkar (2002).

112. Miller (1997, chap. 7). See Elias (1994); on Elias, see also Kim (2001, 158–65).
113. See Bruun (1993). Bruun notes that even today we don't make that separation, wasting high-quality water on toilet flushing.
114. Gandhi also noted that, in terms of real danger, the upper castes were less clean than the lower. During an outbreak of cholera, he went round to inspect the toilet habits of the various residents of his area, and found that the untouchables were doing fine because they defecated in the fields, far from dwelling places, while upper-caste families disposed of the contents of chamber pots in gutters that ran alongside the house, and were thus at high risk for infection. See his *Autobiography*.
115. See Nussbaum (2001a, chap. 15).
116. See Reynolds (1995, 346 ff).
117. Ellis (1890), in the Norton Critical Edition of Whitman, (812). Ellis here contrasts Whitman's attitude to the body with that of Swift, commenting that Swift, not Whitman, "represents . . . the opinions, more or less realized, more or less disguised, of most people even today."

Chapter 3. **Disgust and the Law**

1. See Kahan and Nussbaum (1996, 306–23) for an extensive discussion of this issue.
2. *Maher v. People*, 10 Michap. 212, 220 (1862).
3. *Rivers v. State*, 78 So. 343, 345 (Fla. 1918).
4. See chap. 1 and Kahan and Nussbaum (1996).
5. *Commonwealth v. Carr*, 580 A.2d 1362, 1363–65 (Pa. Super. Ct. 1990). See generally Brenner (1995). On the legal aspects of the case, see generally Pohlman (1999). Judge Spicer emerges as an impressive character, unusually learned and reflective. The case was eventually resolved by a deal, in which Carr waived his right to a jury trial in return for avoiding the death penalty; after a bench trial, he was sentenced to life imprisonment, and he is still in prison. Pohlman points out that the provocation defense was a stratagem chosen by the defense attorney, partly in light of the intensely conservative and homophobic climate of opinion in Adams County, Pennsylvania. The defense attorneys themselves later expressed the view that the crime was probably more a class crime than a hate crime: he was a pathetic loner and drifter, they were prosperous middle-class women who seemed to him to treat him contemptuously during an encounter earlier in the day. Pohlman himself, after interviewing Carr in prison, comes to the conclusion that the crime may well have been a sex crime: Carr admitted that he wanted to rape the women, and masturbated while watching them earlier in the day, as they walked around the campsite naked, unaware that anyone was there. He then says that he rejected the idea of rape, and was afraid to approach them in any other way. Pohlman believes that these sexual motives confused and enraged this very strange mental specimen. (At one point the defense pondered a diminished-capacity defense, but the psychiatric evidence did not seem sufficient to support it.)
6. Carr is an exception to my general claim, above, that male disgust targets male rather than female homosexuals. Often, indeed, female same-sex lovemaking

is found arousing by males, and it is a staple of pornography aimed at males. Carr's psychological history—which allegedly included a lesbian mother, as well as a history of rejection by women and molestation, as a child, by a homosexual man—presumably would explain this anomaly. But we do not need to explain it, if, as Pohlman suggests, this entire account is a defense fabrication.

7. See Mison (1992).

8. *State v. Volk,* 421 N.W.2d 360 (Minn. 1988).

9. As Dressler (1995) argues, some of the cases discussed in Mison (1992) are more indeterminate: A, unsolicited, touches B's groin, or grabs B in an embrace. The line between the aggressive and the nonaggressive is difficult to draw in these cases, although these two should probably be classified as nonthreatening. Even more difficult are cases in which the seduction leads to a scuffle in which blows are traded, and the homicidal assault follows these blows.

10. 570 N.E.2d 918 (Ind. App. 1991). See discussion in Mison (1992).

11. Presumably he understood the perpetrator's interest in a blow job as potentially offering some sort of sexual mutuality, or at least as expressing an interest in seeing him naked.

12. See Mison (1992, 134–35). See also Comstock (1981), but the "homosexual-advance" defense should be distinguished from the "homosexual-panic" defense, which is a diminished-capacity defense, not a heat-of-passion defense, and involves the idea that the violence is the psychotic reaction of a latent homosexual.

13. Once again see chap. 1. We must distinguish between the emotion and the action that follows it: the emotion is appropriate, so we might call it "justified" by the provocation. Nonetheless, violent conduct is not justified. The angry person is supposed to call in the law. So, where the conduct is concerned, the defense provides only a (partial) excuse.

14. See chap. 1. We may consider confining or narrowing the defense in the light of the danger that it will reinforce aggressive male behavior; see Dressler (2002), Nourse (1997).

15. Mison (1992, 177).

16. In the South, even recently, the gaze of a black man at a white woman has sometimes held to be a criminal offense: see Nussbaum (2001a, chap. 15). In 1951, in Yanceyville, North Carolina, a black man named Mark Ingraham was prosecuted for assault with intent to rape for looking at a seventeen-year-old white girl in a "leering manner." The prosecution claimed that he "undressed this lovely little lady with his eyes." (Ingraham's conviction was later reversed because blacks had been excluded from the jury.) In 1953, in Atmore, Alabama, a black man named McQuirter was convicted of the same crime, apparently after simply walking too close to a white woman. The state court of appeals held that racial factors might be considered in assessing the defendant's state of mind. *McQuirter v. State,* 63 So. 2d 388. Although these cases do not directly involve disgust, they do show that what is perceived as threatening or contaminating conduct is highly relative to current social prejudice. Certainly thoughts of contamination are likely to have been involved in these cases, as they so often are in matters of racial mixing. (I grew up in a household in which black servants were forbidden to use the same toilet that we used.)

17. 413 U.S. 15, 93 S. Ct. 2607 (1973).
18. *Miller* n. 1, quoting from the California Penal Code.
19. *Miller* n. 2; the definition in *Roth v. U.S.*, which mentions only appeal to "prurient interest," "does not reflect the precise meaning of 'obscene' as traditionally used in the English language."
20. Note 2.
21. Strictly speaking, Burger represents the "pornographic" as a subcategory of the "obscene": it comprises obscene materials that deal with sex. Thus he allows that there might be other categories of obscenity (perhaps dealing with other disgusting substances? With blood and gore?) that are not relevant to the legal doctrine in question.
22. *U.S. v. Guglielmi*, 819 F.2d 451 (1987). The defense added the argument that even were the standard relativized to zoophiliacs, we could not even conclude that the materials were arousing to "the average zoophiliac," since there was no such thing. They introduced expert testimony on zoophilia that stated that zoophiliacs differ in their preferences for different animals, and most have a preferred animal; thus there was no "average" member of that class for whom the contested materials as a group would be found sexually arousing.
23. Ibid., 454.
24. Miller (1997); Dworkin, "Repulsion" and "Dirt/Death" in Dworkin (1987).
25. James Douglas, *Sunday Express.*
26. The other most criticized portion was Gertie McDowell's exposure of herself to the masturbating Leopold Bloom. Again, the exciting display of (nonmarital) female sexuality is the focus of the critique.
27. For the reaction to Walt Whitman's poetry, see Nussbaum (2001a, chap. 15).
28. See MacKinnon (1987, chaps. 11–16), MacKinnon (1989, chap. 11), and Dworkin (1989). MacKinnon actually says that pornography is not a "moral" issue, because she understands the claim that it is a "moral" issue in terms of the tradition of morals laws, and contrasts the "moral" analysis with her analysis in terms of subordination. In general, MacKinnon follows Marx in dissociating questions of morality from political questions of equality and subordination. I see no reason why we should not say that equality is a moral norm, and many reasons why we should say so. So I describe her position as a moral position, in that sense.
29. Rawls (1996, 340–48).
30. See for example Sunstein (1993).
31. See MacKinnon and Dworkin (1997) for the hearings surrounding the ordinances in Minneapolis and Indianapolis.
32. Ibid.
33. For a fine philosophical study of the relevant issues of causality, see Eaton (manuscript).
34. See Lindgren (1993) for the difficulties average people have in applying legal definitions of pornography to texts: sexually explicit feminist fiction that shows the abuse of women as a bad thing proves difficult to distinguish from violent sexist pornography if we look only at an isolated extract. MacKinnon and Dworkin's definition does a little better than others in making this separation, but this is probably because Lindgren selected an atypical passage

from Andrea Dworkin's fiction, one in which the woman is in control in the sexual encounter. There are many passages from *Mercy*, for example, that would almost certainly be counted as pornographic, taken out of their larger context, according to the MacKinnon-Dworkin definition, but they have insisted that the appeal to the sense of the work as a whole should be rejected—concerned, no doubt, lest pornographers embed violent sexist pornography in an innocuous or uplifting frame, thereby escaping the intent of the ordinance. For the definition itself, see MacKinnon (1987, 262).

35. *Dworkin v. Hustler Magazine, Inc.*, 867 F.2d 1188 (9th Cir. 1989).

36. See Hornle (2000).

37. "Die nach 33a der Gewerbeordnung erforderliche Erlaubnis zum Betrieb einer sogenannten Peep-Show muss versagt werden," BVerwGE 64, 274 Peep-Show (1981), reprinted in Casebook Verfassungs 82 (1991). For an interesting discussion of the case, see Kadidal (1996).

38. "Art. 1 Abs. 1 des Grundgesetzes schützt den personalen Eigenwert des Menschen. Die Menschenwürde ist verletzt, wenn die einzelne Person zum Objekt herabgewürdigt wird."

39. "[W]eil das blosse Zurschaustellen des nackten Körpers die menschliche Würde jedenfalls dann unberührt lasse."

40. "Die Würde des Menschen ist ein objektiver, unverfügbarer Wert."

41. I do not, however, believe that citizens should have a choice to be humiliated by the public sphere: see Nussbaum (2000a, chap. 1).

42. See discussion in chapter 2.

43. *Loving v. Virginia*, 388 U.S. 1 (1967) 3, citing the trial court.

44. See Posner and Silbaugh (1996) for a complete catalogue as of that date; the situation with sodomy laws has, however, been changing rapidly, as many states repeal them.

45. 487 U.S. 186 (1986).

46. Strictly speaking, this amendment did not restrict homosexual conduct as such, but it did make it impossible for local communities to pass ordinances protecting gays and lesbians from discrimination in housing, employment, et cetera, and this move was defended by appeal to the immorality of homosexual conduct.

47. At that stage in the trial, the state was instructed to show a "compelling interest," although later, when the case was argued before the U.S. Supreme Court, the amendment was held to lack a rational basis (a lower level of scrutiny), and the Court ultimately agreed: *Romer v. Evans*, 116 S. Ct. 1620 (1996).

48. 852 P.2d 44 (Hawaii 1993).

49. Testimony of Will Perkins, October 1994, which I heard in person. On the similarity between U.S. prejudice against homosexuals and medieval anti-Semitism, see Posner (1992, 346) and Boswell (1989, 205–8).

50. Fascinating in this regard was the deposition of Harvey Mansfield in the bench trial of Amendment 2 (Deposition 8 October 1993, Civil Action 92 CV 7223). Mansfield repeatedly argued that gays and lesbians are unhappier than other groups in society, appealing to "the Great Books" of Western philosophy as authority. When, after having compared gays and lesbians to African-Americans and women (gays are less happy), he was questioned about "black women," he

no longer chose to ground his statements by appeal to the Great Books, so he appealed to his own experience as a professor at Harvard, seeing happy black women walking around the campus. The plaintiffs' lawyer at this point asked how he knew that these happy black women were not lesbians. (Q: So, if you see a happy black woman at Harvard, you can't know whether she's a homosexual or not, right? A: Not from that. Unless the happiness comes from clearly being with a male"; nobody ever explained why unhappiness should be seen as a sign that there was something wrong with the *unhappy people*, rather than with a social environment that discriminates against them.)

51. Hyde (1956, 339).

52. Similarly, the Marquess of Queensbury repeatedly used the language of disgust to refer to Wilde's conduct with his son and with others: he referred to "disgusting conduct" and a "disgusting letter" (from Wilde to Bosie): see Ellman (1987, 447). At the conclusion of the second criminal trial, he wrote a letter to the press in which he said that Wilde should be treated as "a sexual pervert of an utterly diseased mind, and not as a sane criminal"—thus distancing him even more thoroughly from the normal human community (Ellman, 478).

53. The "gross-indecency" statute was distinct from sodomy laws, which applied only to anal-genital intercourse.

54. The men were typically not actual prostitutes; their occupations included groom, newspaper seller, office boy, clerk, manservant, and bookmaker. Several had literary or theatrical aspirations. Wilde's presents to them included nice clothes, silver cigarette cases, walking sticks, theater tickets, and first editions of his books. The Parker brothers, introduced to Wilde by Taylor, were more like rent-boys. Charles Parker, one of the leading witnesses against Wilde, was an unemployed manservant; after his link with Taylor ended, he went into the army.

55. *Locke v. State*, 501 S.W.2d 826, 829 (Tenn. Ct. App. 1973) (dissenting opinion). (The case concerned the question whether "crime against nature" in a state statute includes cunnilingus; this opinion dissented from the conclusion that it does, and appealed to the fact that even necrophilia, disgusting though it is, has never been illegal in Tennessee. An antinecrophilia law was enacted in Tennessee in 1989.) See Ochoa and Jones (1997).

56. Posner and Silbaugh (1996, 213–16). The states that have such laws, together with the dates of enactment: Alabama (1980), Alaska (1978), Connecticut (1975), Georgia (1977), Indiana (1993), Minnesota (1967), Nevada (1983), New Mexico (1973), New York (1965), North Dakota (1973), Ohio (1978), Oregon (1993), Pennsylvania (1972), Tennessee (1989), Utah (1973), Wisconsin (1987).

57. See *People v. Stanworth*, 11 Cal. 3d 588, 604 n. 15, 114 Cal. Rptr. 250, 262 n. 15, 522 P.2d 1058, 1070 n. 15 (1974) (holding that the crime of rape requires a live victim, but that dead bodies are protected under the "mutilation" provision of the Health and Safety Code). Other case law, however, defines "mutilation" as requiring the cutting off of a limb or some other essential part of the body. See Ochoa and Jones (1997, 544). Posner and Silbaugh accordingly do not count California as having an antinecrophilia law.

58. *People v. Kelly*, 1 Cal. 4th 495, 3 Cal. Rptr. 677, 822 P.2d 385 (1992). Rape, the court held, is a crime whose essential element "'consists in the outrage to the

person and feelings of the victim of the rape' . . . A dead body has no feelings of outrage." The court held, however, that the defendant was guilty of felony murder: "A person who attempts to rape a live victim, kills the victim in the attempt, then has intercourse with the body, has committed only attempted rape, not actual rape, but is guilty of felony murder and is subject to the rape special circumstance."

59. See Ochoa and Jones (1997, 549 n. 63), citing an interview with a California prosecutor.

60. Thus we need not take our stand with Whitman, when he writes, "And as to you, Corpse I think you are good manure—but that does not offend me." (*Song of Myself* 49.1291). See also 52.1339: "I bequeath myself to the dirt to grow from the grass I love, / If you want me again look for me under your boot-soles."

61. Wis. Stat. Ann. 940.225 (1987). See Posner and Silbaugh (1996, 216).

62. For a review of the relevant philosophical literature, see Nussbaum (1994, chap. 6).

63. Wis. Stat. Ann. 940.225 (1987). See Posner and Silbaugh (1996, 43).

64. Tennessee; similar language is used by Alabama ("that would outrage ordinary family sensibilities"), Ohio ("that he knows would outrage reasonable community sensibilities"), and Pennsylvania ("that he knows would outrage reasonable family sensibilities"): in all these cases the statute alludes to "family sensibilities."

65. For a typical example, see *Baltimore v. Warren Mfg.*, 59 Md. 96 (1882), where either danger or the property of being "offensive to taste or smell" is sufficient.

66. *Commonwealth v. Perry*, 139 Mass. 198 (1885). The state argues that "said odors produced discomfort, sickness, and disgust to some of the occupants of said dwelling-houses; that at times they were so intense that some of said occupants were obliged to close their doors and windows; that said odors were the odors natural to swine, described by one witness as 'pig odors,' and by another as 'the odor of one pig multiplied five hundred times,' and by one other as 'the odor of a piggery.' It was conceded that no swill, slops, or unclean food were fed to said swine, but that they were fed only on good grains, beets, and other vegetables."

67. *Kriener v. Turkey Valley Community School Dist.*, 212 N.Y.2d 526 (Iowa 1973). A witness testified that she could not eat when the wind was blowing from the lagoon toward her home: "Well, I know I went home for dinner different times, and I couldn't eat. If I would start frying meat or something, why, it would just about bring my breakfast up, and rather than that I would just quit and forget eating."

68. *Baldwin v. Miles*, 20 S. 618, Conn. 1890.

69. Cited, inter alia, in *Trevett v. Prison Association of Virginia*, 98 Va. 332 (1900), another water-rights case.

70. *State v. Morse*, 84 Vt. 387 (1911), discussing an earlier case, *Dunham v. New Britain*, 55 Conn. 378.

71. 473 U.S. 432 (1985).

72. Language from the Oklahoma statute in question is in *Maynard v. Cartwright*, 486 U.S. 356, 108 S. Ct. 1853 (1988).

73. *Godfrey v. Georgia*, 446 U.S. 420, 100 S. Ct. 1759, 64 L. Ed. 2d. 398 (1980).

74. Ibid. at 428–29, 100 S. Ct. at 1764–65.
75. See *Maynard v. Cartwright,* 1859.
76. See Johnson (2002).
77. See Schulhofer (1995, 850–54), on the connection between "othering" and excessively harsh penalties.
78. *Nicomachean Ethics* VII.5, 1148b24. In a similar category are placed cannibals and people who cut up pregnant women to eat their fetuses. All are called "bestial vice," which is "a different genus from [ethical] vice."
79. Although, as Schulhofer argues (1995), the current tendency of U.S. juries is to respond to this sort of distancing as an invitation to extremely harsh punishment; the insanity defense is only rarely successful. Thus, this argument is an ad hominem reply to Kahan, rather than an argument of immediate pertinence to our current situation.
80. We may, of course, get angry at animals or at small children, but to the extent that we do so, we are typically imputing to them human-like abilities of choice and self-control, whether this imputation is rational or irrational.
81. Goldhagen (1996).
82. Browning (1992), stressing the role of ordinary human reactions such as yielding to peer pressure, the desire not to be thought cowardly, not to lose face, and the like.
83. Hilberg (1985), stressing the psychological importance of a deliberate, ideologically motivated treatment of Jews as similar to vermin, or even to inanimate objects.
84. Bartov (1991), stressing the role of ideology in creating a group capable of carrying out atrocities. See also Bartov (1996a).
85. Goldhagen (1996, 15).
86. See Bartov (1996b), a review of Goldhagen (1996), which sees the falsely comforting message of Goldhagen's work as a possible reason for its enthusiastic reception despite its scholarly faults. See further the exchange between Goldhagen (*New Republic,* 23 December 1996) and Bartov and Browning (*New Republic,* 10 February 1997); also Bartov's review of *The Concentration Camp* by Wolfgang Sofsky, (*New Republic,* 13 October 1997).
87. See Glover (2000) for such reflections.
88. See Bartov (1996b, 37–38): "We are left with the thesis that the Germans were normally monsters, and that the only role of the Nazi regime was to furnish them with the opportunity to act on their evil desires. . . . Goldhagen is actually appealing to a public that wants to hear what it already believes. By doing so, he obscures the fact that the Holocaust was too murky and too horrible to be reduced to simplistic interpretations that rob it of its pertinence to our own time." For discussion of these issues I am grateful to Rachel Nussbaum.
89. Kahan (1998, 1999). Kahan makes it clear that he is interested in this case in part because it is not a death-penalty case and thus helps us focus on the issue of disgust in isolation from the troubling problems of vagueness and capriciousness in the application of the death penalty.
90. *Beldotti v. Commonwealth,* 669 N.E.2d 222 (Mass. Ct. App. 1996).
91. The fact that the items would presumably never again be in Beldotti's possession is no more problematic for this interpretation than it is for Kahan's, since

both of us think, plausibly, that giving them back to his agents in accordance with his wishes is a way of letting him have his way concerning them.

92. See Sunstein, Kahnemann, and Shkade (1998), concluding that judgments and rankings of outrage in punitive-damage cases are surprisingly constant and predictable across experimental juries constructed to reflect variety of many different sorts; financial awards, by contrast, are not at all constant.

93. This is not inconsistent with my claim, above, that giving him back his money or other property would not occasion outrage, even though he might have used money or other property to commit his crime. The sex paraphernalia were intimately connected with the specific nature of the crime and its terrible brutality in a way that other items of property were not. Money is a necessary condition for all actions, good and bad, in a modern society, and thus has no links with crime per se.

Chapter 4. Inscribing the Face: Shame and Stigma

1. Goffman (1963, 128). Notice that he omits income, another source of stigma that might have made his case stronger still: if the "fully employed" college graduate is working as a dishwasher, he is blushing.

2. Ibid., 129, 135.

3. Scheler (1957, 55–148).

4. Bérubé (1996), Minow (1990); see also Wasserman (1998).

5. Whitman (1998); Massaro (1991, 1997); Braithwaite (1989, 1999). Although Braithwaite defends penalties that he calls shaming penalties, he emphasizes that he supports only those that do not stigmatize and that promote reintegration. In chap. 5 I shall argue that Braithwaite actually confuses shame and guilt, and that the punishments he defends should actually be regarded as atonements for guilt at an act, rather than shaming of an individual.

6. I borrow this succinct characterization of Lasch's position from Massaro (1997, 645–80). See notes 2–3 of Massaro's article for references to conservative journalism in praise of shame.

7. Etzioni (2001, 37–47).

8. Kahan (1996).

9. Kahan (1996, 633).

10. This account draws on a more detailed account of emotional development in infancy and childhood in Nussbaum (2001a, chap. 4). See Winnicott (1965, 1986).

11. Morrison (1986a, 1986b, 1989); Kernberg (1985).

12. This section overlaps in some respects with of Nussbaum (2001a, chap. 4), but I have rethought a number of points.

13. If they were: for maternal ill health and malnutrition obviously affect many of the world's children before birth.

14. See epigraph to this chapter.

15. Bollas (1987, 13–29).

16. See Seneca, *Medea*, 329–30.

17. I choose these odd locutions—making the subject the infant's experience-world rather than the infant—to remind the reader that the infant does not yet, in the first eight weeks of life, begin to experience itself as a definite subject. Compare Stern (1985; 1990, chap. 3).
18. Stern (1977, 1985, 1990); Mahler (1968, 1979); Mahler, Pine, and Bergman (2000).
19. Bowlby (1973, 1980, 1982); Lopez and Brennan (2000).
20. Fairbairn (1952); Winnicott (1965, 1986); Kernberg (1985); Bollas (1987).
21. Morrison (1986a, 1986b, 1989). Morrison is a follower of Kohut, but he also owes a large debt to the object-relations tradition, and his book on shame is largely in that tradition, though it also owes something to Kohut's focus on the restoration of the self.
22. In Nussbaum (2001a), following the theorists mentioned above, I argue that the need for comfort is distinct from the need for feeding, and equally primary.
23. The description of the "hunger storm" in Stern (1990) is a very good attempt to put into words an early experience that is inarticulate.
24. On the symbiotic relationship, see Mahler (1979); Mahler, Pine, and Bergman (2000).
25. See Mahler (1979); Balint (1953).
26. See Klein (1984, 1985).
27. See also Bollas (1987, 29): "Transformation does not mean gratification. Growth is only partially promoted by gratification, and one of the mother's transformative functions must be to frustrate the infant."
28. See the analysis of anger developed in chaps. 1 and 2 with reference to Aristotle.
29. See Nussbaum (2001a, chap. 10).
30. *Aidoia* means "shameful parts"; compare Latin pudenda and similar expressions in modern languages. Notice that shame about the genitals for Aristophanes is not shame about sex, but rather about powerlessness over the world, of which the cut parts, the genitals, are a sign. This idea is to be contrasted both with the idea of a shame that is about sexual acts, seeing those as shameful, and with the idea of Velleman (2002) that shame in the Garden of Eden story is a discovery of privacy, of possible insubordination of the body to the will, and thus of the possibility of disobedience to divine command. In my view, shame at one's lack of control over the body in matters sexual would be one specific variety of shame, not covering by any means the entirety of even sexual shame, while the more basic or primitive experience of shame would be in relation to lack of control over external goods generally.
31. For fundamental discussions of shame, see Morrison (1986a, 1989), Wurmser (1981), and Piers (1953).
32. Tomkins (1962–63).
33. Broucek (1991).
34. See the perceptive discussion in Deigh (1996, 226–47).
35. Morrison (1989, 48–49).
36. Piers, in Piers and Singer (1953).
37. Piers (1953, 11, 16).
38. Taylor (1986) connects shame to very elaborate types of perspectival thinking; these may indeed play a role in many instances of shame in adults, but are not necessary in order for the painful emotion itself to be present.

39. For a remarkable treatment of connections between shame and social ostracism, see Kilborne (2002), who focuses on the connection between shame and anxiety about one's appearance.

40. Kaster (1997), discussing the relation of *pudor* to fear, its dynamics within friendship, and much else. Kaster draws particular attention to the link of Roman shame with a social order conceived "in terms of precedence and deference."

41. Scheler (1957).

42. This is at least one way in which the Genesis story has often been interpreted in the history of Christian thought: what the apple reveals to Adam and Eve is their mortality and vulnerability, and their sexuality is simply one aspect of that.

43. See Velleman (2002) for a nuanced and powerful exploration of this type of shame: but see n. 29, above, on the difference between my analysis and his.

44. Thus in general object-relations theorists, like experimentalists Mahler, Stern, and Bowlby, in their account of infantile ambivalence put the accent on issues of control, attention, and rivalry, rather than on sexual desire as such.

45. Mahler (1979) is the primary theorist of these aspects of development.

46. For this concept see Winnicott (1965).

47. Ibid.

48. This issue is more fully explored in Nussbaum (2001a, chap. 4).

49. Klein (1985).

50. Winnicott (1986), with a piece of the early part of the analysis, published as an article in 1972, appended to the text. The patient was nineteen at the time of the beginning of his first analysis; he was referred by his mother, herself in analysis with Winnicott. He made a good recovery. Eight years later Winnicott wrote to the mother to inquire about B's progress; he interviewed her, and she described the pathologies in her own maternal care that she had by now discovered in her own analysis. Some time later the young man, now a medical intern, had had a breakdown and was hospitalized. Winnicott looked him up, and the patient began analysis a week later. During the last six months of the analysis, Winnicott wrote down his extensive notes after five crucial sessions, stating that, though difficult, it was not impossible to remember what had transpired. Fourteen years after the completion of the second analysis, Winnicott wrote to B to ask how he was doing; he had done well in both life and work. This analysis is also discussed in Nussbaum (2001a, chap. 4); it is of sufficient importance that it needs to figure in this argument as well.

51. Winnicott (1986, 10): the patient's symptom was a fear of annihilation as a result of satisfaction itself, as if, once he finished feeding, he had no way of knowing that the good things would ever come again. The interpretation of B's early life that was developing in the analysis was confirmed by Winnicott's interview with his mother, during which she told Winnicott about material she had discovered in analysis with another analyst. As she reported to him during their interview, she became aware of a rigid demand for perfection in her maternal role and of a refusal to tolerate the separate life of the child: she understood perfection as a kind of death of the child, in which he would have nothing more to demand.

52. The mother emerges as an anxious but by no means passive figure: one gets the impression that she is flamboyant. In his last letter to B, responding to the news of the mother's death, Winnicott writes, "She was indeed a personality."

53. Winnicott (1986, 96).
54. As I note in Nussbaum (2001a), other factors can produce excessive shame: for example social stigmatization because of a disability, an issue that I shall take up in chapter 6.
55. Winnicott (1986, 172). See also 163: "The difficulty is the fear of the anger."
56. Ibid., 123.
57. Ibid., 96: "I do not know if I could describe her. I have tended to assume you are not interested in her as a woman. Also I always have a difficulty in describing people. I never can describe a personality, the colour of people's hair, and all that sort of thing. . . . I am always reluctant to use Christian names."
58. Ibid., 97.
59. See ibid., where he describes wanting women to look at him as a perfect lover, and giving up in despair when he realizes that he is seen as human.
60. Here I agree with Piers (1953) against Taylor (1985).
61. On the "false self" see discussion in this section, below.
62. Winnicott (1986, 95).
63. Compare ibid., 147, where the patient gets angry at Winnicott and says he is like "the ogre of childhood play." Winnicott expresses pleasure: "So you have been able to reach play with me, and in the playing I am an ogre."
64. Ibid., 166. Compare the experimental data in Lopez and Brennan (2000), concerning the relationship between early attachment problems and inability to tolerate ambiguity and uncertainty, particularly in romantic life.
65. See also Winnicott (1965) for more extensive treatment of these themes.
66. Chodorow (1978).
67. Morrison (1989, 66).
68. Winnicott (1965, 140–52); Bollas (1987, 135–56).
69. Winnicott (1965, 142).
70. Kernberg (1985, 259–60).
71. See Morrison (1989); also Wurmser (1981), with a wide range of clinical examples.
72. Winnicott (1965, 144).
73. See Mill (1873, 56): James Mill, writes John, had contempt for passionate emotions of all sorts, "and for everything which has been said or written in exaltation of them. . . . He regarded as an aberration of the moral standard of modern times, compared with that of the ancients, the great stress laid upon feeling. Feelings, as such, he considered to be no proper subjects of praise and blame." "My father's teachings tended to the undervaluation of feeling" (97). With this went "an undervaluing of poetry, and of Imagination generally as an element of human nature" (98).
74. This idea is palpable in the published parts of the *Autobiography,* but its clearest statement comes from a passage deleted from the published version:

To have been, through childhood, under the constant rule of a strong will, certainly is not favourable to strength of will. I was so much accustomed to expect to be told what to do, either in the form of direct command or of rebuke for not doing it, that I acquired a habit of leaving my responsibility as a moral agent to rest on my father, my conscience never speaking to me except by his voice. The things I ought not to do were mostly provided for by his precepts, rigorously enforced whenever violated, but the things I ought to do I hardly ever did of my own mere motion, but waited till he told me to do them; and if he forbore or forgot to tell me, they were generally left undone. I thus acquired a habit of backwardness, of waiting to follow the lead of others, an absence of moral spontaneity, an inactivity of the moral sense and even to a large extent, of the intellect, unless aroused by the appeal of some one else,— for which a large abatement must be made from the benefits, either moral or intellectual, which flowed from any other part of my education.

75. For several pertinent texts about Mrs. Mill, see Packe (1954).
76. Cited in Packe (1954). Much evidence about Mill's childhood confirms the picture of a child who did not know how to give and receive affection, and who protected himself by arduous study. The surviving reports of his visit to Bentham's brother and sister-in-law in France at the age of fourteen are of particular interest. The Benthams (a very worldly and fun-loving couple, quite unlike the reclusive Jeremy) form the project of getting John to have fun, and he keeps resisting through anxious retreats into his collection of books—until they conceive the happy idea of saying that they have to box up all the books in preparation for their move to Toulouse. At this point John is lured to the theatre and takes long walks in the mountains. Throughout Mill's later life nature proved a source of rewarding emotional expression. He was much more emotionally at ease with plants than with people, Harriet always excepted.
77. Mill (1873, 117).
78. Marmontel (1999) 63: "'Ma mère, mes frères, mes soeurs, nous éprouvons, leur dis-je, la plus grande des afflictions; ne nous y laissons point abattre. Mes enfants, vous perdez un père; vous en retrouvez un; je vous en servirai; je le suis, je veux l'être; j'en embrasse tous les devoirs; et vous n'êtes plus orphelins.' À ces mots, des ruisseaux de larmes, mais de larmes bien moins amères, coulèrent de leurs yeux. 'Ah! s'écria ma mère, en me pressant contre son coeur, mon fils! mon cher enfant! que je t'ai bien connu!'"
79. Cf. Morrison (1986, 370): "For guilt the antidote is forgiveness; shame tends to seek the healing response of acceptance—of the self despite its weaknesses, defects, and failures."
80. Mill, "Bentham": "In many of the most natural and strongest feelings of human nature he had no sympathy; from many of its graver experiences he was altogether cut off; and the faculty by which one mind understands a mind different from himself, and throws iteself into the feelings of that other mind, was denied him by his deficiency of Imagination. . . . He had neither internal experience nor external. . . . He was a boy to the last."
81. Mill's attitude to his mother remained harsh and contemptuous; it is one of the least likeable aspects of his personality. He refused to visit her after his marriage to Harriet, even though she repeatedly and very kindly invited him to do so. Imagining some slight, he did not even reply or visit when she told him her health was rapidly failing. Nor did he wholly overcome his tendency to relate to others, even relations, in a lifeless and hyperintellectual manner.

82. Concerning Mill's connection of profound emotion with the idea of liberty, a passage from the *Amberley Papers*, describing a visit by Mill in 1870, is significant. After dinner, Mill reads his guests Shelley's *Ode to Liberty.* "He got quite excited and moved over it rocking backwards and forwards and nearly choking with emotion, he said to himself: 'it is almost too much for one!'"

83. Morrison (1986, 33–34).

84. Compare Kernberg (1985, 235): "The greatest fear of these patients is to be dependent on anybody else, because to depend means to hate, envy, and expose themselves to the danger of being exploited, mistreated, and frustrated."

85. Kindlon and Thompson (1999).

86. Morrison (1986a, 19, 86–89).

87. See also Pipher (1994).

88. I discuss these educational ideas more fully in Nussbaum (1995, 1997, 2003b).

89. See Morrison (1986a) for a similar account.

90. Miller (1993, 131–36).

91. For example, Margalit (1996), who connects humiliation with denigration of the level or type of humanity possessed by the person humiliated.

92. See Taylor (1985, 69).

93. Thus I felt not only embarrassment but also shame at the fact that I repeatedly called my colleague Josef Stern by the name Jacob; this shame was dispelled when I was able to come up with a likely explanation for this slip, which he understood and (I think) found amusing and to his credit. (It had to do with my childhood association of Joseph with the Nativity Scene, and thus with my repudiated Christian past, Jacob with my convert's embrace of Judaism.) Now, if it happens, it is merely embarrassing.

94. Williams (1993); see also Annas (manuscript).

95. See the analyses of Taylor (1985, chap. 4) and Piers (1953, chaps. 1–2).

96. Fairbairn (1952), Klein (1984, 1985). See the more detailed account of their views in Nussbaum (2001a, chap. 4). Gabriele Taylor puts the point very well in Taylor (1985, 90): "If feelings of guilt concentrate on the deed or the omission then the thought that some repayment is due is in place here as it is not in the case of shame. If I have done wrong then there is some way in which I can 'make up' for it, if only by suffering punishment. But how can I possibly make up for what I now see I am? There are no steps that suggest themselves here. There is nothing to be done, and it is best to withdraw and not to be seen. This is the typical reaction when feeling shame. Neither punishment nor forgiveness can here perform a function."

97. Winnicott (1986, 165).

98. Ibid., 29.

99. The relationship is further complicated by the fact that guilt and shame can trigger one another, as Piers (1953, chap. 4) argues. For example, suppose C feels guilt about aggressive impulses (or acts). He reacts by inhibiting his aggression, but sometimes, says Piers, this inhibition spreads "from destructiveness proper to assertiveness and in more pathological cases, to 'activity' as such." C now feels passive and useless, and this sense of his inadequacy, especially against the background of social norms, triggers shame. Shame in turn

may lead to overcompensatory aggression, in fantasy or action, which in turn leads back to guilt.

100. In Morrison (1986, 323–47).

101. A. Miller (1986, 342).

102. Kernberg (1985, 232).

103. See Morrison (1989, 103–4) for two such patients.

104. Theweleit (1987, 1989).

105. See Nussbaum (2001a) for more extensive discussion.

106. See the discussion of Ernst Jünger in chap. 2, above.

107. Ehrenreich (2001, 220–21).

108. For a similar case of constructive shame in Camus, see Constable (1997).

109. Meanwhile, the players themselves have expressed shame about their own bad play.

110. For a similar argument, see Williams (1993, 102), though he focuses on respect and shared values, not on bonds of affection. Calhoun (2003) argues that this restriction to those whom one respects and cares for is too restrictive: we should be prone to feel shame before those with whom we share a social world, as part of taking them and their point of view seriously, even if their point of view is racist or sexist, and we ourselves are demeaned by it. Though I admire the essay and find the suggestion interesting, I am not persuaded.

111. On the terminology of penal shaming, see Jones (1987, 2000).

112. See Jones (2000): *stizein* means "to prick," and is related to English *sting* and *stitch,* and German *stechen* ("prick") and *sticken* ("embroider").

113. See epigraph. Quoted by Gustafson (1997).

114. See also the excellent discussion in Warner (1999).

115. At the same time, "normals" will seek to denigrate other members of their own group for weaknesses of one or another sort, thus pushing them "down" toward the zone of the "abnormal."

116. Goffman (1963, 6).

117. Ibid.

118. Kernberg (1985, 232).

119. See Morrison (1989, 116–17).

120. See Gustafson (1997), who gives an exhaustive account of these practices in late Roman antiquity. See also Jones (1987).

121. See Gustafson (1997, 86): tattooing was typically reserved for slaves, so its infliction on an offender or other member of an unpopular group degraded status directly, bringing the person closer to the slave.

122. One remarkable story tells of twelve lines of iambic verse being written on the faces of two allegedly heretical monks (reported from a Byzantine *Life of Michael the Synkellos* [trans. Cunningham] by Gustafson [1997]): "Then the prefect ordered that their faces be inscribed. . . . The executioners came forward and, stretching each of the saints upon a bench, they started inscribing their faces. And pricking their faces for a long time, they wrote the iambic verses on them."

123. Goffman (1963, 3, 5).

Chapter 5. Shaming Citizens

1. See Gustafson (1997) and Jones (1987) on the terminology: very commonly, "in-scriptum" means "tattooed." And Gustafson and Jones both argue cogently that tattooing was by far the most common variety of penal marking (and also of marking slaves). Branding was probably employed only rarely. Cicero's proposal is metaphorical, but only in the sense that he actually wants capital punishment for the conspirators rather than a mere tattoo. As for others, what he wants is that they will clearly take one side or the other: either support the death of the conspirators or confess that they are fellow-travelers.
2. Fairbairn (1952); compare Winnicott's use of the terms "absolute" and "relative" dependence.
3. Rawls (1971, 1996) calls the social conditions of self-respect the most important of the primary goods; my related account of the Central Human Capabilities in Nussbaum (2000a) includes the capacity for emotional health, as well as the social bases of self-respect.
4. At least this is true of the communitarian thinkers under consideration in my argument, such as Etzioni and Kahan. It is probably true of Devlin, and even, perhaps, of Leon Kass.
5. See J. Williams (1999).
6. See Nussbaum (2000a, chap. 1): this is where I reach my limit with the thesis that the political sphere should create capabilities, but not require a particular mode of functioning.
7. Which ones Kahan and Etzioni primarily have in mind is an interesting question. Both focus explicitly on alcohol and drug offenders, but Kahan likes to give examples where the shamed person is powerful: businessmen who urinate in public, well-off men who solicit prostitutes. Etzioni is more likely than Kahan to include the single mother in his list of shameful offenses; certainly many communitarian critics of our current "shamelessness" focus on this case.
8. Kahan (1996).
9. Unlike Braithwaite, who attempts to distinguish shaming from humiliating, Kahan has no qualms about favoring humiliation.
10. This is central to the case for shaming penalties in Etzioni (2001).
11. For examples of shaming penalties actually in use for each of these, see Kahan (1996, 631–34).
12. See Gustafson (1997) and E. Posner (2000).
13. See Massaro (1991, 1997).
14. See Gustafson (1997) on the way in which Christians used the tattoos they received as a positive symbol and even voluntarily tattooed themselves.
15. Annas (manuscript).
16. Whitman (1998).
17. See also Markel (2001), who argues that it is important for reasons of impartiality that punishments be administered by the state.
18. E. Posner (2000).
19. See Gustafson (1997) and Jones (1987).
20. Gilligan (1996); see also Massaro (1991).

21. Braithwaite, personal correspondence, April 2002.
22. Schulhofer, personal communication, June 2002. The general phenomenon is, he says, common in the literature on probation reform and other reform proposals.
23. Whitman (1998).
24. Massaro (1991).
25. Markel (2001).
26. Morris (1968).
27. This parenthesis is me talking, not Markel; he is not responsible for my interpretation of the *Groundwork.*
28. Markel's analysis, and Morris's, are a lot more detailed than this; I have presented only a crude summary.
29. That is what Massaro appears to mean: she conflates retributivism with revenge.
30. Braithwaite (1989).
31. Braithwaite (1999).
32. Braithwaite, personal correspondence, April 2002.
33. See Braithwaite (1989, 185): "[T]he good society is one in which there is consensus about certain core values, including the criminal law, but that has institutions to encourage conflict outside those areas. . . . Among the core values on which the good society must have consensus are freedom, the promotion of diversity and constructive conflict."
34. Braithwaite (1989, 158).
35. Braithwaite (2002, 13).
36. Braithwaite tells me that it was so understood by Etzioni, who sent him the "Communitarian Manifesto" to sign; he refused.
37. Braithwaite himself believes that the main area of disagreement between us is over retribution: he is entirely against it, while I am sympathetic to it, understood in a limited, Kantian way. As I say below, I am not sure that there is such a large difference between the sort of retributivism I favor and the sort of confrontation between victim and aggressor that he favors.
38. See J. Braithwaite and V. Braithwaite (2001).
39. Annas (manuscript); Rhode, in a comment on this chapter at Stanford University, 4 June 2001.
40. Whitman (2003).
41. Archimandritou (2000), written in modern Greek. (My knowledge of the argument derives from conversation with the author.)
42. See my discussion of *Hudson v. Palmer* in Nussbaum (1995). See also Richard Posner's very interesting (dissenting) opinion in *Johnson v. Phelan,* a case involving the privacy rights of prisoners.
43. *Johnson v. Phelan,* 69 F. 3d 144 (1995).
44. Johnson was African-American, and most of the female guards were white; although Posner was not able to mention this fact in the opinion, he told me that it was important to his thinking.
45. His view did not prevail: Judge Easterbrook found against the plaintiff, and the third member of the three-judge panel was a senior judge who was experiencing mental difficulties and voted with Judge Easterbrook under the impression that he was siding with Judge Posner.

46. The states in question are Alabama, Florida, Iowa, Kentucky, Maryland (after the second conviction), Mississippi, Nevada, New Mexico, Virginia, and Wyoming. Delaware removed its restriction recently. Many other states restrict the franchise partially: for example, Texas denies the vote for two years after release from prison. Most states deny the vote to prisoners currently incarcerated.

47. Data from Human Rights Watch (1998) and the *Los Angeles Times*, 30 January 1997. Together with this observation, we should study the classification of offenses as either felonies or misdemeanors. While some states deny the vote for a misdemeanor, the line between felony and misdemeanor is usually crucial, but some drug offenses are classified as misdemeanors, some as felonies, often in ways that, once again, track race. On this issue, see Fletcher (1999).

48. Whitman (2003).

49. Cohen (1972), quoting from an article in the 1964 *Police Review*.

50. Cohen (1972, 95), quoting from Lumbard (1964, 69). Lumbard understands the penalty as a sign that the British police have a sense of humor.

51. Quoted in Cohen (1972, 106); emphasis in original.

52. Ben-Yehudah (1990).

53. Jenkins (1998).

54. Hall et al. (1978).

55. *Evans v. Romer*, Defendants' Trial Brief at 56; Defendants' Motion for Reconsideration and to Alter or Amend Judgment at 1–2; the reasoning is criticized in Plaintiffs' Supplementary Memorandum on the Legal Status of "Morality" as a Governmental Interest at 2: "[M]oral norms are legitimate public purposes only when they are linked in some way with the preservation of public welfare and public order."

56. For detailed investigations of the range of opinion in the major U.S. denominations, see the essays in Olyan and Nussbaum (1998).

57. Equally odd was the repeated claim that no other society has legalized same-sex unions, although by that time at least five European nations had recognized same-sex domestic partnerships that offer most of the benefits of marriage. By now, the number is larger, and the Netherlands has gone all the way to the legalization of same-sex marriage.

58. See Koppelman (2002). Koppelman's argument (in its earlier article form) was accepted by a majority in the Hawaii Supreme Court's decision in favor of gay marriage in *Baehr v. Lewin*, 852 P.2d 44 (Hawaii 1993). See also Law (1988) and Sunstein (2002).

59. See Warner (1999, chap. 1).

60. "Sexual Taboos and the Law Today," quoted in Warner (1999, 22).

61. Of course whether a fundamental constitutional right is or is not involved is an as yet unsettled question, but the ACLU's challenge to the referendum was based on a claim that such a right was involved, so there was no hypocrisy in the ACLU's conduct, as the letter alleged.

62. *Romer v. Evans*, 116 S. Ct. 1628 (1996).

63. *Romer*, 1622, 1628.

64. Rational-basis review is usually highly deferential; generally, when a law is found unconstitutional on equal protection grounds, it is because it does not meet some more exacting level of scrutiny. Laws involving racial and gender-based

classifications need to pass such a more demanding test, but sexual orientation has never been recognized by the U.S. Supreme Court as a "suspect classification" triggering heightened scrutiny.

65. 473 U.S. 432 (1985).

66. See Sunstein (1999, 148): "In both *Cleburne* and *Romer,* the Court was concerned that a politically unpopular gorup was being punished as a result of irrational hatred and fear. Many people appear to think that mental retardation (like homosexuality) is contagious and frightening."

67. See also *Department of Agriculture v. Moreno,* 413 U.S. 528, cited in *Romer. Moreno* concerned Congress's refusal to give food stamps to households containing any individual who was unrelated to any other member of the household. The Court noted that the legislative history suggested a desire to cut off "hippies" and "hippie communes."

68. 388 U.S. 1 (1967).

69. 852 P. 2d 44 (Hawaii 1993).

70. See Nussbaum (1999a, chap. 7), and the comprehensive analysis of the constitutional difficulties with the Defense of Marriage Act in Koppelman (2002, chap. 6).

71. See Sunstein (1999).

72. See Warner (1999 and Nussbaum (2000a, chap. 4).

73. Warner (1999, 159).

74. Andrea Estes, "Massachusetts State Troopers Look the Other Way on Public Sex," *Boston Globe,* 2 March 2001.

75. My argument, then, does not apply to nonconsensual acts, or to acts in which there is deception about HIV status: for those acts are plainly not "self-regarding" in Mill's sense.

76. *Chicago v. Morales,* 177 Ill.2d 440, 687 N.E.2d 53.

77. *Chicago v. Morales,* 527 U.S. 41, 119 S. Ct. 1849.

78. *Chicago v. Morales* (Illinois).

79. Ibid.

80. Meares and Kahan (1998a, 1998b, 1999).

81. See respondents in Meares and Kahan (1999) and Alschuler and Schulhofer (1998).

82. Kniss (1997).

83. Compare Alschuler and Schulhofer (1998, 240)

> Neither race nor geography fully defines a person's communities. Community identity is likely to depend on varied characteristics in varied combinations—religion, race, ethnicity, residence, wealth, gender, sexual orientation, occupation, physical disability, age, and (especially in Chicago) political party and ward organization. Chicago's communities are in fact innumerable. . . . There is usually no way for outsiders to determine which communities are most affected by a legislative measure, . . . to mark the boundaries of informal, unorganized communities, or to assess the dominant sentiment of community members. The concept of community thus provides almost limitless opportunities for creative redefinition and manipulation.

84. In Chicago this is a particularly urgent question since the Mexican community is large and often quite hostile to the African-American community.

Chapter 6. **Protecting Citizens from Shame**

1. Goffman's original citation is to an article by S. Zawadski and P. Lazarsfeld in *Journal of Social Psychology* 6 (1935).
2. TenBroek (1966). TenBroek prefaces his classic discussion by noting: "The views expressed, the author believes, are verified by his personal experience as a disabled individual far more than by all the footnote references put together."
3. Nussbaum (2000a, 2003a).
4. Of course the distinction between the unemployed and the employed corresponded to a distinction between the rich and the poor, and the poor are stigmatized today, whether employed or not, but the change that the Reformation, and the Protestant emphasis on work as a source of value, brought about in Europe should not be underestimated. A Greek gentleman would assiduously avoid doing any work, and whatever he occupied himself doing (politics, say) he defined as nonwork; meanwhile, his wife could run the estate, and running even a large opulent estate was stigmatized activity. A poor person who did not work was in some sense better off in terms of stigma because then he qualified as a beggar, to whom generally understood obligations were felt. Note that the returned Odysseus does not set up as a shepherd or swineherd, but, instead, goes round the table as a beggar (who says he was once a king). Presumably gainful employment would be even more stigmatizing for a hero.
5. See Kindlon (2001), Frank (1999).
6. Ehrenreich (2001).
7. See Sennett (2003).
8. On Roosevelt's views I am greatly indebted to a book in progress by Cass R. Sunstein.
9. 397 U.S. 254 (1970).
10. Ibid., 265.
11. See also *Shapiro v. Thompson*, 394 U.S. 618, invalidating a state residency requirement for receiving welfare.
12. Justice Black's dissent in *Goldberg* argues that welfare rights are an experiment in America, and that such experiments are best carried out by the legislature.
13. See Clark (1997), reporting reasons for Americans' refusal to have sympathy with the poor.
14. I am grateful on this point to unpublished work by my colleague Bernard Harcourt.
15. *Boy Scouts of America v. Dale,* 530 U.S. 640 (2000).
16. See Sunstein (2001).
17. This, of course, is a mixed list, since the members of the list receive different levels of protection, and thus my claims are (intentionally) vague.
18. Notice that we don't encounter many cases in which a man is told to behave in a more feminine way, although in "feminine" occupations we do find a few: see Case (1995).

19. 490 U.S. 228 (1989).
20. Case (1995), 4.
21. Yoshino (2002).
22. Goffman (1963, 102–4).
23. See Comstock (1991), and my discussion in Nussbaum (1999a, chap. 7).
24. Ronald Dworkin expressed this point to me in conversation.
25. *U. S. v. Lallemand* 989 F.2d 936 (7th Cir. 1993). The question was whether Lallemand, who had deliberately set out to blackmail a married homosexual, deserved an upward departure under the Guidelines for choosing an "unusually vulnerable victim": given that all blackmail victims are persons with guilty secrets, what was unusual about this one, a married government employee with two grown children (who had attempted suicide when approached by Lallemand with his blackmail demand)? The answer, Posner argues, lies in current American mores, which treat his sexual secret as more shameful than others. These circumstances indicate a "malevolent focusing in on a particularly susceptible subgroup of blackmail victims." In conversation Posner has mentioned to me that the victim was African-American, and had risen from poverty to a position of respect in the community; these issues also influenced his thinking, although he chose not to put them into the opinion.
26. *Wisconsin v. Mitchell,* 113 S. Ct. 2550 (1993).
27. Comstock (1991).
28. Cornell (1995) calls this space, plausibly, the "imaginary domain."
29. Nagel (1998, 17, 20).
30. See again Yoshino (2002), discussed in chapter 5.
31. Hollander (1994, 61–62).
32. See Nussbaum (2002b).
33. See *Miller v. Civil City of South Bend,* 904 F.2d 1051 (7th Cir. 1990).
34. There was no majority opinion in the case, since Justice Souter wrote a separate opinion.
35. *Barnes v. Glen Theatre, Inc.,* 501 U.S. 520 (1991).
36. See for example Tom Nagel's recent defense of this idea in Nagel (1997).
37. Goffman (1963, 19).
38. TenBroek (1966), see n. 2, above.
39. Morris (1991, 1992).
40. Bérubé (1996) and Kittay (1999).
41. Levitz and Kingsley (1994).
42. I borrow this example from Silvers (2000).
43. As runners know, wheelchair contestants in marathons typically complete the course in a faster time than do runners.
44. This is the central topic of tenBroek's discussion of tort law in tenBroek (1966). He shows that in many instances the analogy between the blind person in the daytime and the sighted person at night has helped guide communities toward inclusionary policy decisions: just as the streets ought to be safe to negotiate at night as well as by day, so too they ought to be safe for the blind as well as the sighted. Definitions of negligence and due care have also evolved to recognize the right of the blind to use public facilities, at least with a cane

or dog, although their right to use these facilities without such an aid is still disputed (see epigraph).

45. See Wasserman (1998). He suggests, following Anita Silvers, that a good question to pose to oneself is how the world would be if the unusual disability were in fact usual. If, for example, most people used wheelchairs, would we continue to build staircases rather than ramps?

46. Morris (1992).

47. Such an account is suggested in Amundson (1992, 2000a, 2000b).

48. See Amundson's criticism of Daniels, Boorse, and others.

49. See Silvers (1998) for this way of putting things.

50. That is my position in Nussbaum (2001a).

51. See Kavka (2000) and L. Becker (2000).

52. See Silvers (1998). The "regarded" clause of the ADA, however, has been interpreted by courts to mean that they must be regarded as having a disability that affects a major life activity, as that clause has been interpreted elsewhere: thus, people who are "regarded as" incompetent because of obesity will not gain relief from this section, except in the most extreme cases.

53. AIDS, for example, has been treated as a disability on the grounds that it limits the major life activity of reproduction—not a bad bottom line, one feels, but perhaps not the most pertinent way of reaching it.

54. Wasserman (2000) argues that such a broadening of the ADA would not lead to a flood of litigation because people will be embarrassed to come forward as litigants declaring themselves obese, or short, or unattractive: thus, he argues, only the most severe cases will present themselves. Yet in today's America, where litigiousness and a confessional mentality are combined, the reticence of which he speaks seems unlikely to prevail.

55. Locke, *Second Treatise on Government,* chapter 8.

56. Gauthier (1986, 18), speaking of "all persons who decrease th[e] average level" of well-being in a society.

57. Rawls (1996, 183 and passim).

58. See Goffman (1963, 17) for a moving first-person account of the stigmatizing of the unemployed: "How hard and humiliating it is to bear the name of an unemployed man. When I go out, I cast down my eyes because I feel myself wholly inferior. When I go along the street, it seems to me that I can't be compared with an average citizen, that everybody is pointing at me with his finger."

59. See Nussbaum (2000b, 2001b). I discuss these issues in detail in my Tanner Lectures, "Beyond the Social Contract: Toward Global Justice," delivered at the Australian National University in Canberra, November 2002, and under contract to Harvard University Press.

60. See Nussbaum (2000a).

61. Francis and Silvers (2000, xix).

62. *Watson v. Cambridge,* 157 Mass. 561 (1893). Watson was said to be "unable to take the ordinary decent physical care of himself." Similar is the oft-cited case of Merritt Beattie, who apparently was not mentally retarded, but whose paralytic condition produced symptoms that were held to have a "depressing and

nauseating effect upon the teachers and school children" (*State ex Rel. Beattie v. Board of Education of the City of Antigo*, 169 Wisc. 231 [1919]). The Supreme Court of Wisconsin upheld the exclusion of Beattie.

63. 343 F. Supp. 279 (1972).

64. 348 F. Supp. 866 (D.C.C. 1972). Technically, because of the legally anomalous situation of the District, they held that it was a due process violation under the Fifth Amendment and that the Equal Protection clause in its application to education is "a component of due process binding on the District."

65. I wish to thank John Brademas, one of the authors of this legislation, for very helpful discussion about the background and history of the law. For discussion of the ensuing educational reforms, see Minow (1990, 29–40).

66. See Bérubé (1996) and Nussbaum (2001b). I describe Jamie at the time of his father's description in the book.

67. See Kelman and Lester (1997). They quote a special educator from Mississippi:

Are there kids who fall through the cracks? Yeah . . . I think that every year we just keep doing it. We're going to reevaluate to see if we can't fit that discrepancy somewhere. "Did we get it yet? Has he fallen far enough behind in achievement now that we can make him eligible for special ed?" . . . I think that somehow, someday we're going to all have to say this is our kid, what we need to do is educate this kid. Whether it's the regular ed teacher taking him into a group for a certain subject or whether it's special ed or Chapter One or whomever, it's necessary.

68. This is Kelman and Lester's conclusion on the basis of their extensive study of IDEA as applied to LD children.

Chapter 7. Liberalism without Hiding?

1. These two alternatives correspond, of course, to Aristotle's two interpretations of pleasure in Books VII and X of the *Nicomachean Ethics*. It is likely that Mill was strongly influenced by these famous ideas. He directs our attention, in *Utilitarianism*, to the fact that the nature of pleasure is far from clear; and there are texts in which he clearly seems to be analyzing pleasure as activity of a sort. He does not, however, devote a sustained inquiry to the conceptual analysis of pleasure, and his position cannot be pinned down with any precision.

2. See my discussion of this view, held by Harsanyi, Brandt, and others, in Nussbaum (2000a, chap. 2).

3. In referring to *On Liberty*, I shall simply cite the chapters because no single edition is in sufficiently widespread use for page references to be helpful.

4. However, the satisfaction of a permanent interest, or unfettered functioning in accordance with that interest, is probably constitutive of happiness in Mill's view, rather than merely instrumental to it.

5. Rawls (1971); Posner (1995).

6. Rawls (1971, 3).

7. See Nussbaum (2000a, chap. 3).

8. See especially *Ad Att.* I.17 (Letter 17 in the numbering by D. Shackleton Bailey in the new Loeb Classical Library edition and translation), where Cicero, having proclaimed that there is perfect trust between him and his friend, says that there is just one thing that divides us: the choice of a conception of life (*voluntatem institutae vitae*). He himself, he says, has been led by a certain *ambitio* to prefer a conception of life that attaches high value to public service; as for Atticus, a *haud reprehendenda ratio* (a reasoning that no one could take issue with) has led him to prefer the Epicurean doctrine, and its urging of a life of virtuous retirement (*honestum otium*). Here we surely see the idea that both conceptions are reasonable, and Cicero amply shows his respect for his friend's doctrine by calling it *honestum*, while gently suggesting the reasonableness of not agreeing with his own choice by mentioning the motive of ambition.

9. See Nussbaum (2001c).

10. Mill then goes on to argue that even the criminal suffers because he loses "the better development of the social part of his nature, rendered possible by the restraint put upon the selfish part. To be held to rigid rules of justice for the sake of others develops the feelings and capacities which have the good of others for their object." This line of defense is probably a mistake on Mill's part. By admitting that some human development may be best advanced by restrictions upon conduct, Mill has let in a consideration that opponents might use to undermine his argument as a whole. (Laws against adultery strengthen the development of marital love, laws against gambling strengthen the capacity for honest work, et cetera.)

11. Rawls (1996).

12. This will be so even if we hold that liberty is not just instrumental to, but partially constitutive of, people's well-being. Consider Aristotle's account of friendship: he explicitly insists that friendship is good in its own right, and yet by far the greatest part of his discussion is devoted to its instrumental benefits.

13. Mill does insist that even correct norms need the stimulus of contestation, but, as I have suggested, that argument is not among his most convincing.

14. See Arneson (2000) and my reply in Nussbaum (2000c).

15. See Nussbaum (2000a, chap. 1). One important exception is in the area of human dignity: I argue that the state must treat citizens with dignity, not simply give them the option to be treated with dignity. If, for example, citizens were asked to pay one cent for dignified treatment, and if they didn't pay they would be humiliated by public officials, this would, in my view, be very bad, a grave violation of the most basic obligations of a liberal state.

16. Although Kahan's recent attack on "rights 1960s style" (see chap. 5) certainly casts doubt on his support for the traditional Bill of Rights.

17. Thus, even insofar as they do not propose to jettison the Bill of Rights, both propose to understand its protections far more narrowly than liberals standardly do.

18. Once again (see chap. 5) these issues are the theme of my current work in progress, tentatively entitled *Beyond the Social Contract.*

19. See Rodman (2003), who even suggests (in his own voice) that this claim is a defense mechanism that manifests the activity of the False Self of analysts.
20. See Maritain (1951), who argues that the ideas behind the Universal Declaration of Human Rights are open to any conception, religious or secular, that thinks the human being is more than a tool or a means.
21. See Nussbaum (2000b).
22. Especially in Nussbaum (2000a).
23. See Nussbaum (2001a, chap. 6). Aristotle defines tragic compassion in terms of the idea of being *anaitios,* that is, not (primarily) responsible for the bad event; other major thinkers follow suit. The notion that a "tragic flaw" causes the hero's downfall is a later Christian misreading of Aristotle, although it may explain the structure of some Christian tragedies.
24. Nussbaum (2001a, chaps. 6–8).
25. See Nussbaum (2001a, chap. 8).
26. See Nussbaum (2001a, chap. 8) for some concrete suggestions.

List of References

Adorno, Theodor, et al. (1950). *The Authoritarian Personality.* New York: Harper and Row.

Ahmed, Eliza, Nathan Harris, John Braithwaite, and Valerie Braithwaite (2001). *Shame Management through Reintegration.* Cambridge: Cambridge University Press.

Alschuler, Albert W., and Stephen J. Schulhofer (1998). "Antiquated Procedures or Bedrock Rights? A Response to Professors Meares and Kahan." *University of Chicago Legal Forum* 1998: 215–44.

Amundson, Ron (1992). "Disability, Handicap, and the Environment." *Journal of Social Philosophy* 23: 105–18.

——— (2000a). "Biological Normality and the ADA." In Francis and Silvers (2000): 102–10.

——— (2000b). "Against Normal Function." *Studies in History and Philosophy of Biological and Biomedical Sciences* 31C: 33–53.

Angyal, Andras (1941). "Disgust and Related Aversions." *Journal of Abnormal and Social Psychology* 36: 393–412.

Annas, Julia (manuscript) (2000). "Shame and Shaming Punishments." Paper for the Workshop on Law and Social Control, University of Minnesota, November.

Archimandritou, Marta (2000). *The Open Prison* (in Modern Greek). Athens: Ellinika Grammata.

Arneson, Richard J. (2000). "Perfectionism and Politics." *Ethics* 111: 37–63.

Averill, James R. (1982). *Anger and Aggression: An Essay on Emotion.* New York: Springer.

Baker, Katharine K. (1999). "Sex, Rape, and Shame." *Boston University Law Review* 79 (1999): 663–716.

Balint, Alice (1953). "Love for the Mother and Mother Love." In Michael Balint, ed., *Primary Love and Psychoanalytic Technique.* New York: Liveright.

Bandes, Susan A. (1997). "Empathy, Narrative, and Victim Impact Statements." *University of Chicago Law Review* 63: 361–412.

———, ed. (1999). *The Passions of Law.* New York and London: New York University Press.

Bartov, Omer (1991). *Hitler's Army.* New York: Oxford University Press.

——— (1996a). *Murder in Our Midst: The Holocaust, Industrial Killing, and Representation.* New York: Oxford University Press.

——— (1996b). Review of Goldhagen (1996). *New Republic*, 29 April, 32–38.

——— (1997). Review of W. Sofsky, *The Concentration Camp. New Republic*, 13 October.

Batson, C. Daniel (1991). *The Altruism Question: Toward a Social-Psychological Answer.* Hillsdale, NJ: Lawrence Erlbaum Associates.

Beale, Joseph H., Jr. (1903). "Retreat from a Murderous Assault." *Harvard Law Review* 16: 567–82.

Becker, Ernest (1973). *The Denial of Death.* New York: The Free Press.

Becker, Lawrence (2000). "The Good of Agency." In Francis and Silvers (2000): 54–63.

Ben-Yehuda, Nachman (1990). *The Politics and Morality of Deviance: Moral Panics, Drug Abuse, Deviant Science, and Reversed Stigmatization.* Albany: State University of New York Press.

Bérubé, Michael (1996). *Life As We Know It: A Father, a Family, and an Exceptional Child.* New York: Pantheon.

Bollas, Christopher (1987). *The Shadow of the Object: Psychoanalysis of the Unthought Known.* London: Free Association Books.

Boswell, John (1989). "Jews, Bicycle Riders, and Gay People: The Determination of Social Consensus and Its Impact on Minorities." *Yale Journal of Law and Humanities* 1: 205–28.

Bowlby, John (1982). *Attachment and Loss.* Vol. 1: *Attachment.* 2d edition. New York: Basic Books.

——— (1973). *Attachment and Loss.* Vol. 2: *Separation: Anxiety and Anger.* New York: Basic Books.

——— (1980). *Attachment and Loss.* Vol. 3: *Loss: Sadness and Depression.* New York: Basic Books.

Boyarin, Daniel (1997). *Unheroic Conduct: The Rise of Heterosexuality and the Invention of the Jewish Man.* Berkeley and Los Angeles: University of California Press.

Brademas, John (1982). *Washington, D. C., to Washington Square: Essays on Government and Education.* New York: Weidenfeld and Nicolson.

Braithwaite, John (1989). *Crime, Shame, and Reintegration.* Cambridge and New York: Cambridge University Press.

——— (1999). "Restorative Justice: Assessing Optimistic and Pessimistic Accounts." *Crime and Justice* 25: 1–127.

——— (2002). *Restorative Justice and Responsive Regulation.* Oxford and New York: Oxford University Press.

Braithwaite, John, and Valerie Braithwaite (2001). "Shame, Shame Management and Regulation." In Ahmed, Harris, Braithwaite, and Braithwaite (2001): 3–69.

Brenner, Claudia (1995). *Eight Bullets: One Woman's Study of Surviving Anti-Gay Violence.* Ithaca, NY: Firebrand Books.

Broucek, Francis (1991). *Shame and the Self.* New York: Guilford Press, 1991.

Browning, Christopher (1992). *Ordinary Men.* New York: HarperCollins.

Bruun, Christer (1993). *The Water Supply of Ancient Rome: A Study of Roman Imperial Administration.* Helsinki: Societas Scientiarum Fennica.

Calhoun, Cheshire (2003). "An Apology for Moral Shame." *Journal of Political Philosophy* 11: 1–20.

Case, Mary Anne C. (1995) "Disaggregating Gender from Sex and Sexual Orientation: The Effeminate Man in the Law and Feminist Jurisprudence." *Yale Law Journal* 105: 1–104.

Cavell, Stanley (1969). "The Avoidance of Love: A Reading of *King Lear.*" In Cavell, *Must We Mean What We Say?.* New York: Charles Scribner's Sons: 267–353.

Chodorow, Nancy (1978). *The Reproduction of Mothering: Psychoanalysis and the Sociology of Gender.* Berkeley and Los Angeles: University of California Press.

Clark, Candace (1997). *Misery and Company: Sympathy in Everyday Life.* Chicago: University of Chicago Press.

Cohen, Stanley (1972). *Folk Devils and Moral Panics: The Creation of the Mods and Rockers.* London: MacGibbon and Kee.

Comstock, Gary David (1981). "Dismantling the Homosexual Panic Defense." *Law and Sexuality* 2: 81–102.

Comstock, Gary David (1991). *Violence Against Lesbians and Gay Men.* New York: Columbia University Press.

Constable, E. L. (1997). "Shame." *Modern Language Notes* 112: 641–65.

Cornell, Drucilla (1995). *The Imaginary Domain: Abortion, Pornography, and Sexual Harassment.* New York and London: Routledge.

——— (2001). "Dropped Drawers: a Viewpoint." In *Aftermath: The Clinton Impeachment and the Presidency in the Age of Political Spectacle.* Ed. Leonard V. Kaplan and Beverley I. Moran. New York: New York University Press: 312–20.

Crossley, Mary (2000). "Impairment and Embodiment." In Francis and Silvers (2000): 111–23.

Damasio, Anthony R. (1994). *Descartes' Error: Emotion, Reason, and the Human Brain.* New York: Putnam.

Darwin, Charles R. (1965 [1872]). *The Expression of the Emotions in Man and Animals.* Chicago: University of Chicago Press.

De Grazia, Edward (1992). *Girls Lean Back Everywhere: The Law of Obscenity and the Assault on Genius.* New York: Random House.

Deigh, John (1994). "Cognitivism in the Theory of Emotions." *Ethics* 104: 824–54.

——— (1996). *The Sources of Moral Agency: Essays on Moral Psychology.* Cambridge: Cambridge University Press.

De Sousa, Ronald (1987). *The Rationality of Emotion.* Cambridge, MA: MIT Press.

Devlin, Patrick (1965). *The Enforcement of Morals.* London: Oxford University Press.

Douglas, Mary (1966). *Purity and Danger.* London: Routledge and Kegan Paul.

Dressler, Joshua (1995). "When 'Heterosexual' Men Kill 'Homosexual' Men: Reflections on Provocation Law, Sexual Advances, and the 'Reasonable Man' Standard." *The Journal of Criminal Law and Criminology* 85: 726–63.

Dressler, Joshua (2002). "Why Keep the Provocation Defense?: Some Reflections on a Difficult Subject." *Minnesota Law Review* 86: 959–1002.

Dworkin, Andrea (1987). *Intercourse*. New York: Free Press.

———— (1989). *Pornography: Men Possessing Women*. New York: E. P. Dutton.

Dworkin, Ronald (1977). "Liberty and Moralism." In Dworkin, *Taking Rights Seriously*. Cambridge: Cambridge University Press: 240–58.

Eaton, Anne (manuscript) (2001). "Does Pornography Cause Harm?" Presented at the annual meeting of the Eastern Division of the American Philosophical Association.

Ehrenreich, Barbara (2001). *Nickel and Dimed: On (Not) Getting By in America*. New York: Metropolitan Books.

Elias, Norbert (1994). *The Civilizing Process*. Cambridge, MA: Blackwell.

Ellis, Havelock (1890). "Whitman." Extract from *The New Spirit*. In *Norton Critical Edition of Whitman*, ed. Sculley Bradley and Harold W. Blodgett. New York and London: W. W. Norton, 1973: 803–13.

Ellman, Richard (1987). *Oscar Wilde*. London: Penguin.

Etzioni, Amitai (2001). *The Monochrome Society*. Princeton: Princeton University Press.

Fairbairn, W.R.D. (1952). *Psychoanalytic Studies of the Personality*. London and New York: Tavistock/Routledge.

Feinberg, Joel (1985). *The Moral Limits of the Criminal Law*. Vol. 2: *Offense to Others*. New York: Oxford University Press.

Fletcher, George (1999). "Disenfranchisement as Punishment: Reflections on the Racial Uses of *Infamia*." *UCLA Law Review* 46: 1895–1907.

Francis, Leslie Pickering, and Anita Silvers, eds. (2000). *Americans With Disabilities: Exploring Implications of the Law for Individuals and Institutions*. New York and London: Routledge.

Frank, Robert (1999). *Luxury Fever*. New York: The Free Press.

Freud, Sigmund (1905). *Three Essays on the Theory of Sexuality*. In *The Standard Edition of the Complete Psychological Works of Sigmund Freud*. Vol. 7. Ed. James Strachey. London: Hogarth Press: 125–245.

———— (1908). "Character and Anal Erotism." In *Standard Edition* 9, 169–75.

———— (1910). *Five Lectures on Psychoanalysis*. In *Standard Edition* 11, 3–56.

———— (1915). "Mourning and Melancholia." In *Standard Edition* 14, 239–58.

———— (1920). *Beyond the Pleasure Principle*. In *Standard Edition* 18.

———— (1930). *Civilization and Its Discontents*. In *Standard Edition* 21, 59–145.

———— (1985). *The Complete Letters of Sigmund Freud to Wilhelm Fliess, 1887–1904*. Ed. and trans. Jeffrey M. Masson. Cambridge, MA: Harvard University Press.

Garvey, Steven (1998). "Can Shaming Punishments Educate?" *University of Chicago Law Review* 65: 733–94.

Gattrell, V.A.C. (1994). *The Hanging Tree: Execution and the English People, 1770–1868*. Oxford and New York: Oxford University Press.

Gauthier, David (1986). *Morals By Agreement*. New York: Oxford University Press.

Geller, Jay (1992). "(G)nos(e)ology: The Cultural Construction of the Other." In *People of the Body: Jews and Judaism from an Embodied Perspective*, ed. Howard Eilberg-Schwartz. New York: State University of New York Press.

Gilligan, James (1997). *Violence: Reflections on a National Epidemic*. New York: Vintage Books.

Gilman, Sander (1991). *The Jew's Body*. New York: Routledge.

Glover, Jonathan (2000). *Humanity: A Moral History of the Twentieth Century.* New Haven: Yale University Press.

Goffman, Erving (1963). *Stigma: Notes on the Management of Spoiled Identity.* New York: Simon and Schuster.

Goldhagen, Daniel Jonah (1996). *Hitler's Willing Executioners: Ordinary Germans and the Holocaust.* New York: Knopf.

Goldhagen, Daniel Jonah, Omer Bartov, and Christopher Browning (1997). An exchange. *New Republic,* 10 February.

Graham, George (1990). "Melancholic Epistemology." *Synthese* 82: 399–422.

Gustafson, Mark (1997). "*Inscripta in fronte*: Penal Tattooing in Late Antiquity." *Classical Antiquity* 16 (1997): 79–105.

Haidt, Jonathan, Clark R. McCauley, and Paul Rozen (1994). "A Scale to Measure Disgust Sensitivity." *Personality and Individual Differences* 16: 701–13.

Hall, Stuart, Chas Critcher, Tony Jefferson, John Clarke, and Brian Roberts (1978). *Policing the Crisis: Mugging, the State, and Law and Order.* London: MacMillan.

Hilberg, Raul (1985). *The Destruction of the European Jews.* New York: Holmes and Meier.

Hollander, Anne (1994). *Sex and Suits: The Evolution of Modern Dress.* New York: Farrar, Straus, and Giroux.

Holmes, Oliver Wendell, Jr. (1992). *The Essential Holmes.* Ed. Richard A. Posner. Chicago: University of Chicago Press.

Hornle, Tatjana (2000). "Penal Law and Sexuality: Recent Reforms in German Criminal Law." *Buffalo Criminal Law Review* 3: 639–85.

Human Rights Watch (1998). *Losing the Vote: The Impact of Felony Disenfranchisement Law in the U.S.* Available online from Human Rights Watch at *humanrightswatch.org.*

Hyde, H. Montgomery (1956). *The Three Trials of Oscar Wilde.* New York: University Books.

Ignatieff, Michael (1978). *A Just Measure of Pain: The Penitentiary in the Industrial Revolution, 1750–1850.* New York: Pantheon.

Jenkins, Philip (1998). *Moral Panic: Changing Concepts of the Child Molester in Modern America.* New Haven and London: Yale University Press.

Johnson, Mark L. (2001). Comment on sentencing and equal protection. *University of Chicago Legal Forum.*

Jones, Christopher P. (1987). "*Stigma*: Tattooing and Branding in Graeco-Roman Antiquity." *Journal of Roman Studies* 77: 139–55.

———— (2000). "Stigma and Tattoo." In *Written on the Body,* ed. Jane Caplan. Princeton: Princeton University Press: 1–16.

Kadidal, Shayana (1996). "Obscenity in the Age of Mechanical Reproduction." *American Journal of Comparative Law* 44: 353–85.

Kadish, Sanford H., and Stephen J. Schulhofer (1989). *Criminal Law and Its Processes: Cases and Materials.* 5th ed. Boston, Toronto, and London: Little, Brown and Company.

Kahan, Dan M. (1996). "What Do Alternative Sanctions Mean?" *University of Chicago Law Review* 63: 591–653.

———— (1998). "*The Anatomy of Disgust* in Criminal Law." *Michigan Law Review* 96: 1621–57.

———— (1999a). "The Progressive Appropriation of Disgust." In Bandes (1999): 63–79.

———— (1999b). "Unthinkable Misrepresentations: A Response to Tonry." *UCLA Law Review* 46: 1933–40.

Kahan, Dan M., and Martha C. Nussbaum (1996). "Two Conceptions of Emotion in Criminal Law." *Columbia Law Review* 96: 269–374.

Kahan, Dan M., and Eric A. Posner (1999). "Shaming White-Collar Criminals: A Proposal for Reform of the Federal Sentencing Guidelines." *Journal of Law and Economics* 42: 365–91.

Kaster, Robert A. (1997). "The Shame of the Romans." *Transactions of the American Philological Association* 127: 1–19.

——— (2001). "The Dynamics of *Fastidium.*" *Transactions of the American Philological Association* 131: 143–89.

Kavka, Gregory S. (2000). "Disability and the Right to Work." In Francis and Silvers (2000): 174–92.

Kelman, Mark (2000). "Does Disability Status Matter?" In Francis and Silvers (2000): 91–101.

Kelman, Mark, and Gillian Lester (1997). *Jumping the Queue: An Inquiry into the Legal Treatment of Students with Learning Disabilities.* Cambridge, MA, and London: Harvard University Press.

Kernberg, Otto (1985). *Borderline Conditions and Pathological Narcissism.* Northvale, NJ: Jason Aronson.

Kilborne, Benjamin (2002). *Disappearing Persons: Shame and Appearance.* Albany: State University of New York Press.

Kim, David Haekwon (2001). *Mortal Feelings: A Theory of Revulsion and the Intimacy of Agency.* Ph.D. Dissertation, Syracuse University, August 2001.

Kindlon, Daniel J. (2001). *Too Much of a Good Thing: Raising Children of Character in an Indulgent Age.* New York: Miramax.

Kindlon, Daniel J., and Michael Thompson (1999). *Raising Cain: Protecting the Emotional Life of Boys.* New York: Ballantine Books.

Kittay, Eva Feder (1999). *Love's Labor: Essays on Women, Equality, and Dependency.* New York and London: Routledge.

Klein, Melanie (1984). *Envy and Gratitude and Other Works 1946–1963.* London: The Hogarth Press.

——— (1985). *Love, Guilt, and Reparation and Other Works 1921–1945.* London: The Hogarth Press.

Kniss, Fred (1997). *Disquiet In the Land: Cultural Conflict in American Mennonite Communities.* New Brunswick, NJ: Rutgers University Press.

Kohut, Heinz (1981a). "On Empathy." In *The Search for the Self: Selected Writings of Heinz Kohut: 1978–1981,* ed. P. H. Orstein. Madison, CT: International Universities Press, Inc: 525–35.

——— (1981b). "Introspection, Empathy, and the Semicircle of Mental Health." In *The Search for the Self: Selected Writings of Heinz Kohut: 1978-1981,* ed. P. H. Orstein. Madison, CT: International Universities Press, Inc: 537–67.

——— (1986). "Forms and Transformations of Narcissism." In Morrison (1986): 61–88.

Koppelman, Andrew (2002). *The Gay Rights Question in Contemporary American Law.* Chicago: University of Chicago Press.

Korsmeyer, Carolyn W. (1999). *Making Sense of Taste.* Ithaca, NY: Cornell University Press.

Larmore, Charles (1987). *Patterns of Moral Complexity.* New York: Cambridge University Press.

———— (1996). *The Morals of Modernity.* New York: Cambridge University Press.

Law, Sylvia A. (1988). "Homosexuality and the Social Meaning of Gender." *Wisconsin Law Review:* 187–235.

Lazarus, Richard S. (1991). *Emotion and Adaptation.* New York: Oxford University Press.

LeDoux, Joseph (1996). *The Emotional Brain: The Mysterious Underpinnings of Emotional Life.* New York: Simon & Schuster.

Levitz, Mitchell, and Jason Kingsley (1994). *Count Us In: Growing Up with Down Syndrome.* New York: Harcourt Brace.

Lindgren, James (1993). "Defining Pornography." *University of Pennsylvania Law Review* 141: 1153–1276.

Lopez, Frederick G., and Kelly A. Brennan (2000). "Dynamic Processes Underlying Adult Attachment Organization." *Journal of Counseling Psychology* 47: 283–300.

Lumbard, J. Edward (1965). "The Citizens' Role in Law Enforcement." *Journal of Criminal Law, Criminology and Police Science* 56: 67–72.

MacKinnon, Catharine A. (1987). *Feminism Unmodified: Discourses on Life and Law.* Cambridge, MA: Harvard University Press.

———— (1989). *Toward a Feminist Theory of the State.* Cambridge, MA: Harvard University Press.

MacKinnon, Catharine A., and Andrea Dworkin (1997). *In Harm's Way: The Pornography Civil Rights Hearings.* Cambridge, MA: Harvard University Press.

Maguigan, Holly (1991). "Battered Women and Self-Defense: Myths and Misconceptions in Current Reform Proposals." *University of Pennsylvania Law Review* 140: 379–486.

Mahler, Margaret S. (1968). *On Human Symbiosis and the Vicissitudes of Individuation.* Vol. I: *Infantile Psychosis.* New York: International Universities Press.

———— (1979). *The Selected Papers of Margaret S. Mahler.* Vol. 1: *Infantile Psychosis and Early Contributions.* Vol. 2: *Separation-Individuation.*

Mahler, Margaret, Fred Pine, and Anni Bergman (2000 [1975]). *The Psychological Birth of the Human Infant: Symbiosis and Individuation.* First paperback edition. New York: Basic Books.

Mandler, George (1975). *Mind and Emotion.* New York: Wiley.

———— (1984). *Mind and Body: Psychology of Emotion and Stress.* New York: Norton.

Margalit, Avishai (1996). *The Decent Society.* Trans. Naomi Goldblum. Cambridge, MA: Harvard University Press.

Maritain, Jacques (1953). *Man and the State.* Chicago: University of Chicago Press.

Markel, Dan (2001). "Are Shaming Punishments Beautifully Retributive?: Retributivism and the Implications for the Alternative Sanctions Debate." *Vanderbilt Law Review* 54: 2157–2242.

Marmontel, Jean-François (1999). *Mémoires.* Paris: Mercure de France.

Massaro, Toni (1991). "Shame, Culture, and American Criminal Law." *Michigan Law Review* 89: 1880–1942.

———— (1997). "The Meanings of Shame: Implications for Legal Reform." *Psychology, Public Policy and Law* 3: 645–80.

———— (1999). "Show (Some) Emotions." In Bandes (1999): 80–122.

Meares, Tracey, and Dan M. Kahan (1998a). "The Wages of Antiquated Procedural Thinking: A Critique of *Chicago v. Morales.*" *University of Chicago Legal Forum* 1998: 197–259.

Meares, Tracy, and Dan M. Kahan (1998b). "The Coming Crisis of Criminal Procedure." *Georgetown Law Journal* 86: 1153–84.

——— (1999). "When Rights are Wrong." In Symposium, "Do Rights Handcuff Democracy?" (with respondents). *Boston Review* 24: 4–8, respondents 10–22, response by Meares and Kahan 22–23.

Menninghaus, Winfried (1999). *Ekel: Theorie und Geschichte einer starken Empfindung.* Frankfurt: Suhrkamp.

Mill, John Stuart (1838). "Bentham."

——— (1859). *On Liberty.*

——— (1861). *Utilitarianism.*

——— (1873). *Autobiography.* (Posthumously published.)

Miller, Alice (1986). "Depression and Grandiosity as Related Forms of Narcissistic Disturbances." *In Morrison* (1986): 323–47.

Miller, William I. (1993). *Humiliation.* Ithaca, NY: Cornell University Press.

——— (1997). *The Anatomy of Disgust.* Cambridge, MA: Harvard University Press.

——— (1998). "Sheep, Joking, Cloning and the Uncanny." In *Clones and Clones,* ed. Martha C. Nussbuam and Cass R. Sunstein. New York: Norton: 78–87.

Minow, Martha (1990). *Making All the Difference: Inclusion, Exclusion, and American Law.* Ithaca, NY: Cornell University Press.

Mison, Robert B. (1992). "Comment: Homophobia in Manslaughter: The Homosexual Advance as Insufficient Provocation." *California Law Review* 80: 133–37.

Morris, Herbert (1968). "Persons and Punishment." Originally published in *The Monist* 52. Reprinted in *Punishment and Rehabilitation,* ed. Jeffrie Murphy. 3d edition. Belmont, CA: Wadsworth Publishing Company, 1995: 74–93.

——— (1971). *Guilt and Shame.* Belmont, CA: Wadsworth Publishing Co.

Morris, Jenny (1991). *Pride Against Prejudice.* Philadelphia: New Society Publishers, 1991.

——— (1992). "Tyrannies of Perfection." *The New Internationalist,* 1 July, 16.

Morris, Norval, and David J. Rothman, eds. (1998). *The Oxford History of the Prison: The Practice of Punishment in Western Society.* New York and Oxford: Oxford University Press.

Morrison, Andrew P. (1986a). *The Culture of Shame.* London and Northvale, NJ: Jason Aronson.

——— (1986b). "Shame, Ideal Self, and Narcissism." In Morrison (1986): 348–72.

——— (1989). *Shame: The Underside of Narcissism.* Hillsdale, NJ: The Analytic Press.

———, ed., (1986). *Essential Papers on Narcissism.* New York and London: New York University Press.

Morse, Stephen J. (1984). "Undiminished Confusion in Diminished Capacity." *Journal of Criminal Law and Criminology* 75: 1–34.

Murdoch, Iris (1970). *The Sovereignty of Good.* London: Routledge.

Murphy, Jeffrie G., and Jean Hampton (1988). *Forgiveness and Mercy.* Cambridge and New York: Cambridge University Press.

Nagel, Thomas (1997). "Justice and Nature." *Oxford Journal of Legal Studies* 17: 303–21.

——— (1998). "Concealment and Exposure." *Philosophy and Public Affairs* 27: 3–30.

Nourse, Victoria (1997). "Passion's Progress: Modern Law Reform and the Provocation Defense." *Yale Law Journal* 106: 1331–1443.

Nussbaum, Martha C. (1990). *Love's Knowledge: Essays on Philosophy and Literature*. New York: Oxford University Press.

——— (1994). *The Therapy of Desire: Theory and Practice in Hellenistic Ethics*. Princeton: Princeton University Press.

——— (1995). *Poetic Justice: The Literary Imagination and Public Life*. Boston: Beacon Press.

——— (1997). *Cultivating Humanity: A Classical Defense of Reform in Liberal Education*. Cambridge, MA: Harvard University Press.

——— (1998). "Emotions as Judgments of Value: A Philosophical Dialogue." *Comparative Criticism* 20: 33–62.

——— (1999a). *Sex and Social Justice*. New York: Oxford University Press.

——— (1999b). "'Secret Sewers of Vice': Disgust, Bodies, and the Law." *In Bandes* (1999):19–62.

——— (1999c). "Invisibility and Recognition: Sophocles' *Philoctetes* and Ellison's *Invisible Man*." *Philosophy and Literature* 23: 257–83.

——— (2000a). *Women and Human Development: The Capabilities Approach*. Cambridge and New York: Cambridge University Press.

——— (2000b). "The Future of Feminist Liberalism." *Proceedings and Addresses of the American Philosophical Association* 74: 47–79.

——— (2000c). "Aristotle, Politics, and Human Capabilities: A Response to Antony, Arneson, Charlesworth, and Mulgan." *Ethics* 111: 102–40.

——— (2001a). *Upheavals of Thought: The Intelligence of Emotions*. Cambridge and New York: Cambridge University Press.

——— (2001b). "Disabled Lives: Who Cares?" *New York Review of Books* 48, 11 January 34–37.

——— (2001c). "Political Objectivity." *New Literary History* 32: 883–906.

——— (2002a). "Millean Liberty and Sexual Orientation." *Law and Philosophy* 21: 317–34.

——— (2002b). "Sex Equality, Liberty, and Privacy: A Comparative Approach to the Feminist Critique." In E. Sridharan, R. Sudarshan, and Z. Hasan, eds., *India's Living Constitution: Ideas, Practices, Controversies*. Delhi: Permanent Black: 242–83.

——— (2003a). "Capabilities as Fundamental Entitlements: Sen and Social Justice." *Feminist Economics* 9: 33–59.

——— (2003b). "Compassion and Terror." *Daedalus* (Winter) 10–26.

——— (2003c). "Genocide in Gujarat: The International Community Looks Away." *Dissent* (Summer) 61–69.

Oatley, Keith (1992). *Best Laid Schemes: The Psychology of Emotions*. Cambridge: Cambridge University Press.

Ochoa, Tyler Trent, and Christine Newman Jones (1997). "Defiling the Dead: Necrophilia and the Law." *Whittier Law Review* 18: 539–78.

Olyan, Saul, and Martha C. Nussbaum, eds. (1998). *Sexual Orientation and Human Rights in American Religious Discourse*. New York: Oxford University Press.

Ortner, Sherry B. (1973). "Sherpa Purity." *American Anthropologist* 75: 49–63.

Ortony, Andrew, Gerald L. Clore, and Allan Collins (1988). *The Cognitive Structure of Emotions*. Cambridge: Cambridge University Press.

Packe, Michael St. John (1954). *The Life of John Stuart Mill*. New York: Macmillan.

Piers, Gerhart, and Milton B. Singer (1953). *Shame and Guilt: A Psychoanalytic and a Cultural Study.* Springfield, IL: Charles C. Thomas.

Pipher, Mary (1994). *Reviving Ophelia: Saving the Selves of Adolescent Girls.* New York: Putnam.

Pohlman, H. L. (1999). *The Whole Truth? A Case of Murder on the Appalachian Trail.* Amherst: University of Massachusetts Press.

Posner, Eric A. (2000). *Law and Social Norms.* Cambridge, MA: Harvard University Press.

Posner, Richard A. (1990). *The Problems of Jurisprudence.* Cambridge, MA: Harvard University Press.

—— (1992). *Sex and Reason.* Cambridge, MA: Harvard University Press.

—— (1995). *Overcoming Law.* Cambridge, MA: Harvard University Press.

Posner, Richard A., and Katharine B. Silbaugh (1996). *A Guide to America's Sex Laws.* Cambridge, MA: Harvard University Press.

Proctor, Robert N. (1999). *The Nazi War on Cancer.* Princeton and Oxford: Princeton University Press.

Rawls, John (1971). *A Theory of Justice.* Cambridge, MA: Harvard University Press.

—— (1996). Political Liberalism. Expanded paperback edition. New York: Columbia University Press.

Reich, Annie (1986). "Pathologic Forms of Self-Esteem Regulation." In Morrison (1986): 44–60.

Reynolds, David S. (1995). *Walt Whitman's America: A Cultural Biography.* New York: Knopf.

Rodman, F. Robert (2003). *Winnicott: Life and Work.* Cambridge, MA: Perseus Publishing.

Rozin, Paul, and April E. Fallon (1987). "A Perspective on Disgust." *Psychological Review* 94: 23–41.

Rozin, Paul, April E. Fallon, and R. Mandell (1984). "Family Resemblance in Attitudes to Foods." *Developmental Psychology* 20: 309–14.

Rozin, Paul, Jonathan Haidt, and Clark R. McCauley (1999). "Disgust: The Body and Soul Emotion." *Handbook of Cognition and Emotion.* Ed. T. Dalgleish and M. Power. Chichester, UK: John Wiley and Sons, Ltd.: 429–45.

—— (2000). "Disgust." *Handbook of Emotions, 2d Edition.* Ed. M. Lewis and J. M. Haviland-Jones. New York: Guilford Press: 637–53.

Sanders, Clinton R. (1989). *Customizing the Body: The Art and Culture of Tattooing.* Philadelphia: Temple University Press.

Sarkar, Tanika (2002). "Semiotics of Terror." *Economic and Political Weekly.* 13 July.

Scheler, Max (1957). "Über Scham und Schamgefuhl." *Schriften aus dem Nachlass.* Band 1: *Zur Ethik und Erkenntnislehre.* Bern: Francke: 55–148.

Schulhofer, Steven J. (1995). "The Trouble with Trials; the Trouble with Us." *Yale Law Journal* 105: 825–55.

Sennett, Richard (2003). *Respect in a World of Inequality.* New York: W. W. Norton.

Sherman, Nancy (1999). "Taking Responsibility for Our Emotions." In *Responsibility,* ed. E. Paul and J. Paul. Cambridge and New York: Cambridge University Press: 1999: 294–323.

Silvers, Anita (1998). "Formal Justice." In Silvers, Wasserman, and Mahowald (1998): 13–145.

——— (2000). "The Unprotected: Constructing Disability in the Context of Antidiscrimination Law." In Francis and Silvers (2000): 126–45.

Silvers, Anita, David Wasserman, and Mary Mahowald (1998). *Disability, Difference, Discrimination: Perspectives on Justice in Bioethics and Public Policy*. Lanham, MD: Rowman and Littlefield.

Spierenburg, Pieter (1984). *The Spectacle of Suffering: Executions and the Evolution of Repression*. Cambridge and New York: Cambridge University Press.

Stern, Daniel N. (1977). *The First Relationship: Infant and Mother*. Cambridge, MA: Harvard University Press.

——— (1985). *The Interpersonal World of the Infant*. New York: Basic Books.

——— (1990). *Diary of a Baby*. New York: Basic Books.

Strawson, Peter (1968). "Freedom and Resentment." In Strawson, *Studies in the Philosophy of Thought and Action*. New York and Oxford: Oxford University Press: 71–96.

Sunstein, Cass R. (1993). *Democracy and the Problem of Free Speech*. New York: The Free Press.

——— (1997). *Free Markets and Social Justice*. New York and Oxford: Oxford University Press.

——— (1999). *One Case at a Time: Judicial Minimalism on the Supreme Court*. Cambridge, MA: Harvard University Press.

——— (2001). *Designing Democracy: What Constitutions Do*. New York and Oxford: Oxford University Press.

Sunstein, Cass R., Daniel Kahnemann, and David A. Schkade (1998). "Assessing Punitive Damages (with Notes on cognition and Valuation in Law)." *Yale Law Journal* 107: 2071 ff.

Sunstein, Cass R., Reid Hastie, John W. Payne, David A. Shkade, and W. Kip Viscusi (2002). *Punitive Damages: How Juries Decide*. Chicago: University of Chicago Press.

Taylor, Gabriele (1985). *Pride, Shame and Guilt: Emotions of Self-Assessment*. Oxford: Clarendon Press.

tenBroek, Jacobus (1966). "The Right to Be in the World: The Disabled in the Law of Torts." *California Law Review* 54 (1966): 841–919.

Theweleit, Klaus (1987, 1989). *Male Fantasies*. Trans. S. Conway. Two Volumes. Minneapolis: University of Minnesota Press.

Tomkins, Silvan S. (1962–63). *Affect/Imagery/Consciousness*. Vols. 1 and 2. New York: Springer.

Tonry, Michael (1999). "Rethinking Unthinkable Punishment Policies in America." *UCLA Law Review* 46: 1751–91.

Tonry, Michael, and Kathleen Hatlestad, eds. (1997). *Sentencing Reform in Overcrowded Times: A Comparative Perspective*. New York and Oxford: Oxford University Press.

Veatch, Robert M. (1986). *The Foundations of Justice: Why the Retarded and the Rest of Us Have Claims to Equality*. New York and Oxford: Oxford University Press.

Velleman, J. David (2002). "The Genesis of Shame." *Philosophy and Public Affairs* 30: 27–52.

Walker, Lenore (1980). *Battered Woman*. New York: Perennial.

Warner, Michael (1999). *The Trouble with Normal: Sex, Politics, and the Ethics of Queer Life*. New York: The Free Press.

Wasserman, David (1998). "Distributive Justice." In Silvers, Wasserman, and Mahowald (1998): 147–208.

——— (2000). "Stigma without Impairment: Demedicalizing Disability Discrimination." In *Francis* and *Silvers* (2000): 146–62.

Weininger, Otto (1906). *Sex and Character.* London and New York: William Heinemann and G. P. Putnam's Sons. (Based on 6th German edition.)

Whitman, James Q. (1998). "What Is Wrong with Inflicting Shame Sanctions?" *Yale Law Journal* 107: 105 ff.

——— (2003). *Harsh Justice: Criminal Punishment and the Widening Divide between America and Europe.* New York and Oxford: Oxford University Press.

Whitman, Walt (1973). *Leaves of Grass. Norton Critical Edition.* Ed. Scolley Bradley and Harold W. Blodgett. New York: W. W. Norton.

Williams, Bernard (1993). *Shame and Necessity.* Berkeley and Los Angeles: University of California Press.

Williams, Joan (1999). *Unbending Gender: Why Family and Work Conflict and What to Do About It.* New York and Oxford: Oxford University Press.

Winnicott, Donald W. (1965). *The Maturational Processes and the Facilitating Environment: Studies in the Theory of Emotional Development.* Madison, CT: International Universities Press, Inc.

——— (1986). *Holding and Interpretation: Fragments of an Analysis.* New York: Grove Press.

Wollheim, Richard (1984). *The Thread of Life.* Cambridge, MA: Harvard University Press.

——— (1999). *On the Emotions.* New Haven: Yale University Press.

Wurmser, Leon (1981). *The Mask of Shame.* Baltimore: Johns Hopkins University Press.

Yoshino, Kenji (2002). "Covering." *Yale Law Journal* 111: 760–939.

Young-Bruehl, Elizabeth (1996). *The Anatomy of Prejudices.* Cambridge, MA: Harvard University Press.

General Index

Index of Case Names